KEITH DARLINGTON

EFFECTIVE
WEBSITE
DEVELOPMENT

Tools and Techniques

KT-163-845

PEARSON

Addison
Wesley

Harlow, England • London • New York • Boston • San Francisco • Toronto • Sydney • Singapore • Hong Kong
Tokyo • Seoul • Taipei • New Delhi • Cape Town • Madrid • Mexico City • Amsterdam • Munich • Paris • Milan

Pearson Education Limited
Edinburgh Gate
Harlow
Essex CM20 2JE
England

and Associated Companies throughout the world

Visit us on the World Wide Web at:
www.pearsoned.co.uk

First published 2005

© Pearson Education Limited 2005

ISBN 0 321 18472 6

British Library Cataloguing-in-Publication Data
A catalogue record for this book is available from the British Library

Library of Congress Cataloging-in-Publication Data
Darlington, Keith
  Effective website development : tools and techniques / Keith Darlington.
     p. cm.
  Includes bibliographical references and index.
  ISBN 0-321-18472-6 (pbk.)
  1. Web sites--Design.   I. Title.

  TK5105.888.D363 2005
  006.7--dc22   2004062820

10 9 8 7 6 5 4 3 2 1
10 09 08 07 06 05

Typeset in 10/12pt Times by 25
Printed and bound in Great Britain by Henry Ling Ltd., at the Dorset Press, Dorchester, Dorset

The publisher's policy is to use paper manufactured from sustainable forests.

To Janice

Contents

Preface

Aims of this book

This book is aimed primarily at undergraduate Internet computing, computing studies and e-commerce students in the field of Web design. It could also benefit students taking courses in computer science, software engineering, business studies or many other academic disciplines. Indeed, some sections could be beneficial to any undergraduate student, not necessarily from a scientific background, wanting to expand their knowledge of the Web. In essence, this book is intended to serve what I believe could be a large potential market of students from all academic disciplines who would want to acquire Web design skills. I also believe that the book will be of benefit to final year degree computing and IT students who may be tackling Web-based projects. Web design is a broad discipline for it can mean anything from XML and CSS to multimedia and graphic design.

I have attempted to provide a cohesive, self-contained book that binds together the many disparate themes in website development. The emphasis, therefore, is on familiarizing readers with the range of website development techniques and tools, rather than too much emphasis on aesthetic issues, such as graphic design. For this reason, I have included many chapters on Web programming techniques and Dreamweaver, as well as discussing themes such as website project management and lifecycle issues. It should also be stressed that no prior knowledge of using the Internet and the Web is assumed in this book, although the reader is expected to have a very basic knowledge of using computers.

Approach

My approach to this book has been guided by the following principles.

- To develop ideas step by step, leading from one idea to the next where possible, and present the material in a manner that will be easy to follow for all readers.

- To avoid the pedantic use of technical jargon where possible and adopt an intuitive approach based on a sound grasp of principles as, in my experience, many students turn off when confronted by an excess of technical jargon. Unfortunately, the Web vernacular is filled with jargon. However, I believe that it is possible to introduce such jargon in a non-intrusive manner, providing the emphasis is on an intuitive approach to learning this subject.

- To take nothing for granted. My experience of teaching Web techniques at this level has shown me that little should be assumed, for there are always unexpected gaps in students' knowledge. For example, I occasionally meet otherwise quite knowledgeable students who have no prior experience of using the Web and no understanding of what a browser is capable of doing other than displaying Web pages. This may be rare nowadays, but it does still sometimes happen. Many authors seem to take such knowledge for granted.

- To try to use plenty of examples to reinforce students' understanding of concepts. For each program example, there is at least one screenshot demonstrating output.

- To use complete Web programs rather than fragments. In my experience, students prefer this because they can then run and test the whole program directly.

- In my coverage of Dreamweaver, I have adopted an approach that is version independent, although I do sometimes make reference to specific version features, such as the Dreamweaver layout – a specific feature of Dreamweaver MX.

Features

- Each chapter begins with a list of objectives. These include the important concepts to be mastered within the chapter. This quick reference to each chapter's contents should provide a useful study aid.

- All chapters conclude with a chapter summary and end-of-chapter exercises.

- Short self-assessment exercises are sprinkled through the chapters. The purpose of these is to encourage the student to reflect on the learning experience at appropriate times.

- End-of-chapter exercises contain short, factual knowledge-testing examples, followed by longer, practical exercises, drawing on programming skills.

- Resources website (www.pearsoned.co.uk/darlington) containing Dreamweaver resources, examples and other relevant material. This book also comes with Microsoft PowerPoint slides for use as a teaching aid for classroom presentations. These slides can be made available to students or can be printed for classroom distribution. Instructors are welcome to add extra topics to these slides if they require.

Chapter layout

Rationale and how to use this book

This book contains 14 chapters, which can be broadly divided into 4 sections, and appendices. The sections are Web design and tools (Chapters 1–4), XHTML and Web programming (Chapters 5–7), Web programming techniques and multimedia (Chapters 8–10) and Dreamweaver (Chapters 11–13).

Each chapter includes exercises that provide a foundation for practice with the chapter material via paper-based tasks and laboratory work where appropriate.

The chapters cover website design, followed by Web programming techniques and three chapters about Dreamweaver towards the end of the book. In my own experience, this is the best way to sequence the material as students need to be familiar with the techniques before applying them using the tools available. Those familiar with the techniques may skip some of the early chapters as many of them are self-contained and then go straight to the part of the book that interests them.

Chapter 1: Introduction to the Internet and Web

The book begins with an introductory chapter that gives an intuitive understanding of the Internet and the WWW, along with an outline of its historical milestones. The evolution of Web standards, tools and browsers is covered during the early part of this chapter. It also provides a light, informal introduction to using HTML to create Web pages. This gives the student a chance to try out hands-on examples from a very early stage. XHTML is studied in a more formal manner in Chapter 5.

The overall purpose of this chapter is to provide a good contextual understanding of the terms and concepts that follow in later chapters.

Chapter 2: Planning and preparation of a website

This chapter looks at planning and preparation issues pertaining to website design. The development stages from conceptualization through to site uploading are studied, with examples of the likely problems that might occur and some possible solutions.

The planning and analysis, design, implementation, testing and maintenance stages – including project management issues pertaining to website development – are looked at in this chapter.

Chapter 3: Designing for visual aspects and navigation

Chapter 3 provides the reader with a general introduction to design principles relating to the user interface. This is supported by contextual illustrations. The topics include designing for text, images, sound and video, navigation principles, feedback and so on, as well as emphasizing graphic and typographical design issues.

Chapter 4: Web development tools

A plethora of tools is now in widespread use for Web development activities, including website development tools and multimedia and graphics software. A range of Web page design tools also exists, such as HTML editors and on to authoring tools, such as Dreamweaver and FrontPage. This chapter looks at the role of Web development tools with examples of their use. It also looks at conversion utilities, such as Word, and briefly at tools for creating and editing graphic and multimedia content, such as Photoshop and Fireworks.

Chapter 5: The basics of XHTML

This chapter provides the reader with an introduction to XHTML. The World Wide Web Consortium recommended XHTML 1.0 as the replacement for HTML 4.0 in January 2001, and it is now the primary means of describing Web content.

The concepts of tags and attributes were introduced in an informal sense in Chapter 1, but in this chapter they are developed by looking at the use of body formatting tags, text structure, using special characters, hyperlinks and graphic tags and attributes. Moreover, this chapter describes the distinction between presentation of a Web document in a browser window and the logical structure of the information in the document. Many students are confused by this distinction and so several examples are provided for clarification. All examples given are supported by screenshots of output in a range of browsers.

Chapter 6: More XHTML techniques

This chapter looks at XHTML applied to tables, frames and forms. A detailed look at how these Web page constructs can be used with XHTML is covered, using a range of examples.

Chapter 7: Web programming

This chapter begins with a rationale for using client-side scripting languages such as JavaScript and VBScript. These languages are compared and examples using both are given, as well as examples of the Java language with Java applets. Also, we take a look at server-side processing and scripting languages, including a brief look at CGI with Perl, and ASP, JSP and PHP.

Chapter 8: Cascading Style Sheets (CSS)

This chapter looks at Cascading Style Sheets (CSS). These provide a mechanism for separating style from content in Web pages and allow HTML and XML authors to control the way Web pages look, irrespective of the browsing device that is used. CSS is therefore covered in some depth in this chapter, beginning with a brief historical contextual section leading to the WC3 specification for CSS2.

This chapter also looks at the role of CSS in providing precision with the styling of Web content, as well as their role in maintaining a consistent style across a site.

A case study is included, demonstrating the power of CSS. The chapter also looks at browser support for CSS, support for JavaScript, CSS tools and offers a brief introduction to DHTML.

Chapter 9: Multimedia and the WWW

The Web has rapidly evolved into a multimedia environment. Web pages include text, graphics, video and sound. This chapter looks at these media with an emphasis on understanding graphic image formats, colours for graphics, as well as sound and video on the Web. It concludes with a look at the use of XHTML tags for multimedia and, briefly, the Portable Document Format (PDF) for the Web.

Chapter 10: Extensible Markup Language (XML)

This chapter looks at XML. Like XHTML, XML is a subset of the SGML language. These relationships are emphasized in relation to the evolution to HTML and the WC3. This not only gives the reader a clear understanding of the reasons for XML but also an idea of how Web content will evolve in the future.

The role of a DTD (Document Type Definition) and well-formed XML documents is demonstrated in this chapter, too, as well as a brief description of derivatives of XML, including XForms. The use of both style sheet languages CSS and XSL in XML is considered, along with examples and validation of XML documents.

Chapter 11: Introduction to Dreamweaver MX

This chapter gives the reader an introduction to using Dreamweaver for the development of a website. The approach to using Dreamweaver is version-independent, although reference is made to particular versions from time to time to discuss particular features.

The approach is hands-on and draws on the techniques examined in previous chapters. Basic WYSIWYG editing with Dreamweaver, site management, setting preferences, using hyperlinks, inclusion of graphic images, adding e-mail links to your site and using Dreamweaver to connect to a remote site are covered in this chapter.

Chapter 12: Intermediate Dreamweaver

This chapter is concerned with extending Dreamweaver's capabilities to add interactivity with forms and behaviours using rollovers and JavaScript to incorporate tables using the standard and Layout views. Using frames in Dreamweaver, as well as using meta-tags to improve the likelihood of detection by search engines, is also covered in detail.

Chapter 13: Improving productivity with Dreamweaver

This chapter looks at more advanced Dreamweaver techniques to improve productivity, including using templates, assets and library items, the HTML tag editor, making design notes and implementing behaviours, as well as giving an insight into layers and Cascading Style Sheets with Dreamweaver. Finally, a study of dynamic database techniques using the PHP/MySQL combination concludes the Dreamweaver section of the book.

Chapter 14: Future technologies

This chapter completes the book by taking a brief look at some emerging Web technologies, as well as looking at search engines in some detail. This is a particularly important theme for the website designer, given the role that search engines now play on the Web.

Appendices

The appendices included in this book provide a quick reference source for the sorts of information that the Dreamweaver user and Web designer are likely to require from time to time. The appendices are:

- Appendix 1, which provides a CSS reference source
- Appendix 2, which provides an XHTML reference source
- Appendix 3 is a quick reference source for Dreamweaver keyboard shortcuts – this is particularly useful for Dreamweaver users who wish to speed up Dreamweaver tasks.

Acknowledgements

I would like to thank my colleagues at South Bank University for their general support and comments. In particular, Dr Val Flynn, who has always been very kind in giving of her time to reviewing and providing useful feedback for this book. I would also like to thank editors Kate Brewin and Owen Knight for their patience and encouragement during this project. I would also like to thank Karen Mclaren and Michelle Clark for their excellent support. Thanks also to the reviewers, who provided plenty of feedback and positive suggestions during the development of this book. Special thanks also to Wendy, my sister, whose support has been tremendous throughout this project. Finally, thanks to my wife Janice and three daughters, Katie, Amy and Rhiannon, for their patience and understanding during those many hours spent typing away at the keyboard.

Publisher's acknowledgements

We are grateful to the following for permission to reproduce copyright material:

Figure 1.4 from http://www.pearsoned.co.uk, reproduced with permission of Pearson Education Limited; Figures 1.5, 1.7–1.9, 1.11, 1.16, 1.18–1.24, 2.3, 3.1, 3.4, 3.9, 4.4–4.9, 4.12, 5.1, 5.3, 5.5, 5.7–5.11, 5.13, 5.14b, 5.15, 5.18, 5.19, 6.2, 6.4, 6.6, 6.7, 6.12–6.14, 6.16, 6.17, 6.19, 6.20, 6.23, 6.25, 7.4–7.8, 7.12, 8.2, 8.4, 8.7, 8.8, 8.10–8.15, 8.17–8.21, 8.24, 8.25, 9.7–9.10, 9.12, 9.16, 10.4, 10.5, 11.1, 11.2, 11.3, 11.37, 12.1, 12.15, 13.34, 13.38, 14.2, 14.4, 14.10 and Listings 8.1, 8.3–8.7, 8.9 and 10.5–10.7 screen shots reprinted by permission from Microsoft Corporation; Figure 1.5 used with permission from http://www.cnet.com and Figure 9.9 used with permission from http://www.mp3.com, copyright © 2004 by Computerworld, Inc., Framingham, MA 01701, all rights reserved; Figure 1.10 from http://www2.excelr8.net/allowell.dcf.html, reproduced with permission of Alan Lowell; Figure 1.11 from http://ciudadquesada.co.uk, reproduced with permission of Archant Anglia; Figure 1.12 from http://www. allexperts.com, reproduced with permission of allexperts.com; Figure 1.12 featuring Opera 7.5 Browser, reproduced with permission of Opera Software ASA; Figure 1.14 from http://www.catalogcity.com, reproduced with permission of Altura International; Figure 1.14 Avant Browser reproduced with permission of avantbrowser.com; Figure 1.15 from http://www.loot.com, reproduced with permission of Loot Ltd; Figures 1.4, 1.15, 1.17, 1.18, 2.13, 3.2, 3.3,

3.6–3.8, 3.12, 3.13, 3.15, 5.4, 5.12, 5.14a, 6.3, 6.5, 6.15, 6.21, 6.22, 6.24, 8.3, 8.9, 10.3, 12.11, 14.5–14.9 featuring Mozilla Browser, reproduced with permission of Mozilla Foundation; Figures 3.1, 3.13, 4.3, 9.1, 9.6, 9.15 and 9.16 Adobe product screen shot(s) reprinted with permission from Adobe Systems Incorporated; Figure 3.2 from http://www.google.co.uk and Figure 14.6 from http://www.google.co.uk/grghp?hl=en&tab=wg&g=, reproduced with permission of Google, Inc; Figure 3.3 from http://www.rspca.org.uk/servlet/ Satellite?page-name=RSPCA/AnimalCare/AnimalCareHomepage, reproduced by kind permission of the RSPCA 2004; Figure 3.4 from www.diy.com/diy/jsp/bq/category/category.jsp?CATID=182628, reproduced with permission of B&Q plc; Figure 3.6 from http://www.templates2go.com/ sample/index.htm, reprinted with permission from Regent Press, http://www.templates2go.com; Figure 3.9 from http://www.guestbook.nu, reproduced with permission of Innovate IT Gothenburg AB; Figure 3.11 from http://www.network54.com, reproduced with permission of Network54; Figure 4.1 from CoffeeCup 9.6 HTML and Figure 8.23 from CoffeeCup StyleSheet Maker, reproduced with permission of CoffeeCup Software, Inc; Figure 4.2 from Homesite 5 and Figures 11.1, 11.4–11.36, 12.2–12.7, 12.9, 12.10, 12.12–12.14, 12.16, 12.17, 12.19–12.25, 12.27, 13.1–13.37, 13.42–13.60 from Dreamweaver, reproduced with permission of Macromedia, Inc; Figure 4.10 from PaintShop Pro V8 and Figure 9.5 from Jasc Animation Shop, © Paint Shop Pro, reproduced with permission of Corel Corporation (formerly Jasc Software); Figure 4.11 from PhotoImpact Editing, reproduced with permission of Ulead Systems; Figures 5.1 and 8.26 from http://validator.w3.org, copyright © 2004 World Wide Web Consortium, (Massachusetts Institute of Technology, European Research Consortium for Informatics and Mathematics, Keio University). All Rights Reserved; Figure 7.11 from http://www.geocities.com/SiliconValley/Bay/6879, reproduced with permission of Louis Schiano; Figure 8.17 and 8.18 from http://www.politics. guardian.co.uk/comment/story/0,,872739,00.html, reprinted by permission of PFD on behalf of the Estate of Roy Jenkins, © Roy Jenkins 2003, as printed in the original volume; Figure 8.20 from http://htmlhelp.com/tools/csscheck, reproduced with permission of htmlhelp.com; Figure 8.21 from http://bobby.watchfire. com/bobby/html/en/index.jsp, copyright © 2002–2004 Watchfire Corporation, used with permission, all rights reserved; Figure 8.22 from TopStyle Lite, reproduced with permission of Bradbury Software LLC; Figure 9.3 from http://pro.corbis.com, reproduced with permission of Corbis; Figure 9.12 from http://www.live365.com/index.live, reproduced with permission of Live365, Inc; Figures 13.38–13.41 and 13.47 from http://www.mysql.com, reproduced with permission of MySQL AB; Figure 14.1 from http://www.att.com/spotlight/broadcast, reproduced with permission of Hewlett Packard; Figure 14.2 from http://www.alltheweb.com/search?cat=web&cs=utf8&q=percent22growing+carrots%22&rys=0&_sb_lang=pref, Figure 14.4 from http://search.yahoo.com/search/dir?p=Welsh+Rugby&y=n&e=1451608f=0%3A2766678%3A2718086%3A14..., Figure 14.7 from http://www.altavista.com/web/ results?itag=wrx&q=title%3A +%22Growing+carrots%22&kgs=0&kls=1, reproduced with permission of Yahoo! Inc., © 2004 by Yahoo! Inc., YAHOO! and the YAHOO! logo are trademarks of Yahoo! Inc; Figure 14.5 from http://search.lycos.com/default.asp, © 2004 Lycos, Inc., Lycos® is a registered trademark of Carnegie Mellon University, all

Chapter

1

Introduction to the Internet and Web

In this chapter you will learn to:

- become familiar with the Internet and the World Wide Web (WWW)
- become familiar with using browsers
- manage cookies
- take a brief look at the Microsoft website
- develop a simple Web page using HTML and a text editor.

The Internet and the WWW

Introduction

The spectacular growth of the Internet and the WWW continue to astonish even the wildest sceptics. There are, at the time of writing this book, estimated to be about 2 billion Web pages in cyberspace and over 100 million Internet hosts. The amount of information on the Web is at least doubling every year (Turban, McLean, Wetherbe 2001). The growth of e-commerce is another remarkable phenomenon. For example, Amazon was formed as a website to sell books. The company now has a turnover in excess of $2 billion with a list of customers in excess of 20 million. Incredible when you think that it was only founded in 1994. E-commerce – that is, shopping on the WWW – is expected to exceed $300 billion by the year 2004. In the UK alone, over 40 per cent of the population now has access to the Internet, with the number being much higher in other countries. In the USA, over 50 million people send at least one e-mail message each day. Yet, this seems like only the beginning.

The dotcom financial crash in the world stockmarkets during February 2000 was seen by many experts to be the result of overestimating the short-term impact of new technology while underestimating the long-term impacts. The burgeoning of this technology during the 1990s was largely a period of experimentation and in-stability. We are now entering a period of maturity where standards, development tools and techniques for the Internet and WWW are becoming more established. To appreciate the impact of the Web, study the Nielson/NetRatings (www.nielsen-netratings.com) research for the week ending 25 January 2004 in Table 1.1. Notice that there are almost 110 million users in the USA alone. Only ten years before, there were fewer than 50,000 Internet users!

Table 1.1 United States: Average home Web usage in the USA for week ending 25 January 2004

Sessions/visits per person	10
Domains visited per person	24
PC time per person	08:34:11
Duration of a Web page viewed	00:00:54
Active digital media universe	109,398,089
Current digital media universe estimate	199,097,176

Some definitions

Let us begin by looking at the terms **Internet** and **WWW**. Many people think that the two terms are synonymous. However, they have different meanings.

∎ The **Internet** is a network of connected computers (see Figure 1.1 for an illustration of networked computers). No one company, organization or nation state owns the Internet. It is a cooperative international effort governed by a system of rules. The purpose of connecting computers is to share information. This can be done in a variety of ways, one of these being electronic mail, or **e-mail**. The e-mail method of sharing information allows different users to communicate with each other using mail delivered electronically over the Internet by storing these messages in recipient mailboxes. There are many other ways of sharing

Figure 1.1
A network of computers

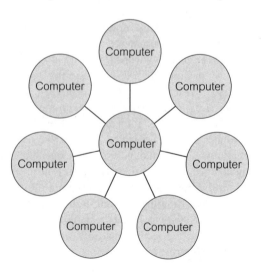

information, but each way requires a special method of communication between computers – known as a protocol. Other Internet communication protocols will be studied a little later in this chapter.

- The **World Wide Web (WWW)** is, like e-mail, simply another protocol that can be used for communication on the Internet. There are several aspects that make the Web unique among other protocols – the main one being that you can link documents together (called **hypertext**) to form a huge 'web' of information. The term that describes the way in which the Web transfers information is called the **Hypertext Transfer Protocol (HTTP)**.

The client

A client is a user of an Internet service, such as the WWW. Most users of the Web simply want to access content on the WWW. To access Web content, the client would need a software application that can receive incoming content and display it. Such an application is called a **browser**. More on browsers follows later in this chapter.

The Web Server

The Web content itself comes from a computer called a **server**. A server is an information provider. It is sometimes called the 'host computer' because it acts as a storage and distribution centre for Web content waiting to be delivered to Web clients. Servers are actual computers physically hooked up to the Internet via cables, telephone lines and so on.

A Web server is a 24-hour, 7 days a week communication application that works something like an automated telephone switchboard. It waits for requests placed by people using Web browsers asking for Web pages. Once a request is made by a browser, the server returns to the client – if it can find it – the requested page. However, this request is not made to one central computer, because the Internet is a network of connected computers that are not owned by any one company – it is said to be '**non-proprietary**'. Many of the computers connected to the Internet are themselves servers. The servers could be commercially based – that is, providing their services to fee-paying customers. These are called **Internet Service Providers (ISPs)** and examples of these are familiar names, such as AOL, Freeserve, Microsoft Network (MSN) and so on. Other types of server service providers may be organizations that have their own servers, such as universities and colleges, local authorities, businesses and so on.

Historical development of the Internet and World Wide Web

Table 1.2 shows some of the significant milestone dates following the history of the Internet and the WWW during its relatively short life.

Table 1.2 Significant milestones in the development of the Internet and World Wide Web

Year	Development
1969	During the Cold War, the US military was concerned with how to communicate in the aftermath of a nuclear war. The Pentagon's Advanced Research Projects Agency (ARPA) agreed to develop a centralized network of computers that became known as ARPANET. It was originally commissioned to investigate research communications to enable dissemination of information in the scientific community.
1972	The INWG (Internet Working Group) was formed. Some agreed protocols for the Internet were devised, Telnet being the first (RFC 318). This protocol lets users access their accounts from remote sites. The same year, other uses for the Internet began to emerge – a researcher wrote a program that could send and receive messages over the Internet, known nowadays as e-mail.
1975	The INWG established the FTP (File Transfer Protocol). This protocol enables users to transfer files from one computer to another.
1977	TCP/IP protocol was invented for networking computers and became the standard. The network itself became known as the Internet.
1989	Tim Berners-Lee was working at the European Laboratory for Particle Physics in Switzerland (known as CERN). He was concerned with finding a method for the distribution of documents for scientists using networked computers. He described hypertext as 'a way to link and access information of various kinds as a Web of nodes in which the user can browse at will. It provides a single user-interface to large classes of information'. The Web was born. IETF (Internet Engineering Task Force) formed – the primary organization developing Internet standards. It meets three times a year.
1990	World Wide Web spec released to the public after ARPANET ceased to exist. First text-based browsers emerged, structure defined by hypertext using HTML (Hypertext Markup Language) – the standard means of displaying Web pages.
1991	The HTTP protocol (Hypertext Transfer Protocol) was devised, enabling the transfer of hypertext documents to remote sites.
1993	The first graphic-based browser, called Mosaic, was created by Marc Andreessen. The Mosaic Communications corporation was formed – later to become Netscape. In the autumn of 1994, the W3C was formed, proclaiming its goal to 'lead the Web to its full potential'.
1994	There was a total of about 50 Web servers at the start of this year. By the end of 1995, this figure had increased to over 200,000.
1995	AltaVista – probably the first search engine used for general purposes – was implemented.

An overview of other common Internet protocols or services

Although this book is primarily concerned with the World Wide Web, Web designers need to be aware of other Internet protocols in common use. The following are some of these.

- **E-mail**, or electronic mail, is by far the most widely used Internet service. The e-mail method of sharing information allows different users to communicate with each other using mail delivered electronically over the Internet by storing these messages in recipient mailboxes. The messages can be read at the convenience of the reader.

- **FTP – (File Transfer Protocol)** – is a method of sending files between computers. It is the most common protocol used to bring files from a particular location on the Internet on to your computer. FTP is required by website designers who would want to transfer their files from their local computer to a server.

- **Usenet** derives its name from the words 'user's network' – for it is a network, the traffic on which moves over the Internet as well as other networks to facilitate discussion and exchange of information on subjects of interest – called **Newsgroups**. Usenet has its roots in the **Unix** operating system and was first used in 1979, although today non-Unix machines participate in Usenet. Usenet boasts a huge variety of topics. These newsgroups are open to all and cover everything from artificial intelligence to landscape gardening.

- **Gopher** is a system that was very popular in the early 1990s. It displays Internet documents and services as menu options. You just select a menu choice and the Gopher either displays a document or another menu or transfers you to a different Gopher site. Gopher predates the Web as a means of organizing and displaying files on Internet servers. A Gopher server presents its contents as a hierarchically structured list of files. When the Web began its ascendancy, many Gopher databases were converted to websites, which can be more easily accessed via Web search engines (see Chapter 14).

- **Telnet** is another program that has been around since the 1960s and enables you to log on to another computer on the Internet and use its resources as though they existed on your machine. For example, you could access a library's computer via Telnet to use the electronic version of its card catalogue. Telnet was very popular in universities for making campus information available to students, but nowadays this sort of information is usually available on the Web. Even so, Telnet is still frequently used by website designers who might want to view file directories on Web servers.

Internet and WWW standards

Many people think that the Internet is an anarchic, unstructured entity. This is a false perception. The Internet has an open architecture network but this is only made possible by standards that apply and allow different proprietary technologies to work seamlessly together. There is no single central point of control on the

Internet, but there are several groups that pull together from a community of Internet users. These organizations work together for a perceived benefit to the Internet and WWW. These organizations include the following.

- **RFC (Request For Comments) (www.rfc-editor.org)** is an organization that provides a set of technical papers for users of the Internet. It is a vital conduit that enables Internet experts to pool their abilities and focus on how best to move the technology forward. Documents are submitted as an Internet draft and considered by members for publication.

- **ISOC (Internet Society) (www.isoc.org)** is perhaps the most influential group behind the scenes of the Internet. ISOC is the international organization responsible for cooperation and coordination on the Internet. It acts as an administrative glue, holding together a host of groups responsible for Internet infrastructure standards and protocols.

- **W3C (World Wide Web Consortium) (www.w3.org)** is probably the most important from the Web designer's point of view and something all Web designers need to become familiar with. The W3C is now appropriately led by Tim-Berners Lee – the man who invented the Web – and acts as an archive of Web information for developers and users. The W3C also promotes standards and develops prototype applications to demonstrate the use of new technologies. Working in accordance with ISOC procedural guidelines, W3C helps to develop and maintain anything that can impact the evolution of the Web. This means that not only do Web languages, such as HTML, come under W3C scrutiny but also Web television and various other emerging Web technologies, such as mobile phones or other wireless devices, which are vying for Web access.

The WWW addressing system

Each document on the Web has its own unique address so that it can be identified, called a **Uniform Resource Locator (URL)**. A typical URL is made up of four parts. For example, 'http://www.lsbu.ac.uk/graphics/my_file.html' is a URL. The four component parts are as follows.

- The first part – http:// – refers to the Internet protocol to be used. In this case the **Hypertext Transfer Protocol**.

- The second part – www.lsbu.ac.uk – names the connecting server where the document will be found. This is called a **domain name**, which is itself broken up into a number of parts. The 'www' refers to the World Wide Web, which means that a file will be obtained from the lsbu Web server. Both 'ac' and 'uk' are known as domain suffixes. The 'ac' means that the server represents an academic institution, such as a university, in the country called the 'uk' (United Kingdom). Table 1.3 describes commonly used domain suffixes that are recognized by the W3C.

- The third part – /graphics – refers to the **path name** – that is, it specifies which directory on the server to search for the required file. Note the way that the '/' character – called **forward slash** – is used to separate the component parts.

- Finally, the fourth part is the name of the file itself – in this case, 'my_file.html'. The part before the full stop is the **filename** itself, while the part after the full stop tells us that the file is an HTML document (see later in this chapter). It must end in '.htm' or '.html' in order to be recognized as an HTML Web document. If a file-name is not specified, then the home page is usually selected by default. The **home page** represents the front door entrance to a website (see note to Figure 1.2).

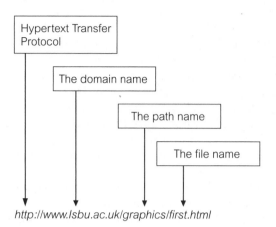

Figure 1.2
What the parts of a Web address mean

http://www.lsbu.ac.uk/graphics/first.html

NOTE

If a file name is not specified in a URL, then the server will search for a default file, usually called 'index.html' or 'default.htm'.

Table 1.3 Domain suffix names

Domain name extension	Intended purpose
.com	Used primarily for commercial sites. It is supposed to be international, but has become synonymous with the USA. Use this if required domain is international
.org	Used by non-profit-making organizations, such as charities, user groups and so on
.ac	Used by academic institutions, such as universities and other higher education colleges
.net	Used by various network organizations
.edu	Used by education and higher education institutions, such as schools, colleges and so on
.gov	Used to describe various government sites

NOTE

In practice, some websites use extensions that do not always match their intended uses. One of the reasons for this is that a name using a particular extension might already be registered and therefore a domain name using a different extension might be used instead. However, it is not always possible to get the extension you want because some domain name extensions are monitored, such as .gov and .ac. On the other hand, domain extensions such as .com are under no such scrutiny.

Browsers

Anyone who has any experience of using the Web will have used a browser. A **browser** is a software program that enables users to view Web pages. It does this by reading and interpreting HTML files to display text, graphics and other resources on the user's display from the WWW.

Several browsers are available and they run on a variety of platforms, including PCs, Macintosh and mainframe computers. However, the most commonly used browsers on the PC are Microsoft Internet Explorer (IE) and Netscape Navigator. On the Macintosh, the major browser is currently Apple Safari. IE – at the time of writing – is also very popular, but development of this browser has currently been discontinued. Other well-known browsers include Opera, Mozilla and Lynx, which all run on both PC and Macintosh hardware.

IE and Netscape are the two most successful **graphic user interface (GUI)**-based browsers, while Opera is more popular with Web developers because of its testing facilities. The Mozilla browser with its Gecko engine will form the basis of all future Netscape browsers and has been increasing its market share consistently for the last two years (see www.w3schools.com/browsers/browsers_stats.asp). Lynx is a text-based browser. It was developed in 1990 and is still used mainly in academic institutions. WebTV was specifically developed for use with television set Internet access.

Browser statistics

There is no standard browser in use, but Internet Explorer (IE) has about 80 per cent of the total market share at the time of writing (see www.netmechanic.com). Netscape (including Mozilla) has most of the remaining 20 per cent of market share. Web designers should note that, although Lynx and WebTV have less than 1 per cent of overall market share, they do, nevertheless, have over 1 million users worldwide.

Browser vendors are constantly improving their products by releasing newer versions – on average, a new version of IE and Netscape is released every 18 months. Each successive version of a browser introduces more features, as well as providing compatibility with the more recent Web technologies.

The pie chart in Figure 1.3 depicts the Web browser statistics for the USA during the early part of 2004 (note that the proportion for Netscape includes the

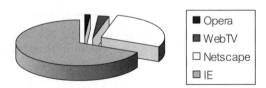

Figure 1.3 Browser statistics for January 2004
Source: www.webmechanic.com

Mozilla browser). For more on browser usage and other up-to-date statistics, visit http://browserwatch.com. For browser utilities, visit www.browsers.com

Browser problems for Web designers

Browsers arouse much debate in the Web community because what you see on your screen depends to a great degree on how your browser is able to interpret and display the HTML files and associated graphic, sound and multimedia resources. Lynx, for example, is a text-based browser and provides facilities that are little more than digital teletypes, sending text from the file to your screen. Lynx would not be able to render graphic or video facilities. On the other hand, Lynx consumes very little memory and so is fast in operation and, as Lynx is only text-based, it does not require expensive hardware or software to run. Moreover, Lynx users would be well aware of its limitations and might only be interested in viewing text content anyway. Also, disabled users may require a text-only browser or have the graphics turned off because of some sight disability, say.

From the website designer's point of view, one of the greatest challenges comes from designing pages that display properly when using different browsers. This is because browsers sometimes display pages differently because of the way that they interpret HTML tags and some browsers use their own proprietary tags. Moreover, each successive version of a browser introduces more features and compatibility with newer Web technologies. One of the problems, then, confronting Web designers is not just ensuring that their websites display correctly with newer technologies, but that alternative technologies are provided to work with older browsers that do not support these newer technologies – a formidable task for designers, as we shall see in Chapters 8, 9 and 10. The choice and version of the browser that is selected by a Web page viewer is an unknown quantity, so browser support requires careful thought by the website designer.

Using browsers

Web browsers are generally easy to use and require little training. To use a browser to view a website, you would normally enter the URL of the website into the **location** or **'Address' bar** (see Figure 1.4). For example, if you wanted to view, in IE, the Web page with the URL www.pearsoned.co.uk, then you would simply type the name directly in the Address bar.

Within the browser window, you will see the familiar title bar at the top of the window, which is called the **page title**. As you skim the mouse over a viewable page, you will see that the mouse pointer changes to the hand shape and sometimes these items are underlined and coloured blue. These are called **hypertext links**. The user can transfer from one page to another using hypertext. Hypertext is a special word or phrase in a Web page that acts as a link to other Web resources, such as a different Web page. When you select the link (usually by clicking on it with your mouse), the linked resource automatically appears on your computer. Any word or phrase can be designated a hypertext link. Indeed, it is also possible to use a graphic

Figure 1.4
Using a browser
Address bar to
go to a URL

The
Address
bar

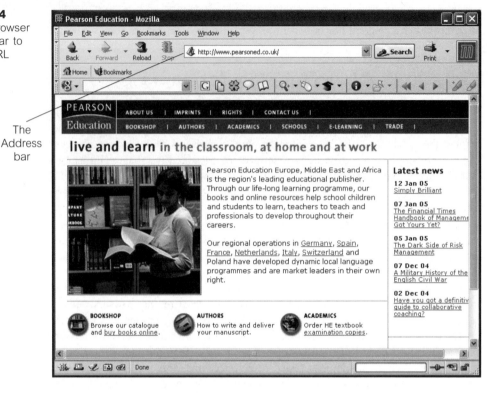

picture or button to do this as well. There is also no reason for the link to point only to other Web documents – you could use a hyperlink to point to an e-mail program or many other Internet-based activities.

Browser navigational facilities

Browsers facilitate navigation in several ways. For example, Figure 1.5 displays the IE 6 standard toolbar, which contains both **Forward** and **Back** buttons. The Back button will link with the previous page visited, while the Forward button will return to the page after the Back button – that is, it will link forward to the next page.

The **Home** button takes the user to the Home page that has been set by the browser (more on this below).

The **Search** button on the standard toolbar is another established browser component (see Figure 1.6). Any query can be entered, with references given following the click of the Search button.

Other features provided by browsers

GUI-based browsers provide a variety of other features. These are implemented in a variety of ways depending on the browser and include the following.

∎ **History** gives users the opportunity to search through recently visited sites. Clicking the History button, as shown in Figure 1.5, divides the browser window

The History list   Forward and Back buttons   The Home button   Other standard toolbar buttons

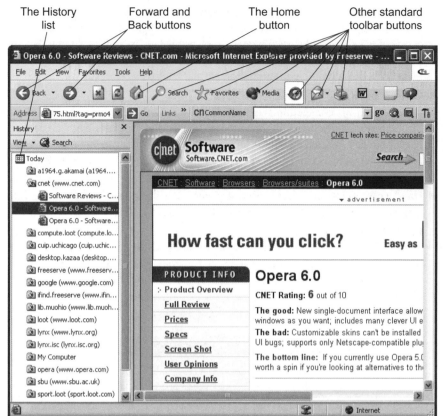

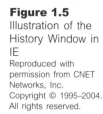

Figure 1.5
Illustration of the History Window in IE

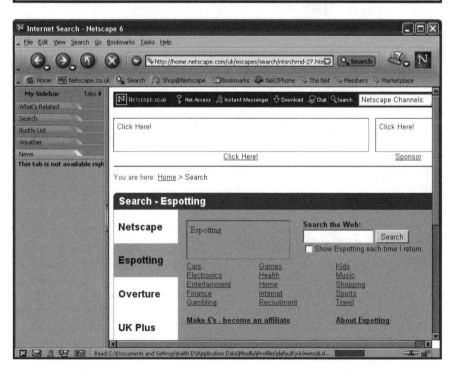

Figure 1.6
The Search facility on Netscape

into two vertical sections. Using the left-hand window, the user can search through the contents and select previously visited pages. The user can then categorize the pages in all sorts of ways – such as by date, by order visited today, by site or even by most visited. The History window is useful for finding previously visited URLs without having to remember the address.

■ **Offline browsing** is another handy facility for users who have access to a metered dial-up connection. Using File / Work Offline sets the browser into offline mode by disconnecting the modem connection. The user can then browse pages already visited without incurring any additional telephone charges. Alternatively, pages can be permanently saved by using File / Save As from the File menu.

■ **Hard copy printing** is used to print pages by using File / Print from the File menu or by clicking the Print button on the standard toolbar.

■ **Favorites** provides another feature that has been around for many years but has been improved with successive browser versions. Users can designate favourite websites for easy access without having to remember their URLs. When you add a page to Favorites, you will see that there is also an option to make it available offline (see Figure 1.7). By clicking the Customize option, you can ensure that when you view the page offline, it is still up to date.

Figure 1.7
Adding a page to
Favorites on IE

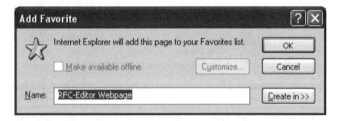

■ **Controlling access** The Internet provides unprecedented access to a wide variety of information. Some information, however, may not be suitable for every viewer. For example, you might want to prevent children from seeing websites that contain violent or sexual content. Figure 1.8 illustrates how IE would let you do this by setting values in the **Content Advisor**.

■ **Customizable toolbar buttons** empower the user with the capability to move or remove toolbars as the user likes.

■ **Search assistants** enable users to find out if, and where, some text item appears on a Web page.

■ **Refresh** (on IE) or **Reload** (on Netscape) is a browser feature that ensures you have the latest version of the current Web page. This is particularly useful if you are viewing, for example, news broadcasting sites.

■ **AutoSearch** facilities enable users to type a simple phrase into the address bar of a browser and the correct URL will – quite often – be found (see Figure 1.6).

■ **E-mail** is a feature that lets you send the page that you are currently viewing to a colleague by clicking on the **Mail** button on the standard toolbar and selecting **Send a link**.

Figure 1.8
Setting viewing
content on IE

Setting browser preferences

Browsers can be customized to reflect an individual user's preferences. This means the user can control the way that text, colours, images, the choice of home page to go to during startup and so on are displayed.

It is very likely that the default home page set up by the system is not appropriate for every user. All browsers can be customized to display any choice of default home page. On IE 5, this can be done by (see Figure 1.9) following these steps:

Figure 1.9
Setting default
home page in
the Internet
options dialogue
box on IE

1 from the **Tools** menu choose **Internet options**

2 click the **General** tab and select the **Home page default** and set as required (in Figure 1.9, I have set my Home page to www.icwales.com)

3 click the **OK** button.

Many other user preferences can be set, but there are too many to list them all here, so you are advised to refer to the online browser **Help** for more details. Moreover, it is advisable to become familiar with one or more browser features. The main browser Web addresses are included in the following sections and more details can be found there.

General tips for using browsers

Familiarity with the scope of facilities provided by browsers can save time and effort. Here are some general tips for using browsers.

- Get into the habit of using the History list when trying to retrieve recently visited pages. This is a useful browser facility that enables you to find a Web page from the current or previous session of use. To use this facility, simply click the History button on the toolbar (see Figure 1.5). History options can be adjusted by using the General tab of the Internet Options dialogue box. By clicking the Settings button (see Figure 1.9), the amount of disk space allocated to stored Web pages can be set. This is called the **cache**. The cache is an area on the hard disk that a browser designates for saving Web pages so that they can be retrieved rapidly and read offline.

- If you get errors when trying to open a Web page with a lengthy URL, such as http://www.sbu.ac.uk/graphics/documents, don't despair – it might still be there, but stored in a different place on the server. It might be worthwhile trying to break it down, perhaps by trying http://www.sbu.ac.uk/graphics, and then, if you enter the Web page for this section, you might find the link to the required page. This often happens because organizations move hyperlinks to different directories for reasons such as restructuring to reflect changes in the organization.

Popular browsers

Netscape Navigator (http://channels.netscape.com/ns/browsers/default.jsp)

When Netscape Navigator was first released in December 1994, its impact was enormous. Netscape was the first really successful commercial graphical Web browser that ran on the Windows, Macintosh and Unix operating systems. The browser came with built-in newsgroup access and basic e-mail capabilities as well as search facilities, favourites and many other features.

During the mid-1990s, Netscape was the most successful Web browser in use. However, it took Netscape over three years after the release of 4.0 to produce its next generation browser (Version 6.0) and this delay gave Microsoft's Internet Explorer (IE) time to establish itself as the most popular Web browser. Figure 1.10 displays the Dave Clark Five's website, using the Netscape 7 browser.

Figure 1.10
Illustration of the Dave Clark Five's webSite, using Netscape 7.0

Internet Explorer (IE)
(www.microsoft.com/windows.ie/default.mspx)

Internet Explorer has now established itself as the market leader in the browser market.

Version 5 and above contain built-in IntelliSense technology, which can save you time with routine Web tasks, such as automatically completing Web addresses and forms for you and automatically detecting your network and connection status. IntelliSense technology also provides a means of eliminating unnecessary keystrokes, such as circumventing the need to type the 'http://' part in a URL. IE also includes plenty of support for security and privacy when using the Web.

The Accessibility Wizard presents features sorted by disability, making it easy to customize Windows to each individual's needs. The Accessibility Wizard also enables you to save your settings to a file that can be used on another computer.

The Content Advisor provides a way to help you control the types of content that your computer can gain access to on the Internet. After you turn on Content Advisor, only rated content that meets or exceeds your criteria can be viewed. You can adjust the settings.

Automating common tasks is another feature that is prominent on IE 5+. The Autocorrect feature, for example, automatically corrects misspelled Web address components, such as 'http://'.

IE 6 also contains advanced control facilities for cookies (see later in this chapter). Figure 1.11 displays a screenshot of a Spanish tourist destination page using IE 6.

Figure 1.11
A Web page on an IE 6 browser

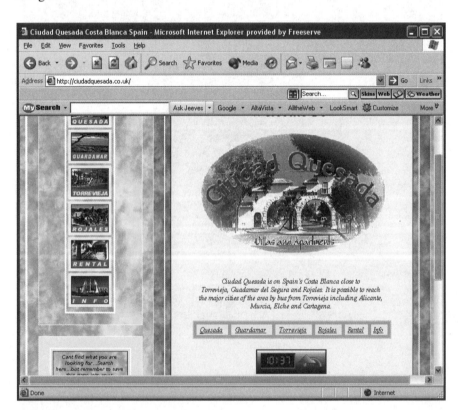

Opera (www.opera.com)

Opera has established itself as one of the most popular browsers in current use (see Figure 1.12). It is particularly popular with Web designers because of its capability to monitor browser statistical information, such as speed of download time and size. Opera runs very fast on a PC with Windows or Linux or a Macintosh computer and contains a built-in e-mail client, along with many other features.

Figure 1.12
The Opera 7.5
browser in use

Lynx (www.lynx.browser.org)

Lynx is a text-based browser and, despite its limitations, has a fairly large user base, especially in academic institutions. Lynx cannot render graphics, sound or video facilities. On the other hand, it consumes very little memory and is, therefore, fast in operation and, as it is only text-based, it does not require expensive hardware or software to run. Figure 1.13 displays a configuration screen using the Lynx browser.

Figure 1.13
The Lynx text-
based browser
configuration

Mozilla (www.mozilla.org)

Mozilla is an **open source** browser, which means that its code is shared publicly so that other programmers can contribute to improvements. Mozilla is rapidly gaining in popularity for it includes Web-browsing facilities, e-mail and newsgroup support, privacy support, facilities for customization and even a built-in Web page development program called Composer. Future versions of Netscape will be based on the Gekko engine, underlying the operation of Mozilla, so both browsers are closely linked.

Other browsers

There are many other browsers available for use on the PC and Macintosh. However, the combined market share of the others is tiny. The Avant browser (www.avantbrowser.com) (see Figure 1.14) is used to display a Santa Claus website. NeoPlanet (www.neoplanet.com) works closely with IE and screenshots using NeoPlanet are sometimes displayed in later chapters in this book.

Figure 1.14
A Web page on the Avant browser

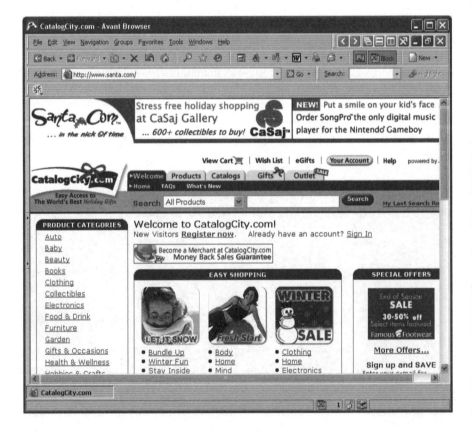

Managing cookies

A **cookie** is a small text file generated by a Web server, stored locally by a Web browser and made available to the originating server on demand whenever a user downloads Web pages from that Web server.

The purpose of a cookie is that, whenever a user revisits a site, the server could use the cookie information to make decisions regarding the user. For example, suppose you visited a computer retailer site and spent a great deal of time reading pages on notebook computers, the cookie may contain this information so that the next time you visit the site you could be alerted to any special offers on notebooks that are available to customers. As another example, suppose you wanted to place regular advertisements in a newspaper using a website. You would probably need to register at the site with a name and password for identification. For security reasons, these would be checked by the server every time you revisit the site and the server could then manage your advertisements. Figure 1.15 shows how a registered visitor to the Loot advertising (www.loot.com) website would be able to read and manage previously placed advertisements. Cookies are unpopular with some Web users because they might be seen as an infringement of privacy. One of the new features on IE 6 browser versions is cookie management.

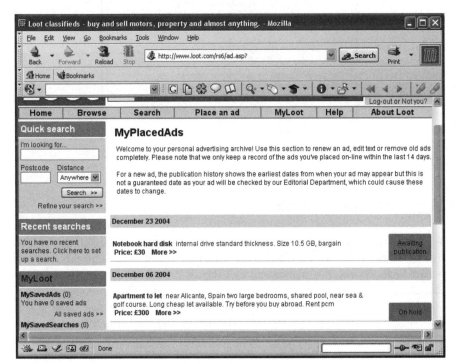

Figure 1.15
Using cookies to store user data

To manage cookies on IE 6, go to **Tools / Internet options** and select the **Privacy** tag. Figure 1.16 shows how you can control cookies entering your system hard disk. Notice how the user can move the slider so that the control varies between complete blockage of cookies and complete acceptance of all cookie content. The user can now control the cookie content on a host machine on IE 6 by selecting the **Security** tab of the Internet Options dialogue box. There are four levels of security. The most lenient permits downloading of all cookies, while the other extreme prevents any cookies from being stored on your PC.

Figure 1.16
Setting cookie
controls

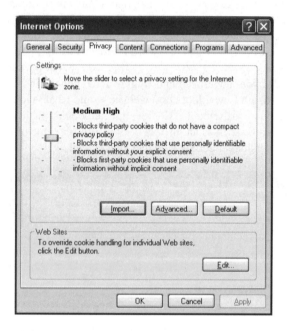

How cookies work

When a URL is requested by the user, the browser sends the request in the form of **header lines** to the server. The server responds with a Web page preceded by header lines. A cookie is transmitted invisibly as extra header lines. The browser then stores the cookie information on the user's terminal. Cookies contain names and values. A cookie name can contain alphanumeric characters and underscores. The value is a text string. The domain comes next and, for security reasons, cookies can only be read by scripts on the same site that created the cookie – they cannot be read by documents on other sites. A cookie is stored for the duration of the browser session. If you specify an expiry time, the cookie will exist even if the browser session has ended until the specified time required. You can find out what cookies are stored on your system by visiting the website http://privacy.net/analyze – Figure 1.17 displays a screenshot from this site.

Figure 1.17
Finding out how
many cookies are
stored on your
system

A brief look at the Microsoft website

The Microsoft website is one of the largest sites in the world and the most visited. For these reasons, we will look briefly at it – not just to gain an understanding of what to expect to find on large websites but also to provide some pointers for Web design issues in the following chapters. In the sections that follow, we will focus on the **user interface** – that is, the visual communication aspects of the site – and the **support** provided to the user community to enable users to deal with problems.

The home page

The home page (see Figure 1.18) contains about 30 menu headings, leading to innumerable options and pages. It also contains many article links, news, five main features and a search engine. There is also a very extensive download centre included so that users can download anything from try-out software to program fixes.

Figure 1.18
Microsoft's home
page

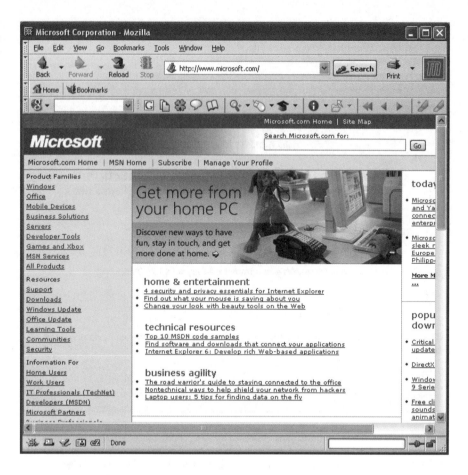

The user interface design

The user interface design includes a consistent blue and white background layout
throughout, with some areas using different colours to easily identify the sections.
For example, Figure 1.18 shows Microsoft's home page. If you look at this page on
your computer, you will see a black menu bar in the top of the page window. This
gives quick access to certain key areas of the entire site and is always there, re-
assuring the user who may feel lost. These menus are called **navigation bars** and
are a familiar feature of many websites to enable easy navigation.

Immediately below the black menu is a blue menu bar running across the page
that includes an option for the home page. The purpose of this is to take the user
quickly to the most useful sections or parts of the site that the user is currently
surfing. There is another more substantial navigation bar on the left-hand side
(coloured grey) that is specific to the area you are currently in.

There is also a built-in **search engine**. A search engine enables you to search for
sites containing certain keywords and, thus, get quick access to relevant information. In the case of the Microsoft site, the user can do both an internal and external

site search. The basic search box is below the blue bar, from where you can enter any query, word or phrase and then references will appear, if available. An **advanced search** accompanies the **basic search**, allowing refinements such as excluding particular words, words occurring together and so on. There is also a **quick search** facility.

Support

Clicking the black menu bar's Support option (see Figure 1.19) gives a number of choices, including the 'Knowledge Base'. The Knowledge Base is of particular interest because it gives the user access to the support provided by Microsoft. Figure 1.19 displays a screenshot of the page called 'Product Support Services' and the left-hand navigation bar contains an 'I want to ...' set of options. Selecting the 'Find a Solution using ...' option on this screen gives the 'Find a solution – Overview' support screen, as shown in Figure 1.20.

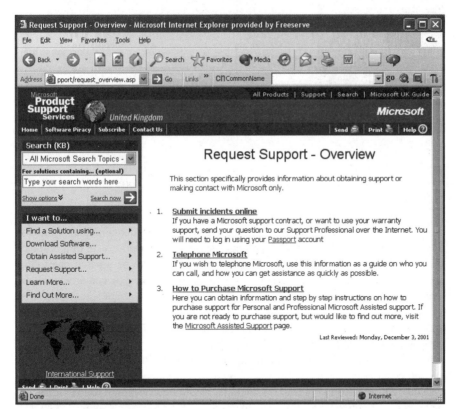

Figure 1.19
Microsoft's main page for user support

Overview of support

The support section provides an overview of the types of support available from Microsoft's website. Figure 1.20 shows the self-support overview. Notice that there

Figure 1.20
The 'Finding a
solution –
Overview' page

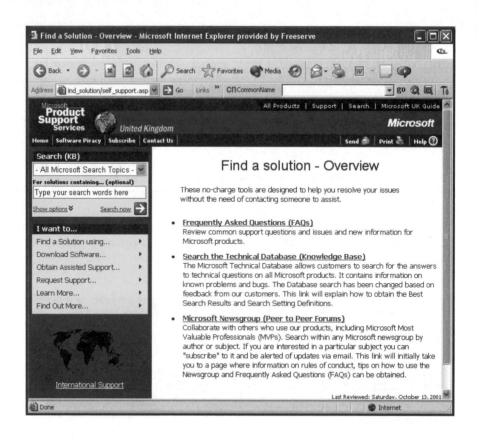

are three parts to self-help. They are 'Frequently Asked Questions (FAQs)', 'Search
the Technical Database (Knowledge Base)' and the 'Microsoft Newsgroup (Peer to
Peer Forums)'.

The FAQs page is divided into categories that lead to many Microsoft-specific
products. The Knowledge Base is an invaluable search tool, containing a vast repository of information pertaining to product support, descriptions of tools, update
fixes and so on. If a solution to your problem turns out to be a patch or product
update, you will be referred to the Download Centre, where you can download the
item to install on your PC.

Finally, the Microsoft Newsgroup could well turn out to be a useful last resort for
those who fail to solve their problem cases adequately. The Newsgroups are discussion forums that are populated by Microsoft users and very often might include
someone who has experienced an identical problem to the one that you might be
encountering.

You will see from Figure 1.21 that the 'Community Newsgroups' left-hand
menu bar is organized into different categories – 'Desktop Applications', 'Games',
'Hardware', 'Internet Applications', 'Reference', 'Windows' and so on. These
categories are subdivided into products, such as – in the case of Windows
products – items such as Windows XP, Windows 2000, Windows NT and so on.
Figure 1.22 displays a page from the Community Newsgroup discussing problems
pertaining to the Photodraw application.

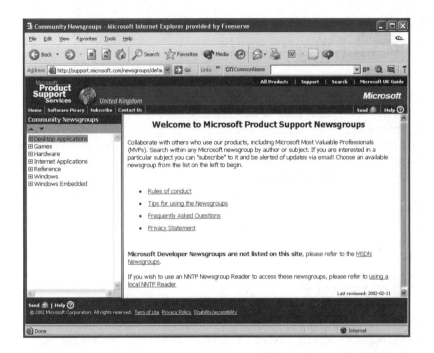

Figure 1.21
The Microsoft
Product Support
Newsgroups
page

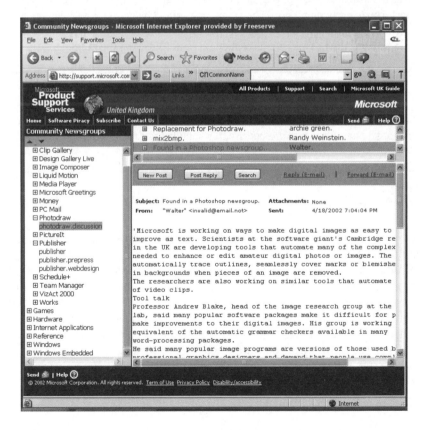

Figure 1.22
Selecting a
Microsoft
newsgroup

A brief introduction to Hypertext Markup Language (HTML)

If you already have some familiarity with the HTML language, you may skip this section, for its purpose is to get you briefly acquainted with the Hypertext Markup Language (HTML) via a hands-on example before studying XHTML in some depth in Chapters 5 and 6.

Before a Web page can be rendered using a browser, it has to be created in a language such as HTML, the purpose of which is to describe how that page should be displayed by the browser. Languages that do this are called **markup languages** and HTML is one example. HTML is the major language of the World Wide Web, with most websites and Web pages using this language. All HTML files are **plain text files** – that is, they contain only standard keyboard text characters, so they can be edited on any type of computer.

HTML **elements**

An HTML file is composed of elements. An **element** is a block of code that is marked with special characters called **tags**. Elements are used to add content to a Web page, such as inserting text on a page, making text bold and so on, instructing the browser to perform a particular task. The HTML tags are always enclosed inside angle brackets < >. For example, the tag for making text bold is <B>. The letter B inside the tag informs the browser to make the text item following the tag bold.

NOTE

Browsers will accept upper-case or lower-case elements in HTML tags. In the <B> tag above, <b> would also be accepted by the browser. However, when using XHTML, lower-case characters must be used for tag elements. This means that the upper-case characters that are used in this section are prohibited from Chapter 5 onwards.

Container tags

HTML uses two types of elements: **container tags** and **empty tags**. These tags differ because of what they represent.

Container tags define a section of text in the document itself and specify the formatting or construction for all of the selected text. A container tag has both a beginning and an ending. The **ending tag** is identical to the beginning tag, with the addition of a forward slash preceding the end tag. For example, the bold tag <B> is a container tag that will be used to mark a section of a document to be rendered bold. This means that when you use the bold tag, it will have a begin tag <B> and an end tag </B>. Hence, if you wanted to render the line of text 'Have a happy day!' in bold in a browser window, the HTML code would be written as:

```
<B> Have a happy day!</B>
```

Empty tags

Empty tags, on the other hand, are tags that are defined in such a way that they contain no end tag. Examples would be line breaks and horizontal rules in a document. Clearly, a line break doesn't have an end tag associated with it. These tags indicate 'one time' instructions that WWW viewers can read and execute without having a finish.

A template for HTML documents

HTML documents must follow a defined pattern of elements if they are to be interpreted correctly. It is a good idea to create a template to use for each page so that you are less likely to leave out an important detail.

Listing 1.1 is an example of a basic HTML template. Detailed explanations of these tags will be given in Chapter 5.

Listing 1.1 A basic HTML template

```
< HTML>

<HEAD >
   < TITLE> My First Web Page</TITLE>
</HEAD >

<BODY >
This is where all visible page items appear.

</BODY >

</HTML >
```

Notice how all HTML documents contain the <HTML>, <HEAD> and <BODY> tags. The HEAD contains the TITLE tag. The contents of the TITLE tag will be displayed in the Window document bar of the browser window. These tags will be examined in detail in Chapter 5. HTML tags used assumed default values. For example, the <BODY> tag displays the body of a document and the background colour of the document is assumed to be 'white'. However, you might want to change this default value to some other colour instead – for example, yellow. You can do this by changing the background colour attribute. Setting attribute values is described next.

Attributes

Attributes are used to control some aspect of a tag's actions. For example, when a heading tag is used, an attribute could control the alignment. Most attributes take values that follow an = sign after the attribute's name. The syntax for using an attribute is:

```
<BODY BGCOLOR ="Red">
```

The above line has the effect of changing the background colour of the Web page from white to red.

Using hyperlinks

The most important capability of HTML is its ability to create hyperlinks to documents elsewhere on the server and different servers and make possible a worldwide network of linked information.

A hypertext link really has two different parts. First, there's the part you see on the Web page, called an **anchor**. There's also the part – the **URL reference** – that tells the browser where to go if you click that link. When you click a link's anchor, the browser loads the file or document given by the link's corresponding URL reference.

The following example shows the HTML tag format for using a hyperlink:

```
<A HREF="http://microsoft.com">The Microsoft Web Site</A>
```

Creating HTML documents

HTML files are plain text files – standard 8-bit ASCII, which means that it is possible to create an HTML file using a simple text editor on virtually any computer. A text editor is normally supplied with a computer's operating system software. Notepad is an example of a text editor that is supplied with Microsoft Windows.

The hands-on task that follows uses the Microsoft Windows NotePad program to create a simple HTML Web page. The example contains links to my favourite search engine websites. Notice in the listing that the first two lines after the <HTML> tag contain:

```
<!--Introduction to HTML and hyperlinks   -->
<!--Author Keith Darlington 2003 -->
```

These are examples of **comment tags**. Their purpose is to provide information to the HTML writer and are ignored by the browser. There are many other new tags used in this listing that will be described in later chapters. The purpose of the task is to enable you to become familiar with using a text editor and running HTML files.

Hands-on task

Create the HTML file shown in Listing 1.2 using the NotePad text editor by following these steps.

1 Right-click any area of the Windows Desktop and, from the given menu, choose **New / Text Document**.

2 A new window will appear enabling you to enter the file. Use the keyboard to enter the file as it is shown in Listing 1.2 – use your own name and favourite search engines if you wish.

3 When the typing is complete, save the file using **File / Save As**. Save the file using the filename **links.html**.

4 Test the file using Internet Explorer. Do this by entering Internet Explorer, choose **File / Open**. Click the **Browse** button (see Figure 1.23) in the pop-up window that follows. Select the **filename links.htm** that will then be displayed in the desktop window contents list that follows.

Figure 1.23
Opening a file on
the Browser

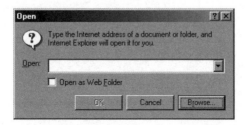

NOTE

If your browser displays the HTML source code in the window instead of showing the actual Web page itself, then the cause of this problem is probably due to inadvertently saving the file with a `.txt` extension instead of using the required `.html` extension. Be careful when saving HTML files. Many text editors, such as NotePad, use the .txt extension by default.

Listing 1.2 A hands-on example

```
<HTML>
<!-- Introduction to HTML and hyperlinks    -->
<!--Author Keith Darlington 2003-->

<HEAD>
<TITLE > Accessing Search Engines with Hyperlinks</TITLE>
</head>
<BODY bgcolor="red">
<CENTER>
<H2>Here are Keith Darlington's favourite Search Engines</H2>
<P><STRONG>Click on the Search Engine link to go to that
site.</STRONG></P>
<!--Hyperlink form: <A HREF ="address">-->
<P>Lycos: <A HREF ="http://www.lycos.co.uk">
http://www.lycos.com</A></P>
<P>AltaVista: <A HREF ="http://www.altavista.com">
http://www.altavista.com</A></P>
<P>Dogpile: <A HREF ="http://www.dogpile.com">
http://www.dogpile.com</A></P>
<P>Webcrawler: <A HREF ="http://www.Webcrawler.com">
http://www.Webcrawler.com</A></P>
</CENTER>
</BODY >
</HTML >
```

The output from this listing is shown using IE 6 in Figure 1.24.

Figure 1.24
Screenshot of
Listing 1.2
using IE 6

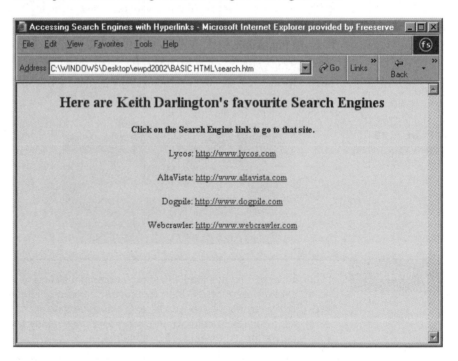

Useful Web learning resources

The following is a list of Web resources that the reader might find useful for getting a better understanding of some of the topics covered in this chapter.

W3Schools (www.w3schools.com)   This site contains a very useful set of online tutorial Web resources for developing a website. W3Schools provides an interactive-style tutorial covering everything from HTML to virtually every other Web technology. Most of the tutorials include a quiz inviting the user to test their knowledge of the material covered. There is also an online HTML editor, which means you can experiment with code and see the results very easily. There is also a good tutorial on browsers on this site.

thesitewizard.com (www.thesitewizard.com)   This site contains a large collection of documents for all aspects of Web design.

Webmonkey (http://www.webmonkey.wired.com/webmonkey)   This is another extensive website that contains many tutorials on every aspect of Web design. Well suited to the intermediate user with plenty of emphasis on W3 standards.

PageTutor (www.pagetutor.com)   This site is well suited to the beginner and presents the material in a novel, humorous manner. All aspects of Web page design are covered, with particular emphasis on HTML and scripting languages.

SitePoint (www.sitepoint.com)   This is an online magazine for designers and includes many practical articles. Lots of these have tutorials for Dreamweaver, QuickTime and JavaBeans. The site also includes an e-mail newsletter for subscribers. Several book reviews are also included on this site.

HTMLCenter (www.htmlcenter.com)   This site is better suited to the intermediate user who will find many specialist articles as well as discussion boards concerning many aspects of Web programming and other techniques.

Summary

- A browser is a software program that lets you view Web pages on the World Wide Web.
- A URL is the address of a website. For example, www.bbc.co.uk/wales.
- A URL is made up of four parts.
- A home page is the first page visitors reach when visiting your website.
- A Web page title appears at the top of the browser window in the Title bar.
- It is recommended that Web page file names should be kept to under eight characters so that they are compatible with older systems.
- A cookie is a text file generated by a Web server, stored locally by a Web browser and made available to the originating server on demand whenever a user downloads Web pages from that Web server.
- The purpose of a cookie is that, whenever a user revisits a site, the server can use the cookie information to make decisions regarding the user.
- Cookies can be controlled with the most recent wave of browsers by setting Internet options within the browser.
- Web page authors can use HTML to provide the content and layout of their pages.
- HTML files can be created by using a text editor.
- HTML files can have the '.htm' or '.html' extension.

Exercises

1 Distinguish between the World Wide Web and the Internet.

2 Explain what is meant by a Web server. What is the HTTP protocol and why is it used?

3 Describe the constituent parts of a URL.

4 Briefly describe the purpose of a browser.

5 Visit the websites www.ietf.org and www.w3.org using either the Internet Explorer or Netscape browsers. From your visits, write a short paragraph describing what the purpose is of both the Internet Engineering Task Force and World Wide Web Consortium.

6 Visit and compare the Netscape and Internet Explorer browsers. Try to find out if each browser contains the following facilities and, where they are available, comment on their effectiveness:

> Favorites
> History
> Search
> Help

Can you see any differences that are likely to have implications for website designers?

7 Explain the difference between a bookmark page and a history list. Find out, using the IE browser, the different ways in which you might be able to view a history list.

8 You can see a list of all cookies that are stored on your system by visiting http://privacy.net. Click on the link at the top left-hand side of the page that says 'For a full analysis click here'. You will see that the report contains a great deal of information about the presence of cookies and other items. State two other items that are described in the analysis, indicating how they might help the browser user.

9 Download the Opera Web browser from the website www.opera.com, then evaluate the browser using the following criteria:

> speed of download
> history facility
> clarity of menu bars.

10 Create an HTML file using a text editor and type the following text within the body element:

> If $x < 0$, then x is a negative number.

Test the page using a browser and comment on what happened. Can you see why?

Chapter

2

Planning and preparation of a website

In this chapter you will learn to:

- be aware of website development lifecycle stages
- understand the stages of prototyping and testing
- be familiar with website planning issues
- establish functions of your website
- create a site map
- apply a range of information design paradigms for website development
- know how to upload files on to the Web.

Introduction

Many website projects are no different from any other software development project in that their development will follow formal processes in terms of a cycle of stages – known as the **development lifecycle**. These stages are interdependent and follow a particular sequence. In this chapter we look at these stages in some detail before getting acquainted with basic design issues.

NOTE

There are plenty of websites that have not been formally developed. These tend to be small sites – where an ad hoc approach is possible – or sites where the goal is simple information exchange, such as artists, photographers and so on, who may use graphic design tools to create their sites to display their material. While an experimental approach may suffice for these groups, in general, a formal approach is necessary in most cases – especially with larger sites as, without formal planning and development, it would be very difficult to manage such a project.

Lifecycle development issues

A typical Web project lifecycle might involve several stages, including the following:

- planning and analysis
- design and prototyping
- development
- testing
- implementation – running the site online.

Before looking at these stages in some detail, we shall first look briefly at some development methodologies that could be applied to the development of a website.

The waterfall approach to development

A commonly used approach to the development lifecycle is the waterfall-type model – so called because each completed stage trickles into the next stage, resembling a waterfall (see Figure 2.1).

Figure 2.1
Illustration of the waterfall approach to development

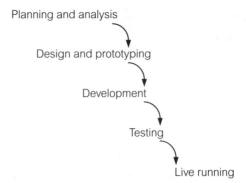

Planning and analysis

Design and prototyping

Development

Testing

Live running

In practice, developing websites using the waterfall method is difficult because the users might not be clear about how they would want the site to look. Developing a prototype can help with this problem.

Prototyping

The word **prototype** refers to the first conceptual version of a product. A prototype can be very useful for website development because it provides a starting point for subsequent development. In doing so, a prototype can provide a platform for discussion with users, the project management team and others who are involved in the project so that potential problems can be identified at an early stage and resolved. Any possible misunderstandings with regard to the functional requirements, navigational issues and visual aspects can also be clarified with the aid of a prototype.

Website projects' stages are not always successful at the first attempt. When a stage is not successful, previous stages will often require revision. For example, errors that are identified in the testing stage of a project might be due to problems in the development stage or some earlier stage. This is known as a feedback loop and, because of the experimental nature of website design, the loop may well extend beyond the previous stage (see Figure 2.2). Moreover, several iterations may be necessary before the system reaches the desired state.

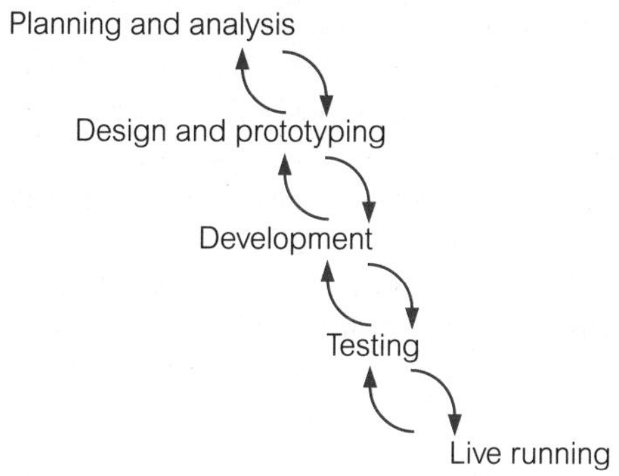

Planning and analysis

Design and prototyping

Development

Testing

Live running

Figure 2.2
Prototyping and
feedback loops

Stage 1: Planning and analysis

Like many other projects, developing a website requires planning and analysis. The purpose of planning and analysis is to:

- establish the feasibility of the project
- determine the users' requirements
- create a work plan.

The feasibility of the project

A Web project must begin with a list of criteria to determine whether or not the project is worthwhile. Given the diverse nature of websites, these criteria can vary considerably. Almost all organizations nowadays have some Web presence, but this can vary from sites containing a few pages describing what the organization does, to a site that contains several hundreds of pages of details. Clearly, the beneficiaries of the site will have a limited budget to allocate to the development of a site. Development and maintenance costs would clearly be an important factor, but so too would the anticipated requirements of the users, which are described in the next section.

Determine the users' requirements

The starting point of any website project is to establish precisely what the users want, but ideas for websites can originate from a variety of sources – management, customers, employees and all sorts of other people who may have an interest in a website project. Moreover, visitors to a website are not always a simple homogeneous group. The reasons for users visiting a website can differ greatly. They may require specific information from a site, want to purchase some product or just be casually browsing. This means that managers must be clear about who the users are and what they want from the site from the start.

The design of a website should not begin until the likely visitors to that site have been identified. The website designer will need to understand who the likely visitors are going to be and what they will be wanting from the site. The purpose and motives for the site have to be established from the very beginning.

The British Broadcasting Corporation (BBC) once defined its role as being to 'inform, educate and entertain'. The purpose of a website could be any combination of these or more. For example, the primary purpose of a retailer's website might be to inform customers about the product range available. The primary purpose of a children's website, on the other hand, might be to entertain the children. This may be achieved by providing online games, puzzles, jokes and so on (see Figure 2.3). The primary purpose of an academic distance learning website might be to educate via online tutorials. In each case, the purpose has to be clearly established before anything else.

Figure 2.3
Disney's website –
its purpose is to
entertain children

Methods for researching the users' requirements

The users' requirements can only be found by gathering information from the potential users of the site. A variety of techniques can be used and some are these are briefly described below:

- questionnaires
- focus groups
- interviews.

Questionnaires

Questionnaires come in a variety of formats, from postal mail to e-mail and Web formats. This method of eliciting information is quite efficient and comparatively cheap. It is also possible to obtain large numbers of responses – although it often takes some effort to encourage participants to complete questionnaires. The more responses, the more information is obtained and, hence, the more indicative this is of likely success. However, the downside of questionnaires is the low response rate often attained. The challenge is to design questionnaires so that the responses to questions are easy to complete, thus minimizing the effort required by the respondent, resulting in a higher response rate.

Focus groups

Focus groups involve gathering a group of people together to discuss related issues. The advantage of using focus groups is that you can get one person's reaction to an idea and then it can be developed further by another member of the group.

Interviews

An alternative way to get an understanding of users' requirements would be to carry out individual interviews. Interviews provide scope to explore issues that could be difficult by using questionnaires and/or focus groups. For example, points of ambiguity or imprecision can be clarified by interviews. Also, interviews can pick up on other points that have not been considered or overlooked.

Prepare a work plan

Having determined the users' requirements, the next stage is to write a description of what your site will provide, along with the functions of each part. This is a description of the **functional requirements** and, from it, a work plan setting out how they will be implemented can be formulated.

The **work plan** is a document that details the project tasks, resources and time allocated to the development of each of the tasks. Normally, a Gantt chart (see Figure 2.4) or some other project management chart along with project milestones and development schedules would be produced.

A **Gantt chart** is a bar chart graph that depicts how long a task is scheduled to take in relation to the other proposed tasks. A Gantt chart is scaled so that the anticipated duration of each task is proportional to the length of the bar. The Gantt chart is a very useful project management tool in that it can be used as a guide to the project's progress. Figure 2.4 depicts a number of general activities, such as 'Feasibility study initial team discussions', 'Analysis and interviews' and so on. However, in practice, it is better to include as much specific detail in the Gantt chart as possible so that designers can be very clear about what each general task entails.

EWD Web Site Project Gantt Chart

		Qtr 1			Qtr 2		
Project Steps:		Jan	Feb	Mar	Apr	May	Jun
Feasibility study initial team discussions	▬						
Analysis and interviews	▬						
Design and prototyping		▬					
Development and production		▬					
Testing			▬				
Documentation			▬				

The purpose of this work plan is to give you the tools for managing the project so that you maintain a schedule and complete the project on time.

Stage 2: Design and prototyping issues

Web site design is an iterative process. This means that you will probably have to make many revisions to a design before it appears in the desired form. Prototyping, as we have seen earlier in this chapter, is the name given to the process of producing a model of a system followed by refinements. The design stage of a website project will normally consist of the following steps.

1 Creating a site map from the functional requirements. More on this follows in the next section.

2 Creating the visual design and user interface. Understanding how this is done is explored in the next chapter.

3 Implementing the technical design. Once you know what functions are required, you will need to examine the tools and techniques so as to ensure that these functions are implemented in the best possible way. There is more on this in Chapters 4, 7, 8, 9 and 10.

Creating a site map

Once the users' requirements have been established, you will know what you want your website to do and need to make sure that your site fulfils these functions. You will need to produce a **menu tree diagram** or **site map**.

It is called a menu tree diagram because it describes a page-by-page layout of your site, with the home page at the top of the tree. Below the home page, the sub-menus are broken down into their component pages. The menu tree diagram shows pages, links and some description of content. For example, the menu tree diagram in Figure 2.5 shows a menu tree diagram of a section of a landscape artist's Web page. You will see that below the home page, the user can link to any one of the options 'Galleries', 'Techniques', 'Purchase items' or 'Contact us'.

Figure 2.5
An example of a menu tree diagram

The menu tree diagram is a useful visual aid for discussion of the initial ideas. However, you will need to think carefully about an informational structure so that the required functions are achieved in the most efficient manner.

Designing a site information structure

As previously stated, after creating a menu tree diagram, you will need to give careful thought to how users could best access information in your site.

As we have already seen, hypertext is the means by which the user can navigate around the WWW. A user can click on a hypertext link on a Web page and transfer to some other page or position in a page. This is a very different organizational structure to that of, for example, guiding the reader through the pages of a book – the contents of which are read page after page. A book-like information structure is called a **linear structure**. Hypertext links give the user total freedom to go wherever they want, although navigating familiar structures will frequently make life much easier – depending on the task that they are performing. For example, if a user is using an online presentation, then it may be necessary to implement a linear structure for presenting the information. There are many structures that could be applied to website architecture, as we will now see. In practice, most sites are a hybrid combination of these structures.

Linear structure

The linear structure – illustrated in Figure 2.6 – guides the user along as if they were turning the pages of a book. Once into the content, the user can navigate forwards or backwards. Each page can contain a link to the main page if required.

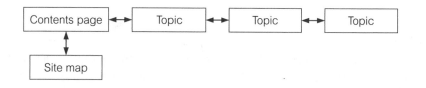

Figure 2.6
A linear structure

Such a structure could be easily implemented by ensuring that a single forward link is visible to the next page and a backward link to the previous page. This could be accompanied by a site map page that is linked to the main page so that the reader could become familiar with the structure of the material being presented.

This type of structure could be well suited to a website segment that involves completing a process in some specified order, such as a purchasing process.

Hierarchical structure

The hierarchical structure – illustrated in Figure 2.7 – is well suited to large sites with extensive content collections because section pages can be used to break up and organize the content at different levels throughout the site.

Figure 2.7
A hierarchical structure

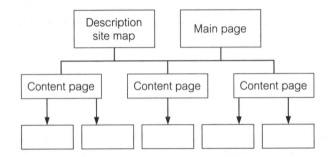

Navigation is primarily linear within the content sections. Users can scan the content on the section page and then choose the content page of their choice. A description site map page may be linked to the main page so that the user can see what the site contains.

The advantages of a hierarchical structure are that it is possible to describe the structure easily and it is also relatively easy to add, or delete, elements from the structure.

Cluster structure

The cluster structure attempts to isolate each topic as an individual group of pieces of information. In Figure 2.8, there are two topic entry pages, although this would vary in practice. All the pages in each cluster would be linked to each other. The user is thus encouraged to browse through all (or some) of the information within a topic area. In a cluster structure, you might have a link from the main page to the site map (as shown in Figure 2.8).

Tutorial structure

The tutorial structure is commonly used in online training programs. It is frequently linear in presentational format. However, there would generally be other pages, allowing the user to choose the order of lessons or start at any concept point they may want (see Figure 2.9). So, this structure would probably best be supported by a table of contents, an index page and a site map, as shown in the illustration.

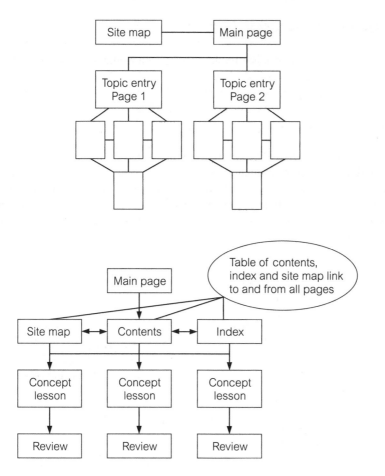

Figure 2.8
A cluster structure

Figure 2.9
A tutorial structure

Web structure

The web structure has links to and from every page on the website (see Figure 2.10). This means that a user can navigate to and from any page. If this structure is adopted for design, then some form of navigation, applicable to all pages, must be included.

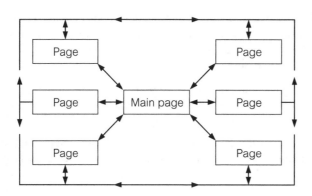

Figure 2.10
A web structure

Stage 3: Development

During the development stage of your website, you would normally create the Web pages and store them on your own computer before transferring the files to a Web server. These pages would be created either by using a text editor with HTML or Web development tool(s) such as Dreamweaver. Further HTML techniques are studied in Chapters 5 and 6. Web development tools are explored in more detail in Chapter 4.

When the website has been completed and tested (see next section), it is then transferred to the server computer – this is called **uploading**. To upload files to the server, you will need to use **File Transfer Protocol (FTP)** software. This is often incorporated inside Web development tools. Figure 2.11 describes the relationship between the website developer building the website on a computer, the server and the end user.

Figure 2.11
Relationship between your computer, Web server and your end user

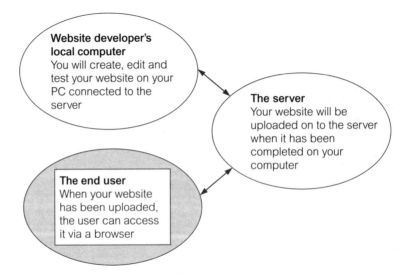

Stage 4: Testing

When developing a website, most of the site development would be completed on a local machine before being uploaded to a Web server for use on the WWW. More will be said about testing in later chapters, but, in essence, the following tests should be carried out before running the site live.

- Test all your pages thoroughly for correctness of spelling, grammar, layout and consistency of style. Many website development tools currently in use provide facilities for spellchecking, grammar checking and more.

- Test your pages using all targeted browsers. Again, many Web development tools – including Dreamweaver – can automatically test the pages using different browsers.

- Test all hyperlinks for correctness. Again, many Web development tools can automate link testing.

- Test for correct graphic rendering in all targeted browsers and test for text-only rendering with graphics turned off and/or using the Lynx browser.

- Test all program scripts (see Chapter 7) thoroughly.

Stage 5: Implementation – posting the site

How Web servers work

A **Web server** is a computer connected to the Internet and running software that serves up Web files. Any server is usually operating 24 hours a day, 7 days a week and used only for serving files to Internet users.

Servers are actual computers, physically hooked up to the Internet via cables, telephone lines and so on. A server can cease functioning without affecting the stability of the rest of the Web/Internet.

When a request is made by a browser, the server checks to see if it can find the requested page. If it can find the page, the server sends it back to the browser and the browser displays it. If the server can't find the page or there is some other problem, it sends back an error response in the form of a numeric code. Some of these responses may be '404 – the Web server can't find the page you asked for' or '403 – you're not allowed to access the page you asked for without authorization'.

The role of the Web server is to run software that responds to requests for Web content and return messages and data and perform other tasks when required, such as run program scripts, query databases and so on, before responding to clients. However, the main purpose of the Web server is to serve the XHTML pages to user requests. This is how it happens.

1 The user clicks a link to another page or enters a URL location in the browser. This will cause the browser to send a message to the server's Internet Protocol (IP) address. The message will request from the server, the address of which might be '256.196.250.005', to find and send the required file to the computer with the address ID '128.880.240.240'. The server will also recognize the ID of the user making the request from his/her username ID.

2 The message, when received by the server, will travel through cyberspace looking for the required computer file.

3 The server with IP number 256.196.250.005 receives the message and sends the required file to the computer with IP address 128.880.240.240.

4 The Web page of this ID can then be viewed with the browser to be displayed on the screen. The server will know who to send it to because it knows the ID username of the requestor.

Figure 2.12
A Web hosting
service

Figure 2.13
Registering a
domain name

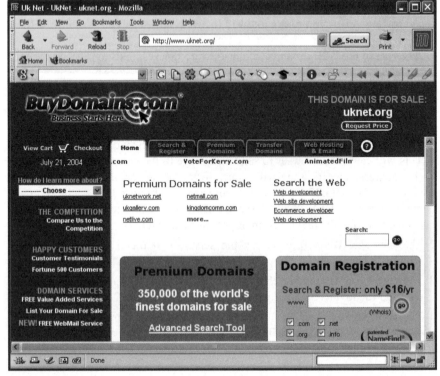

Types of Web servers

The most commonly used Web servers are the following.

- **Apache** is a Web server that is based on the Unix operating system and was originally the only Web server computer. MacOS X – a more recent version of the Mac operating system – uses a variant of Unix and includes Apache as its built-in Web server. Furthermore, an Apache server is also available for the Windows operating system.
- **Internet Information Server (IIS)** is a Microsoft Web server that runs on Windows XP and NT operating systems.
- **Personal Web Server (PWS)** is a slimmed-down Microsoft Web server that was used on the Windows 98 operating system. Its use is very limited nowadays.

Web page hosting

After you've created your website and before you upload the files to the Web server, you will need to consider how you are going to host the site. For small sites, it might be possible to use space allocated by your ISP, but larger organizations would probably want to own their own website. This has the advantage that your site name can closely resemble the name you require. It is possible to do this by buying a **domain name**. A domain name is the equivalent of a mail address. For those who want to use their own hosting service, a number of sites are available for this purpose. They include FreeWebspace.net at www.freeWebspace.net (see Figure 2.12), and GeoCities at http://geocities.yahoocom. Alternatively, you could purchase your own domain name. If you want to see if a domain name is available or register your own domain name, there are several Web services that can be used. You can visit www.uknet.org (see Figure 2.13) or NetworkSolutions at www.networksolutions.com is another possibility. These sites would normally provide a simple interface that lets you enter a name to see if it is already registered. You can then register a name, if it is available, for a small fee.

Domain names are normally renewed every two years. Network Solutions and others repossess many names every year due to non-payment and these are for sale, often at a reduced price.

NOTE

Scheduling for analysis and design, development and testing

The rule of thirds

Research has shown (Strauss and Hogan 2001) that the relative amounts of time and effort spent on design, development and testing of a website project are approximately equal. Put another way, you could expect that, in a project expected to last for one year, you would spend four months on design, four months on production and development and four months on testing. Of course, this is only a guide and could not be used to determine the exact time taken for a Web project.

Summary

- A typical website development will consist of several stages, which include:
  - planning and analysis
  - design and prototyping
  - development
  - testing
  - implementation.
- Several approaches are used with regard to the website development lifecycle. These include the waterfall and prototyping methods.

- The planning and analysis phase will often involve a feasibility study as well as an attempt to determine the users' requirements and the production of a work plan.

- The design phase involves deciding on an appropriate information structure for the site. Among the possible configurations are the linear, hierarchical, tutorial and web structures.

- Web pages are normally created and edited on a personal computer before uploading to a Web server. When uploaded, the user can access the site via a browser.

- Web pages can be hosted using Web space allocated by your ISP or, alternatively, it is possible to buy a domain name.

- The most commonly used Web servers are Apache, (Unix) IIS and PWS (Microsoft).

Exercises

1 Describe the stages of the website development lifecycle.

2 What are the key factors to consider when identifying your target audience?

3 Describe two of the methods that could be used to elicit the information required for finding out what your target audience of a new website would want.

4 You have been asked to evaluate a company's website. Make a list of all the criteria that you believe should be considered in your evaluation. Include a justification for each of the criteria that you have listed.

5 What are the benefits of purchasing a domain name?

6 What are the benefits of creating a site diagram before building a new website?

7 Visit the website www.cahoot.com. This site enables visitors to apply for an online personal loan. What type of organizational structure is suited to this task?

8 Browse the Web and find examples of the following site structures:

   a linear
   b hierarchical.

9   PetHelp is a UK-based pet and animal welfare charity that is considering setting up a website. The charity offers many services, including finding new homes for abandoned pets, neutering and providing educational information regarding the welfare of animals. Write a brief report that outlines the likely development stages for this project and describe an information structure that may be appropriate for this site.

10 You have been consulted by a friend – who is an expert on growing large vegetables – about setting up a website. He believes his many years' experience in this field should be promoted on the Web. He has won several prizes for his entries and hopes to display lots of photographs of prize-winning vegetables and develop links with other vegetable growers. He also wants to display pages containing tips and advice and other vegetable-growing articles of interest. What type of site structure would be suitable and why? Draw an outline site map that you think might be appropriate. Your friend also needs advice on how to upload the site – whether to use an ISP or host his own site using his own domain name. Briefly explain the advantages and disadvantages of each.

Designing for visual aspects and navigation

In this chapter you will learn about:

- human computer interaction (HCI) issues
- design for page layout
- design for text
- design for graphics
- design for colour
- design for inclusivity
- design for feedback
- design for navigation
- being aware of the general principles of good website design.

Introduction

Every day more and more people are using the Internet and World Wide Web. As the Web develops, people are expecting more from the websites they visit. To attract users and maximize repeat visits, websites must be easy to navigate, attractive and compelling to use. Otherwise, with such a vast choice on offer, the user will simply go elsewhere. To make sites attractive and easy to use, Web designers need to be aware of the general principles of human computer interaction, for these principles apply as much to the design of websites as they do to any other computer software design.

Human computer interaction (HCI) issues

HCI has been defined as being 'about designing computer systems that support people so that they can carry out their activities productively and safely'. Computers are complicated creations that have the potential for realizing an unlimited range of

behaviour and interactions with human users. However, making computer interaction with humans easy and productive – like other systems that have been developed over time – is about careful thought to the design of the human–computer
interface. 'User-centred design' is a term that is used to describe 'the user' as being
in control rather than the system. In practice, it is often difficult to achieve. However,
the following criteria are considered to be necessary in HCI design.

■ Make it easy to determine what actions are possible at any moment (make use of
  constraints or make idiotproof option choices). In the case of Web page design,
  this would mean using navigation bars that are clearly labelled so that the user
  knows exactly where they can go to.

■ Make things visible, including the conceptual model of the system, alternative
  actions and results of actions. In the case of Web design, this would mean
  including a site map of the system, a clear written description of each action
  occurring from skimming over an option choice with the mouse and the consequence of that choice.

■ Make it easy to evaluate the current state of the system. From the point of view
  of website design, this would mean making sure that the user knows what page
  they are on and where it fits into the site hierarchy. In practice, this could mean
  displaying titles in the browser title bar, for example, or something similar.

■ Follow natural mappings between intentions and the required actions, between
  actions and the resulting effect and between the information that is visible and
  the interpretation of the system state.

These principles – important as they are – are by no means a panacea for good
design. There are many other issues, such as choice of text style, fonts, layout,
graphics, colours, that, of course, will affect the user's perception of your site. The
next section focuses on these issues.

Page layout design

The exponential growth of the Web has given viewers the luxury of choice,
meaning that site designers have to give much thought to aesthetics if they are to
attract visitors. Page layout plays a big part in this for it partly determines the look
and feel of the site and, despite being a subjective issue, can affect the way the user
interacts with the site.

As a general rule, you need to determine the components that are to be included
in your pages, such as headers and footers, page titles, navigation bars, images,
logos, sound, and so on, before prototyping for a page layout.

Page layout should adhere to the following guidelines (Brink, Gergle and Wood
2001).

■ *Consistency*
  Consistency is a key design component in page layout. Consistency gives
  confidence to viewers from their familiarity with the system, for they will know
  what to expect and this should make the site easier to use. A consistent layout
  will also improve the viewer's perception – called a **mental model** – of the site.

A consistent layout will aid navigation and give the site a greater sense of structure. Hence, Web designers should strive to give a consistent look and feel to pages. To help achieve this, avoid using different colours for the background on each page. The same applies to navigation bars and other Web page components. Try, too, to make sure that they are consistently positioned from page to page, as well as ensuring that the text sizes and fonts are consistent, as with other page objects, such as buttons, click boxes and so on. For example, the header menu graphic navigation bar is present on every page of the Adobe site and the company logo appears in the same position on every page (see Figure 3.1). This creates a consistent user interface and corporate identity.

Figure 3.1
Illustration of
Adobe's website
logo

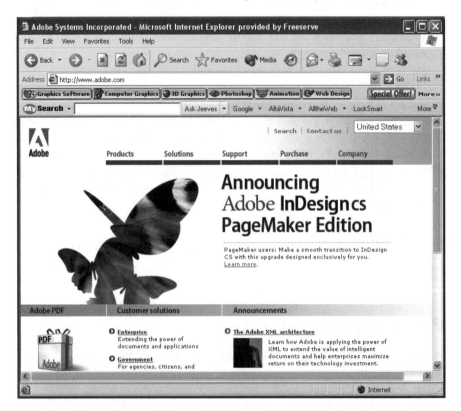

- *Simplicity*
  Try to keep the page structure simple and uncluttered. A simple page ensures that the viewer will recognize the distinct parts, such as the title and navigation bars, and identify the information content. Research has shown that users are alienated by too much clutter on Web pages. A good example of an uncluttered page is the Google home page (see Figure 3.2).

- *Focus*
  Focus is defined as ensuring that key elements on the page are brought clearly into view. These elements of emphasis could be a title, a label, icon or whatever. The main point to make is that they should immediately communicate the information

Figure 3.2
Google's home
page interface

contained on that page. Focus enables you to control the viewer's gaze on the page. Figure 3.3 is an example of a Web page incorporating these features. The page is immediately identified by visitors from the familiar logo in the top left-hand corner. The user can easily understand where they are from the page contents heading and the navigation bar indicates other possible places to go. The clear animal focus enables the visitor to grasp the site's contents very quickly.

- *Use metaphors when appropriate*
  A **metaphor** is used to associate a new concept, such as a navigational tool, with a familiar idea. The metaphor could be verbal. For example, if we consider a website that quotes stock market prices, then the system might be designed in such a way that the site visitor would enter a 'dealing room' page instead of a 'home page'. The 'dealing room' metaphor would clearly be more appropriate for this type of site than a 'home page' metaphor. Another type of metaphor that is very popular is an icon metaphor – that is, a graphical icon could be used to represent a metaphor. An example of the use of this type of metaphor is shown in Figure 3.4 for a DIY home improvement website. You will see that on this site, a tool metaphor is being used for 'Your basket'. Both these icons provide a clear association with the real-world entities. Despite their obvious advantages, metaphors can have misleading consequences, in that not every section of a website will perhaps have a logical association with the metaphorical landscape. Furthermore, they can often be costly to implement, in that much effort might be required in their design. If they are to be used, make sure that they add to the information content of the site. Good metaphor design means using interface metaphors that are simple, familiar and intuitive for the audience. For example,

Figure 3.3
Elements of good page layout design

Figure 3.4
Illustration of the use of metaphors

if you want a metaphor for a home page, then choose a graphic house icon, not a television set or camera. It might sound like an exaggerated example, but sometimes happens in practice. The best information designs are the ones that most users never notice. A good example of a website applying these principles is that of the Adobe Corporation (www.adobe.com).

- *Functional stability*
Functional stability in your Web design means keeping the interactive elements of your site working reliably. Functional stability has two components: getting things right the first time you design your site and then keeping things functioning smoothly over time. This is more difficult than it may sound because links within sites often change (as do external links). There are many reasons for this, one of which is that Web pages are sometimes moved on the server, while another is that an organization may change its domain name and, in so doing, cause links to it to change. As you create your design, you will need to constantly check to be sure that all of your links work properly. This is because things can change quickly on the Web, both internally and externally. There are software checkers available for this purpose in Web development tools, such as Dreamweaver. You will need to check for this periodically to be sure that your links are still working properly and that the content they supply is still relevant to your needs.

Page layout techniques

Before embarking on a page layout plan, you will need to give some thought to the page components that will be required. Remember the components will include such things as text headers, footers, logos, navigation bars, images, diagrams and various interactive elements, such as forms. When you are clear about the likely page contents, you can plan the layout.

Planning your layout

A **mockup** is an interface prototype – often created using paper and pencil – that represents the navigation, interaction and look and feel of the site. A mockup is a useful tool for planning your website layout. By creating one, you can gain quick feedback from interested parties on these important issues without incurring a great deal of cost and time. Mockups can be created with layout explorations using paper and pencil or design explorations using software tools, such as Photoshop or Pro.

When beginning the design of a site, it is often a good idea to start with a mockup using a sketched layout with paper and pencil. Try to make sure that you use a grid or graph paper pages instead of blank paper so that you get your proportions correct and that space is allocated for navigation, headers and footers, body text and whatever other elements will be repeated throughout the site. This mockup sketch will serve as a pattern for the site's appearance and should not change very much, if at all, from page to page.

Once you have decided where everything will go, you can establish, and pencil in, the cell widths that will be required for fixed elements; you can also decide which elements can be included in the page using shared borders and make a note of this, too. An example of a sketched mockup is given in Figure 3.5.

Figure 3.5
An example of a
sketched mockup

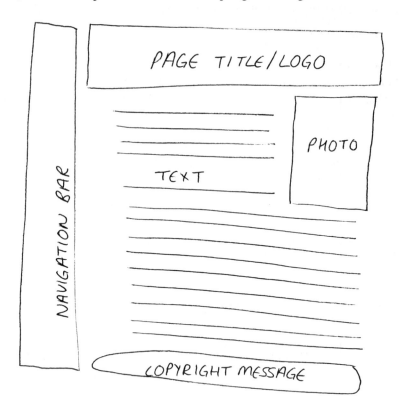

Using a page template

One of the easiest ways to achieve consistent page layout is to use a **page template**. Many Web development tools provide templates, including Dreamweaver, which will be used for this purpose in Chapter 13.

A template can be thought of as a stencil or pattern, the structure of which can be copied from page to page so that a consistent look and feel to the site can be maintained. The use of a template can be of tremendous benefit to the site designer because, once a common page structure has been established, it is then easier to create new pages and, if a change is necessary to the template, then all the pages that are based on the template will also change. A wide range of page templates are in common use. As a general rule, once you have identified the basic requirements, you can formulate an appropriate page template. A sample Dreamweaver template is shown in Figure 3.6. Notice that the template contains a navigation bar and headings that can be changed for the business in question. If you use templates, you will need to test your site content to see how it fits into the structure that you wish to use.

Figure 3.6
A sample
Dreamweaver
template

Designing for text

The Web is still primarily a visual medium, so the main method of presenting information is by using text. The way in which text is presented is, therefore, an extremely important consideration. Which font(s), sizes and colour contrasts to use are important elements to think about when designing your Web pages.

Choice of text size

Normally, people do not read text one word at a time. Text is read in groups of words. The size of the text is a key element in determining how easy it is to read sentences. Text that is displayed too large is just as difficult to read as text that is too small. When text is too large, it means that the reader can only read a few words at a time. When text is too small, on the other hand, it can be difficult to focus the eyes comfortably.

Web page text size varies in a range from 1 to 7, with 1 being the smallest, and 7 the largest. The default text size for a Web page is 3. As we will see in Chapter 5, text size can be specified using HTML. It is sensible for the Web designer to state the text size – even if just confirming the default – so that the browser settings do not override the designer's intentions. Some examples of font sizes are shown below:

This text is specified as 'default'.
This text is specified as '3'.
This text is specified as '4'.
This text is specified as '2'.

Choice of text font

Text in Web pages is displayed by browsers using the fonts available on the viewer's computer. Most PC users have Arial, Verdana and Times New Roman, plus others, installed. Macintosh computers, apart from the much older models, usually have Arial, Verdana and Times New Roman installed. It is nowadays safe to use these fonts plus some other Microsoft fonts, such as Trebuchet, Georgia and Tahoma. Some of these fonts are displayed in Figure 3.7. The vast majority of text presented on Web pages is limited to these fonts for both practical and technical reasons.

Fonts used on Web pages are broadly classified into **serif** and **sans serif** fonts Serif fonts are the old-style or traditional-looking fonts and have a flick added to the tips of the lines making up the letter. Times New Roman and Palatino are examples of serif fonts. Sans serif fonts (meaning without serifs) do not contain any flicks added to the tips of the lines making up the letters and are the most appropriate family for general text reading on the Web, as their simpler letter forms remain readable at low resolutions, whereas serif fonts need more pixels to display their extra details. Arial and Trebuchet are examples of sans serif fonts.

Figure 3.7
Illustration of some Web text fonts

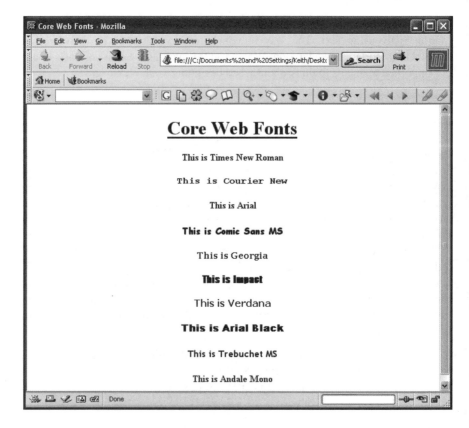

As a general rule, when it comes to text on the Web, serif fonts are suitable for headers and sections designed to stand out, whereas sans serif fonts are suited to main body text (there is more on this in Chapter 5). A good choice of Web body font is Verdana. Research has shown that it is not advisable to use more than two fonts on a page for it can make the contents more difficult to read.

Choice of text contrast

Strong contrast between text and background makes the text easier to read. Black text on white is the easiest to read. White on black is also a marked high contrast but is a little harder to read, especially for those with poor vision. Sometimes, successful sites are designed by breaking up pages with these different combinations when sectionalizing Web content. Colour combinations, such as red and blue, should be avoided for, as can be seen from Figure 3.8 – the same page as that in Figure 3.7 – the effect is discomfort with reading the text.

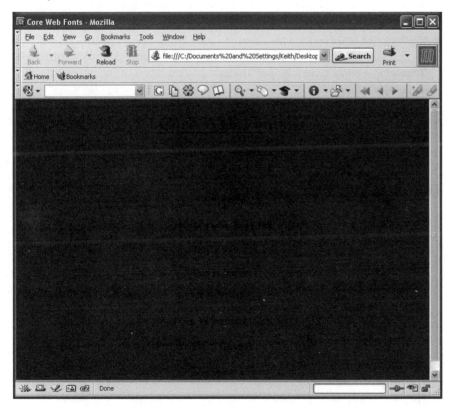

Figure 3.8
The same page as shown in Figure 3.7 using a different colour contrast

Guidelines for preparing text for the Web

Writing for the Web is very different from traditional printing, such as a newspaper. When you read a newspaper, you have the full newspaper canvas to read from, but, in the case of the Web, you are restricted by the size of the monitor display. As a general rule, the following guidelines should be considered when writing for the Web.

- Make good use of headings and subheadings. Readers of Web pages are often in a hurry and so will scroll through text looking for a reference to a particular concept. Good use of headings and subheadings will make this task easier for them.

- Brevity is an important consideration in designing text for the Web as research has shown that people spend less time reading a Web page than they do reading printed articles. To make text more appealing for the Web, you should strive to write short, focused paragraphs, providing hyperlinks to further explanations for the reader.

- Try to ensure that the text presented on a page is autonomous, for the reader could arrive at your page from a variety of sources, including a direct link from a search engine. You cannot assume that the reader has arrived at your page via the previous page and, therefore, need to make allowances for this in the text that you prepare for your site.

- Use lists and other styles where appropriate. Lists are very effective on the Web because they provide a succinct mechanism for conveying an explanation. Readers in a hurry generally find lists easier to read than sifting through detailed paragraphs of text.

- Try to use more conversational language for the Web. Avoid the use of abbreviations or other constructions that could make reading difficult. Remember, the Web is a very different medium to conventional print.

Designing for graphics

Before we look at some guidelines for using graphics on the Web, you will need to become familiar with the graphic formats in use.

Graphic formats for the Web

There are three main graphic formats used on the Web. They are all discussed in more detail in Chapter 9, but are briefly summarized here.

- **GIF (Graphic Interchange Format)**   This is an 8-bit format, allowing a range of 256 colours. File sizes are small because of high compression.

- **JPG or JPEG (Joint Photographic Experts Group)**   Uses 24-bit or true colour for storing images.

- **PNG (Portable Network Graphic)**   A versatile format recommended by the WC3.

Guidelines for using graphic files on the Web

Graphics are explored in some detail in Chapter 9, so in this section we will summarize the important points regarding the use of graphics on the Web.

Graphics on the Web serve much the same function as they do in traditional publications, with some additional requirements.

■ A Web graphic must add to the communication of information. If a Web graphic is being used only as a decoration, it must generate the desired effect in the reader, not simply take up space.

■ A Web graphic must be appropriate in content, scale and style. For example, you might use line drawings to convey abstractions, which might encourage the reader to focus on the relevant information in the graphics. On the other hand, you might use a photograph when information of substance is needed. When it comes to size, sometimes a symbolic graphic is required, in which case a small image will suffice. Conversely, if you want to convey information in a graphic, it may be necessary to use a larger image.

■ A Web graphic must be matched to the visual and technical skills of the intended client. This means that the website designer must address the question 'What is the visual insight and competency of the client?' before using graphics on a website.

■ A graphic interface must be intuitive. Users must easily determine how to navigate through the site and know what elements are clickable.

■ Use graphics sparingly. Remember, images take substantially longer to download than text because they consume more memory.

■ Use graphic icons for navigation where necessary, such as home, back and forwards in a tree hierarchy).

Designing for the use of colour on the Web

Guidelines for using colour on the Web

When it comes to using colour on the Web, virtually all display monitors have a minimum of 256 colours. However, 40 of these colours are reserved by the operating system and these are unsafe to use in Web pages, which leaves 216 colours. These are called **safe colours** and will be examined in more detail in Chapter 9.

When you use safe colours on your Web pages, they should display correctly in all main browsers. However, most monitors nowadays can handle 16-bit colour or higher, so the need to work with the restrictions of the Websafe palette is rapidly diminishing.

Other points to note when using colours include the following.

■ Avoid overusing colour – it can confuse the message. Think carefully about the reason for using each colour on your page.

- Use colour in the correct context. For example, bright orange, yellow and green might be well suited to a children's website, but is hardly likely to help convey the message in a text information-dominated site.

- Think carefully about colour combinations. For example, colour contrasts such as red text on a green background are not recommended as the contrast makes text difficult to read. On the other hand, black text against a white background gives a good contrast for reading.

- Use colours consistently so that regular visitors can associate colours with particular meanings. For example, on Microsoft's website (see Figure 3.3), consistent use is made of the colour black for banners in the Games area of their site.

- Consider the visitors to your site who may be colour blind or suffer from some other colour visual disability. See the www.w3.org website for more information on designing for disabilities.

Designing for inclusivity

One of the greatest problems facing website designers is uncertainty about users' interaction with the Web. There is uncertainty about viewers' choice of browser, viewers' speed of connection, the size and resolution of the viewers' monitors and the viewers' hardware – PCs or Macs – and the operating system software that is being used, such as Windows, Linux, MacOS, and, finally, the types of users visiting your site – whether they are disabled or not. All of these issues will clearly affect the quality of the users' experiences with the Web – not only in the way that pages are viewed but also in the speed and quality of their interaction with the Web. Each of these issues is briefly discussed below.

Designing for browsers

Design pages to work in as many browsers as you possibly can and check your site thoroughly with different browser and version combinations. Consideration of the following points will help to ensure that your pages will render properly with different browsers:

- If you are going to use state-of-the-art technologies, then you might have to create alternative pages if you want to ensure that your pages will work on as many older browsers as possible. If you use Cascading Style Sheets, Frames or Layers, then your pages will only be supported by IE and Netscape browsers above Version 4 (see later chapters). This would, of course, involve a great deal of effort, but could pay dividends in the number of visitors attracted to your site. Dreamweaver behaviour, or JavaScript, could then be used to check the browser version that the reader is using. Care must also be taken with technologies such as Microsoft ActiveX, which is only supported by one browser – IE.

- Try to make sure that alternatives are always provided to those visitors who have to be ignored for practical reasons. For example, if it is impractical to design complete site pages that run in the Lynx browser, then try to include an alternative page that runs in this browser.

■ The tools that you use to create Web pages can sometimes affect the way that they are rendered. For example, FrontPage can sometimes cause pages to look different in IE than in Netscape. This is because many features of FrontPage are designed to work only with IE. You can, however, disable the features that do not work in Netscape and thus circumvent this problem.

Connection speeds

Human factors research has shown that, for most computing tasks, the threshold of frustration is around ten seconds. Web page designs that are not well 'tuned' to the network access speed of your typical users will only frustrate them. Home computer users will, in general, surf the Web via 56k, or less, modem connections, so it is risky to place huge bitmap graphics on your pages. The average user will not be patient enough to wait endlessly while your graphics download over the phone line. However, universities and large organizations' sites frequently access the Web at Ethernet speeds, in which case the designer could be more ambitious in the use of graphics and multimedia. Much has been made of broadband Internet access, but it still has not, as at the time of writing, made a huge impact. Broadband and other connection technologies are discussed in a little more detail in Chapter 9. The benefits of a broadband connection compared to a dial-up modem at home are:

■ an 'always on' connection

■ connection speeds up to 20 times faster than those of analogue modems

■ it does not require the use of a telephone line

■ fast audio and video streaming becomes a reality by virtue of the faster download speeds

■ unmetered access to the Internet.

Monitor resolution and size

Monitors are available in many sizes – 15-, 17- and 19-inch being the most common – and the size will affect the screen area – called the **resolution**. The screen area determines the pixel resolution that is possible (see Chapter 9).

Pixel is an acronym taken from the words 'picture element' and it is a small dot on a two-dimensional display that can contain a colour and brightness value. The more pixels used, the better the resolution.

Each size of monitor has the capability to display varying numbers of pixels, as shown in Table 3.1. The table shows that 640 × 480 is the lowest resolution and so this is the value that Web designers have traditionally conformed to in order to ensure that the most important Web page content fits into the page without forcing the user to scroll to see everything. However, the more modern approach to this is to use **liquid pages**. These are pages that expand and contract according to the available screen area of viewers' monitors. This means that viewers should see no white space when the window is large or see scrollbars when the window is small. Liquid pages can be implemented by specifying relative values for resolutions rather than fixed values, as with using pixel sizes. Liquid pages can be implemented in Dreamweaver and Chapter 13 briefly explains how to do this.

Table 3.1 Monitor size and resolution

Monitor size	Resolution
15-inch screen	640 × 480 or 800 × 600
17-inch screen	Up to 1024 × 768
19-inch screen	Up to 1280 × 1024

Hardware and operating system issues for Web design

When it comes to designing for users using different hardware, such as PCs or Macs, or different operating systems, such as Windows, Unix, DOS or MacOS, the main point to note is the different file naming systems that they use.

Web page file naming

Before naming files for use on the Web, bear in mind that the DOS, Windows, Mac and UNIX operating systems have traditionally used different standards for naming files. These are summarized in Table 3.2. This means that care has to be taken when naming files because they could be running on different operating systems when transferred between sites. It is safer, therefore, to adopt the ISO 9660 Standard as described below.

The ISO 9660 standard

The International Standards Organization (ISO) uses a file naming convention designed to avoid file name problems. This is known as the **eight-dot-three method**. This means that any file name will contain a maximum of eight characters, followed by a dot, followed by a three-character extension. Furthermore, only alphabetical, lower-case letters, numbers and the underscore character are allowed to be used in a file name. No spaces should be used in file names.

In practice, however, if you find the ISO 9660 standard a little restrictive, you should be able to use longer file names, of up to 20 characters, with 4-character extensions without encountering problems, but still be careful not to use spaces in your file names.

Table 3.2 File naming standards for operating systems

Operating system	Standard
DOS	Maximum of 8 letters plus 3-character extension after the dot
Windows 95, 98, 2000, XP	Maximum of 255 letters. Most characters permitted in file names
UNIX, MacOS X	Case-sensitive, all characters allowed except '/' and white space
Older Macintosh systems	Maximum of 31 characters. Most characters allowed in file names

It is also best to use lower-case characters only in Web file names because, if your server is upgraded from Windows to Unix, then, as can be seen from Table 3.2, Unix is case-sensitive and, therefore, problems may occur.

NOTE

Designing for accessibility

The W3C has issued accessibility guidelines (see www.w3.org/TR/WAI-WEBCONTENT) to help Web designers decide what accessibility issues to consider in website design. They have listed the following user categories that should be accommodated, if possible:

- those who may not be able to see, hear, move or may not be able to process some types of information easily or at all
- those who may have difficulty reading or comprehending text
- those who may not have or be able to use a keyboard or mouse
- those who may have a text-only screen, a small screen or a slow Internet connection
- those who may not speak or understand fluently the language in which the document is written
- those who may be in a situation where their eyes, ears or hands are busy or interfered with – for example, those working in a loud environment
- those who may have an early version of a browser, a different browser entirely, a voice browser or a different operating system.

Later chapters in this book have adopted techniques that encourage working with W3C standards that facilitate designing for accessibility.

Designing for feedback

Well-designed websites should always provide direct links to the site's editor or the 'Webmaster' responsible for running the site. An indication of when the site was last updated also helps so that the viewer will know if it contains current information.

There are many facilities that can be added to a Web page to encourage feedback – an e-mail link is probably the most obvious that comes to mind, but there are many others, some of which are described below.

Guestbooks

The **guestbook** concept is the same as that of completing the visitor's book in a hotel – anyone can leave a message in your guestbook and the book is open for anyone who visits your site to view.

Guestbooks normally work as follows. The message database is stored on a third-party guestbook server system, which also generates the guestbook's Web pages. You place hyperlinks on your site to dummy page URLs on the guestbook server. When a visitor clicks on a link, the server intercepts the message and generates the appropriate viewing or data entry page. Unwanted messages can be removed using the guestbook server.

There are several websites that provide users with free guestbook facilities. These include www.guestbook.nu (see Figure 3.9). This site lets you customize

Figure 3.9
Guestbook.nu's
home page

your guestbook page with your own background and graphics incorporated into your site, so that it really looks like part of your site. Other websites providing guestbook facilities include www.efreeguestbooks.com (this is well suited to e-commerce guestbooks) and www.htmlgear.lycos.com

User response forms

Providing an e-mail contact name on a Web page is likely to elicit some feedback, but not the kind of structured feedback that will give you enough information to maintain a quality site. A user response form can be added to a website for this purpose.

The contents of a user response form – called **fields** – can vary from checkbox-type responses to the provision of **text areas**, which can elicit lengthy text messages.

Some system servers provide a standard forms-to-e-mail service, in which data captured from a form is sent to you in an e-mail message (one message per completed form). The system works by providing a form for the user to complete and, when the user completes the form, the data is sent to the forms-processing server, which in turn sends it to the e-mail address that you have specified during the completion of the form. In most cases, the user then sees a 'thank you' page and a link back to your site. More on forms processing follows in Chapters 6 and 7.

Forms processors are available on the Web and vary in the amount of help they give you in building your form. One of the easiest to use is www.freedback.com

Figure 3.10
Freedback.com's home page

(see Figure 3.10). This site generates HTML source code for your form, which you can paste into your own pages and modify to provide your own site's 'look and feel'. You can also use as many fields as you like. Other form processor sites include www.response-o-matic.com and www.TheFreeSite.com, which offers a range of poll services for visitors to your site.

Forums

Forums – sometimes also called **bulletin boards** or **newsgroups** – provide discussion forums for people with similar interests. They can also serve as a source of feedback as someone can start a discussion by posting comments about a subject, another person may answer, to be followed by other people joining and so on, so a **thread** of linked messages develops.

As with guestbooks, the databases of forum messages are stored on a third-party server, which also generates the display and data-entry HTML pages. Like guestbooks, forums need regular supervision. You can log into the forum server to remove unsuitable messages and some forum servers let you ban unwanted participants.

You can choose from many sites to create your own forums, including www.network54.com (see Figure 3.11). Using this site, you can customize the forum page with your own graphics, giving it the 'look and feel' of your site. As well as serving forums, this site will serve chatrooms, Web logs and other facilities. There are plenty of other forum servers to choose from, too, including http://beseen.net.

Figure 3.11
Network54's
website

Chatrooms

Chatrooms – also called **Internet Relay Chat (IRC) Channels** – allow groups of people to exchange live text messages.

When you log on to a chatroom, you will see a scrolling window containing messages from everyone else in the room. Any user can participate by typing messages that appear immediately in the scrolling window. The interchange of messages is handled by a central IRC server.

There are many servers around that will host a chat channel for your site. Chatting via an IRC server used to require a standalone IRC client application, but not any more.

Sites offering chat hosting include www.chatplanet.com and www.parachat.com (see Figure 3.12).

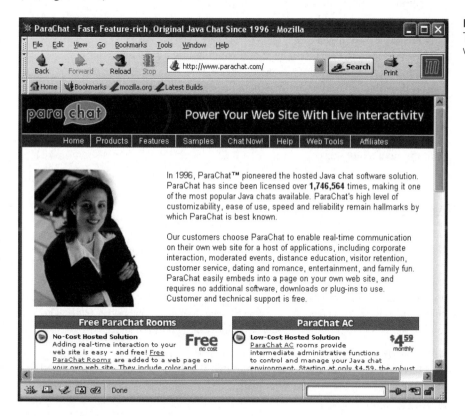

Figure 3.12
The ParaChat website

Other Web technologies

Before moving on to the next section, we need to be familiar with some other Web technologies. These are briefly discussed below.

- **Cascading Style Sheets (CSS)** provide a method for advanced style and formatting. Note that these are not a replacement for HTML, they work with HTML. See Chapter 8.

- **Dynamic HTML** provides a method for adding interactivity (or animation) to Web pages by combining HTML with scripting languages, such as JavaScript and CSS.
- **Extensible Markup Language (XML)** provides authors with a means of defining customized tag sets that make content perform as databases or some other functionality not possible with HTML.
- **Java** is a cross-platform programming language developed by Sun Micro-systems. Typically used for developing large, enterprise-scale applications, but it can also be used for creating small applications for the Web in the form of applets (see Chapter 7).
- **JavaScript** is a scripting language developed by Netscape that adds inter-activity and conditional behaviour to your Web pages. Unlike Java, it is not a compiled language, but a language interpreted by the browser. Frequently used for implementing rollovers, pop-up windows and so on.
- An **Applet** is a self-contained and executable program often written in Java. Note that a Java applet:
  - is written in the Java language and compiled by a Java compiler
  - can be included in an HTML document
  - is downloaded and executed when the HTML document is viewed
  - requires the Java runtime system to enable it to execute.
- **ActiveX** is a Microsoft technology that enables self-contained software components, similar to Java applets, to be used on the Web. ActiveX is a complement to the Java technology.

Navigational issues

Navigation is a very important issue to address in website design, for the user has to be able to find what they are looking for as quickly as possible. This means that the user should be able to move around the site with the greatest of ease, being able to go forwards or backwards, having clear visual indications as to where they have been, and gain easy access to important pages, such as the home page. The fol-lowing list is a general guide to how to achieve navigational success.

- *Use navigation bars on the left-hand side of the Web page*
  It has become an accepted convention that the main site's navigation should be on the left-hand side of the Web page.
- *Always include back links*
  Links should be two-way, thus, any link taking the user into a site should have a back link. It should not be necessary for the user to have to click the back button on the browser.
- *Always include a home page link*
  A home link should be included on all pages as this gives the user the option to go to a familiar page in the site and not feel lost. Users should always be able to return to your home page easily and to other major navigation points on your site. Viewers often make or follow links directly to subsection pages buried deep in

the hierarchy of websites. Thus, they may never see your home page or other introductory information on your site. The basic links mentioned here should be present on every page of your site. Often graphic buttons are used as these both provide basic navigation links and should also help to create the graphic identity that signals to the user that they are still within your site domain. For example, on Adobe's corporate website, the bar of buttons shown in Figure 3.13 appears at the top of every page.

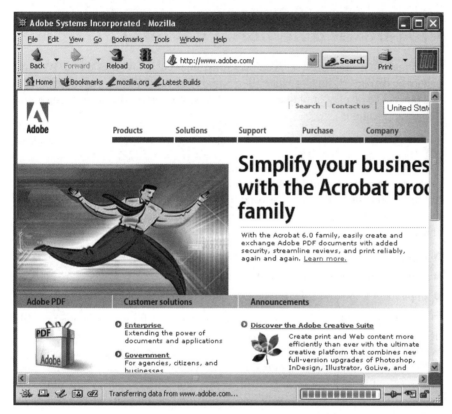

Figure 3.13
Adobe's home page

- *Use a consistent style for links*
  Links should always look like links – keep using a consistent style for them so that the user can recognize them without too much difficulty.

- *Build clear navigation aids*
  Most users' interactions with Web pages involve navigating hypertext links between documents. The main interface problem on websites is the lack of a sense of where you are within the local organization of information. Clear, consistent icons and graphic or text-based overview and summary screens can give the user confidence that they can find what they are looking for without wasting time.

- *Avoid dead end pages*
  Every Web page should contain at least one link. **Dead end pages** – pages with no links to any other local page on the site – can frustrate and annoy visitors, especially inexperienced users.

■ *Try to give users direct access*
Users often know exactly where they want to go and want to do it in the fewest possible steps, in the shortest time. This means that you must design an efficient structure of information to minimize the number of menu pages they have to click through. Human Computer Interaction studies have shown that users prefer menus that present a minimum of five to seven links and a few very dense screens of choices rather than many layers of simplified menus.

Plug-ins and helpers (viewers)

When you are using a browser, you may sometimes encounter files on the Web that cannot be displayed, such as video files, audio files, non-Web format graphics files and others. To display or play these files, you need to install the proper **plug-ins** or **helper** applications.

Plug-in applications

Plug-ins are external software applications that work with or inside Web browsers to provide functionality that is beyond the browser's built-in capabilities. Plug-ins are normally free applications that can be downloaded by users who want to enhance their browser. Plug-ins:

■ represent an extension to a Web browser

■ normally operate within the browser window

■ implement a specific MIME type (see later) in an HTML document.

The purpose of a plug-in is to extend and complement a browser's native capabilities, expanding and enhancing the type of content that can be delivered over the World Wide Web. Using plug-ins, your Web browser can display animation, multimedia, audio, interactive applications and video directly on the Web page. However, unlike a browser's built-in display capabilities, which are limited to generic file formats, such as GIF and JPEG images, plug-ins offer open-ended expansion that can include any content type.

Many vendors have released plug-ins capable of displaying their own proprietary multimedia, application, animation and other data format files enabling them to include on their Web pages any type of content that they require. Examples of supported formats include Macromedia Director multimedia presentations, Adobe Acrobat portable documents, Apple QuickTime movies format, and RealAudio audio files. There are also plug-ins for applications such as spreadsheets and word processor files. Figure 3.14 displays the Netscape plug-ins page (http://channels.netscape.com/ns/browsers/plugins.jsp).

Helper applications

Early in the history of the Web, it became obvious that website developers and Web surfers wanted more variety in Web page content than Web browser programs could

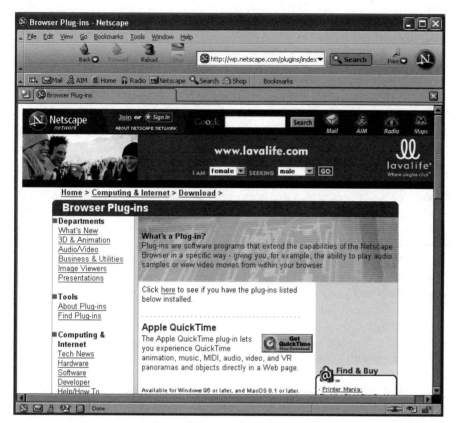

Figure 3.14
The plug-ins finder page on Netscape's website

provide. Text, graphics and elementary forms were not enough. **Helper applications** filled the gap. Unlike a plug-in, a helper application is not part of the browser, but a separate application that runs a required file type. Almost all Web browser programs enable you to set up external, standalone programs as helper applications. Once properly installed and configured, a Web browser launches the helper application when it encounters a file of the defined type.

Helper applications have many of the same uses and advantages as plug-ins:

■ they extend the Web browser's capability to deal with additional file types

■ they load into memory only when needed, then unload to free up system resources when they are no longer useful

■ you need to install only the helper applications that you want

■ many plug-ins are self-installing; some are distributed as archive files that you must first decompress before you run the installation.

However, helper applications have some disadvantages. They are that:

■ helper files run on external programs, so they are more conspicuous – they display files in a separate program window

■ helper applications are not integrated into your Web browser, which means that you have to learn how to use each one separately and the learning curve can be steep

■ installing a plug-in is much easier than setting up a helper application because you do not have to worry about defining MIME types (see next section) or file name extensions as you do with some helper files.

A brief introduction to MIME types

Before browsers of the likes of Netscape can tell whether they can display a file internally or need a helper application or plug-in, they must determine the kind of data that they are encountering.

You can probably identify many file types by their file name extensions. You know that a file named blah.exe is an executable program, because the file name ends with the extension .exe, and that a file named beh.doc is a Microsoft Word document, because it ends with the extension .doc. Browsers identify files on the Web by their MIME type.

MIME is an acronym for **Multipurpose Internet Mail Extensions**, but this is a little misleading because MIME type definitions are not just for Internet mail – they are used to identify any file that can be transmitted over the Internet.

How browsers use MIME type definitions

Web pages usually consist of not just a single file, but a collection of several files. For example, the text portion is usually a single Hypertext Markup Language (HTML) text file, while each graphic is a separate .gif or jpeg format file. When your browser reads a Web page, the server sends all this data as a stream, identifying each section with a preceding MIME type definition header. A MIME type definition consists of two parts. They are:

type/subtype – for example image/jpeg

Figure 3.15
Setting MIME type
file extensions
with Mozilla

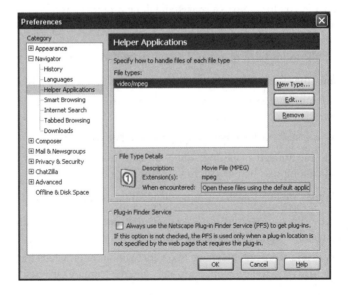

As you can see, this MIME type definition describes an image file in jpeg format. Before sending a file to a browser, a Web server invisibly sends the MIME type definition for that file. The browser reads this definition and looks it up to see if it can handle the file internally or a helper application or plug-in is required for the file. In this example, the browser knows that the file it is about to receive is an image in jpeg format, which, of course, it can display internally.

You can see a complete list of the MIME types that a browser – such as Mozilla – recognizes natively by choosing **Preferences** from the **Edit** menu, then selecting the **Helper Applications** tab. There are only seven sanctioned MIME types: text, audio, image, video, multipart, message and application. Any new program or data file type must fit into one of these seven MIME types before a MIME-enabled application such as Mozilla can recognize it. The screenshot shown in Figure 3.15 that the MIME type extension for video/mpeg default application is a Movie File.

Adding a counter to your Web pages

Another useful feedback facility is a Web page counter. **Web counters** keep track of how many people have visited your site. The basic method of operation involves putting an image tag on your page that links to a 'virtual image' file on the Web counter server (the HTML for this is supplied by the counter system when you create your account – you just paste it into your page source). When someone views your page – called a **hit** – their browser asks the counter server for the 'image'. The counter system intercepts the request, updates your hit count and generates a graphic representing the new count value, which is then displayed on your page.

Adding a counter to your home or index page lets you monitor overall site traffic, although there's a danger that people will bookmark specific pages within your site, then visit them directly, which will not update your home page counter. If your site has major sections, then it is a good idea to put counters on the section header pages, too.

Counters have been around for a long time, but the latest generation provide detailed statistics. These can tell you at what times your visitors came, where they came from, which operating systems they were running and which browsers they used. The latter detail is especially useful, as it helps you decide which browser-specific features – such as Dynamic HTML – are worth using on your pages.

It is worth checking your ISP/Webspace provider first for a hit counter. Many ISPs now provide them and an in-house counter will normally give the fastest response. Alternatively, a 'FastCounter' service, with statistics, is available from Microsoft's Small Business Center, at www.microsoft.com/smallbusiness/products/online/fs/plans.mspx (see Figure 3.16). Another site, www.thecounter.com, provides neat counter graphics and carries no adverts. Its statistics are excellent – you can view them from its website, and have a summary sent to you by e-mail each week.

Figure 3.16
FastCounter's
home page

Summary

■ To make sites attractive and easy to use, Web designers need to be aware of the general principles of Human Computer Interaction (HCI).

■ A mockup is an interface prototype – often created using paper and pencil – that represents the navigation, interaction and look and feel of the site.

■ One of the easiest ways to achieve consistent page layout is to use a page template. See more on this in Chapters 11, 12 and 13.

■ The Web is still primarily a visual medium and the main means of presenting information is text. Which font(s), sizes and colour contrasts to use are important considerations when designing your Web pages.

■ Writing for the Web is very different from traditional forms of writing and printing, such as newspapers. When you write for a newspaper, you have the full newspaper canvas to read from; in the case of the Web, you are restricted by the size of the monitor display.

■ Most monitors can display a minimum of 256 colours. However, there are only 216 Websafe colours.

- When you use safe colours in your Web pages, they should display correctly for all the main browsers.

- One of the greatest problems facing website designers is uncertainty about the users' interaction with the Web. This uncertainty can arise because of differences in browsers, monitors, connection speeds and other things.

- Navigation is a very important issue to address in website design, for the user has to be able to find what they are looking for as quickly as possible.

- File names created for the Web should conform to the ISO 9660 standard. This is known as the eight-dot-three format, because file names are restricted to eight characters followed by three-character extensions.

Exercises

1   Browse the Web and find a site that appeals to you. Write a short paragraph on how the site focuses on its users' needs.

2   Visit the website www.rspca.co.uk and write a mission statement for it that summarizes the site's goals.

3   Enter the www.loot.com website. Discuss the user interface design with regard to both browsing the contents of the magazine electronically, and the ease with which a customer may place a free advertisement.

4   Find the Lexmark (printer manufacturer) website and try to download the printer driver for the Lexmark 2050 printer. Did you find the experience easy? If not, how do you think it could be improved?

5   You have been asked to evaluate a company's website with regard to the user interface. Make a list of all the criteria that you believe should be considered in your evaluation. Include a justification for each of the criteria that you have listed.

6   Visit the website www.cnn.com (an American TV news channel). Apply the criteria that you described in question 5 to evaluate this website. Write a short paragraph summarizing your findings.

7   Describe three feedback utilities that could be incorporated into a website. Discuss the appropriateness of each.

8   Explain the difference between the terms plug-in file and helper file, and give two examples of plug-ins.

9   You can see a list of all plug-ins on your system by visiting http://privacy.net. Click on the link at the top left-hand side of the page that says 'For a full analysis click here'. You will see that the report contains a great deal of information about the presence of cookies and other items. As you scroll down the page, you will also see a list of your browser plug-ins. Write down the list of plug-ins on your system and try to understand what they might be doing.

10   Explain how you would use your browser (Netscape, for example) to change a video plug-in.

11 Using the Netscape browser, go to the following websites and evaluate them with respect to the criteria displayed in each column of the table below. Mark a tick in each column if each is, in your opinion, adequate.

www.volvo.com
www.walmart.com
www.thesimpsons.com

Website	Text	Text formatting	Colour	Animation	Images	Speed of download
www.volvo.com						
www.walmart.com						
www.thesimpsons.com						

Chapter

4

Web development tools

In this chapter you will learn to become familiar with:

■ the software tools required for the Web

■ the range of Web page development tools

■ conversion tools, such as Word

■ the range of Web graphic creation tools.

Introduction

Use the wrong tool for the job and you pay a high price in cost and time. Many of us who have tried using the wrong screwdriver to insert a wall screw can relate to this. Selecting appropriate software tool(s), whether it is for HTML coding, graphic creation, editing Web music file(s) or anything else related to Web development, is an essential prerequisite for success. The problem is that, with such a plethora of software available, how do you set about choosing the right tool(s)? In this chapter, we will look at the range of software used for Web development and the criteria that determine choice when selecting tool(s).

Software used on the Web

The software used on the Web broadly falls into the following categories.

■ *Browsers*
Browsers are tools that enable users to view Web pages. Familiar examples of browsers were seen in Chapter 1 and include Internet Explorer, Netscape Navigator, Opera and Mozilla.

■ *Web authoring tools*
These are broadly described as programs that create the Web pages. They can vary in functionality between so-called HTML **editors** (examples of these tools include BBEdit by Bare Bones Software – www.barebones.com – or HotDog Professional – www.sausage.com) to **WYSIWYG (What You See Is What You Get)** Web

page creation tools (such as Macromedia Dreamweaver – www.macromedia.com – or Adobe GoLive – www.adobe.com). These categories are discussed in more detail later in this chapter.

- *General Internet tools*
  These are other general categories of tools that facilitate Web development. For example, there are tools that facilitate the uploading/downloading of files from a computer's hard disk to a Web server. Examples are Fetch on the Macintosh and cuteFTP (www.cute.com) for Windows. Other tools, such as Telnet, provide remote access to server files.

- *Multimedia and graphic creation tools*
  These are programs that enable the creation of graphic and multimedia files for use in Web pages. Examples of these tools include Adobe Photoshop (www.adobe.com) and Macromedia Fireworks (www.macromedia.com).

Web authoring tools

HTML development tools fall into three categories:

- text editors
- HTML editors
- Web authoring environments
- conversion utilities.

Text editors

We have already used text editors, such as NotePad, in Chapter 1. **Text editors** provide very limited features – their main purpose is to provide a means of hand coding XHTML in plain-text format.

Text editors are very easy to use but leave all the hard work to the coder. Nevertheless, they do offer some advantages. First, they are a ubiquitous component of any operating system and therefore offer mobility in that, irrespective of platform – PC, Mac, Unix – code modifications are always possible. Second, text editors provide coders with access to fine-tuning control that would sometimes not be available with more sophisticated Web coding tools. Moreover, no additional costs are incurred with text editors because they are provided with the operating system of a computer. On the other hand, text editors do offer only very basic editing facilities, such as cut, copy paste, find and replace and, sometimes, a few other features. Examples of familiar editors include the EMACS editor, which runs on the Unix, Macintosh and Windows operating systems, and the NotePad editor, which runs on Microsoft Windows.

HTML **editors**

HTML **editors** provide a step up from text editors in both functionality and user interface. They provide HTML coders with rapid text entry facilities via a number of features, such as a **graphic user interface (GUI)** for tag selection, to tag templates to speed up the coding. Figure 4.1 illustrates some of these features using the Coffee Cup Editor.

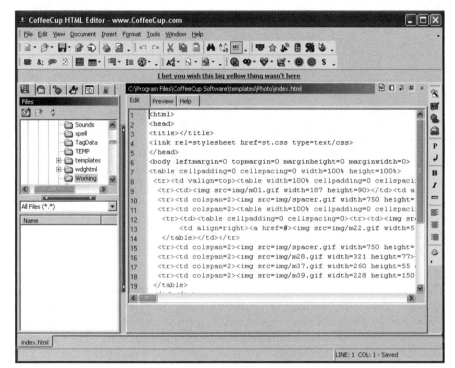

Figure 4.1
Illustration of the Coffee Cup 9.6 HTML editor

HTML editors are ideally suited to coders of smaller websites who have a fairly good knowledge of HTML code and want to speed up development. Typically, HTML editors would also include facilities such as **syntax checkers** – used for checking the syntax of code – spellcheckers and colour coding to distinguish different categories of tags and attributes, none of which would be provided with simple text editors. Another useful feature provided with many HTML editors is a **Multi-File Search and Replace facility**, allowing the coder to search through many files or Web pages and carry out a global search and replace. Figure 4.2 illustrates this feature using the Macromedia HomeSite HTML Editor. This is a very useful time-saving feature.

HTML editors come in all shapes and sizes. Macromedia HomeSite is an example of one that is available on both PC Windows and Macintosh environments. BBEdit by Bare Bones Software (www.barebones.com) runs on PCs and HotDog Professional (www.sauages.com) and CoffeeCup (www.coffeecup.com) are available for Windows (see Figure 4.1). Many browsers themselves are bundled with an HTML editor. For example, Netscape contains an HTML editor called Composer.

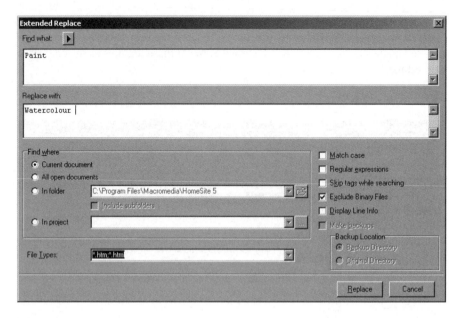

Web authoring environments

These are sometimes called **WYSIWYG tools** for they provide a 'What You See Is What You Get' interface for website development. Popular examples are Macromedia Dreamweaver (www.macromedia.com) and Adobe GoLive (www.adobe.com) or Microsoft FrontPage (www.microsoft.com). Most of these tools run on a PC and Macintosh.

The main advantage of using this type of tool is that the tool user may never need to learn any HTML code for these tools enable the user to enter text, graphics and so on, with the tool generating the code behind the scenes so to speak. However, Web authoring environments do much more than mark up pages. Many provide extensions for all aspects of Web project development, with support for project management, uploading, testing and a multitude of other facilities. However, Web authoring tools do have disadvantages, too, and one of these is the likelihood of the tool including HTML code that is surplus to requirements – remember, the tool does the coding, not the tool user. The tendency to include proprietary tags in this way annoys many because the code is more likely to reflect the application than the coder's choice. For example, Figure 4.3 includes a screenshot of the Adobe GoLive tool. Notice that it displays the HTML code generated and the code includes proprietary tags and attributes, such as '<met name="generator" content="Adobe GoLive 5">' and the '<title>Welcome to Adobe GoLive 5</title>'. A detailed study of a Web authoring environment is given with Dreamweaver in Chapters 11 to 13.

Web authoring environments vary in cost but are, in general, more expensive than HTML editors or other Web development tools.

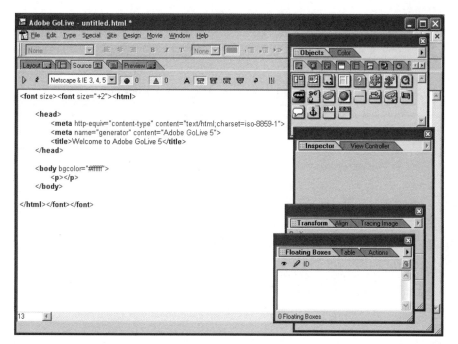

Figure 4.3
Illustration of
proprietery tags
inserted in GoLive

HTML **conversion utilities**

Conversion utilities are tools that are often integrated within another application. For example, the Microsoft Word program contains a utility to use a 'Save As' option that allows the user to convert a Word document into HTML. For small- to medium-sized documents, FrontPage 2000 provides conversion to HTML. Further information can be obtained from www.its.monash.edu.au/web/resources/conversion.html

Converting a Microsoft word document to Web page format

To convert a Word document to HTML format, follow the steps below:

1 Open the document that is required to be converted in Word (see Figure 4.4).

2 On the Word menu, select **Save As ...**

NOTE

You will notice that not all the parts of the Word document in Figure 4.4 have correctly converted to HTML. The text in the document has converted correctly, but the hand-drawn diagram has not. This is because the diagram is not a browser readable file, as GIF or JPEG images are, so care needs to be taken when attempting to convert documents of this type. There are other formats, such as Portable Document Format (PDF), that might be used for storing this type of file, as we shall see in Chapter 9.

Figure 4.4
Converting a
Word document
to HTML

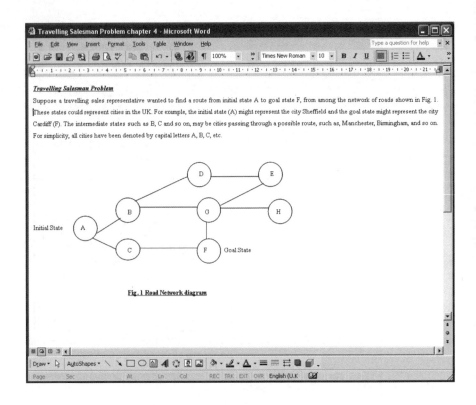

Figure 4.5
The Save as
dialogue box to
convert document
to HTML

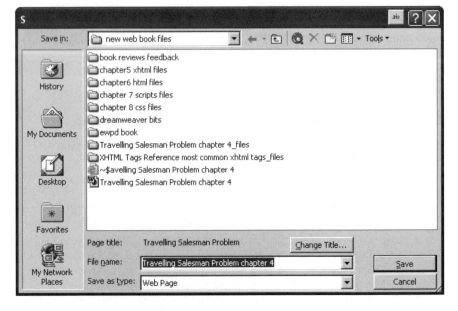

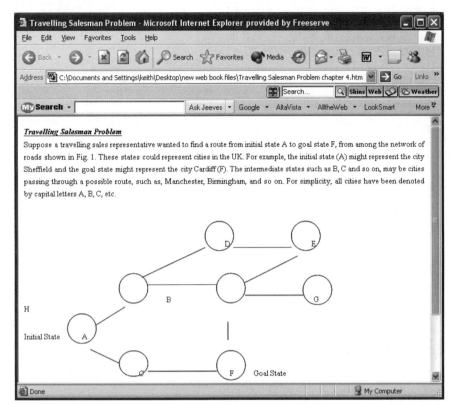

Figure 4.6
The converted file
displayed in the
IE 6 browser

3 In the dialogue box that follows, make sure that, in the **Save as type:** list box, you choose **Web Page**. Choose an appropriate file name and click the **Save** button (see Figure 4.5).

4 Test your page in both main browsers (the travelling salesman page displayed in Word in Figure 4.4 is displayed using the IE 6 browser in Figure 4.6).

Creating a new Web page using Microsoft Word

Create a Web page based on a template as follows.

1 On the **File** menu, click **New**.

2 A template can be selected from the **New From Template** window, which will appear in the **Document** window (see Figure 4.7). Alternatively, a Web page document can be opened (below the **Blank Document** option).

Entering and formatting text

Entering text in a Web page Word document follows the same pattern as entering text in a normal Word document. Remember that Word provides the facilities for choosing a wide range of fonts, colours, layout, style, lists and so on, all of which can be converted to Web page format.

Figure 4.7
Choosing a Web
template for
opening a new
document with
Word

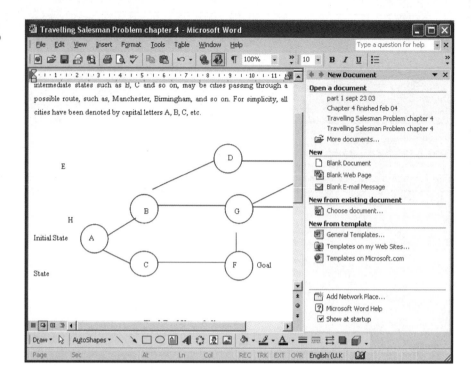

Creating hyperlinks using Word

Hyperlinks can be inserted into Word documents in the following ways:

∎ the creation of links in the same page – a bookmark
∎ the creation of links to different pages on the same website
∎ the creation of links outside the site in the WWW.

Text hyperlinks

In Word, you can insert, edit or delete hyperlinks using the **Hyperlink ...** option in
the **Insert** menu or click the keyboard combination **Ctrl + K** – called the keyboard
shortcut. You can insert a hyperlink in another document, file, Web page or e-mail
address. You can also create a hyperlink to an existing file or a new file or set up a
hyperlink to a point elsewhere on the same page. These are called **bookmarks**.
Figure 4.8 displays the **Insert Hyperlink** dialogue box. You will notice that I have
linked the selected item in the Word document to an existing file called XML1.htm.
After you've specified a name for the new file, you can choose to open the file for
editing immediately or come back to it later. As we have previously seen, text
hyperlinks are usually underlined in blue.

To expand on the above process, if you want to use Word to insert a hyperlink,
the method for doing this is as follows:

1 select the text or drawing object you want to display as the hyperlink, then click
  Hyperlink ... in the **Insert** menu

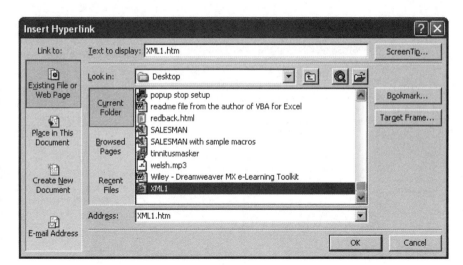

Figure 4.8
The **Insert Hyperlink** dialogue box in Word

2 when the **Insert Hyperlink** dialogue box appears, do one of the following:
   - to link to an existing file or Web page, click **Existing File** or **Web Page**
   - to link to a file that you haven't created yet, click **Create New Document**, under **Link to**
   - to link to a position that is in the same document, click **Place in This Document**
   - to link to an e-mail address, click **E-mail Address**
3 next, do one of the following:
   - if you clicked **Existing File** or **Web Page** in step 2, locate and select the file you want to link to
   - if you clicked **Create New Document** in step 2, type a name for the new file – you can also specify the path to the new file and choose whether you want to open the new file for editing now or later
   - if you clicked **Place in This Document** in step 2, then you will see a list of all the points in your document where it can be inserted – shown in Figure 4.9 in the **Select a place in this document** window – and you can now select the required position
4 to assign a tip to be displayed when you rest the mouse over the hyperlink, click **Screen Tip**, then type the text you want – Word uses the path or address of the file as the tip if you do not specify one
5 click **OK** twice
6 test the new hyperlink in your Word document by moving the mouse over the hyperlink, then hold down the keyboard Ctrl key and click the mouse button.

You can quickly create a hyperlink to a Web page without knowing the address. Click **Web page** to switch to your Web browser, open the World Wide Web page you want, then switch back to Word – the link is then created.

NOTE

Figure 4.9
Using the Insert
Hyperlink
dialogue box to
link to a Bookmark
in the same
document

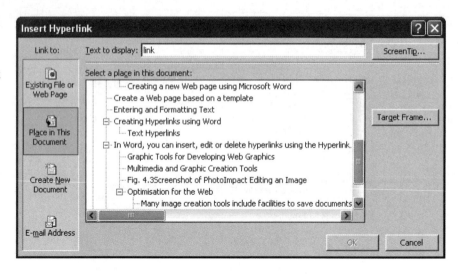

Preparing text in Word for use in a Web authoring tool

Word is a fairly ubiquitous program, so many writers prefer to prepare text with it that is to be used in a web authoring tool, such as GoLive or Dreamweaver. Word contains many facilities to make writing and formatting documents easier – and, indeed, many documents that would be transferred to the Web might already be in Word format. However, the transfer is not always as simple as it sounds. The following guidelines will help make the transition less troublesome:

- as we have already seen, do not include handwritten diagrams or non-standard format pictures in the document as they do not transfer very well
- avoid formatting the text in Word because it will probably look crooked when it gets to Dreamweaver
- take care with white space – remember, repeated spaces are ignored on the Web
- avoid using tables because tables that are created in Word are not easily imported into Web authoring tools
- many Web authoring tools include spelling and grammar checkers but it is advisable to do this in Word, because it is a program that is more suitably dedicated to these tasks.

Adding images

The majority of graphic files used on Web pages are JPEG and GIF formats, although the PNG format is beginning to make an impact (more on this in Chapter 9). These are all compressed formats. Adding images to a page can make it eye-catching and interesting. You can use images from a variety of sources, including scanned photographs and artwork. To add a graphic in Word, select **Insert** / **Picture** / **From file**, and then choose the required image for opening, or click the image icon on the standard toolbar.

If you are incorporating graphic images on Web pages, bear in mind that GIF only supports 256 colours. For this reason, Word automatically converts all images into GIF if the file uses fewer than 256 colours, but will store it in JPEG format if the file contains more than 256 colours.

Multimedia and graphic creation tools

The term **multimedia**, as the name suggests, refers to multiple communication media methods that include text, graphics, animation, video, sound and music. A wide range of tools is available for developing and editing multimedia graphics for websites. Here are descriptions of a few of the most popular ones.

- **Adobe Photoshop (www.adobe.com)** is often seen as the standard for editing and compositing bit-mapped (see Chapter 9) Web graphics. The program takes time to master but delivers many features, one of which is the ability to create and edit Web-optimized bit-mapped graphics (an example of optimization is given in the next section). Photoshop **layers** provide a powerful way to work with images. Also, Photoshop has excellent facilities for manipulating and filtering photographs to improve their quality. A Web-safe palette, ability to create transparent and interlaced GIFs (see Chapter 9) and many more features make Photoshop well suited to professional Web development. Photoshop is available for the Windows and Macintosh environments.

- **Macromedia Fireworks (www.macromedia.com)** is a stable-mate of the Web authoring program Dreamweaver and both programs, as you would expect, integrate their features well. Fireworks was the first major program to be designed from the ground up for producing graphics for the Web (Crowder and Crowder 2001). Fireworks can be used for editing anything from photographs to drawings and animation. It also can be used for HTML generation for graphic positioning and generating code for JavaScript rollovers. Fireworks runs on both the PC and Macintosh.

- **Jasc Paint Shop Pro (www.jasc.com)** is a popular choice for many Web developers. Paint Shop Pro has many features, including layers, a built-in tool to create GIF animations called Animation Shop and extensive features for editing photographs (see Figure 4.10), as well as painting and drawing facilities. Paint Shop Pro is also a little easier to use than some of its competitors, which makes it a very attractive choice for many Web developers. Paint Shop Pro runs only on Windows-based systems.

- **Ulead PhotoImpact (www.ulead.com)** is a low-cost tool well suited to Web-based graphics. Features include Imagemap support, a Web button maker and Web optimization facilities (see Figure 4.11). It runs only on Windows-based systems.

- **Flash (www.macromedia.com)** is a Macromedia software product that is a multimedia authoring tool (see Chapter 9) and has become the de facto standard for

Figure 4.10
Screenshot of a photograph edited using Paint Shop Pro Version 8

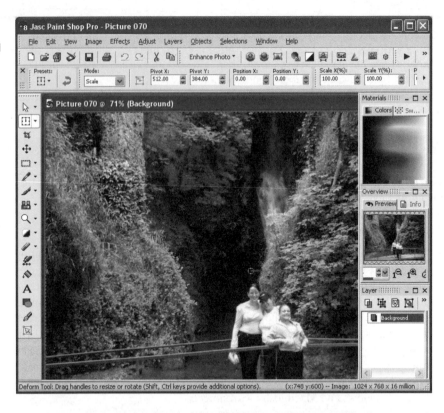

Figure 4.11
Screenshot of a PhotoImpact editing an image

interactivity and short animation for websites. Flash movie files use an .swf extension and audio can also be embedded into Flash movies. However, Flash is not particularly well suited to streaming applications (see Chapter 9). Flash files can be played with a Flash player, which nowadays is built into browsers, making the need for a plug-in redundant.

■ **Director (www.macromedia.com)** is another Macromedia multimedia authoring tool for displaying slide presentations and movie and animated applications on the Web. Director files can be played back with Shockwave players. The Shockwave format may contain sound and streaming audio in the format (see Chapter 9).

To become proficient with a graphic editing tool such as Photoshop takes more than just acquiring the software tool skills. Creating sophisticated graphics often requires art and design skills as well.

NOTE

Summary

■ A range of software tools is required for Web development.

■ Browsers render pages to view on the Web.

■ Web development tools are used to build websites and these include the following general categories:
  - text editors, used for writing complete HTML
  - HTML editors, to remove much of the donkey work that coding with text editors requires by providing tag templates and more to speed up coding
  - Web authoring environments provide a WYSIWYG interface for website development
  - conversion utilities, tools – such as Word – that can be used to convert from a non-Web format to a Web-suitable format.

■ Word can be used to save documents as HTML Web page documents.

■ Word can be used to edit simple HTML files and prepare them for use in a Web authoring tool, such as Dreamweaver.

■ Web graphic tools provide the means for creating and editing graphics on the Web.

■ Web optimization tools can be used to reduce the size of graphic images so that they may download faster for use on the Web.

Exercises

1 Briefly describe the varieties of tools that can be used to create Web pages.

2 Check with your browser(s) to see if there is a default editor that is used to create Web pages. Hint: you can do this in IE by selecting **File** / **Edit** from the menu.

3   Create the page shown in Figure 4.12 in Word exactly as it is (the background colour is yellow). Check the document's correctness using the IE and Netscape browsers. Save the file using an appropriate file name and create linked pages (but only include the title inside each page) for each of the categories of food shown at the end of the page – Rolls and Sandwiches, Burgers, and Kebabs and Pitta. Check the correctness of the links using your browser.

Figure 4.12
Document for
question 3

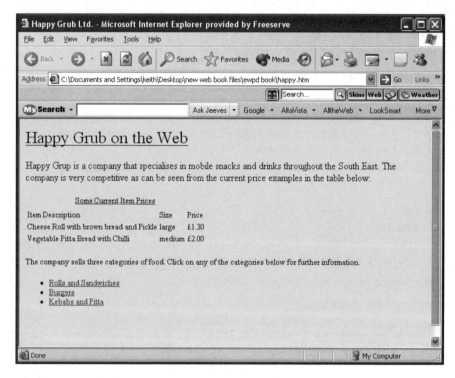

4   Repeat the above exercise using the Netscape Composer editor. Check the page using both Netscape and IE.

5   View the file in HTML form using the **View** / **HTML source** menu option and see if you can make sense of the code before we begin HTML in the next chapter.

6   Prepare a formatted text document in Microsoft Word using a variety of fonts, font sizes, bulleted list points and headings. Save the file using a suitable file name and convert the file into HTML format. Now, open the file using both the IE and Netscape browsers. Describe any differences in your results.

7   Create the above Web page using Word. Save the page using the file name 'engine'. Test the page by using the **Web Page Preview** option in the **File** menu of Word. You should find that Word will automatically identify hyperlinks as soon as you begin to type in the http://www

8   PetHelp is a UK-based pet and animal welfare charity that is considering setting up a website. The charity offers many services, including finding new homes for abandoned pets, neutering pets and other vetinary services, as well as providing educational information regarding the welfare of animals. The charity is very low on funds and cannot afford to spend a great deal on the site's development. On the other hand, the chief

executive has stated that she would like to get the site up and running very soon. Of the eight volunteers who work for the charity on a part-time basis, only two have any knowledge of website development – both attended an introductory-level course in Dreamweaver. Neither has any knowledge of HTML or other development tools. Write a brief report recommending suitable tool(s) for this task. You should comment on the time constraints, costs and the likely learning curve emanating from your recommendation.

9 You have been consulted by a friend – who is an expert on growing large vegetables – about setting up a website. He believes his many years' experience in this field should be promoted on the Web. He has won several prizes for his entries and hopes to display lots of photographs of prize-winning vegetables, as well as developing links with other vegetable growers. He also wants to display pages containing tips and advice and other vegetable-growing articles of interest, but does not want to invest too much in time and costs. Comment on the viability of using an HTML editing environment for this task, such as Macromedia's HomeSite. You have recommended using Adobe's Photoshop for editing and preparing his vegetable photographs for the Web. Why would a program like this be necessary before using photographs on Web pages?

Chapter

5

The basics of XHTML

In this chapter you will learn:

- about XHTML and its evolution on the WWW
- how to create a basic template for an XHTML document
- about text formatting elements
- about physical and logical formatting elements
- how to add hidden comments to XHTML
- how to add lists to your Web pages
- how to incorporate graphic images in a Web page
- how to incorporate hyperlinks in a Web page
- how to use image maps in Web pages
- how to understand the tree structure of an XHTML document.

Introduction

XHTML stands for **Extensible HyperText Markup Language** and it evolved from HTML as the primary means of describing Web content. World Wide Web sites and Web pages are written in HTML. All XHTML files are plain text files so that they can be edited on any type of computer. XHTML is not really a programming language – it is more a set of rules stored within the browser that defines how to structure the elements of a page by using embedded tags.

Using XHTML is not very different from using HTML. Indeed, it is identical to HTML in many respects. According to the W3C, 'XHTML 1.0 is a reformulation of HTML. It is the first major change to HTML since HTML 4.0 was released in 1998'. XHTML also brings the rigour of XML to Web pages and is the keystone in W3C's work to create standards that provide richer Web pages on an ever-increasing range of browser platforms, including mobile phones, televisions, cars, wallet-sized wireless communicators, kiosks and desktops.

However, XHTML imposes more discipline in the way that it is written because, unlike HTML, it will not interpret language code that does not conform strictly to the rules. Moreover, XHTML can also be extended beyond the range of tags and attributes available. If you're familiar with HTML, XHTML will be easy to learn and use.

XHTML 1.0 was released on 26 January 2000 as a Recommendation by the W3C. However, another version – XHTML 1.1 – was released as a W3C recommendation in May 2001 and represents a big change, in that specific modules are defined to handle particular tasks. Modules facilitate a more structured approach to development because systems can be broken down into smaller parts independently of each other and bolted together, so to speak. The spirit behind this approach is that authors can use the standard XHTML modules and create their own XML modules. This means that authors who write code for devices such as PDAs or mobile phones can restrict themselves to the use of a subset of modules that meet their needs and thus reduce the complexity of the task. Indeed, modularization has gone one step further with the release of XHTML 2.

Why use XHTML rather than HTML?

There are many advantages to using XHTML rather than HTML.

- XHTML encourages a more structured, disciplined approach because, unlike HTML, it does not tolerate violations in the rules. This is good practice because it forces the website developer to conform to the rules and, thus, circumvent possible non-compatibility with browsers. Some browsers will accept sloppy HTML, such as non-closing tags and so on. By accepting ill-formed HTML, more unpredictable outcomes are likely when rendered with different browsers. Unlike HTML, XHTML will not accept such ill-formed documents.

- XHTML offers the best of both worlds in the sense that it gives compatibility with previous versions of HTML (for this reason some have called it HTML 5), yet gives developers the power and flexibility to define their own tags and, thus, extend the language to their requirements.

- XHTML is another application of XML (Extensible Markup Language). Chapter 10 looks at XML in detail, but it should be known at this stage that XML is a structured set of rules for how one might define any kind of data to be shared on the Web. It is called 'extensible' because anyone can invent a particular set of markup for a particular purpose and, as long as everyone uses it (the writer and an application program at the receiver's end), it can be adapted and used for many purposes, including describing the appearance of a Web page.

- Using HTML, authors had a fixed set of elements to use, with no variation. Unlike HTML, however, XHTML can be extended by anyone who uses it. New tags and attributes can be defined and added to those that already exist, making possible new ways to embed content and programming in a Web page. With XHTML 1.0, authors can mix and match known HTML elements with elements from other XML languages, including those developed by W3C for applications such as multimedia.

- XHTML will help make pages more readable for disabled users. For those who are, for example, visually impaired or blind or are likely to rely on speech synthesizers or Braille readers to render the text, XHTML provides support for Cascading Style Sheets (CSS). These provide a means with which to separate the presentation of the document from its structure and will be studied in more detail in Chapter 8.

- XHTML accommodates new devices and technologies, such as PDAs, mobile phones, pagers – all of which are increasing their share of access to the Internet in relation to the PC.

- XHMTL supports style sheet technologies such as XSL (see Chapter 8).

The origins of HTML and XHTML

HTML is actually a descendant (or subset) of **Standard Generalized Markup Language (SGML)**. This markup language was created to structure technical documents, primarily for government and military establishments.

SGML is a versatile language created so that it would be easier to exchange text-based information across multiple computer platforms than had been possible previously. However, SGML is very general and difficult to learn. For more on SGML, see www.oasis-open.org/cover/general.html

The birth of HTML began with Tim Berners-Lee (1989), who was working at the European Laboratory for Particle Physics in Switzerland (known as CERN). He was concerned with finding a method for distributing documents for scientists over networked computers. He realized that scientists and, therefore, the larger Internet community would be reluctant to learn SGML because of its difficulty and looked for a simpler alternative markup language.

His idea was to link documents using the hypertext worldwide Web concept. His work led to the HTML derivative that he believed would be sufficient for the distribution of hypertext documents using text and graphics to be viewed in a non-linear way. This system was implemented so that it could be viewed on any computer, for HTML could be written as a simple ASCII text file.

The Web was originally developed for CERN, but rapidly expanded and the World Wide Web consortium – W3C – was formed. Berners-Lee was, and continues to be, an active member of the consortium. The W3C became responsible for the evolution and standardization of HTML. From the beginning, HTML has been evolving to allow for the incorporation of new techniques and changes in technology. Table 5.1 outlines the milestone stages in the evolution of XHTML.

The elements of XHTML

XHTML, like HTML, is composed of **elements**, or instructions, to WWW browsers to perform a defined task. Examples of these elements could be, perhaps, to make text bold or insert a paragraph break or format a list of items in a predetermined manner. As we have already seen in Chapter 1, these elements are called **tags**. XHTML tags

Table 5.1 The evolution of HTML and XHTML

Year proposed	Recommendation	Remarks
1993	HTML Version 1	Rapidly superseded by Version 2. Originally contained 12 tags
1994	Version 2.0 developed to codify common practice	Significant additions agreed, including table elements and forms (see Chapter 6)
1995	Version 3.0 proposed a much richer version, including greater page format control	Never got off the ground – superseded by HTML 3.2
1996	Version 3.2 developed to codify common practice	Tags such as `<font>` were introduced and caused more problems than they solved. Problems revolved around the separation of presentation from structure of the document. Also, browser proprietors such as Netscape had much influence over HTML 3.2. Many of Netscape's extensions were approved by the W3C
1998	Version 4.0 was viewed as a watershed development by many in the Web community	HTML 4.0 was the first to provide support for CSS, enabling all formatting to be moved out of the HTML document and into a separate style sheet. This marked a new direction for the W3C HTML working group. Other extensions include support for frames and scripting tools as well as improved support for internationalization of documents
2000	XHTML Version 1.0 replaces HTML as the primary means of describing Web content	XHTML essentially a reformulation of HTML 4
2001	XHTML Version 1.1 recommended in May	A reformulation of XHTML 1.0 consisting of modules that separate sets of elements. This adds more structure. Also known as Modular XHTML
2002	August, the first public Working Draft of XHTML 2.0 was published	XHTML becomes a modular language, going back to its roots by encouraging the use of tags only for structure and leaving presentation to style sheets

consist of individual elements inside angle brackets <>. However, the following rules must be strictly applied when writing XHTML-compliant documents.

- Lower-case characters *must* be used in any XHTML element or attribute names. This is very different to HTML, which is case-insensitive. The reason for making XHTML case-sensitive is that it is a particular case of XML. As XML was made case-sensitive by the HTML working group, it became inevitable that XHTML would follow suit.

- Attribute values must be enclosed in either single quotes or double quotes. Moreover, all attributes must be assigned to explicit values. An example of this is given later in this chapter under the heading 'Adding horizontal lines', which deals with the <hr> tag and its attributes.

- In Chapter 1, in the brief introduction to HTML, we discussed two types of elements: **empty** and **container tags**. Just to recap, **empty tags** generally represent constructs such as horizontal rules or line breaks, both of which do not have the defined use of an end tag. **Container tags**, on the other hand, define a section of text and specify the formatting or construction for all of the selected text. A container tag has both a beginning and an ending – the ending tag is identical to the beginning tag, with the addition of a forward slash. Most containers can overlap and hold other containers. In XHTML, *all* tags are required to be container tags, even when no ending tag is necessary. If you use an empty element that does not contain any content, then you must include an end tag. For example, `<tag>,</tag>`. Alternatively, you can use the abbreviated form `<tag />`. Note that the space must be used before the terminating slash when using this form.

- Nested tags must be terminated in the reverse order to the way in which they are written. So, `<tag1><tag2> ... </tag2></tag1>` is a correct construction, but `<tag1><tag2> ... </tag1></tag2>` is incorrect.

NOTE   Strict XHTML-compliant code will not be interpreted unless all the above restrictions are met.

The three variants of XHTML

It is possible to use XHTML without conforming to the strict rules discussed earlier, for there are three variants available. The variants are:

- strict
- transitional
- frames.

Strict version

Use this variant when you want really clean structural markup, free of any tags associated with layout.

When you use this version all deprecated tags and attributes are taboo also. The reason for this is that the goal of separating structure from presentation is strictly observed. This means the Cascading Style Sheet (CSS) language needs to be used to get the font, colours and layout effects you want.

In general, it is desirable to use strict XHTML, although one has to trade this off against practical considerations, such as browser compatibility and so on.

Transitional version

The transitional version permits the use of deprecated tags and attributes and is more relaxed on the application of the rules of XHTML.

The main idea here is to take the advantages of XHTML features, including style sheets, but, nonetheless, make small adjustments to your markup for the benefit of those viewing your pages with older browsers, which can't understand style sheets.

Frameset version

This, the final of the three versions of XHTML, is for when you want to use frames (see Chapter 6) to partition the browser window into two or more frames. This is exactly the same as the transitional version, apart from its support for frames.

A template for XHTML documents

Before you begin your XHTML document, you need to lay out a basic working frame-work. XHTML documents must follow a defined sequence of tags if they are to be interpreted correctly. It is a good idea to create a template to use for each of your pages so that you are less likely to leave out an important detail.

The document declarations

If you are writing XHTML documents, then they must conform to the proper XHTML syntax. To ensure that they conform, you must include in any document a group of tags called **document declaration tags**. Before we look at the syntax in detail, we need to understand why these tags must be included.

There are three tags that must be declared and they are shown below with descriptions of each of them following. (*Note*: the frameset version tags are given in Chapter 6 when frames are discussed in detail.)

```
<?xml version = "1.0"?>

<!DOCTYPE html PUBLIC "-//WC3//DTD XHTML 1.0 Transitional //EN"
"http://www.w3.org/TR/xhtml11/DTD/xhtml11-transitional.dtd">

<html xmlns = "http://www.w3.org/1999/xhtml">
```

The document version declaration tag

For an XHTML browser to correctly parse and display your XHTML document, you need to tell it which version of XML is being used to create the document. You must also state which XHTML DTD (see under next heading) defines the elements in your document. To declare that you are using XML Version 1.0, place this directive in the first line in your document:

```
<?xml version="1.0"?>
```

This tells the browser that you are using XML 1.0. You will often see this element used with the encoding attribute, as shown below:

```
<?xml version="1.0" encoding="UTF-8"?>
```

The purpose of this attribute is to indicate which character set is being used. In the above example, the 8-bit Unicode character set – the most common – is used (this is explained further in Chapter 10 on XML).

NOTE Some XHTML authors leave out the encoding attribute. This is not to be recommended, however, because it specifies the character set and, therefore, some special characters may not render properly without its inclusion.

The document type declaration tag

The tag `<!DOCTYPE html PUBLIC "-//WC3//DTD XHTML 1.0 Transitional //EN" "http://www.w3.org/TR/xhtml11/DTD/xhtml11-transitional .dtd">` is a document type definition, which must be included with your XHTML listings. As we have seen from the above, the W3C has defined three types of XHTML documents. This means that there will be three ways to implement, or carry out, your XHTML markup. You must specify which of these variants you are using by inserting this line along with the other document declaration tags. This tag specifies something called a **Document Type Definition (DTD)**, which can be thought of as an interpreter of the language version. The purpose of this tag is to inform the browser what variant of XHTML you are conforming to so that it can turn on the strict compliance formatting, if required, and only render documents that conform to the DTD.

The Namespace tag

The tag `<html xmlns = "http://www.w3.org/1999/xhtml">` is called the

root element and **namespace attribute tag**. Every XHTML document must begin with the root element html. The reason for having a namespace attribute in this tag is that, as stated earlier, XHTML is another application of XML, which means that anyone can create a set of markup elements for a particular purpose and, as long as everyone uses it (the writer and an application program at the receiver's end), it can be adapted and used for many purposes, including describing the appearance of a Web page.

However, for this to happen a Document Type Definition (DTD) is required to define elements and attribute names that make up this markup language. These elements and attribute names are stored in a **namespace** that is unique to the DTD. As you reference elements and attributes in your document, the browser looks them up in the namespace to find out how they should be used. For example, in Chapter 1 we used the tag <body> and attributes such as colour = 'Red '. These are defined in the XHTML DTD and their names are placed in the DTD's namespace so that the browser will know what the markup means and what it should do with the markup. However, with XML, your document could use more than one DTD and so may need more than one namespace. For example, suppose you created a transitional XHTML document, but also included special XML markup for human body health tags. If both the XHTML DTD and the XML human body health tags use the same name to define different <body> elements, such as for the XHTML body of a program and <body> for a human body, then ambiguity will clearly arise. This ambiguity can be resolved by using the xmlns attribute, so that their meanings will be separated.

You can use this attribute to define one or more alternative namespaces within your document. It can be placed within the start tag of any element within your document and its URL-like value defines the namespace that the browser should use for all content within that element.

If you are using XHTML, you should at the very least include an xmlns attribute within your document's <html> tag that identifies the primary namespace used throughout the document:

```
<html xmlns="http://www.w3.org/1999/xhtml">
```

The majority of XHTML authors will never need to define multiple namespaces and so will never have to use fully qualified names containing the namespace prefix. Even so, you should understand that multiple namespaces exist and that you will need to manage them if you choose to embed content based on one DTD within content defined by another DTD.

The Unicode standard

Characters in XHTML follow the Unicode standard. Unicode is an extension to the ASCII (American Standard Code for Information Interchange) character set, which has long been a computer standard. However, ASCII does not support other international character sets and that is why XHTML conforms to the Unicode standard. Unicode supports all spoken languages as well as mathematical and other symbols. However, unlike ASCII which uses an 8-bit character set, Unicode uses a 16-bit code format so that the increased range of language characters can be accommodated.

In many cases, you will not need to use the 16-bit and can work with 8-bit encoding instead. That is why we have the attribute `encoding="UTF-8"` in the XML declaration tag. In some of the examples that follow, the document declaration tags have been omitted for simplicity. You should always include them if your code is conforming to XHTML standards.

A basic document template

Listing 5.1 A basic XHTML document template

```
<?xml version = "1.0"?>
<!DOCTYPE html PUBLIC "-//WC3//DTD XHTML 1.0 Transitional
//EN"
"http://www.w3.org/TR/xhtml11/DTD/xhtml11-transitional.dtd">
<html xmlns = "http://www.w3.org/1999/xhtml">

<!-- my first XHTML page written by Keith Darlington -->
<!--Date written 12th June 2002 -->


<head >
<title > My First XHTML page </title>
</head >
<body >
Put the body text in here.
</body >
</html>
```

Listing 5.1 begins, as already stated, with the `<html>` tag that is necessary for every XHTML document. Next is the `<head>` tag, which opens up the heading part of the document. This contains the `<title>` element, which is used for adding a title to your document. This element is not required, but using it represents good practice as it helps readers of your document to know what they are reading. The heading is closed with the `</head>` tag. Finally, the `<body>` element follows. This will be where you place the bulk of the material in your document. Remember to close the body element with the `</body>` tag and to finish the page with the `</html>` tag.

Because XHTML is a markup language, the body of your document is turned on with the start tag `<body>`. Everything that follows this tag is interpreted according to a strict set of rules that tell the browser about the contents to be displayed. The body element is closed with the end tag, `</body>`. In the basic template shown above, the body text is a single line. In your document, you will replace this line with the main text of your document. Unless you are using a special XHTML editor, you must enter your text using a strict ASCII format. This limits you to a common set of characters that can be interpreted by computers throughout the world. The text that you enter here – whether for the first time or from an existing document – must be completely free of any special formatting.

The `<html>` tag

XHTML documents are platform-independent and can be accessed with any compliant WWW browser. One way to indicate this independence is the `<html>` tag. Because XHTML documents are not compiled (or processed) for execution, some applications need a hint to know how to interpret the plain text in a home page. That's where the `<html>` tag comes into play. The `<html>` and `</html>` tags should be the first and last elements of your XHTML document.

The head section: using the `head` element

XHTML provides the `head` element to define the head section in a document. The `<head>` tag encloses or contains the head section (which is enclosed by the `<html>` tag). The closing `</head>` tag sets the bounds for the head section.

The head section often contains tags that would not cause anything to be displayed on the Web page. For example, tags for validating the HTML (see Note below). The only tag in the head section that would be displayed by the end user's viewer is the value of the `<title>` element.

Try to get into a habit of using the XHTML template to create Web pages – it will make your work easier.	**TIP**

Deprecated tags

The WC3 often discourages the use of older tags and attributes that have been replaced by more appropriate tags. These are known as **deprecated tags** and we will come across some of them in this chapter.

The WC3 discourages the use of particular elements because it may be more efficient to implement some tasks by using Cascading Style Sheets (see Chapter 8) or some other techniques. It is important to know that using deprecated elements will not necessarily result in faults in the way that your document is rendered in a browser, unless you have specified the strict version in the declarations, but it does mean that, by not using them, you will be conforming to standards that will often improve the readability of the document as well as making it easier to maintain. See Appendix 2 for a complete listing of tags and attributes and those that are deprecated in XHTML 1.0.

You can check the correctness of XHTML code by using an XHTML validation service, such as the W3C's XHTML marking Validation Service at (see Figure 5.1):	**NOTE**

http://validator.w3.org

Most validation services want to know which version of HTML or XHTML your Web page should be checked against (see Figure 5.1).

Figure 5.1
XHTML code
validation
service's website

Attributes

Attributes, as we saw in Chapter 1, are used to control some aspect of a tag's actions. For example, a heading tag could use an attribute to control the alignment. When a heading tag is used, the assumed alignment – called the **default** – is assumed to be left justified. A heading could be centred or right aligned. Most attributes take values that follow an = sign after the attribute's name.

The way in which an attribute is used within a tag is shown in the following examples:

```
<h1 align ="center">Keith's Favourite Music Page</h1>

<body bgcolor ="red"> (Note: #000000 is colour black)
```

NOTE   Some XHTML tags use many optional attributes, some use none, while some tags require attributes for their use, as we shall see throughout this chapter.

Adding hidden comments to your XHTML file

It is possible to add comments to your XHTML document that will not be seen by a reader. This is a convenient way to leave notes for yourself or others and aid XHTML readability. An example might be to add a comment when new material is added to a document that shows the date of the new addition.

To add a comment tag, start with the usual angle bracket symbol,<, then an exclamation mark followed by two hyphens: <!--. After the comment is completed, finish with two hyphens and closing angle bracket: -->. An example of an XHTML comment is given below:

```
<!--This is a comment tag and will not be displayed in the
browser -->
```

Self-assessed exercise

Write two XHTML comment tags. The first should state your name and the second should state today's date.

Get into the habit of inserting plenty of comments in your XHTML documents. Comments will help with the readability of the document, as well as enable you to include other important information that may be of use in the future.

TIP

The body element of an XHTML document

Despite the graphical nature of the Web, most information on it is in the form of text documents. Most people who view your documents will be interested in what you have to say. Hence, as a Web designer, you will spend much of your time working in the body, entering text. Much of the remainder of this chapter and the next looks at XHTML techniques for incorporating text and graphic elements. In the next section, we will look at basic body text formatting.

XHTML text formatting

Text is by far the most common way of providing information on the Web. So, it is clearly very important to be familiar with the elements that can enable the text to be formatted and presented. The main XHTML elements that are used to achieve this are considered in the following sections.

Using text in the body section

Any printed text-based document will normally be divided into a number of paragraphs. Web-based documents can also break up text into paragraphs by using paragraph elements.

To use a paragraph element, insert the tag <p> at the beginning of each new paragraph, and the browser will display a new paragraph at the point of insertion of the <p> element. Remember to add the </p> tag at the end of your paragraph to follow the XHTML standard.

Adding line breaks

XHTML does all of the formatting at the browser rather than at the source. This has the advantage of device independence, but what do you do if you have a reason to break up a line of text at a certain point?

The way to end a line where you want is to use the line break tag, <br>. This forces the browser to start a new line, regardless of the position in the current line. Unlike the paragraph element, the line break does not double-space the text. In other words, the <br> element has the effect of creating a carriage return without getting the blank line associated with the <p> element.

NOTE   XHTML interprets only up to two consecutive spaces (from the spacebar key). Also, it ignores tabs and carriage returns *unless you use the 'previously formatted text' tag.*

Creating a text outline

Adding structure to a Web page document can make it more readable. Users of the Web want to be able to quickly scan a document to determine whether or not it has the information that they are looking for. The way to make this scanning easier is to break the document up into logical sections, each covering a single topic.

After you have broken up the document, the next step is to add meaningful headings to each section, which enables your reader to quickly jump to the material of interest.

Adding headings

Headings in XHTML provide an outline of the text that forms the body of the document. As such, headings direct the reader through the document and make your information more interesting and usable. They are probably the most commonly used formatting elements that you will find in XHTML documents.

XHTML has six levels of headings – h1 (the most important), h2, h3, h4, h5 and h6 (the least important). Each of these levels will have its own appearance in the viewer's browser, but you have no direct control over what that appearance will be. This is part of the XHTML philosophy, that you, as the document writer, have responsibility for the content, while the browser has responsibility for the appearance.

To use a heading element of the largest possible size, begin with a start tag of the form <h1> and end the heading container with a corresponding end tag – </h1>. See the example in Listing 5.2.

Listing 5.2 An XHTML document displaying the use of heading tags

```
<?xml version = "1.0"?>
<!DOCTYPE html PUBLIC "-//WC3//DTD XHTML 1.0 Transitional //EN"
"http://www.w3.org/TR/xhtml11/DTD/xhtml11-transitional.dtd">
<html xmlns = "http://www.w3.org/1999/xhtml">

    <head>
    <title>Creating an XHTML Document</title>
    </head>
    <body>
    <h1>Level 1 Heading</h1>
    <h2>Level 2 Heading</h2>
    <h3>Level 3 Heading</h3>
    <h4>Level 4 Heading</h4>
    <h5>Level 5 Heading</h5>
    <h6>Level 6 Heading</h6>
    </body>
</html>
```

> **NOTE**
>
> Handling white space has always been a problem for Web page designers. A browser will only leave one space when rendering text, even if more than one space is included. If you want the browser to insert more than one space, there are techniques that can be used later in this chapter.

The screenshot in Figure 5.2 shows how Listing 5.2 looks when rendered in Netscape 7.

Hands-on exercise

Create the file shown in Listing 5.2 and run the file using Netscape and Internet Explorer. Check the fonts and the sizes of the headings. Note any differences that you can see.

> **NOTE**
>
> The best way to use headings is to think of them as an outline for your document. Generally, it is good practice to use a new level whenever you have two to four items of equal importance.

Figure 5.2
Heading level
tags shown in
Listings 5.2 output
in Netscape 7

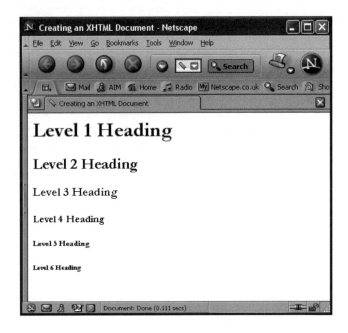

Adding horizontal lines

Another method for adding divisions to your documents is the use of horizontal lines. These provide a strong visual break between sections and are especially useful for separating the various parts of your document.

A horizontal rule can be created using the horizontal rule element, `<hr />`. This tag draws a shaded horizontal line across the browser's display. However, its appearance is at the mercy of the browser. There is an implied paragraph break before and after a horizontal rule.

Table 5.2 Attributes of the `<hr>` tag

Attribute	Possible value(s)	Purpose of attribute	Default value
Align =	Left, right, center	To justify or centre the position of the horizontal rule	Center
Noshade =	True, false	Eliminates the 3D effect on display	True
Size =	Any integer value	To set the thickness of the rule in pixels	Two pixels
Width =	An integer value representing the number of pixels across the screen or a percentage of the screen width	To assign width to an element across the screen	None

There are four main attributes that can be used with the `<hr>` tag. They are summarized in Table 5.2. However, the size attribute is deprecated in XHTML, since its effects can be achieved with the CSS specification (see Chapter 8). Nevertheless, examples that include the size attribute have been included here.

The `<hr>` tag is deprecated and should not be used with strict XHTML. The W3C recommends the use of style sheets instead.

NOTE

The tag `<hr>` creates a horizontal rule using the default attribute values, giving the following effect:

The tag `<hr noshade ="noshade" size="10" width="75%">` creates a horizontal rule without 3D shading with a thickness of 10 pixels and a width of 75, giving the following effect:

The tag `<hr noshade ="noshade" size="2" width="85%">` creates a horizontal rule without 3D shading with a thickness of 2 pixels and a width of 85, giving the following effect:

The tag `<hr  size="20"  width="45%">` creates a horizontal rule without 3D shading with a thickness of 20 pixels and a width of 45, giving the following effect:

The tag `<hr  size="20"  width="55">` creates a horizontal rule without 3D shading with a thickness of 20 pixels and a width of 55 pixels (not expressed as a percentage of the total length of the line, but the absolute number of pixels), giving the following effect:

Overlapping tags is incorrect and will produce errors – always nest them in the opposite order to that at the beginning. For example:

```
<p><h1> text </p></h1> is incorrect
<p><h1> text </h1></p> is correct
```

NOTE

Example

The example in Listing 5.3 shows how to combine the use of some of the text layout elements – such as the `<p>` and `<hr>` – to achieve the correct divisional balance. The document output is shown in Figure 5.3. Listing 5.3 includes the XHTML code required to achieve this effect.

Figure 5.3
Output of
Listing 5.3 using
basic text
formatting tags

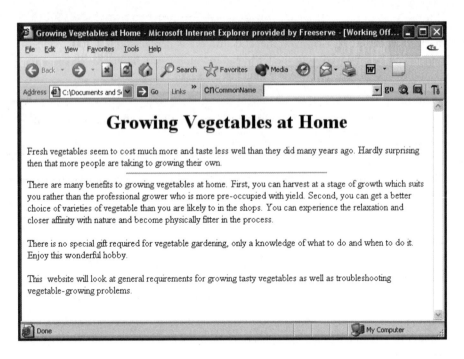

Listing 5.3 Example of the use of basic formatting tags

```
<?xml version = "1.0"?>
<!DOCTYPE html PUBLIC "-//WC3//DTD XHTML 1.0 Transitional //EN"
"http://www.w3.org/TR/xhtml11/DTD/xhtml11-transitional.dtd">
<html xmlns = "http://www.w3.org/1999/xhtml">

<!-- Example of text layout using the paragraph, break and
horiz line -->
 <!--written by Keith Darlington Date June 2003 -->

<head>
 <title>Growing Vegetables at Home</title>
</head>
<body>
<h1 align = "center"><b>Growing Vegetables at Home</b></h1>
</head>
 <p>
  Fresh vegetables seem to cost much more and taste less well
  than they did many years ago. Hardly suprising then that
  more people are taking to growing their own.

 <hr align ="center" width ="50%"></hr>

  There are many benefits to growing vegetables at home.
```

```
    First, you can harvest at a stage of growth which suits you
    rather than the professional grower who is more pre-
    occupied with yield. Second, you can get a better choice of
    varieties of vegetable than you are likely to in the shops.
    You can experience the relaxation and closer affinity with
    nature and become physically fitter in the process.
</p>
<p>
    There is no special gift required for vegetable gardening,
    only a knowledge of what to do and when to do it. Enjoy
    this wonderful hobby.
</p>
<p>
    This website will look at general requirements for growing
    tasty vegetables as well as troubleshooting vegetable
    growing problems.

</p>
</body>
</html>
```

Using fonts with XHTML

The main categories of **fonts**, or typefaces, used on computers are as follows.

- **Serif typefaces** The serif characters include small strokes at the ends of the letters. An example of a serif font is Times (illustrations of this and other fonts are given later in this section). Research has shown that serif fonts are the easiest to read for long blocks of text. They are thus used a great deal in newspapers and magazines.

- **Sans serif typefaces** The sans serif typeface has traditionally been successful for use in newspaper headlines. An example is the Arial font. The sans serif font does not contain the small strokes used in serif fonts. Sans serif fonts are quite popular in Web page design.

- **Monospaced typeface** Monospace fonts allow equal spaces for all the characters, irrespective of the space that each character takes us. An example is the New Courier font. For example, the character 'M' is given the same space in a line of text as the character 'J', even though 'M' is wider than 'J'. Monospace fonts may or may not have serifs.

Web page designers are free to work with virtually any desired font. The problem is that not all fonts are installed on the computers that users are viewing the Web page on and, therefore, the browser may deliver unpredictable results. Different computers come with different preinstalled fonts.

As a general rule, it is probably safer to use common fonts that are likely to be found on all computer platforms. However, the same font on different platforms might be known by different names. For example, on modern computers, the main sans serif font is called Arial, but on the older computers it was called Geneva. Table 5.3 lists the names of the fonts associated with each of the standard font option groups.

Table 5.3 Main font groups

Font group	Modern computers	Older computers
Sans serif	Arial	Geneva
Serif	Times New Roman	Times
Monospaced	Courier New	Courier

Core Web fonts

In addition to the above font groups, another set of fonts has been designed specifically for use on the Web – core Web fonts. An illustration of what these fonts look like is given in Figure 5.4 later in the chapter. However, some Web viewers may not have access to them on their computers, so, if used, it is advisable to specify alternative safe fonts, as given in Table 5.3.

NOTE

Avoid the use of the font tag. The font tag – introduced in HTML 3.2 – is now a deprecated tag because of the difficulties associated with the separation of presentation and layout. As noted earlier in this chapter, tags that contain specific display information have been discarded in favour of style sheets. Unfortunately, you are still likely to encounter many pages that use the <font> tag and, for this reason, examples given below illustrate how this tag is used.

Using font properties in XHTML

The <font> tag, despite being deprecated, is still frequently visible when older authoring tools generate HTML. For this reason, we will briefly look at the <font> tag before going on to look at style sheet font properties.

The <font> tag can be used in association with the attribute face to specify a font associated with text to be displayed in a browser. For example, the line shown below will display 'This is the sans serif Arial font' in a Windows browser.

```
<font face = "Arial"> This is the sans serif Arial font
</font>

<font face = "Arial, Geneva, Helvetica"> This is an example
of a sans serif font Arial/Geneva/Helvetica </font>
```

Other font element attributes

You can also use the size and colour attributes with the font tag. For example, the following container:

```
<font size = "3", color = "blue", face = "Arial"> Blue
Text</font>
```

will assign an Arial font, with a size assigned to it of 3, making the colour of the font blue for the text 'Blue Text'.

Using font properties with the style element

CSS provide six font properties that modify the appearance of text. These are font-family, font-height, font-style, font-size, font-weight and font-variant.

Here we will look at how to use these properties to affect inline font properties. The paragraph tag below shows how to use an inline style attribute to render the sans serif Arial font. However, this sans serif font might display differently on non-Windows platforms, so it is better to amend the style properties so that the alternatives are given when using a Macintosh or other platform. The example given below includes the alternatives Arial, Geneva and Helvetica and, finally, the generic sans serif font. Notice that the style attribute can itself contain font properties and values. More on this in Chapter 8, when we look at CSS in detail.

```
<p style ="font-family: Arial, Geneva, Helvetica, sans
serif"> This is an example of a sans serif font.
</p>
```

The next example does the same for a serif font, Times, along with alternatives. Notice how the Times New Roman alternative is surrounded by the single quote marks. Then, the generic alternative serif would be used in the event that none of the alternatives are available.

```
<p style = "font-family: Times, 'Times New Roman',
Palatino, serif"> This is an example of a serif font.
</p>
```

Listing 5.4 and Figure 5.4 show examples of the font tags discussed so far and how the fonts are rendered on a Web page.

Listing 5.4 Example of the use of codes for font properties

```
<?xml version = "1.0"?>
<!DOCTYPE html PUBLIC "-//WC3//DTD XHTML 1.0 Transitional //EN"
"http://www.w3.org/TR/xhtml11/DTD/xhtml11-transitional.dtd">
<html xmlns = "http://www.w3.org/1999/xhtml">
```

```
<head>
<title>Core Web Fonts</title>
</head>
<body>
<h1 align = "center"> <u>Core Web Fonts </u></h1>
<font face="Times New Roman"><h4 align = "center"> This is
Times New Roman </h4></font>
<font face="Courier New"><h4 align = "center"> This is
Courier New </h4></font>
<font face="Arial"><h4 align = "center"> This is Arial
</h4></font>
<font face="Comic Sans MS"><h4 align = "center"> This is
Comic Sans MS </h4></font>
<font face="Georgia"><h4 align = "center"> This is Georgia
</h4></font>
<font face="Impact"><h4 align = "center"> This is Impact
</h4></font>
<font face="Verdana"><h4 align = "center"> This is Verdana
</h4></font>
<font face="Arial Black"><h4 align = "center"> This is Arial
Black </h4></font>
<font face="Trebuchet MS"><h4 align = "center"> This is
Trebuchet MS </h4></font>
<font face="Andale Mono"><h4 align = "center"> This is Andale
Mono </h4></font>
</body>

</html>
```

Logical format elements

One of the ideas behind HTML was that documents should provide structure so that they can be used over the Web. With this in mind, the designers of XHTML created a number of formatting elements that are labelled according to the purpose they serve rather than by their appearance. The advantage of this approach is that documents are not limited to a certain platform. Although they may look different on various platforms, the content and context will remain the same. If the proper font is not available, then the browser must render the text in the closest possible manner.

Some of the more commonly used logical format elements are shown and described briefly below.

∎ `<cite>` The citation element is used to indicate a quotation. It can also be used to indicate the title of a book or article. An italic font is normally used to display citations.

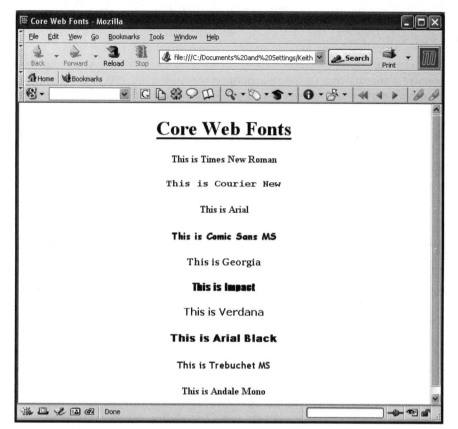

Figure 5.4
Font rendering
with IE 6

- `<code>` The code element is used to indicate a small amount of computer code. It is generally rendered in a monospace font, such as Courier.

- `<em>` The emphasis element is used to indicate a section of text that the author wants to identify as significant. Emphasis is generally shown in italic font.

- The `<div>` element divides a document into distinct divisions. Div tags allow you to demarcate a portion of your page so that you can do things to it. Anything enclosed within the `<div>` `</div>` container will begin on a new line and gives the developer scope to divide documents with specific formatting and so on. We will see much more of this element in Chapter 8.

- `<span>` The span element has a similar effect to `<div>`, except that it is an inline element and does not, like `<div>`, create a line break.

- `<strong>` The strong element normally renders text in bold.

Physical format elements

The problem with logical formatting tags is that you do not know how their use will be rendered in a browser. For this reason, a range of elements is provided in XHTML that give limited control over what the reader sees. These are known as **physical formatting elements** and they change the appearance of the text in the browser. Some physical elements provide specific display instructions, such as the 'underline' element. Other elements only affect the size of the text, such as the 'big' element. Others change the position of the text as well as the text size. An example of this is the 'subscript' element. Some of the most commonly used physical elements are shown below.

- ∎ **The bold element `<b></b>`** uses a bold font to display the text. For example, `<b> This is bold text </b>`.
- ∎ **The italic element `<i></i>`** renders text using an italic font. For example, `<i> This is italic text </i>`.

NOTE

`<b>` and `<strong>` are likely to produce the same effect, but, in the case of the logical formatting tag `<strong>`, it is the browser that makes the decision about how to render the tag.

Table 5.4 contains a list of the logical and physical formatting elements that have not been discussed in this section.

NOTE

The underline element is deprecated in XHTML. Style sheets are recommended for underlining text, but use the underline element with care, because it can sometimes result in ambiguity. For example, underlining is also used for hyperlinks.

Additional text elements

Some text symbols that you might want to use in your documents are reserved as special XHTML symbols. For example, if you wanted to display the angle bracket symbol '<' in the browser, there would be a problem as its use is reserved as a tag element! The solution is to use the symbol '&' with other combinations of characters. The following examples illustrate how this works.

In the case of the '<' symbol, we would use '&lt'. In the case of the '>' symbol, we would use '&gt'. Hence, if you wanted to display a sentence such as 'The number 7 is > than 4' in the browser, you would write in the body section 'The number 7 is '&gt' than 4'.

Listing 5.5 demonstrates the effect of some of the various text formatting tags. Study the XHTML code in the listing, then view the output in the IE browser (Figure 5.5). Notice that the `&lt` and `&gt` are special character sequences that produce the less than '<' and greater than '>' characters respectively. This means that you can use this format if you want these characters to appear on the browser screen without the browser interpreting them as tags.

Table 5.4 Logical and physical formatting tags

Tag	Description	Style	Purpose
`<abbr>`	Abbreviation	Logical	Enclosed text is an abbreviation
`<acronym>`	Acronym	Logical	Enclosed text is an acronym
`<b>`	Bold font tag	Physical	To display contained text in bold font
`<big>`	Big	Physical	To display contained text in larger size than surrounding text
`<blink>`	Blink tag	Physical	Causes the contained text to blink on and off the display
`<code>`	Program code tag	Logical	Often used to indicate program code segment in page. Usually rendered as monospace font
`<del>`	Deleted text	Logical	Usually rendered as strike through text
`<dfn>`	Defining instance	Logical	Body text (requires CSS for style information)
`<ins>`	Inserted text	Logical	Body text (requires CSS for style information)
`<i>`	Italic	Physical	Used to render enclosed text in italic
`<kbd>`	Keyboard text	Logical	Used to render enclosed text in keyboard-like input
`<q>`	Inline quotation	Logical	Inline quotation to specify URL of source of quoted material
`<samp>`	Sample text	Logical	The enclosed text is a sample
`<s>`	Strike through	Physical	The enclosed text is struck through with a horizontal line. *Note*: the `<s>` element replaces the now deprecated `<strike>` element
`<small>`	Smaller text	Physical	Formats the enclosed text as of a smaller typeface than the surrounding text
`<sub>`	Subscript text	Physical	Displays the text as subscript
`<sup>`	Superscript text	Physical	Displays the text as superscript
`<tt>`	Teletype	Physical	Displays the text in the user's default monospace font
`<u>`	Underline text	Physical	Underline the text enclosed within the `<u>` element
`<var>`	Variable text	Logical	The text enclosed within the `<var>` container is a variable's name

Listing 5.5 XHTML tags for text formatting fonts

```
<?xml version = "1.0"?>
<!DOCTYPE html PUBLIC "-//WC3//DTD XHTML 1.0 Transitional //EN"
"http://www.w3.org/TR/xhtml11/DTD/xhtml11-transitional.dtd">
<html xmlns = "http://www.w3.org/1999/xhtml">

<head>
<title>Text formatting tags</title>
</head>
<body>
<h1 align = "center"> <u>Some Text Formatting Tags </u></h1>
<h3>
<div align = "center">
&lt;B&gt; is <b> Boldface </b><br>
&lt;I&gt; is <i> Italic </i><br>
&lt;U&gt; is <u> Underline </u><br>
&lt;tt&gt; is <tt> Teletype</tt><br>
&lt;sub&gt; is <sub> Subscript </sub><br>
&lt;sup&gt; is <sup> Superscript </sup><br>
&lt;s&gt; is <s> strikethrough </s><br>
&lt;big&gt; is <big> big </big><br>
&lt;big&gt;&lt;big&gt; is <big><big> Bigger </big></big><br>
&lt;small&gt; is <small> Small </small><br>
&lt;small&gt; &lt;small&gt; is <small><small> Smaller
</small></small><br>
</div>
</h3>
</body>
</html>
```

The address element

The **address** element is used to let you identify yourself as the author of the document and possibly let people know how they can get in touch with you. Any copyright information for the material in the page can be placed here as well.

The address element is normally placed at either the top or bottom of a document and is used to identify the author or maintainer of the document.

Using preformatted text – the `<pre>` container

It is not always necessary to use paragraph and line break elements for formatting text, because XHTML provides a container tag that can hold preformatted text. This gives you more control over how the browser displays your text in a document.

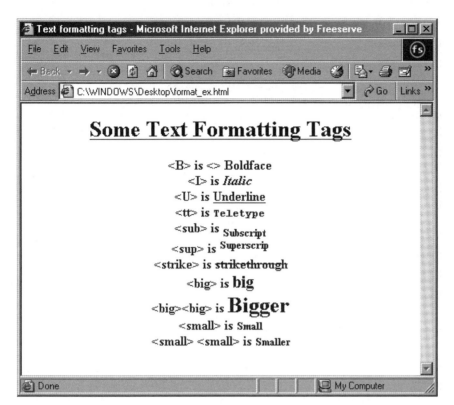

Figure 5.5
Output of the text
formatting tags

The most useful and commonest of the preformatting tags is the `<pre>` container. Text in a `<pre>` container is basically free form, with line feeds causing the line to break at the beginning of the next clear line – line breaks and paragraphs can be used within a `<pre>` container. This versatility enables you to create items such as tables (see Listing 5.6) and precise columns of text.

Another common use of the `<pre>` element is to hold large blocks of computer code that would otherwise be difficult to read.

As Listing 5.6 shows, text in a `<pre>` container can use any of the physical or logical text formatting elements. You can use this feature to create tables that have bold headings or italicized values.

The biggest drawback to the `<pre>` container is that any text within it is displayed in a monospaced font in the browser. This is because changing to a monospaced font, such as Courier New, can result in text alignment problems. Also, monospaced fonts do not look as aesthetically pleasing as proportionally spaced fonts. However, monospaced fonts are well suited to lists where exact text alignment is important. This is why the output from Listing 5.6, shown in Figure 5.6, is so well aligned.

NOTE

The use of paragraph formatting elements, such as `<Address>` or any of the heading elements, is not permitted with the `pre` element. However, anchor elements, which are described in Chapter 6, can be included within a `<pre>` container.

Listing 5.6 Illustration of the use of the `pre` container

```
<?xml version = "1.0"?>
<!DOCTYPE html PUBLIC "-//WC3//DTD XHTML 1.0 Transitional //EN"
"http://www.w3.org/TR/xhtml11/DTD/xhtml11-transitional.dtd">
<html xmlns = "http://www.w3.org/1999/xhtml">


<head>
<title>Text entry using the pre container element </title>
</head>
<body>


<pre>
<h1>        <u>Happy Grub Prices</u></h1>
      <p><b><u>Item</u><u>Description</u>         <u>Price</u>
</b>
      <p> Cheese Roll            Food                 1.50
      <p> Large Coke             Drink                 .90
      <p> Cornetto               Ice Cream            1.20


</pre>
</body>
</html>
```

Figure 5.6
Using the `pre` element for formatting a table-like structure

Text positioning

One of the biggest additions to the standard in the HTML 3.0 specification was the ability to control the positioning of text horizontally across the page. This will give you the option of placing your headings either against the left-hand margin, in the centre of the page, or against the right-hand margin. The flexibility to locate your headings where you want them will enable you to make your documents more appealing.

Alignment is specified for headings in the same way that it is for paragraphs, using the align attribute. The acceptable choices for heading alignment are left, right, centred and justified. Setting alignment to justify will start the heading at the left-hand margin and add spaces to fill the entire line length, if possible.

Creating lists in XHTML

Lists have long been used in traditional text documents for achieving layout in the form of contents pages and so on. The same effect is often desired in Web documents.

XHTML offers Web authors three types of lists:

- unordered list (ul)
- ordered list (ol)
- definition list (dl).

The three types of tag corresponding to these are <ul>, <ol> and <dl>. These lists can be nested to give greater flexibility to Web authors. Examples of XHTML code using lists follow in the next sections.

Creating an ordered list by using the <ol> tag

An **ordered list** – also called a numbered list – is used to create a sequential list of items or steps. When a Web browser sees the tag for an ordered list, it sequentially numbers each list item using standard numbers, such as 1, 2, 3, or i, ii and iii and so on. Figure 5.7 displays a screenshot of a Web page containing an ordered list using IE 6.

Ordered (or numbered) lists begin with the <ol> tag, and each item uses the standard list item <li> tag. Close the list with the </ol> tag to signal the end of the list to the browser. List containers provide both a beginning and ending line break to isolate the list from the surrounding text. It is not necessary (except for effect) to precede or follow the list with the paragraph <p> tag.

Attributes associated with the ordered list include type and start. The type attribute is used to define the numerical type of each item in the list – the default value is Arabic numerals. Other possible values of a label include upper- and lower-case alphabetic letters, and upper- and lower-case Roman numerals. In Figure 5.7 the type attribute has been set to Roman lower-case numerals. Listing 5.7 displays the XHTML code containing these attributes. The start attribute defines the starting value for the list to begin from – the default value is 1.

Figure 5.7
Example of
ordered list tags
at work

Listing 5.7 Example of ordered list tags

```
<!-- Example using ordered lists Date Feb 2003   -->
<!-- By Keith Darlington Date Feb 2003   -->

<html>
<head>
<title>A Simple Illustration of an ordered list in a Web
page</title>
</head>
<body>
<h1>My Favourite Growing Vegetables:</h1>
        <ol type = "i">
            <li>Carrots - the Early Nantes variety</li>
            <li>Marrows - the Green Bush variety</li>
            <li>Welsh Onions </li>
            <li>Broad Beans - the Dwarf Sutton Variety</li>
        </ol>
</body>
</html>
```

NOTE   The XHTML has been deliberately indented from the `<ol type = "i">` tag so that you can see how the list items are nested within the `<ol>` tags. You can use leading blanks and extra lines to make your list code easier to read, but Web browsers will, of course, ignore them.

Creating an unordered list by using the `<ul>` tag

An unordered list can be created if the `<ol>` tag is replaced by the `<ul>` tag. The `<li>` tag lists each item, as with the previous `<ol>` example.

Unlike an ordered list, items in an unordered list will not be preceded by numerical values, but by some other symbol assigned with the `type` attribute. The possible values of the type attribute can be `disc`, `square` or `circle`. The purpose of this attribute is to change the shape of the bullet for each item in the list. The default value is `disc`.

The following is an example of the use of an unordered list. The XHTML code is shown in Listing 5.8, followed by the output shown in Figure 5.8 using IE 6. Study the XHTML – make sure that you can understand the way it works before proceeding to the next section, which uses definition lists.

Listing 5.8 Example of the use of unordered list tags

```
<!-- Example using lists    written by Keith Darlington   Date
Feb 2003
-->

<?xml version = "1.0"?>
<!DOCTYPE html PUBLIC "-//WC3//DTD XHTML 1.0 Transitional //EN"
"http://www.w3.org/TR/xhtml11/DTD/xhtml11-transitional.dtd">
<html xmlns = "http://www.w3.org/1999/xhtml">

<head>
<title>List Processing Example using nested unordered
lists</title>
</head>
<body>
<h1>My favourite rock groups and tracks:</h1>
    <ul>
        <li>REM</li>
        <li>U2
          <ul>
              <li>It's a beautiful day</li>
              <li>One love</li>
              <li>The sweetest thing</li>
          </ul>
        </li>
        <li>Rush</li>
        <li>Phil Collins</li>
        <li>Manic Street Preachers</li>
    </ul>
</body>
</html>
```

Figure 5.8
Output of
Listing 5.8

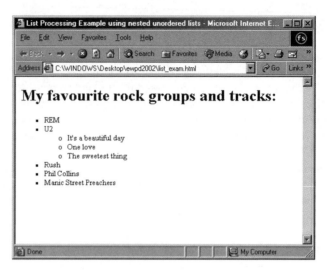

In the example below, we look at how to use a list to produce a contents page layout (see Listing 5.9 and Figure 5.9). Something like this could be used for, perhaps, preparing a Web-based tutorial.

Listing 5.9 Illustration of a contents page compiled using list tags

```
<html>
<head>
<title> A Document Contents Page </title>
</head>
<body>
<h1>Contents</h1>

<h2>Section 1</h2>
   <ul>
                  <li><b>Topic One</b></li>
                  <li><b>Topic Two</b></li>
                  <li><b>Topic Three</b></li>
   </ul><h2>Section 2</h2>
   <ul>
                  <li><b>Topic One</b></li>
                  <li><b>Topic Two</b></li>
                  <li><b>Topic Three</b></li>
   </ul><h2> Section 3</h2>
   <ul>
                  <li><b>Topic One</b></li>
                  <li><b>Topic Two</b></li>
                  <li><b>Topic Three</b></li>
   </ul>
</body>
</html>
```

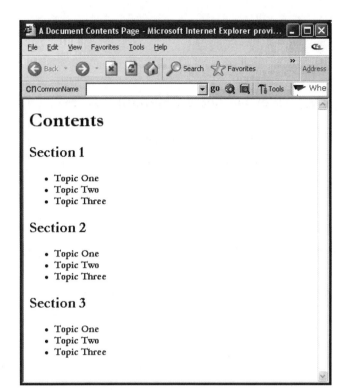

Figure 5.9
The output
resulting from
Listing 5.9

Definition lists

Definition lists are not as common as ordered or unordered lists, but they can sometimes be very useful. They consist of a pair of terms and definitions. They are particularly useful on scientific and academic websites, although they also turn out to be helpful in other circumstances – for example, when a retailer wishes to list products and descriptions. Moreover, they can be used for indenting, as definition lists do not insert bullets or numbers for each item. However, use definition lists with care here, because, as we have already seen, the effects can be unpredictable with different browsers.

Definition list tags

The basic definition list tag is <dl>, which is a container tag and needs to be closed with the </dl> tag. However, in place of the list item tag <li>, definition lists use the <dt> and <dd> tags. The <dt> tag means 'definition term', while the <dd> tag means 'definition description'. These are also container tags. Figure 5.10 is a screenshot showing how information created with definition lists would be displayed and Listing 5.10 should give you a clear understanding of how these tags work in relation to this example.

Figure 5.10
Output resulting
from the definition
list tags example

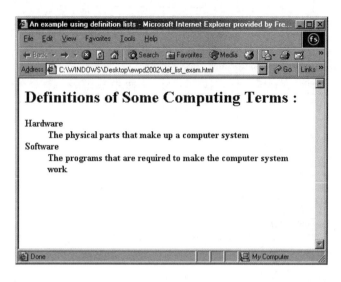

Listing 5.10 Use of definition list tags in an XHTML example

```
<?xml version = "1.0"?>
<!DOCTYPE html PUBLIC "-//WC3//DTD XHTML 1.0 Transitional //EN"
"http://www.w3.org/TR/xhtml11/DTD/xhtml11-transitional.dtd">
<html xmlns = "http://www.w3.org/1999/xhtml">

<!-- Example definition lists   written by Keith Darlington
Date Feb 2003   -->

<head>

<title>An example using definition lists</title>

</head>

<body>

<h1>Definitions of Some Computing Terms :</h1>

<dl>

<h3><dt>Hardware</dt>

<dd>The physical parts that make up a computer system</dd>

<dt>Software</dt>

<dd>The programs that are required to make the computer
system work</dd>

</h3>

</dl>

</body>

</html>
```

XHTML **graphic tags and attributes**

Adding images to a page can break up the monotony of text and add areas of interest to the page's viewer. In this section, we will look at elements that enable the positioning of an image on a Web page.

You can use transitional XHTML tags, although, like many other tags, they are moving out in favour of style sheets.

Images can be created in a number of ways – by using digital cameras, scanned images or by the Web author using appropriate software. We have already seen in Chapter 4 that software used for the latter could include Adobe Photoshop, Macromedia Fireworks and so on.

Adding a basic inline image to your XHTML document

Putting an image into an XHTML document is achieved by using the <img> tag. This is an empty tag and, therefore, in XHTML, would be written as <img/>. However, the img element must be accompanied by a src (source) attribute, which points to the URL of the graphic file to be displayed (see Listing 5.11). For example, the following tag, when added to your XHTML document where you want to display the image, will result in the file name 'beetroot.jpg' being displayed in the browser using the image's actual height and width.

```
<img src ="beetroot.jpg"/>
```

Note that this line will work correctly as long as the image is located in the same directory as the XHTML document containing this line. If your image file is located in another directory, perhaps as a subdirectory of the directory containing the index.html page, then you would need to include the directory reference in the src attribute reference, like so:

```
<img src = "images/beetroot.jpg"/>
```

Using height and width attributes with the image tag

If you wanted to scale the display of the image by using a height and/or width that were not the actual size of the image, then you could use the height and width attributes. These attributes are optional but desirable (see Notes, below). Here is an example:

```
<img src ="beetroot.jpg" height = "220" width = "150"/>
```

In the above example, the file name 'beetroot.jpg' will be displayed in the browser, but the maximum height and width will be assigned 220 and 150 pixels respectively. The image parameters are measured in pixels – taken from the words 'picture elements'. Any computer monitor resolution is measured in pixels, which represent the number of distinct coloured dots filling the two-dimensional screen. In the example shown, the height is 220 pixels and width 150 pixels.

Using an alternative text attribute

Even if you want to use graphics, your documents should be usable by readers who do not have access to Web graphics. Some viewers might be using text-based browsers or may have turned off the graphics in their browser to improve the page download speed. Whatever the case, you can provide a text alternative for such viewers by adding the `alt` attribute to an `<img>` tag, as illustrated by the following example:

```
<img  src = "beetroot.jpg" alt = "Beetroot Photograph"/>
```

The effect of the above tag is to display alternative text – 'Beetroot Photograph' – if the graphics have been turned off or the user has a text-only browser. Otherwise, the image called 'beetroot.jpg' is displayed.

NOTES

1 `<img/>` is one of the few tags that must have an attribute – namely the source `src` attribute. However, it is recommended that you also use height and width attributes with `img` tags. For the designer, control over the layout on the page will result in a faster download.
2 For strict conformance to XHTML, you must use the `alt` attribute with the image tag.

Image wraparound

By default, the browser displays the image inline. That is, the browser displays it immediately to the right of any text or any other object that immediately precedes the image. For example, take a look at Listing 5.11. It shows the same image three different times. Each time, the image is shown inline – that is, the browser displays the image immediately to the right of any text preceding it, as seen in Figure 5.11. The figure displays a screenshot using IE 6 and shows how images can be displayed using height and width attributes with the `img` element. Listing 5.11 shows how the `img` element would be used to create this result.

Listing 5.11 Use of XHTML image tags

```
<?xml version = "1.0"?>
<!DOCTYPE html PUBLIC "-//WC3//DTD XHTML 1.0 Transitional //EN"
"http://www.w3.org/TR/xhtml11/DTD/xhtml11-transitional.dtd">
<html xmlns = "http://www.w3.org/1999/xhtml">
```

```
<!-- Example using incorporation of graphical images into
XHTML written by Keith Darlington  Date Feb 2003  -->

<head>
  <title>Using the Image tag</title>
</head>
<body>
  <p>
    <img src="phone.gif" height="220" width = "150"/>
    This text immediately follows the image.
  </p>
  <p>
    This text is interrupted
    <img src="phone.gif" height="220" width = "150"/>
    by the image.
  </p>
  <p>
    In this case, the image appears inline after this text.
    <img src="phone.gif" height="220" width = "150"/>
  </p>
</body>
</html>
```

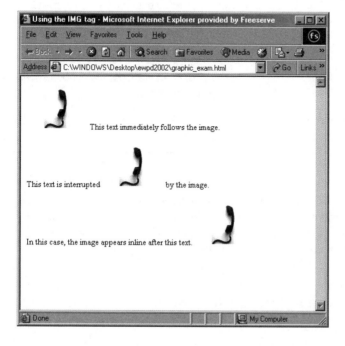

Figure 5.11
Output resulting
from Listing 5.11

NOTE	Although it is not essential to include the height and width attributes, it is always good programming practice to do so. One reason is that the image will be loaded and rendered faster in the browser because it will know immediately how much screen space to allocate to the image without having to do internal calculations itself.

Summary of other attributes used with the image tags

Table 5.5 More attributes of the `img` element

Name of attribute	Example use	Description of purpose
border	border = "3"	Used to add or remove a border around an image. This attribute takes a numerical value, which determines the thickness of the border
align	align = "top"	Used to align an image either horizontally or vertically. The values that can be used with this attribute include right, left, top, middle and bottom. See Figure 5.12
title	title = "My graphic Image"	Used to name a title for an image. The value assigned to this attribute will be displayed when the user skims over the image with a mouse
horizontal space	hspace = "5"	Used to add space around the horizontal axis of the image
vertical space	vspace = "2"	Used to add space around the vertical axis of the image

Listing 5.12 extends Listing 5.11 by including `alt`, `border`, `hspace`, `vspace` and `align` attributes. The output is shown in Figure 5.12 and should give you a better idea of how they work. Notice how the `align` attribute has been set to top, middle and bottom for each display of the phone image and the corresponding text is positioned accordingly.

Listing 5.12 img attributes

```
<?xml version = "1.0"?>
<!DOCTYPE html PUBLIC "-//WC3//DTD XHTML 1.0 Transitional //EN"
"http://www.w3.org/TR/xhtml11/DTD/xhtml11-transitional.dtd">
<html xmlns = "http://www.w3.org/1999/xhtml">

<!-- Example using incorporation of graphical images into
XHTML written by Keith Darlington  Date Feb 2003   -->

<head>
   <title>Using the Align attribute with the Image tag</title>
</head>
<body>
  <p>
     <img src="phone.gif" height="100" width = "70" alt =" My
phone" border ="2" vspace = "5" hspace ="5" align = "top"/>
     This text is displayed from the top of the image
     by setting the align attribute to the value "top"
  </p>
  <p>
     <img src = "phone.gif" height = "100" width = "70" alt ="
My phone" border ="2" vspace = "5" hspace ="5" align =
"middle"/>
     This text is displayed from the middle of the image
      by setting the align attribute to the value "middle"
  </p>
  <p>

     <img src="phone.gif" height="100" width = "70" alt =" My
phone" border ="2" vspace = "5" hspace ="5" align =
"bottom"/>
     This text is displayed from the bottom of the image
      by setting the align attribute to the value "bottom"
  </p>
</body>
</html>
```

NOTE

When you use the alt or title attributes, you will get the alternative text displayed when the user passes the mouse over the image. However, there is a subtle difference in the way that they work. The alt attribute will display the text value in the event that the image is not available to display, whereas the title attribute will not. The alt attribute will also display the text while the graphic itself is loading – this will often sustain the user's interest in what is coming.

Figure 5.12
Using other img
attributes

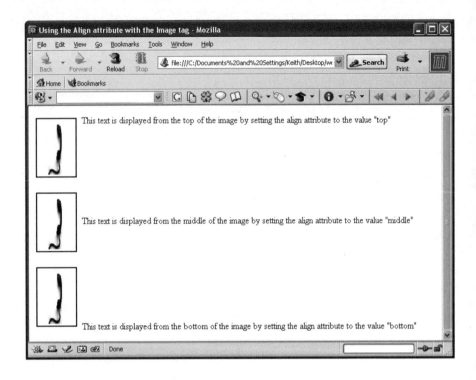

The ID attribute

In HTML, you can also use an attribute called name with the <img> tag.

The purpose of this attribute is to refer to the image in JavaScript (see Chapter 7) for doing things like image rollovers. This attribute has been changed to the id attribute when used in XHTML. So, for example, the HTML code:

```
<img src="carrots.jpg" name="my_carrots ">
```

would need to be written in XHTML as:

```
<img src="carrots.jpg" id="my_carrots "/>
```

Hyperlinks in XHTML

Introduction

The most important capability of XHTML is its ability to create hyperlinks to other Web documents. These may be elsewhere on the server or on different servers and make possible a worldwide network of linked information. When the user positions the cursor over an area that is defined as a hyperlink, the page, graphic or whatever it is linked to is displayed. A hyperlink can link to another website, another page on the current site or to another position in the current page or even to some given position in another page. The referencing system for linking to files on the WWW is as follows.

- To reference a domain name only, you would use a link of the form: www.somesite.com The default file on the server, such as index.html or home.html, would then be selected.

- To reference a specific file, such as somefile.html, you would link to something of the form www.somesite.com/somefile.html on the specific domain www.somesite.com

- To reference a specific file in the current directory called somefile.html, you would simply write the file name to link.

- To reference a specific file (somefile.html) in the specific subdirectory under the current server directory, you would write subdirectory/somefile.html – that is, if you wanted to reference a file called somefile.html on the server whose hard disk is C:, and which is in the subdirectory called images, then you would write c:\images\somefile.html.

- To reference a specific place in a specific file, called somefile.com, then you would write somefile.com# placeinpage, where placeinpage is the position on the page where the link would transfer to (note the use of the # symbol for achieving this).

NOTE

The links themselves may be text in the form of words or sentences or even graphic images. Figure 5.13 displays four hyperlinks, all of which are links to search engines. The reader will note that the bottom link to Webcrawler has already been visited – its colour has changed. The other three links have not been visited yet.

Figure 5.13
Example of some hyperlinks

Anatomy of a hyperlink

A hypertext link really has two different parts. First, there's the part you see on the Web page, called an **anchor**. There's also the part – the URL reference – that tells the browser where to go if you click that link. When you click a link's anchor, the browser loads the file or document given by the link's corresponding URL reference.

The following example shows the XHTML tag format for using a hyperlink.

```
<a href = "http://www.disney.com">The Disney Web Site</a>
```

Listing 5.13 displays the XHTML source document for the hyperlink document displayed in Figure 5.13. Notice how the <div> tag has been used to 'center' all the lines in the document. The first hyperlink tag to the search engine uses the tag:

```
<a href = "http://www.lycos.co.uk">
http://www.lycos.com</a>
```

Anchors

A link's anchor can be a word, group of words or a picture. Exactly how an anchor looks in the browser depends largely on what type of anchor it is, how the user has configured the browser to display links and how you created it. There are only two types of anchors:

∎ text

∎ graphical.

Listing 5.13 XHTML hyperlinks

```
<?xml version = "1.0"?>
<!DOCTYPE html PUBLIC "-//WC3//DTD XHTML 1.0 Transitional //EN"
"http://www.w3.org/TR/xhtml11/DTD/xhtml11-transitional.dtd">
<html xmlns = "http://www.w3.org/1999/xhtml">

<!-- Introduction to hyperlinks     -->
<!--Keith Darlington March 2003    -->

<head>
<title> Accessing Search Engines with Hyperlinks</title>
</head>

<body>
<div align ="center">
<h2>Here are my Favourite Search Engines</h2>
<p><strong>Click on the Search Engine link to go to that
site.</strong></p>
```

```
<p>Lycos: <a href = "http://www.lycos.co.uk">
http://www.lycos.com</a></p>

<p>AltaVista: <a href = "http://www.altavista.com">
http://www.altavista.com</a></p>

<p>Dogpile: <a href = "http://www.google.com">
http://www.dogpile.com</a></p>

<p>Webcrawler: <a href = "http://www.Webcrawler.com">
http://www.Webcrawler.com</a></p>
</div>
</body>
</html>
```

Text anchors

A **text anchor** is indicated by one or more words that the browser underlines to make clear the fact that it represents a link. The browser also displays a text anchor using a different colour to the rest of the surrounding text (the colour and appearance of links are under the author's and user's control).

The XHTML for a text link is given in the example shown below. The <a> tag is called the anchor tag.

```
<a href ="http://microsoft.com">The Microsoft Web Site</a>
```

Graphical anchors

A **graphical anchor** is similar to a text anchor. When you click a link's graphical anchor, the browser loads the Web page that the link references. However, graphical anchors are not underlined or displayed in a different colour, but they can be displayed with a border by setting a border attribute. No two graphical anchors need to look the same, either. It depends entirely on the picture that you choose to use.

To make a graphic linkable, all that is necessary is to place the image within the context of the anchor tag, such as:

```
< a href ="f514.html"><img src="carrots.jpg" alt="Carrots
picture"/></a>
```

We can see that the linked file here is 'f514.html' and an image file called 'carrots.jpg' is the item to be clicked. Figure 5.14a displays the carrots file and transfers to the html file called f514.html, as shown in Figure 5.14b.

Figure 5.14a
Using an image
as a hyperlink

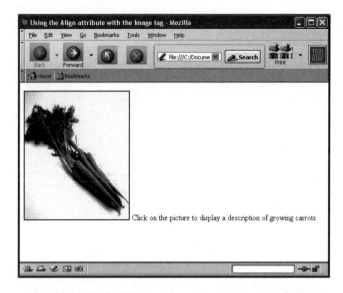

Figure 5.14b
File linked to the
carrots image in
Figure 5.14a

Hyperlink maintenance

All absolute links should be tested regularly to verify that they work correctly. Externally linked pages are sometimes removed, reorganized into different directory structures or experience a domain name change. Whatever the case, manual checking with a large site would be very time-consuming and tedious. Automated link checking programs are available for helping with this task. Many such checkers are available on the Web, and include www.seventwentyfour.com (see Figure 5.15) and http://home.snafu.de/tilman/xenulink.html.

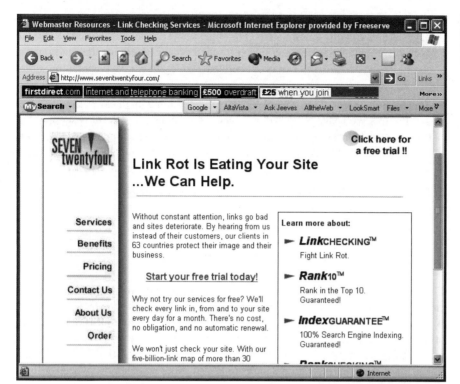

Figure 5.15
SeventyTwenty
Four.com – a link
checking service

Image maps

Any graphic can be broken down into areas that can be linked to different URLs. These areas are known as **image maps**. An image map is defined as the dissection of a graphic into a mutually exclusive set of regions, each of which is individually clickable and might link to a separate URL. Image maps are images on Web pages that include regions – known as **hotspots**.

An image map has three components:

- an image
- a set of map data
- an XHTML host entry.

The image is a normal Web image, typically stored in the GIF or JPG format. The map data set is a description of the mapped regions within the image and the XHTML host entry is code that positions the image within the page.

The regions in a map can include shape descriptors, such as a rectangle, circle, polygon or others, and their associated link URLs. Maps can also include a layer order, defining which regions take precedence when overlap occurs. In a client-side map, regions can be defined as nohref. When a nohref region overlaps other regions, the region is subtracted – or cut out – from the other regions. Image maps can be **client-side-based** or **server-side**. These are defined as follows:

- A **client-side image map** is one where the map data is embedded in the host page. When you click an image on the page, the processing is carried out by the Web browser without interaction with the server. The client-side map data is stored in XHTML files and can be embedded directly into a page containing other XHTML elements.

- **Server-side image maps** are processed by interaction with the Web server. When a visitor to a Web page clicks within a server-side image map, the browser program transfers the coordinates of the click to a program running on the Web server. This program then examines the map data and determines the link. The way in which server-side maps are stored depends on software installed on the Web server.

In this book, we will confine our attention to client-side image maps because these are the most commonly used in practice.

Creating client-side image maps

The client-side image map process is fairly straightforward. When the user clicks on an image, the browser compares the cursor's coordinates with the image map and, if it occurs within one of the defined shapes, the appropriate link is activated. In other words, it indicates an area where visitors can choose to link to another document. As an example, Figure 5.16 displays a map of Wales that includes some image maps representing national parks in Wales. Note that these have been defined as rectangles to be displayed and not regions bordering each other, although they could be if required.

Figure 5.16
Image maps of
some national
parks in Wales

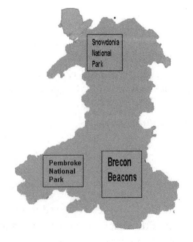

XHTML **image map tags**

To create and use image map regions in Web page design, you will need to become familiar with a number of image map tags and their attributes.

The <map> tag specifies a container for client-side image map data. Inside the <map> container, you place instances of the <area> tag. The <area> tag defines an area within a client-side image map. Each <area> tag defines one hotspot.

There are several attributes associated with the <area> tag. The shape attribute defines the shape of the hotspot area. The possible values that shape can take are 'circle', 'rect' and 'poly'. In the Wales map (Figure 5.16), there are three marked hotspots – all shown as rectangles – that are used to describe the approximate positions of the national parks at Pembroke, the Brecon Beacons and Snowdonia.

To define the position of a rectangular hotspot, you need to specify the start and end coordinates of the region. To define the position of a circular hotspot, you need to define the coordinates of the centre and the radius of the circle. To define the position of a polygon, you need to define the coordinates of each point along the path that surrounds the area. In the national parks of Wales example, we are using only rectangles.

Client-side image maps do not require the presence of a server-side script in order to interpret the coordinates of the 'hot' regions of your multi-clickable image. The client-side image map is much more efficient than the server-side image map and it allows the visitor to see the actual URL associated with the mapped regions in the hotspot.

In the case of server-side image maps, the list of shapes is held on the server so the browser has to send the coordinates to the server. The server then decides what page to show.

Here is the XHTML segment for describing the hotspots in the map of Wales example (the method for finding the rectangular coordinates of each of the hotspots is described later):

```
<map name="wales ">
<area shape="rect" coords="20,27,82,111"
href=" snowdon.html">
<area shape="rect " coords="129,285,207,346"
href="pembroke.html">
<area shape="rect"
coords="245,277,325,367"href="Brecon.html">
<area shape="default" nohref="nohref">
</map>

<img src = "wales.gif" usemap ="#wales">
```

Note the following points.

- The tag <map name="wales "> along with the name attribute is required because each map that is going to be used must be given a name.
- Each area tag contains the shape identifier – in this case they are all rectangles – along with the position description. Also, each area tag must contain the URL for the link. So, the first area tag defines the coordinates of the first rectangle – Snowdonia – as being 20,27,82,111 with (20, 27) representing the start coordinates and (82,111) representing the finish coordinates (see Figure 5.17).

Figure 5.17
Coordinates of
rectangle for area
tag

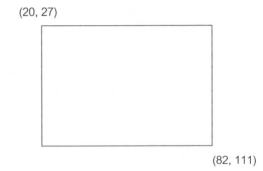

(20, 27)

(82, 111)

- Note how the attribute in the tag `usemap = "#wales"` is used. This attribute is required to show that the graphic is an image map that uses the `<map>` named 'wales'.

- The `nohref` attribute used with `<area shape = "default nohref">` indicates that no document is associated with this area: it is a non-clickable area.

Using the `ismap` attribute to find image map coordinates

You may be wondering how we found out what the coordinates for each of the rectangular hotspots on the Wales map were. One way to do this is to use the `ismap` attribute by following these steps.

1 Set up an `img` tag with an `ismap` attribute and make it a link label for an anchor tag. For the Wales map this could be:

```
<a href = "dummy.html"><img src="wales_parks.jpg" alt ="
Wales map" ismap = "ismap"/></a>
```

Note that the file `dummy.html` does not have to exist because the purpose of this task is to find the hotspot coordinates, not to visit links.

2 Display the html file that contains this link (see Figure 5.18).

3 Place the mouse cursor over each of the top left-hand and bottom right-hand corners of the park hotspot rectangles and record the x and y coordinates. The coordinates will be displayed in the bottom of the browser window to the right of the status message (again see Figure 5.18). Repeat the process for each of the required points on each of the hotspots to get all the required coordinates.

Alternatives to image maps

Image maps are quite difficult to use in practice and, for this reason, they are now often being replaced by tables (see next chapter). Tables enable an image to be broken up and sliced into segments, each of which can be referenced in an altogether easier way than by using image maps.

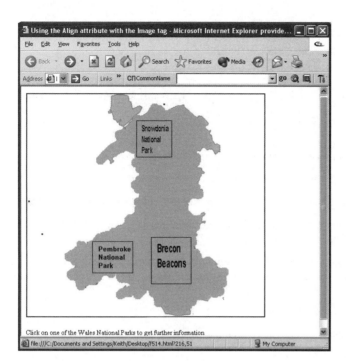

Figure 5.18
Using `ismap`
to find the
coordinates of a
hotspot

Summary

This chapter looked at some of the basics of XHTML. The main points to remember are the following.

- You only require a text editor (such as Windows' NotePad) and a brand new text file to create a Web page with XHTML.

- XHTML is nothing but a series of tags that take the form `<tag>text</tag>`.

- Stricter conformance to rules is necessary when writing XHTML as opposed to HTML. This means that:
  - all tag elements and attributes must contain lower-case characters only
  - all attribute values must be enclosed in single ' ' or double " " quote marks
  - no empty (non-closed) tags are permitted in XHTML.

- All XHTML pages begin with the document declaration tags and end with the `</html>` tag.

- There are two sections in an XHTML document. The first section is the head and you define it by the `<head>` and `</head>` tags. The second section is the body and you surround it with the `<body>` and `</body>` tags.

- The title of your Web page is inserted between the `<title>` and `</title>` tags and placed within the head section of an XHTML document. Indeed, this is the only part of a head section that is visible on the Web page.

- Attributes are often associated with tags. An attribute is a value that changes a default setting associated with a tag. For example, the background colour on the body of a page would normally be white.

To change this setting to yellow would mean setting the background attribute to yellow. Attribute values must be enclosed within quote marks. The tag syntax for this, then, would be:

```
<body bgcolor ="yellow">
```

■ Tag attributes are often optional – one exception is the source attribute associated with the image tag.

■ The <img> tag is used for displaying a graphic image on a Web page.

■ Graphics can enhance Web pages, but bear in mind that they consume substantially more memory than text and, therefore, the download time can be substantially longer.

■ Always use the alt attribute with the <img> tag.

■ The displayed sizes of images can be controlled by setting the width and height attributes.

■ A border can be set with the <img> tag. If the border attribute has the value 0, then the border is absent, otherwise a default border has a width of 2 pixels.

■ A hyperlink consists of a link label and a link destination and is created by using the anchor container tags <a> </a>. The link label is the clickable part of the link within the tags, while the destination is a value of the href attribute.

■ A hyperlink can be either text or via an image.

■ Links enable users to transfer to a bookmark on the same page, load a different page on the same site or load to an external site.

■ An image map is defined as the dissection of a graphic into a mutually exclusive set of regions, each of which is individually clickable and might link to a separate URL.

■ Image maps are images on Web pages that include regions – known as hotspots.

■ The regions on a map can include shape descriptors, such as rectangle, circle, polygon or others, and their associated link URLs.

■ Image maps can be client-side-based or server-side-based.

Quick summary of tags and attributes used in this chapter

Basic template tags

`<html></html>`	Creates an HTML/XHTML document
`<head></head>`	Displays the page title and processes other information that is not displayed on the Web page itself.
`<title></title>`	Puts the name of the document on the title bar.
`<body></body>`	Displays the visible portion of the document in the browser.

Body attributes

`<body bgcolor=?>`	Sets the background colour, using name or hex value.
`<body text=?>`	Sets the text colour, using name or hex value.
`<body link=?>`	Sets the colour of links, using name or hex value.
`<body vlink = ?>`	Sets the colour of followed links, using name or hex value.
`<body alink=?>`	Sets the colour of links on click.

Text tags

`<pre></pre>`	Creates preformatted text.
`<h1></h1>`	Creates the largest header font.
`<h6></h6>`	Creates the smallest header font.
`<b></b>`	Creates bold text.
`<i></i>`	Creates italic text.
`<tt></tt>`	Creates teletype or typewriter-style text.
`<cite></cite>`	Creates a citation, quote, usually in italic text.
`<em></em>`	Emphasizes the container text – usually in italic or bold.
`<strong></strong>`	Emphasizes the container text – in italic or bold.
`<font size=?></font>`	Sets size of font, varying from 1 to 7 (default size is 4).
`<font color=?></font>`	Sets font colour, using name or hex value.

Link tags and attributes

`<a href="URL"></a>`	Called the anchor tag and creates a hyperlink.
`<a href="mailto:EMAIL"></a>`	Creates an e-mail link.
`<a name="NAME"></a>`	Creates a target location within a document.
`<a href="#NAME"></a>`	Links a target location to some other position in the same document.

Formatting tags

`<p></p>`	A new paragraph container.
`<p align=?>`	Aligns a paragraph to the left, right or centre.
` `	Inserts a line break in the document.
`<hr/>`	Inserts a horizontal rule.
`<hr size=?/>`	Sets size (height) of rule.
`<hr width =?/>`	Sets width of rule, in percentage or absolute value.

`<hr noshade = "noshade"/>`	Creates a rule without a shadow.
`<blockquote></blockquote>`	Indents text from both sides, producing document quotation structure.

List processing tags

`<ul></ul>`	Creates a bulleted list.
`<ol></ol>`	Creates a numbered list.
`<dl></dl>`	Creates a definition list.
`<li></li>`	Precedes each list item, and adds a number.
`<dt>`	Precedes each definition term.
`<dd>`	Precedes each definition.

Graphical elements

`<img src="name">`	Adds an image with attribute.
`<img src="name" align=?>`	Aligns an image – left, right, centre; bottom, top, middle.
`<img src="name" border=?>`	Sets size of border around an image.
`<img src="name" alt =?>`	Sets alternative text for browsers that cannot display graphic.

Exercises

1 Why had the W3C developed the XHTML 1.0 specification?

2 Use the `<p>` and `<hr />` tags to write XHTML code to render the text shown in Figure 5.19.

3 Look at the following XHTML file. Predict the output using the IE 6 browser.

```
<html>
<body bgcolor="yellow">
<h2>Look: Colored Background!</h2>
</body>
</html>
```

4 Look at the following XHTML file. First, predict the output using the Netscape browser. Would you expect the same with IE 6? Now run the file using the IE 6 browser. Was the output as predicted? If not, try to explain.

```
<html>
<body>

<p>
 Humpty Dumpty
    Sat on the wall.
  Humpty Dumpty
```

Figure 5.19

```
        Had a great fall.
      </p>

    </body>
  </xhtml>
```

5   Write an XHTML document that, under a suitable heading, produces an ordered list of your three favourite books. Save the file and include a screen dump of the output in your work book.

6   Go to the www.w3.org website. Try to find out about the differences between the HTML 3.2 and HTML 4.0 specifications.

7   Give three examples of deprecated tags and attributes from the XHTML 1.0 spec, and give an example of one in the HTML 4.0 spec.

8   What creates spaces in your browser? Create a document that uses multiple <br> and <p> tags, plus returns between <pre> tags to add blank lines to your document. Then, test the page in your browser to see which are the most reliable. (In most cases, it should be <pre>, but it's interesting to note the differences from browser to browser.)

9   When would you use a definition list instead of an ordered or unordered list? What XHTML elements are required for creating an XHTML definition list?

10   Why is it important to include an alt attribute with the img tag?

11   Explain the difference between an absolute URL and a relative URL.

12   Explain why regular link maintenance is necessary.

13   Write the XHTML code for the following page. The page should have a background colour of yellow (code #FFFF00). The main page title should be 'Happiness is Effective Web Design'. The main heading should be header level 4, centred. Below this heading, a horizontal line should be inserted followed by the next lower-level heading, which should read 'Welcome to the study of Web page design'. This should be followed by this text:

This unit has now enrolled more than 30 students.
It is a coursework-based unit.
The coursework specification is based on a Web tutorial.

Test the page in both Netscape and IE browsers. Include comments if there are any differences. Include a screen dump of the output in either browser (but not both).

6

More XHTML techniques

In this chapter you will learn how to:

■ use tables with XHTML

■ create frames with XHTML

■ create forms with XHTML.

Introduction

The last chapter looked at the basics of XHTML. In this chapter, you will gain some familiarity with three XHTML techniques that can improve the appearance of Web pages as well as expand the Web experience for many users. Tables help to control the layout of Web pages, frames divide the available browser space so that the user can view more than one page on the screen at any time and forms provide visitors with a means of interacting with your website. These three techniques are discussed in detail in this chapter.

Tables with XHTML

Introduction

Tables have played a very significant role in creating Web documents, for they have until recently been used as a basic design element. This is because the grid system in tables can be used to control the layout of a Web document. The traditional role for tables has been to present data in rows and columns because they make comparative analysis more understandable. They can also be used – albeit invisibly – to divide the printed page into sections for layout purposes. Tables can be used to:

■ display data – as was originally intended – in rows and columns

■ improve text alignment by putting text into tables (with borders turned off) – it is possible to format indents and add white space to a page

- achieve a consistent page layout structure – for a page can be divided up into different sections using tables, so, for example, you can have a contents section on the left-hand side for navigation and information on the right-hand side and so on.

- hold together a multipart image – an image to enable animations, rollovers and so on (more on this in Chapters 11, 12 and 13).

Using tables

Figure 6.1 describes the general architecture of a table structure. In this example, there are three rows and three columns. The top row contains headings – these are optional in XHTML tables. Each of the rows below the top row will contain some kind of data – text, numbers or even images. Each box in the table item is referred to as a **cell**.

Figure 6.1
The structure of a table

Heading A	Heading B	Heading 3
Cell content for row 1, column 1	Cell content for row 1, column 2	Cell content for row 1, column 3
Cell content for row 2, column 1	Cell content for row 2, column 2	Etc...

Table tags and attributes

XHTML defines tables in much the same way that it defines list containers. The <table> element is the container tag for the table's data and layout.

XHTML tables are composed row by row and you indicate a new row with the <tr> (table row) tag, and separate the data with either the <th> (table header) or <td> (table data) tags. Think of the <tr> tag as a line break, indicating that the following data starts a new table row.

Table headings are generally shown in bold and centred by WWW browsers. Table data is shown in the standard body text format. Whereas you can think of a row as a line in a table, a cell is a box within the table.

The following points summarize the basic XHTML table tags and attributes that you are likely to use with tables.

- To create a table structure, use the <table> </table> tags, which serve as a container for the rest of the table data. The table tag <table> marks the start and end of the table.

- You can specify how many rows and columns to display by using the cols and rows attributes of the <table> tag. For example, <table cols="3" rows="7"> will create a table containing three columns and seven rows.

- You can use the tags `<th></th>` to create table headings. These are usually inserted in the first row or column of the table.
- Each row in the table is contained by the tags `<tr></tr>`.
- Use the tags `<td></td>` to define a cell. Table data is contained within these tags. You can also nest additional tables within a single cell if required.

To see how these tags work in browser display, study the layout below:

```
<table>
    <tr><th> Header 1</th> <th> Header 2 </th>    <th>
    Header 3 </th></tr>

    <tr><td> Cell content </td> <td> Cell content </td> <td>
    Cell content </td></tr>

    <tr><td> Cell content </td> <td> Cell content </td> <td>
    Cell content </td></tr>
</table>
```

If you don't tell the browser how many columns to display, it works out the number itself by finding the maximum number of `<th>` tags or `<td>` tags on any one row in the table. If any row contains fewer cells than the row with the maximum, then it fills it up with blank cells to the right.	**NOTE**

Here are some useful table attributes.

- *Border* = *n* (an integer)   Sets the width of the border drawn around the table (default = 0).
- *CellPadding* = *n* (an integer)   Sets the width for the margin inside the boundaries for each cell (default 2).
- *CellSpacing* = *n* (an integer)   Sets the width of the boundary separating adjacent cells (default 2).
- *Colspan* = *n* (an integer)   Allows the cell to span *n* table columns.
- *Rowspan* = *n* (an integer)   Allows the cell to span *n* table rows.

Illustration of the basic table tags

An XHTML example of the use of tables is given in Listing 6.1 and the output shown in Figure 6.2.

Listing 6.1 Example of simple table elements in use

```
<?xml version = "1.0"?>
<!DOCTYPE html PUBLIC "-//WC3//DTD XHTML 1.0 Transitional //EN"
"http://www.w3.org/TR/xhtml11/DTD/xhtml11-transitional.dtd">
<html xmlns = "http://www.w3.org/1999/xhtml">
```

```
<head>
<title> Table Example Using Birds of Prey in Wales</title>
</head>
<body>
<h1> Birds of Prey in Wales </h1>
<table border width="358">
  <tr>
    <th width="754">Birds of Prey</th>
    <th width="447">Population</th>
    <th width="656">Region of Wales</th>
    <td width=""></td>
  <tr>
    <td>Red Kite</td>
    <td>Very low </td>
    <td>Mid Wales</td>

  </tr>
  <tr>
    <td>Peregrine Falcon</td>
    <td>High </td>
    <td>All Wales</td>
  </tr>
 <tr>
    <td>Buzzard</td>
    <td>Moderate</td>
    <td>West Wales</td>
  </tr>
</table>
</body>
</html>
```

Figure 6.2
Output of listing
6.1 in IE 6

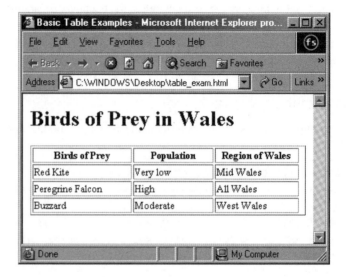

Using `rowspan` and `colspan` attributes

Sometimes, you may want a particular row or column to span multiple rows or columns. You can use the `rowspan` and `colspan` attributes of the `<th>` and `<td>` tags to accomplish this. For example, suppose we wanted to obtain the tabular output shown in Figure 6.3. You will notice that the table is used to describe two main heading data items called 'Symptom' and 'Likely Causes'. The first describes the symptoms affecting each part of the spinach and the second column is the likely causes of the problem.

However, if you look at the first column – Symptom – you will see that it spans the two columns beneath it. Similarly, the row containing the seedlings data item spans the two rows to its right, in order to describe the two possible symptoms and causes, and the row containing leaves spans four rows and so on. Listing 6.2 shows how the `rowspan` and `colspan` attributes can be used to achieve this effect in XHTML.

The column span can be implemented in the table by using the line `<th colspan="2" width="354">Symptom</th>`. The effect of this line is to create a table heading containing 'Symptom' and then a two-column span for this heading using the attribute `colspan="2"`. Note that a width attribute – `width = "354"` – has also been assigned to this heading tag.

Similarly, spanning the 'Seedlings' data tag can be implemented by using the line `<td rowspan="2">Seedlings</td>`, and the 'Leaves' data tag can be spanned over four rows by using the line `<td rowspan="4"> Leaves </td>`.

To summarize, the `rowspan` and `colspan` attributes can be used to span rows and columns associated with table data items.

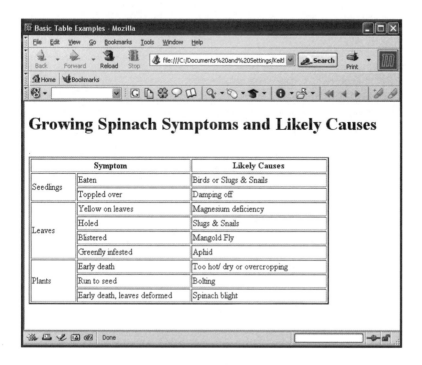

Figure 6.3
Screenshot
illustrating some
advanced
features of tables

Listing 6.2 A more advanced example of using table tags

```
<?xml version = "1.0"?>
<!DOCTYPE html PUBLIC "-//W3C//DTD XHTML 1.0
Transitional//EN"
"http://www.w3.org/TR/xhtml1/DTD/xhtml1-transitional.dtd">
<html xmlns = "http://www.w3.org/1999/xhtml">
<head>
<title>Basic Table Examples</title>
</head>
<body>
<h1> Growing Spinach Symptoms and Likely Causes </h1>
<table border"border" width="558">
 <tr>
  <th colspan="2" width="354">Symptom</th>
  <th width="247">Likely Causes</th>

 </tr>
 <tr>
  <td rowspan="2">Seedlings</td>
  <td>Eaten </td>
  <td>Birds or Slugs & Snails</td>

 </tr>
 <tr>

  <td>Toppled over</td>
  <td>Damping off</td>
 </tr>
<tr>
  <td rowspan="4">Leaves</td>
  <td>Yellow on leaves</td>
  <td>Magnesium deficiency</td>
 </tr>
  <tr>
  <td>Holed</td>
  <td>Slugs & Snails</td>
 </tr>

  <tr>
  <td>Blistered</td>
  <td>Mangold Fly</td>
 </tr>
```

```
  <tr>
  <td>Greenfly infested</td>
  <td>Aphid</td>
  </tr>


  <tr>
<td rowspan="3">Plants</td>
  <td>Early death</td>
  <td>Too hot/dry or overcropping</td>
  </tr>


  <tr>
<td>Run to seed</td>
  <td>Bolting</td>
  </tr>
  <tr>
  <td>Early death, leaves deformed </td>
  <td>Spinach blight</td>
  </tr>
</table>
</body>
</html>
```

The `border` table attribute

Earlier in this chapter, the `border` attribute was introduced. This sets the thickness of the border around a table. The assumed default for the border thickness is 1. In the event that no border is used, the corresponding border thickness is 0, and values above 1 increase the thickness of the border, with values between 0 and 1 giving a border thickness that is less than the default value.

Another attribute that can be used with `<table>` is the `bordercolor` attribute. This attribute, as you would expect, allows you to change the colour of the border. It can also be used with row and cell tags.

In the event that you don't want all four sides of a table's border to be displayed, it is possible to specify which ones to display. This can be done using the `frame` attribute of the `<table>` tag. For example, if we modify the `table` element in Listing 6.2 to read `<table border="2" frame="above" width="558">`, this will have the effect shown in Figure 6.4, displaying only a border across the top. A complete list of the values that the `frame` attribute can take is shown in Table 6.1.

Figure 6.4
Illustration of the
`frame` attribute
used with the
`table` tag

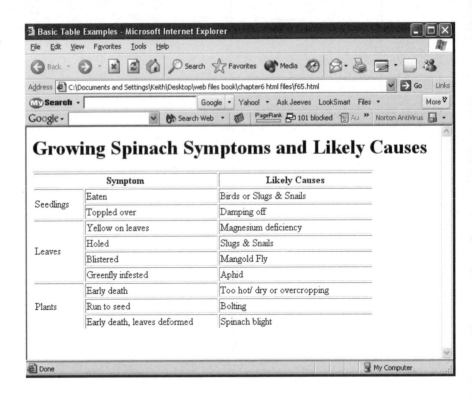

Table 6.1 The possible values the `frame` attribute can take

Name of attribute	Applies to
above	Top border only
below	Bottom border only
hsides	Top and bottom only
lhs	Left-hand side only
rhs	Right-hand side only
vsides	Left-hand and right-hand sides
box	Full border all sides (default)
void	No border
border	Full border all sides

The `rules` attribute

You can also control the thickness of the internal lines between cells by using the `rules` attribute of the `<table>` tag. For example, if we modify the `table` element in Listing 6.2 once again to read `<table border="2" frame="above" width="558" rules="rows">`, the effect will be as shown in Figure 6.5 (i.e., no vertical or column lines will be included only rows. Note that the default value is `all` – that is, to draw borders around all cells. The possible values of the `rules` attribute are given in Table 6.2.

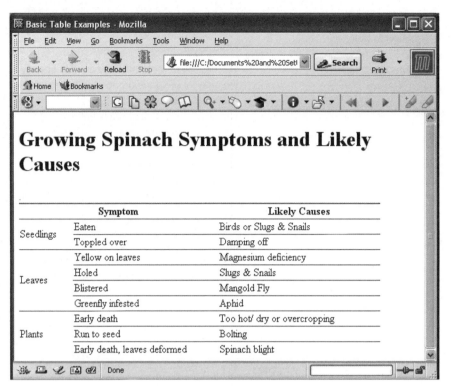

Figure 6.5
Illustration of the
rules attribute
used with the
table tag

Table 6.2 The possible values of the rules attribute

Value	Effect
none	No internal lines
rows	Horizontal lines only
cols	Vertical lines only
all lines	Horizontal and vertical
groups	All

Other table attributes

There are many other attributes that can be used with the <table> tag, including cellpadding, cellspacing, width align and bgcolor. These are among the most well-known attributes and are described in Table 6.3. Some of these are examined in more detail when we look at tables in Chapters 11, 12 and 13. For the complete list of table tags, see Appendix 2.

Table 6.3 Other useful table attributes

Attribute and value	Effect on Web page
cellpadding="option value"	The cellpadding attribute is used to specify the amount of space around the edges of each cell within the table
cellspacing="numeric value"	The cellspacing attribute is used to specify the amount of space between each individual table cell
align="numeric value"	The align attribute is used to align tables on a Web page. The possible option values are left, right and center, with the default value being left
bgcolor="hex value or name"	The bgcolor attribute is used to specify the background colour used in a table. The attribute could be in hexadecimal format – #FFCC00 – or a named colour value, such as 'red'
width="pixel value or %"	Sets the width of the table

Frames with XHTML

Introduction

Frames provide a means of dividing the available browser space into independent, separate windows.

Frames were first introduced with Netscape Version 2.0. Since their introduction, frames have often been subjected to a great deal of controversy in the Web development community. Some designers believe them to be confusing and that they take the focus away from the content. On the other hand, there are others who believe that they can be a useful tool for improving navigation on the World Wide Web.

We will look at the merits and problems of frames later in this chapter, but first let us try to gain an understanding of the frame concept and the way in which frames are implemented in website design.

The frame concept

Frames enable the Web designer to create independently changeable and (sometimes) scrollable windows that tile together to break up and organize a display. The idea is similar to that of a picture frame, rendered by constructing the image from a number of windows.

An example of a Web page using frames is shown in Figure 6.6. You can see that the document window is divided into different 'windowpanes', separated by rules

Figure 6.6
An example of
frames in use, with
three scrollable
and one static
frame

and scroll bars. These 'windowpanes' are called **frames**. In this particular example, the main window is divided into four frames. The Web designer is free to decide both the number and size of each frame. Notice that, in this particular example, the screen has been divided into three horizontal frames (rather like rows in a table), with the middle horizontal frame split into two vertical frames (columns), giving a total of four frames. The top frame, encompassing the 'Garden magic' logo, is a fixed, non-scrollable frame; the two middle frames, containing the headings 'Essential Jobs' and 'Fruit Garden', both have vertical scroll bars so that the user can scroll through the content of each, if required. Finally, the bottom row frame is, again, a vertically scrollable frame, containing four graphic hyperlink images.

NOTE

When working with frames, Netscape sometimes behaves unexpectedly after loading changes. Often, the **Reload** button alone does not work, but closing the browser window and opening a new window works most of the time. Clearing the cache is another possible solution to this problem.

Although it is not immediately apparent in the example shown in Figure 6.6, each frame in the window is displaying an independent XHTML document. If the user selects a hypertext link in any of the frame windows, then it is possible to reference and replace content in that same frame window or replace content in another frame or affect more than one frame's content, or even replace the entire browser window with a single XHTML document. For example, the website shown in Figure 6.6 has been constructed in such a way that, if the user clicks the 'Winter' hyperlink image in the fourth frame, then the content is altered in all three non-fixed frames to reflect the seasonal changes in each of the aspects of 'Essential Jobs', 'Fruit Garden' and 'General Advice' for the winter season. Figure 6.7 displays these results.

Figure 6.7
The changed frames that result from Clicking the 'Winter' graphic hyperlink

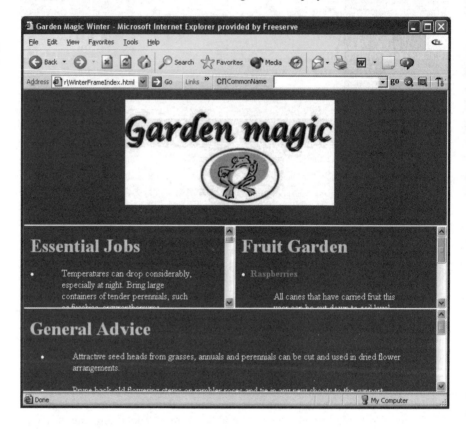

XHTML **for frames**

The first important point to make about using frames with XHTML is that you must use the `frameset` declaration in the prologue, as described in the earlier part of this chapter. The document declaration tags required for frames are:

```
<?XML version = "1.0"?>
<!DOCTYPE html PUBLIC ".//W3C//DTD XHTML 1.0 Frameset//EN"
http://www.w3.org/TR/xhtml1/DTD/xhtml1-frameset.dtd>
<html xmlns = http://www.w3.org/1999/xhtml>
```

Constructing XHTML for frames requires two components:

- a `frameset`
- individual `frames`.

A **frameset** is an XHTML page that defines the structure of a set of frames within a document. This frameset definition includes information about the number of frames displayed on a page, the size of the frames, the source of the page loaded into a frame, and other definable properties.

A **frameset** XHTML page isn't displayed in a browser – it merely stores information about how the frames on a page will display. The frameset XHTML page, therefore, does not contain the <body> </body> container, but is replaced by the <frameset> container. The individual frame pages are just XHTML pages that occupy frame space.

The frameset container

If you wish to develop XHTML for a frame-based website, then you need to create a frameset XHTML document. This replaces the <body> container on a frames-formatted page. The purpose of the frameset page is to define the layout information, as well as the names of the pages that will occupy the frame.

The <frameset></frameset> container surrounds each block of frame definitions. Within the <frameset> container, the only tags that can be used are frame (see the next section) tags or nested <frameset> containers.

Defining frames layout by using rows and cols attributes

The <frameset> tag uses two major attributes:

- rows – rows
- cols – columns.

These attributes are used to describe how the frames will be formatted on the page. You can use either the rows attribute or the cols attribute or a combination of both. The frame page will then be divided according to the values entered into the rows or cols attributes, which can then be either an **absolute value** – meaning a set size in pixels – a **relative value** – where size is determined by percentages – or a **proportional value** – where elements are relative in size to each other.

The generic syntax for a <frameset> container is:

```
<frameset rows ="value_list"  cols ="value_list">
```

Where value_list can be a numerical pixel value, a percentage value or a size value.

The following examples illustrate how these frameset attributes work.

Example 6.1

Suppose you wanted to design a frame Web page system consisting of rows in the proportions 25, 50 and 25 per cent. In other words, the top row contains 25 per cent of the total length, the middle 50 per cent and the bottom row 25 per cent, as shown in Figure 6.8.

In this example, three horizontal rows are to be created in the proportions 25, 50 and 25 per cent of the available screen length respectively. There are no columns in

Figure 6.8

Frameset divided
into three rows in
the ratio 1 : 2 : 1

the example and, therefore, the frameset tag and attributes producing the required effect in Figure 6.8 would be:

```
<frameset rows = "25%,50%,25%">
```

Absolute and relative values

The rows attribute given in Example 6.1 specifies relative values for the row proportions consumed by each frame, because the attribute values make no reference to a figure for the actual width of any display. It is possible to specify absolute values that specify the number of pixels used instead. For example, the tag: <frameset rows ="125,250,125"> specifies that the rows would be divided into 125 pixels, 250 pixels and 125 pixels respectively. These are called **absolute values**.

The problem with absolute values is that the Web designer would need knowledge about the monitors used because, if the screen size changed, the positions of the frames would remain the same with the possibility of producing peculiar results. You could overcome this problem by specifying **relative values** for the frame layout. This means that when the screen size is changed, the rows will stay the same relative size to one another. One way to do this would be to use proportional values.

Proportional values

You can also specify frame layout values proportionally. **Proportional values** are also relative. Using an asterisk (*) to indicate each part of the screen, separated by commas, a value indicating three equal rows would be as shown is the following XHTML syntax (see Figure 6.9).

```
<frameset rows ="*,*,*">
```

Figure 6.9

Frameset divided
into three equal
rows

As another example, if we want three rows, with the middle row twice the height of the top and bottom rows (see Figure 6.10), the values could be written like this:

```
<frameset rows ="*,2*,*">
```

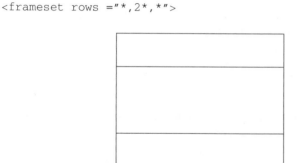

Figure 6.10
A frameset divided into three rows, using equal absolute values, relative values, and proportional values with the centre row twice the height of the top and bottom rows

The frame tag

In the previous section, we learned how to define the layout for the insertion of frames in a Web page. However, we now need a way to get the required content inserted into each frame. To do this we use the frame container. The <frame></frame> tags are enclosed by the <frameset></frameset> tags and are used to define each individual frame. There must be one set of <frame></frame> tags for each frame defined in the cols and rows attribute in the <frameset> tag.

Each of the frame tags gives a separate browser window within a large browser window. Each frame has own content and its own set of scroll bars that can be resized by the user. Both the scroll bars and the resizing can be turned off by setting their attributes, as we shall see when we look at the range of attributes that can be used with the frame tag.

The source – src – attribute

In order to have a page appear in each of the individual frames, we have to tell each <frame> tag which page to load into each frame. This is done by entering the src attribute followed by the URL of the XHTML document to be included. For example, if we wanted to insert the XHTML document called "header.htm" into the top frame, then we would use the tag:

```
<frame src = "header.html">
```

The scrolling attribute

Scroll bars will automatically be created for a frame if the content that has been specified is too large to fit within the frame. Scroll bars can be controlled by including the scrolling attribute within the <frame> tag.

The possible values for this attribute are 'yes', 'no' or 'auto'. These attribute value choices are self-explanatory in the sense that selecting 'yes' will force the scroll bar to be inserted (whether necessary or not), the 'no' choice will result in no scroll bars (again whether necessary or not) and, finally, the 'auto' choice is the default choice – namely, insert the scroll bars if the amount of content to be viewed exceeds the size of the display window. As an example of how this works, if you wanted to turn the scrolling off for the frame named `header.html`, then the required tag format would be written as:

```
<frame src = "header.html" scrolling = "no">
```

The `noresize` attribute

Frames can be resized – that is, you can use the mouse to move the borders of the frame, resizing it when viewing a Web page.

There is a good reason for allowing the resizing of frames and it is that frames will appear different when seen in different browsers. Therefore, resizing allows the viewer to expand the frame if it is blocking part of the content. If you want to turn off this capability for the viewer, the `noresize` attribute should be included in the `<frame>` tag, in the form:

```
<frame noresize ="noresize">
```

However, you should be careful about turning off resizing – don't, unless you can be sure that your frame pages work well on a wide range of browsers and monitors.

Other `frameset` and `frame` attributes

There are many other attributes that can be used with the `frameset` and `frame` tags. It is beyond the scope of this book to look at each of these in detail, but, in Table 6.4, some of the more useful attributes are briefly described.

Example 6.2

Suppose we wanted to create a `frame` definition document that contains the layout information depicted in Figure 6.11. Suppose, too, that the names of the XHTML documents that would occupy each frame are `header.htm`, `label.htm`, `info.htm` and `footer.htm`, respectively.

The XHTML `frameset` that will accomplish this layout is shown in Listing 6.3 and includes four frames. The top frame spans the width of the page window and 25 per cent of the length of the window and will contain the XHTML content from the file called `"header.html"`. There are two central frames – one that will contain the content for the `"label.html"` file, which takes up 25 per cent of the screen width, and the side frame that will contain the content from the `"info.html"` file, which takes up the remaining 75 per cent column space. Another frame containing the content from `"footer.html"` fills the entire width of the bottom 25 per cent of the screen.

It's important to note that this document calls four other XHTML documents – `header.html`, `label.html`, `info.html`, and `footer.html` – containing the actual information displayed in each of the individual frames. Figure 6.12 shows the output in IE 6 from this listing. Note that all the frames are blank because the calling frames have not yet been created.

Table 6.4 Some `frameset` and `frame` attributes

Other `frameset` tag attributes	Format for use	Notes
`border`	`border="x"` Where x is a number representing the number of pixels	Originally a Netscape attribute used to control border width around frames. Use with care – effect unpredictable with different browsers
`frameborder`	`frameborder="x"` Where x can take the values 'yes' or '1', which enable the `frameborder`, or 'no' or '0', which disable the `frameborder`	Used to define the presence or absence of a border. Use with care – effect unpredictable with different browsers
`framespacing`	`framespacing="x"` Where x takes a numerical value representing the number of pixels	Works with Netscape only. Use with care – effect unpredictable with different browsers
`bordercolor`	`bordercolor="x"` Where x takes a colour value either in text form or as a string	Works with Netscape only. Use with care – effect unpredictable with different browsers
`frameborder`	`frameborder="x"` Where x can take the values 'yes' or '1', which enable the `frameborder`, or 'no' or '0', which disable the `frameborder`	Use this attribute to control borders around individual frames (contrast with that for the `frameset` use for this tag)
`title`	`title="x"`	Provides a readable description of the frame's function. Use the `title` attribute with a descriptive value, such as `title = "navigation"`

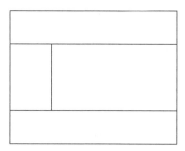

Figure 6.11
Desired frame layout

Note also that XHTML requires that you identify the `frameset` document by including the version information. This means that you are required to insert the following tags as a prologue to the `frameset` declaration:

```
<!DOCTYPE html PUBLIC ".//W3C//DTD XHTML 1.0 Frameset//EN"
"http://www.w3.org/TR/xhtml1/DTD/xhtml1-frameset.dtd">
```

Listing 6.3 Example of a `frameset` document

```
<?xml version = "1.0"?>
<!DOCTYPE html PUBLIC ".//W3C//DTD XHTML 1.0 Frameset//EN"
"http://www.w3.org/TR/xhtml1/DTD/xhtml1-frameset.dtd">
<html xmlns = "http://www.w3.org/1999/xhtml">

<head>
</head>
<frameset rows ="25%,50%,25%">
        <frame src ="header.html">
        <frameset columns ="25%,75%">
                <frame src ="label.html">
                <frame src ="info.html">
        </frameset>
        <frame src ="footer.html">
</frameset>
</html>
```

Figure 6.12
Output in IE 6
from Listing 6.3.
Blank frames are
due to uncreated
XHTML file names

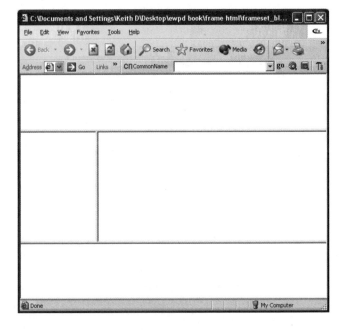

The `noframes` tag

Listing 6.3 assumes that the user has a browser that can display frames and will not inform the user if their browser does not support frames. Most browsers in use today do support frames. However, frames were not supported by the early versions of IE and Netscape. Other browsers, such as Lynx, will also have problems displaying frame-based pages. This may be a small minority of users, but, nevertheless, designers should try to provide an explanation to those users whose browsers cannot display frames. The noframes tag can be used – as shown in the extended Listing 6.4 – to display an appropriate message to browsers that do not support frames.

Listing 6.4 Frameset document with noframes tag

```
<?xml version = "1.0"?>
<!DOCTYPE html PUBLIC ".//W3C//DTD XHTML 1.0 Frameset//EN"
"http://www.w3.org/TR/xhtml1/DTD/xhtml1-frameset.dtd">
<html xmlns = "http://www.w3.org/1999/xhtml">

<head>
</head>
<frameset cols ="25%,50%,25%">
        <frame src ="header.htm">
        <frameset cols ="25%,75%">
                <frame src ="label.htm">
                <frame src ="info.htm">
        </frameset>
        <frame src ="footer.htm">
</frameset>
<noframes>
Your browser cannot display frames.
</noframes>
</html>
```

NOTE

An XHTML document that contains a frameset definition has no body section in its XHTML code, and a page with a body section cannot use the <frameset> tag. If you define a body section for a page that you compose with frameset and frame commands, the frame structure is completely ignored by browser programs and none of the content contained in the frames is displayed. Instead, you see only the content contained in the body section. Because there is no body container, frameset pages can't have background images and background colours associated with them. (Remember, these are defined by the background and bgcolor attributes of the body tag, respectively.) However, the XHTML files that contain the content for the individual frames use background colours and images as they *do* use the <body> tag.

Targeting Windows using frames

When you click on a link in a frame-based system, you need to know which page is to go where. For example, when you click on a link in a particular frame window, would you want the required page to load in the same window or in a different one or in a new blank page?

One way to deal with this problem is to use so-called **magic target names**. There are several predefined target names that will cause certain results to occur when a target link is created. These are:

- `target="_self"` This is used when you want the targeted document to load in the same window as the original link
- `target="_parent"` This is used when you want the targeted document to load the link's parent frameset
- `target="_blank"` This is used when you want the targeted document to open in a new browser window.

Example 6.3

Suppose we wish to develop a frame-based system to display vegetable trouble-

Figure 6.13
Frames layout for vegetable troubleshooting website

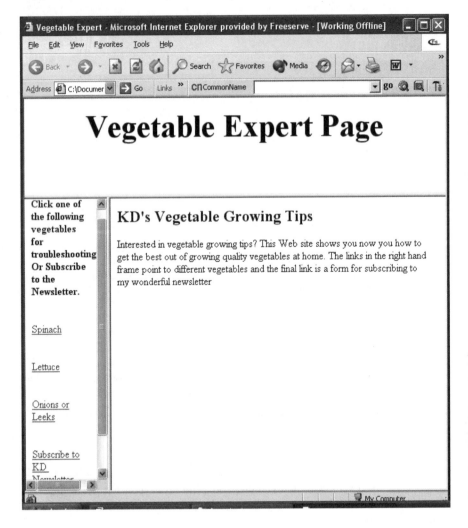

shooting frames. This is a continuation of the vegetable website theme that was started in Chapter 5.

Suppose we require the page structure to contain three frames. The top frame will be static and contain the website title, the lower left-hand side frame will be used to store an index of vegetables and other relevant links, while the lower right-hand side frame will contain the text itself.

The required home page layout is depicted in Figure 6.13. Note in Listing 6.5 that this example uses the same `frameset` description as displayed in Listing 6.3, and that the scrolling has been turned off in the tag:

```
<frame name="header" scrolling="no" src="header.html">
```

The frame border has also been turned off in the tag:

```
<frameset frameborder="0" cols="20%,80%">
```

Listing 6.5 The `frameset` coding for the Vegetable Expert home page, with scrolling and frame border turned off

```
<html>
<head>
        <title> The Vegetable Expert </title>
</head>
        <frameset rows="25%,*">
            <frame name="header" scrolling="no"
src="header.html">
            <frameset frameborder="0" cols="20%,80%">
                <base target="top">
                <frame name="vegetable" src="vegetable.html">
                <frame name="contents" src="contents.html">
            </frameset>
        </frameset>
</html>
```

Figure 6.14 displays the directory contents of the files required for this system. You will notice that, as well as the `frameset` frame, we have frames for each of the vegetables described in the left-hand side frame index. So, these include the vegetable HTML files, such as `spinach_ex` (Figure 6.15), `lettuce_ex` and `onion_ex`, as well as `form`, for the feedback form (Figure 6.16).

The `margin` attributes

The margins of a `frame` tag can be modified by using `marginwidth` and `margin-height` attributes. The margin values would be specified in pixels.

Consider Listing 6.6.

Figure 6.14
Directory content
for frames for
vegetable website

Figure 6.15
Frame that opens
when user clicks
on Spinach
hyperlink

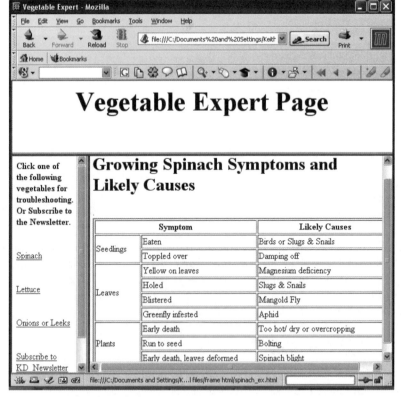

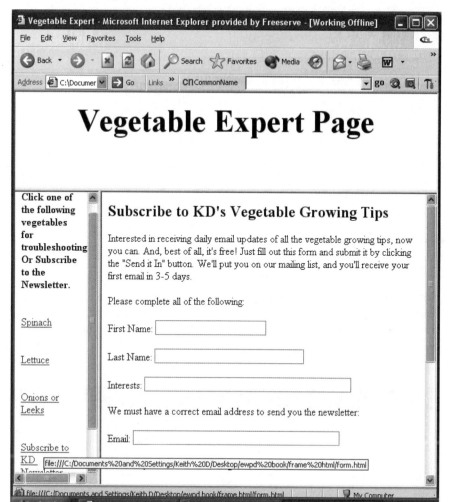

Figure 6.16
Formframe on
vegetable website

Listing 6.6 Inclusion of frame margins

```
<?xml version="1.0" encoding="iso-8859-1"?>

<!DOCTYPE html PUBLIC '-//W3C//DTD XHTML 1.0 Frameset//EN"
"http://www.w3.org/TR/xhtml1/DTD/xhtml1-frameset.dtd">

<html xmlns="http://www.w3.org/1999/xhtml">

<head>

<title>Frame Test</title>

</head>
```

```
<frameset cols="*,*">

 <frame noresize="noresize" marginwidth="15" marginheight="5"

scrolling="Yes" src="f514a.html" />

 <frame marginwidth="50"

marginheight="50" scrolling="yes"

src="f514a.html" />

<frame src="margframe.htm"></frameset><noframes>

</noframes>

</html>
```

Notice in Figure 6.17 how the two identical images in each frame are positioned differently. This is because the `marginwidth` and `marginheight` attributes have been given different settings. Notice also that the `noresize` attribute has been set for the right-hand frame.

Figure 6.17
The effect of
margins

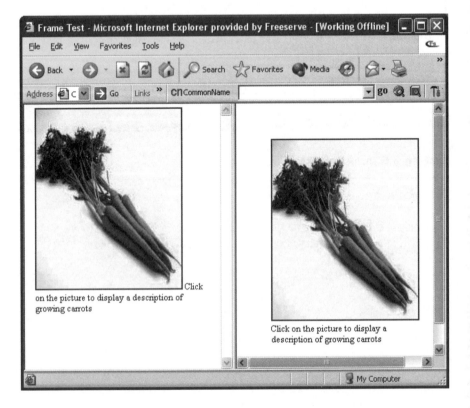

The name attribute

The name attribute gives the frame a name. In this way, the frame can be targeted from other links within the frame page.

Inline frames, or I-frames

It is possible to use another kind of frame with your Web pages called **inline frames**. These were originally developed by Microsoft and recognized in IE 4.0, but later were adopted by HTML 4.0. They don't work with versions of Netscape before version 6.0.

Unlike traditional frames, **I-frames** can float and be positioned within a page just like a graphic or other object, but their content could be changed by clicking links, like a frame. Here's an example of how they work:

Listing 6.7 An XHTML I-frame

```
<html>
  <head><title>In Frame Example</title></head>
  <body>
  <iframe name="iframe" width="400" height="70" src="kd.txt">
  </iframe>
  </body>
  </html>
```

Figure 6.18
Screenshot of output of Listing 6.7

As you can see from Listing 6.7, the iframe element contains a number of attributes. These include the width and height attributes, which, as with a standard image element, define the dimensions of the frame. The source attribute src specifies the source – in this case, a text file called "kd.txt". Make sure that this file is in the same directory as the iframe file. As with traditional frames, you can also use frameborder or scrolling attributes with the iframe element. Figure 6.18 displays the output using the Netscape browser.

Using forms in XHTML

Introduction

Forms provide a means for Web users to send information to the server, as well as receive information to view from the server. They offer an opportunity to gather information from people reading your Web page. Just as XHTML provides many mechanisms for receiving information from the server, so forms provide a mechanism for sending information to the server.

The idea of a Web form is not dissimilar to ordinary everyday paper forms. For example, a job application form will require that the applicant fills in details such as their name, address, age, present employment and so on. These are known as **fields**. You can add forms to your Web page with many different results in mind. You can do something simple, like asking visitors to sign a guestbook or comment about your website. You can also use forms to gather input for a discussion group or some other purpose or design a form to gather statistical data from a large sample of users, maybe using simple 'yes' or 'no' checkbox-type questions.

Creating a form

You create forms by providing a number of fields in which a user can enter information or choose an option. Then, when the user submits the form, the information is returned to a server-side script. A **script** is a short program that is written specifically for each form. More on scripts follows in Chapter 7.

XHTML form elements and attributes

The <form> tag must be used at the start of any form that you use in XHTML code. When you create a <form> tag, you also define the script that it uses and how it sends data using the action and method attributes.

The action attribute

This attribute points the form to a URL that will accept its information and do something with it. If you don't specify an action, it sends the information back to the same URL the page came from. It is a compulsory to use this attribute with this element.

The `method` attribute

This attribute tells the form how to send its information back to the script. The most common method is `post`, which sends all the information from the form separately from the URL. The other option for `method` is `get`, which attaches the information from the form to the end of the URL.

The following is an example of a `<form>` tag:

```
<form method="post" action="/cgi-bin/comment_script">
...
</form>
```

This says that you want the browser to send the completed form to the script `comment_script` in the `cgi-bin` directory on your server and to use the `post` method to send it.

The `input` tag

The `<input />` is an empty tag and is used for managing the input controls that will be placed within it. This element contains other options for acquiring information, including simple text fields, password fields, radio buttons, checkboxes and the buttons to submit and reset the form.

Many attributes are used with the `<input>` tag and these are described below.

- The `name` attribute defines the name for the control. This field is required for all types of input except `Submit` and `Reset` (see examples later in this chapter).
- The `size` attribute specifies the size of the input field in terms of the maximum number of characters to be allowed for a text or password field. The required format is `size = "num"` where `num` is the number of pixels.
- The `Value` attribute can be used with a text or password field. It defines the default text displayed. For a checkbox or radio button, it specifies the value that is returned to the server if the box or button is selected. For the `Submit` and `Reset` buttons, it defines the text inside the button.
- The `type` attribute sets the type of input field you want to display (see the types in the following section).
- The `maxlength` attribute specifies the maximum number of input characters allowed in an input control. The required format is `maxlength = "num"` where `num` is the number of pixels.

Input control attributes

Various input controls are available for use with forms. These include the following.

- The `text` control creates an input text box that allows the user to input any text on a single line. This is ideal for many forms of input, such as a person's name, address, postcode, e-mail address and so on. You can control the width of the box by using the `size` attribute. An example of its use would be:

```
<input type="text" name="Firstname" size ="20"/>
```

In the above `input` tag example, a `text` control is created, the name of which is `"firstname"` and its size is 20 characters.

∎ The `checkbox` attribute creates a box that can be clicked. This control is easy to use for it is either checked or unchecked. Checkboxes are well suited to situations where more than one choice is likely. For example, if you were setting up a selection of choices that would be used for the number of vegetables eaten with your last meal, then more than one choice is possible. Use a checkbox when the choice is 'yes' or 'no' and doesn't depend on anything else. An example of the use of the `input` tag that uses a checkbox is:

```
<input type="checkbox" name="checkbox1" checked =
"checked"/>
```

In the above example, a checkbox input type is created, the name of which is `"checkbox1"` and the checkbox will be checked by default.

∎ The `password` attribute is a modified text field and displays typed characters as bullets instead of the characters actually typed, so its value remains private. Possible attributes to include with the typed password are `name` (required), `size`, `maxlength` and `value`. Although it might appear a little different with cross-browsers, the `password` element hides the text that is typed. An example of the use of the `password input` tag attribute is:

```
<input type="password" name "mypass" size="8"/>
```

In the above example, we have a password input type, the name of which is `"mypass"` and it has a maximum size of eight characters.

∎ The radio button creates a control similar to that of a checkbox in that it can either be set or unset. However, unlike a checkbox, radio buttons allow only one of a related set to be chosen. You can group radio buttons together by using the `name` attribute – this keeps all buttons in the same group under one `name`. Possible attributes to include with the `type` text are `name` (required), `value` and `checked`. An example of the use of the radio buttons is:

```
<input type="radio" name="choice" value="choice1"/>
```

In the above example, a radio button has been created, the name of which is `"choice"` and its value is `"choice1"`.

∎ The `submit` attribute displays a push button with the preset function of sending the data in the form to the server to be processed by a server-side script. As with the reset button – see below – you can use the `value` attribute with `submit` to provide text other than `Submit Query` (the default) for the button. An example of the use of the `reset button` attribute used with the `input` tag is:

```
<input type = "submit" value = "Transmit data"/>
```

- The `reset` attribute displays a push button with the preset function of clearing all the data in the form to its original value. You can use the `value` attribute with the `reset` tag to provide text other than `reset` (the default) for the button. An example of the use of the `reset button` attribute with the `input` tag is:

```
<input type = "reset" value = "Clear form"/>
```

In the above example, a reset button has been created, but the text inside the button has been changed from "`reset`" to "`Clear form`".

For functional forms, or those that result in some processing, you will have to run a CGI script. In the examples that follow, the HTML just creates the appearance of a form.

NOTE

Example of using the form `input` tag

Listing 6.8 is an example using the `input` element along with the `input` tag's `type` attribute assigned to the value "`text`". This input type gathers a simple line of text. You can use other attributes with the text input type, including the attribute's `name` (this is required), `size` and `maxlength`. All these attributes are included in the listing. Figure 6.19 shows the output using IE 6.

Listing 6.8 Use of text input boxes

```
<?xml version = "1.0"?>
<!DOCTYPE html PUBLIC "-//WC3//DTD XHTML 1.0 Transitional //EN"
"http://www.w3.org/TR/xhtml11/DTD/xhtml11-transitional.dtd">
<html xmlns = "http://www.w3.org/1999/xhtml">

<head>
<title>Illustration of the Use of Text Input with Forms
</title>
</head>
<body>
<h3>An example of the use of text input with a form </h3>

<form>
Input your name:  <input type="text" name="Firstname" size
="20" maxlength="20"/>
<br>
Input your telephone number: <input type="text" name="Phone"
size="14" maxlength="12"/>

</form>
</body>
</html>
```

Figure 6.19
The text input
boxes resulting
from Listing 6.8

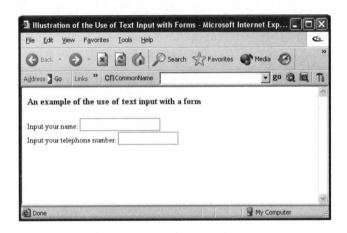

Example of using checkboxes

This example displays two checkboxes – one that has been labelled "A pre-selected checkbox" and checked, the other labelled "A checkbox", which is unchecked. Possible attributes to include with the type text are name (required), value and checked, which defaults the checkbox as unchecked. Listing 6.9 contains the XHTML code and Figure 6.20 displays the output in IE 6.

Listing 6.9 Use of checkboxes input type

```
<?xml version = "1.0"?>
<!DOCTYPE html PUBLIC "-//WC3//DTD XHTML 1.0 Transitional //EN"
"http://www.w3.org/TR/xhtml11/DTD/xhtml11-transitional.dtd">
<html xmlns = "http://www.w3.org/1999/xhtml">

<head>
<title>Illustration of the use of Checkboxes in Form</title>
</head>
<body>
<form>
<h3>An example of the use of checkboxes with a form </h3>
<input type="checkbox" name="checkbox1"
value="checkbox_value1"/>
A checkbox
<input type="checkbox" name="checkbox2"
value="checkbox_value2"
checked = "checked"/>A preselected checkbox
</form>
</body>
</html>
```

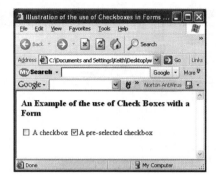

Figure 6.20
Checkboxes
output in IE 6 from
Listing 6.9

Example of using radio buttons

This example shows how radio buttons can be used. The browser window will display two groups of radio buttons. The first illustrates a group of two radio buttons, labelled 'Yes' and 'No', neither of which has been checked. The second group shows the same labelled buttons, 'Yes' and 'No', with the 'Yes' button checked by default. In the top half of the browser display, without selecting 'Yes' or 'No', the user can send back a 'blank' value for this selection because none of the boxes were preselected with the `checked` field. Listing 6.10 contains the XHTML code and Figure 6.21 displays the output in Mozilla.

Listing 6.10 Use of radio button input type

```
<?xml version = "1.0"?>
<!DOCTYPE html PUBLIC "-//WC3//DTD XHTML 1.0 Transitional //EN"
"http://www.w3.org/TR/xhtml11/DTD/xhtml11-transitional.dtd">
<html xmlns = "http://www.w3.org/1999/xhtml">
<head>
<title>Illustration of Radio Buttons </title>
</head>
<body>
Illustration of Radio Buttons unchecked:
<form>
     <input type="radio" name="choice" value="choice1"/ >
Yes.
     <input type="radio" name="choice" value="choice2"/ > No.
</form>
<hr/>
Illustration of Radio Buttons checked:
<form>
     <input type="radio" name="choice" value="choice1"
checked = "checked"/ > Yes.
     <input type="radio" name="choice" value="choice2"/ > No.
</form>
</body>
</html>
```

Figure 6.21
Radio buttons
output using
Mozilla

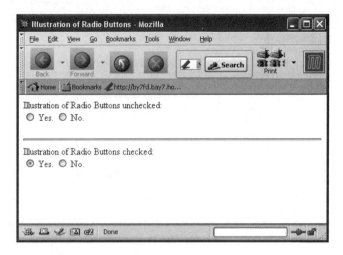

Example using reset buttons

This example shows how reset buttons can be used. The reset value of the type attribute displays a push button with the preset function of clearing all the data in the form to its original value. The browser will display two reset buttons. The second button displays the value attribute with the input tag to provide text other than reset (the default) for the button. Listing 6.11 contains the XHTML code and Figure 6.22 displays the output using the Mozilla browser.

Listing 6.11 Use of reset buttons input type

```
<?xml version = "1.0"?>
<!DOCTYPE html PUBLIC "-//WC3//DTD XHTML 1.0 Transitional //EN"
"http://www.w3.org/TR/xhtml11/DTD/xhtml11-transitional.dtd">
<html xmlns = "http://www.w3.org/1999/xhtml">

<head>
<title>Illustration of the use of Reset Buttons</title>
</head>
<body>
<form>
      <input type="reset"/>
      <br/>
      <input type="reset" value="Clear that form!"/>
</form>
</body>
</html>
```

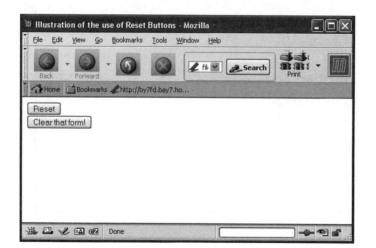

Figure 6.22
Use of reset
buttons output
using Mozilla

Example of using submit buttons

This example shows how submit buttons can be used. The submit value of the type attribute displays a push button with the preset function of sending all the data in the form to the server. The browser will display two submit buttons. The first button displays the default text. The second button displays the value attribute with the input tag to provide text other than submit (the default) for the button. Listing 6.12 contains the XHTML code and Figure 6.23 displays the output using IE 6.

Listing 6.12 Use of radio buttons input type

```
<?xml version = "1.0"?>
<!DOCTYPE html PUBLIC "-//WC3//DTD XHTML 1.0 Transitional //EN"
"http://www.w3.org/TR/xhtml11/DTD/xhtml11-transitional.dtd">
<html xmlns = "http://www.w3.org/1999/xhtml">

<head>
<title>Illustration of Submit Buttons </title>
</head>
<body>
<form>
      <input type="submit"/>
      <br/>
      <input type="submit" value="Send in the data!"/>
</form>
</body>
</html>
```

Figure 6.23
Use of submit
buttons output
using IE 6

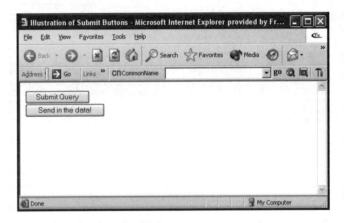

Example of using list boxes

This example shows how list boxes can be inserted as a form control. In Listing 6.13 you will notice that a `<select>` tag has been used to implement this control using the `name` attribute, which is useful for scripting, as we will see in the next chapter, and a `size="1"` attribute setting the size of the list box. Notice that the `<option>` container is then used to specify the choices in the list box, along with the `value` attribute, which specifies each value used in the list box. Figure 6.24 displays the output using Mozilla.

Listing 6.13 Use of menu list input type with a `select` tag

```
<?xml version = "1.0"?>
<!DOCTYPE html PUBLIC "-//W3C//DTD XHTML 1.0
Transitional//EN"
"http://www.w3.org/TR/xhtml1/DTD/xhtml1-transitional.dtd">
<html xmlns = "http://www.w3.org/1999/xhtml">
<head>
    <title>Illustration of Creation of a Form Menu
List</title>
</head>

<body>
Select a Tools website to browse
<p> </p>
<hr />
<form>
<select name = "SiteSelector" size = "1">

    <option value = "http://www.inprise.com">
        Inprise home page for Delphi</option>
```

```
   <option value = "http://www.oracle.com">
       Oracle Corporation for Oracle program
   </option>

    <option value = "http://www.macromedia.com/ ">
     Macromedia Home page for Dreamweaver
    </option>
    <option value = "http://msdn.microsoft.com/vstudio/ ">
       Microsoft Visual Studio start page
    </option>

</select>

</form>
</body>
</html>
```

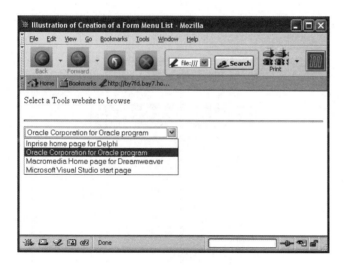

Figure 6.24
Use of menu list output using Mozilla

The button container

In the last section, we used the `input` tag with the `type` attribute set to `button` in order to use a button component on a form. However, a more flexible form of button element – `<button>` – is available with form controls. This is a container tag that was introduced with HTML 4.0. A `type` attribute is associated with the `<button>` tag that has a default value of 'button'. This means that it does nothing other than function as an ordinary button by default. However, it is possible to attach scripts (see the next chapter) to `<button>` and attach images to the `<button>` tag. The example in Listing 6.14 illustrates how this might work. Note that the output from this listing attaches an image that behaves like a button rather than a hyperlink – that is, the content is raised and sinks when pressed. Figure 6.25 displays the output in IE 6.

Listing 6.14 Use of the button element

```
<?xml version="1.0" encoding="iso-8859-1"?>
<!DOCTYPE html PUBLIC "-//W3C//DTD XHTML 1.0
Transitional//EN" "http://www.w3.org/TR/xhtml1/DTD/xhtml1-
transitional.dtd">
<html xmlns="http://www.w3.org/1999/xhtml">
<head>
<title>Using the BUTTON element</title>
</head>
<body>
<form>

<button type="submit" value="mysubmit"/></button>
 <img src="phone.gif" alt = "The telephone image"/> <br />
   Press this!
</form>
</body>
</html>
```

Figure 6.25
The button
element output in
IE 6

> **NOTE** You cannot insert an image map into the <button> container.

The advantages and disadvantages of the techniques discussed in this chapter are summarized in Table 6.5.

Table 6.5 Summary of the advantages and disadvantages of the XHTML techniques discussed

Technique	Advantages	Disadvantages
Tables	Can display data. Data much easier to read when structured properly using tables because its formatting is likely to be preserved	Can take a great deal of effort to create a complicated table structure. Tables are not supported by all browsers. Tables are now being replaced by CSS as the main means of delivering structured content on the Web
Frames	Allow Web designers the scope to present several documents in one window. Unlike tables, each frame's contents can be static or scrollable. Frames can be used to keep important elements – such as navigation buttons – visible at all times	Some users feel overwhelmed by frame systems – especially those containing several scroll bars. Site maintenance can be more complicated than for other options and time-consuming because of the plethora of document interactions involved in frame-based systems. Some search engines have problems with frames and may not be able to index a framed site properly. Printing can also be a problem with frame systems because users might not realize that they have to click on the frame required to be printed before choosing to print
Forms	Adds interactivity to Web pages, providing a means of obtaining feedback from users	Dependent on scripting languages to use. A newer W3C recommendation called XForms (see Chapter 10) is less dependent on scripting languages than are forms

Summary

- The standard text and image formatting tags that were explored in the previous chapter give only limited control over the layout of a page.

- Tables and frames give more control over the accuracy of layout.

- A table consists of a grid of rows and columns, but only the number of rows, along with the highest number of cells in a row, would be specified in XHTML – that would be enough to determine the number of columns in the table.

- The <table> tag can be combined with the table heading <th> tag, table row <tr> tag and table cell data <td> tag to accomplish the required layout for a table.

■ There are several table formatting attributes available with the `<table>` tag that provide for the specification of width, alignment background and spacing around cells.

■ Cells can be merged across columns or rows by using the `colspan` and `rows` attributes when used with the `<th>` and `<td>` tags.

■ Frames provide a means of breaking up the browser window into independent areas – called **panes**. A frame page layout can be defined using the `<frameset>` tag. The `<frameset>` container will contain `<frame>` tags, which will specify the names and size of the frames.

■ Frames can be arranged either vertically or horizontally in any combination.

■ Frames can be of fixed size or variable and can be set using `frame` tag attributes.

■ Attributes are also available for setting the scroll bars of a frame.

■ A named frame can be the target for a link, so that the linked document is displayed within the frame.

■ The target frame can also be displayed in a new browser window if required.

■ Forms provide a means of sending information to the server.

Quick summary of `forms` tags and attributes

For functional forms, you'll have to run a CGI script – the XHTML just creates the appearance of a form. Nevertheless, the following summarizes the main controls that can be used with forms.

`<form>`	Creates a form in an XHTML document.
`<input type=text name="abc" size="n">`	Creates a one-line text area. Size sets length of string in characters.
`<select multiple name="NAME" size="n"></select>`	Creates a scrolling menu. Size sets the number of menu items visible before you need to scroll.
`<option>`	Sets off each menu item used with a list box.
`<select name="NAME"></select>`	Creates a pulldown menu or list box.
`<textarea name="NAME" cols="n" rows="m"></textarea>`	Creates a text box area. Columns set the width; rows set the height.
`<input type="checkbox" name="NAME">`	Creates a checkbox. Text follows tag.
`<input type="radio" name="NAME" value="n">`	Creates a radio button. Text follows tag.

```
<input type="submit" value="NAME"                          Creates a submit button.

<input type="image" border="n" name="NAME" src="name.gif">  Creates a submit button
                                                           using an image.

<input type="reset" value="NAME">                          Creates a reset button.
```

Exercises

1 Give three reasons for using tables to create Web pages.

2 Explain the difference, using an illustration, between the `cellpadding` and `cellspacing` attributes of the `table` element.

3 What table attribute would you use to create a borderless table and what value would you set the attribute to?

4 Explain how you would implement the table structure shown in Figure 6.26. What `table` tags and attributes would be required?

Figure 6.26
Table structure to implement for question 4

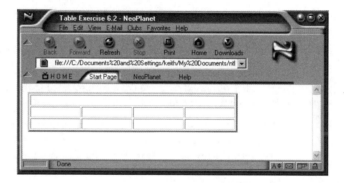

5 Write the XHTML code to create a table consisting of two rows and one column. The top row should contain the text heading 'Look at this', while the bottom row should contain the text message 'Now look at this'. Save your file using the file name 'table_ex.html' and check your code using the IE browser.

6 Write the XHTML code to create a table consisting of one row and two columns. The left-hand column should contain the text 'West' and the right-hand column should contain the text 'East'. Set the border of this table to 2 units. Save the file using a text editor with the file name 'direct_ex.html' and check the code using both the IE and Netscape browsers.

7 Give three possible benefits of using frames in the development of a website. What are the main problems with using frames?

8 Find a website that uses frames. Study the site carefully and state why you think frames have been used.

9 With reference to XHTML frames, explain what is meant by a frameset. Which two attributes determine how many frames appear within a frameset definition?

10   What XHTML element would you use to check that a user has a browser that can display frames?

11   Explain the purpose of the frame tag. What attribute would you use to insert a specified frame name into the frame tag? What attribute would be used to turn scrolling off within a frame and what are the possible values that this attribute takes?

12   Use the frames concept to write XHTML code for the following Web page. Create three horizontal windows in the ratio 2 : 1 : 1. The top window should be a heading window, containing the message 'This is a heading'. The middle window should contain the message 'This is the middle', and the bottom window should contain the message 'This is the bottom'.

13   Which attribute would you use to send a link destination to a different frame?

14   Name two standard XHTML form buttons.

15   Explain the purpose of the action and method attributes that are used with the form element.

16   When would you use radio buttons instead of a checkbox control on a Web page? Give an example of when you would use a checkbox in preference to radio buttons, and vice versa.

17   Find out what the textarea element does with regard to using forms.

18   Run the example listings given in this chapter for both the checkbox and radio buttons. What is the difference between a checkbox and radio button?

19   Create a form that offers the following choices: a pop-up menu, a series of radio buttons and a list of checkboxes. Make a different value the default in each. The choices are North, South, East and West.

20   What controls would you use in order to implement the form design shown in Figure 6.27, taken from an e-commerce website? Give reasons for your answer. Write the XHTML code to display this layout and save it on your PC. Test it using your browser. What additional controls do you think might be necessary in order to complete the design?

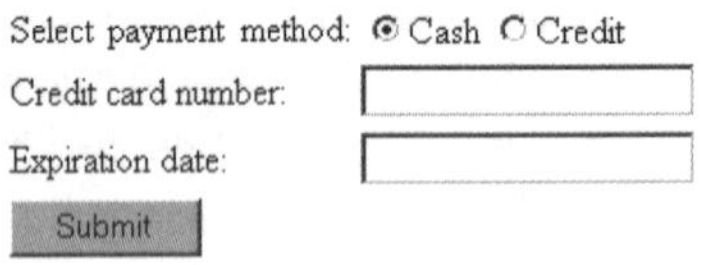

Select payment method: ⊙ Cash ○ Credit
Credit card number: [   ]
Expiration date: [   ]
[Submit]

Figure 6.27 Form design

21   Write the XHTML to set up a Web page that includes three text fields, as shown in Figure 6.28. Note that the name field should be restricted to 30 characters, the employee ID should be restricted to 12 characters and the telephone number to 10.

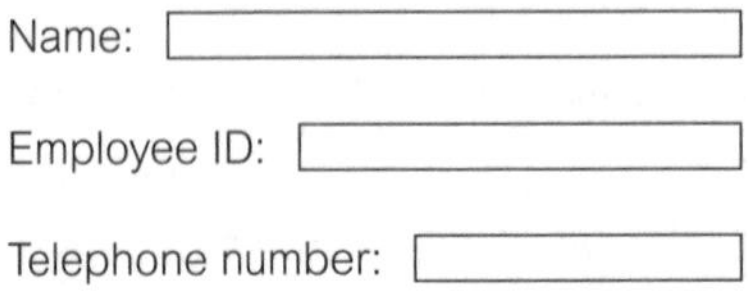

Name: [   ]

Employee ID: [   ]

Telephone number: [   ]

Figure 6.28 Text fields

22   Write the XHTML code to reproduce the table shown in Figure 6.29. Save the XHTML code and check it using the Internet Explorer 6.0 browser.

Examples taken from a life assurance expert

Example number	Age	Smoker?	Gender	Risk
1	Young	No	Female	Low
2	Old	Yes	Male	High
3	Middle	No	Male	Low

Figure 6.29 Table

23   Show how a table can be used to divide a Web page into two halves, split down the middle, with two different background colours and separate columns of text inside each half. Which attribute and attribute values would you use to ensure that a 20-pixel space appeared between the columns of text? Write the XHTML code for the table that fulfils these criteria.

Web programming

Introduction

When the Web was first being used in the mid-1990s, the interaction was very much one-way: the user would request a Web page from the server and then view its content. At that time, Web usage was mostly a reading process – the user would read pages supplied by the server. However, as Web technologies improved, the communication became more interactive by enabling the user to do things such as completing a form online with the browser.

When a form is completed online, the data is sent to the server and it then needs to be processed in some way. The problem is that XHTML has evolved from a markup language, the purpose of which is to present information on the screen, not to process data sent to the server. However, a solution to this problem has been found in the form of scripting languages. These will be explored in some detail in this chapter.

Scripting languages

A number of Web programming languages have evolved that are capable of handling Web interactivity, called **scripting languages**. A **script** is a small program that might run on the server or the user's browser that provides a way to make Web documents interactive.

Scripts can be written in many languages and can be **server-side** or **client-side**. Server-side scripts execute on the Web server, feeding XHTML to the browser as a product of their computations, while client-side scripts execute on the user's computer. Clearly, client-side scripts are more limited in scope than server-side ones because they do not have access to server-wide information. Nevertheless, they can perform useful jobs, as we will see throughout this chapter.

Client-side Web scripting languages include **JavaScript** – compatible with Netscape, IE and most browsers – and **VBScript** – which is IE compatible only. Given that JavaScript is browser-independent, it has become the de facto standard for client-side scripting and is recommended for this purpose.

There are many other scripting languages that are used on the Web. These include **Java applets** which may be included in client-side or server-side Web pages for even more flexible interactivity. On the server-side, the main scripting languages are **Perl** for CGI, while VBScript is quite popular for ASP and Java for JSP. Finally, **PHP** is establishing itself as a popular server-side non-proprietary language. In this chapter, we will take a brief look at all of these scripting languages.

When to use a server-side or client-side script

A **server-side script** would be appropriate to use if any of the following requirements exist:

- you need to include output from a database or some other legacy application in your XHTML documents
- you're writing a client-side script just to generate XHTML as the user opens the Web page
- you have to process a user's form input on the server (transaction processing, for example).

Writing a server-side script will not always be possible – particularly if the service that is hosting your Web pages doesn't support server-side scripts, although that's very unlikely nowadays. In such cases, you have no choice but to write a client-side script or relocate your Web pages to a service that does support scripts.

NOTE

Client-side scripts interact with the XHTML while the user is viewing it. In general, you should write a client-side script whenever either of the following conditions prevail.

- You want to change the appearance of the Web page as the user interacts with it by, for example, replacing one image with another as the mouse passes over image – called a **rollover**.
- You want to prevent frequent round trips to the server by validating form input before submitting it. For example, you could ensure that a name field only contains upper- or lower-case letters or, perhaps, a date field is entered in a specific

format, such as dd/mm/yyyy. If the user enters the first two digits (dd) > 31, then you could use a client-side script on the browser to respond appropriately. This is clearly faster than sending the data to the server and then carrying out the checks before sending it back.

Client-side scripting languages

There are two main languages that are used for client-side scripting. These are **JavaScript** and **VBScript**.

JavaScript is loosely based on C++ and has gained worldwide acceptance on the Web. You can use JavaScript to interact with the user's environment, change the appearance of the content while the user interacts with it – known as rollovers (see Chapter 12), process or calculate values to be entered in the browser window and many other things. Most browsers support JavaScript.

VBScript is based on Microsoft's Visual Basic and is currently only supported by IE. It is most commonly used with Microsoft's Active Server Page technology for server-side scripting. You use it to create client-side scripts that interact with the user's environment, change content dynamically and glue together objects.

VBScript's biggest advantage is that Visual Basic is a fairly ubiquitous language. However, Internet Explorer is the only Web browser that supports VBScript at the present time. Figure 7.1 outlines the stages a client-side script goes through as it is processed. These stages are outlined below:

1 The author creates the Web page containing the client-side script and uploads it using the Web server.

Figure 7.1
The stages a client-side script passes through as it is being processed

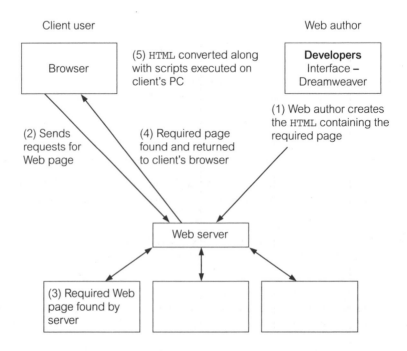

Client user   Web author

Browser

(5) HTML converted along with scripts executed on client's PC

Developers
Interface –
Dreamweaver

(1) Web author creates the HTML containing the required page

(2) Sends requests for Web page

(4) Required page found and returned to client's browser

Web server

(3) Required Web page found by server

2 At some time in the future, a client requests the page using his or her browser.

3 The request is sent to the server, which searches through the Web to try and find the required page.

4 When the page is found, the server sends the page back as HTML to fulfil the client's request.

5 The HTML is converted so that the client can view the page on the display, along with any scripts in the HTML code that are executed on the client's machine (see Figure 7.2).

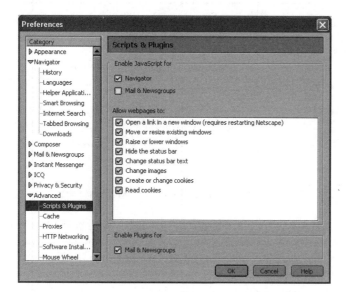

Figure 7.2
Controlling JavaScript preferences with Netscape

Choosing between JavaScript and VBScript

JavaScript is now widely recognized as the de facto standard for client-side scripting, but VBScript is still used. When choosing between these languages, consider the following criteria before making your decision. Do your scripts have to run on both Internet Explorer and Netscape? If so, use JavaScript. If you do not yet know how to program and you want to learn quickly, start with VBScript because it has a shorter learning curve – particularly if you already know Visual Basic.

The client-side examples that follow focus on JavaScript. VBScript examples are looked at in the server-side scripting section later in this chapter.

Uses of JavaScript

JavaScript is well suited to the following programming situations, some of which will be considered in the examples that follow:

■ reacting to 'events' such as mouse movements

- calculations, such as time differences between countries
- updating parts of Web pages, such as image replacement when something has happened
- detecting browsers and browser versions that are being used
- displaying pop-up messages to alert the user that something has happened
- handling cookies
- validating form data, as described earlier in the chapter.

NOTE

1 JavaScript is case-sensitive – take care when typing program code characters as you are writing code with JavaScript. Lower-case text is required for JavaScript commands.
2 Always comment out JavaScript code – this will prevent any non-compatible browsers from displaying the code on the display. Knowing how to do this is explained later in this chapter.
3 As Figure 7.2 shows, it is possible to turn off JavaScript, even if the browser is JavaScript enabled. You need to be aware of this and plan accordingly.

Interpreted and compiled languages

JavaScript and VBScript are interpreted languages as opposed to **compiled** languages, such as Java. A **compiled language** actually translates each instruction in the program into machine code. This means that the computer executes the program directly – as an executable file. This means that compiled programs run faster than interpreted programs and can run independently of the program that compiled it. **Interpreted languages**, on the other hand, execute a script instruction by instruction. An interpreted language is therefore slower than a compiled language. In practice, however, the scripts that are interpreted by the Web browser are usually very small, so therefore the user is not likely to notice any difference. Moreover, scripts often only execute in response to something that the user does – such as clicking the mouse – instead of executing continuously as compiled programs sometimes do.

Objects and events

Events are things that happen on the Web page – for example, a mouse action, such as clicking or skimming over something (called an object) on a page, will trigger events, as will a keyboard action, such as typing a character, but other types of events that do not involve some physical action can also occur on a Web page, such as a timer finishing its countdown.

When you write scripts, you embed instructions into your Web pages that describe how you want the browser to handle certain events.

Events have three key parts – an **object**, the **event** itself, and what is known as the **event handler**.

- An **object** can be anything on the Web page – a button or form field, perhaps, or an image or text label.

- Objects raise **events** in response to something that the user does to an object. For example, if the user clicks a button, the button raises a click event or if the user skims the mouse over some object, then the object raises the mouseover event.

- **Event handlers** take action when there is an event. To create an event handler, you associate a function with the event. This means that the browser then executes that function whenever that event occurs.

Learning to program: writing scripts

You can write scripts in two ways. The first is to use a wizard, such as the Scripting Wizard that comes with Microsoft FrontPage and FrontPage Express. Wizards enable you to write very simple scripts and associate them with events and objects using an intuitive mouse-driven interface. You can also write scripts using a text editor. Doing so requires that you have an intimate understanding of the script language that you are using. You can type your scripts directly into a file using your XHTML editor, or type them into a plain text file that you link to your XHTML file.

How to write JavaScript code into your pages

JavaScript can be written into XHTML pages in a number of ways.

Embedding it within the `<script>...</script>` tags in the body of the document

You can embed scripts in an XHTML file using tags, much like any other content you put on a Web page. Scripts are placed between the `<script>` and `</script>` container tags, as shown below. The commands or individual lines in a JavaScript program are called **statements**. As you can see in this example, there is only one statement to be executed: `alert("Welcome to JavaScript")`. The effect of this statement will be to display a message box containing the message 'Welcome to JavaScript'. The scripting language you are using will be specified by using the language attribute.

```
<body>
<script language = "JavaScript">
   alert("Welcome to JavaScript")
</script>
</body>
```

The problem with writing JavaScript into pages in this way is that the code is executed as soon as the script is being loaded and if a large page is being loaded and the JavaScript code tries to access an object before it has loaded, the script might crash.

Embedding scripts into the head section

It is more common for scripts to be written in the `<head>` section of a program by using **functions** than other options.

A **function** is a self-contained block of JavaScript statements that will be executed when it is called from a JavaScript statement in a `<script>`...`<script>` block, or attached to an object somewhere in the `<body>` part of the document. The function must be given a name – in this case, I have called it `displayMessage()`. The purpose of the round brackets after the function name is to enable data to be passed to the function. The function code must be enclosed in curly brackets – { } – and the function itself will be called (or executed) from the `displayMessage()` statement in the `<script>` block. When the `<script>` block is executed in the `<body>` section of the document, the `<displayMessage()>` statement will cause the program to transfer to the function with the same name and the program enclosed within the curly brackets will then be executed, causing the message box to be displayed there as shown in Figure 7.3. The way that this would be written in `<html>` listings is as follows:

```html
<html>
<head>
    <script>
        function displayMessage()
        {
            alert('Welcome to JavaScript')
        }
    </script>
</head>
<body>
    <script>
        displayMessage()
    </script>
</body>
<html>
```

Figure 7.3
Displaying a
message box by
using a JavaScript
alert statement

Take care with quotation marks when writing JavaScript code. Remember, double quotation marks " " are used for enclosing attribute values in XHTML and therefore single quotation marks ' ' are used for enclosing JavaScript text items.

Embedding inline code within an XHTML object

You can attach JavaScript code directly into an event handler of an XHTML object. The code will then be executed when the event occurs.

The example below shows how this is done using JavaScript code embedded in an XHTML anchor tag. In the example, some text is displayed on a Web page as a hyperlink and the JavaScript inline code should cause the display of the next hyperlink page name in the status window at the bottom of the browser window when the mouse runs over the hyperlink. Running the mouse over a hyperlink causes the onMouseOver event to occur – it is triggered by the mouse passing over the hyperlink, not clicking it.

When this event happens, the JavaScript code will invoke the action, that is, display the message 'Go to next page' in the status window at the bottom of the screen. When the user passes the mouse out of the hyperlink, the onMouseOut event will be active and the window status will no longer display a message.

(Table 7.1 displays a subset of JavaScript events, their descriptions and an example illustrating their purpose.)

The JavaScript code for this example is inline and contained in the anchor tag, and each event is written as an attribute with the return true required to display the message. The output from this example is shown in Figure 7.4 using IE 6. The anchor tag is written as:

```
<a href="next.html"
            onMouseOver="window.status='Goto next page';
            return true"
            onMouseOut="window.status='';
            return true">
Click here for next page </a>
```

Figure 7.4
Output for JavaScript event handler showing link via status window at the bottom of page on an IE 6 browser

This example shows that you can include event handler JavaScript code as an attribute of the XHTML tag that initiates the event. The general syntax of an event handler within an XHTML tag is:

```
<tag eventHandler="JavaScript code whatever it is"
```

NOTE	Event handler names are the same as the name of the event, except that they have the prefix 'on'.

Table 7.1 Some common JavaScript events

Event	Description	Example of use
Click	The mouse is clicked over some page hyperlink	`<a href="next.html"` `onClick="alert('JavaScript is fun!!');"` `Click here to discover something about` `JavaScript <a>` This event `onClick` will trigger the appearance of a dialogue box containing the message 'JavaScript is fun!!' (see Figure 7.5)
MouseOver	Mouse is moved over some element on the page	`<a href="next.html"` `onMouseOver="window.status='Goto` `next page';` `return true"`
MouseOut	Mouse is moved out of some element on the page	`onMouseOut="window.status='';` `return true">` `Click here for next page </a>` This `onMouseOut` event handler will display a message 'Go to next page' when the mouse moves over the anchor element. When the mouse moves away from the element, the message will disappear
Load	On loading the Web page by the browser	`<body onLoad= "alert('Welcome to this` `page');">` This event `onLoad` will trigger the appearance of a welcome message box when the page is first loaded
Change	The value of an element changes, often a field in a form	`<input type ="text" onChange` `="alert('The value of the text field has` `now changed');"/>` This `onChange` event handler displays a dialogue box containing the message 'The value of the text field has now changed'

Understanding how a browser executes scripts

When a user opens a Web page, the browser makes note of every script in the XHTML document. It translates the scripts into **intermediate code**, which represents the keywords in the script as **tokens** – these are binary values representing the keywords – which can be interpreted more efficiently because they are smaller than the original keywords.

It also creates a table called a **symbol table**, which contains the name of each script function (scripts that are called by name from other scripts).

The browser looks up functions in the symbol table as they are invoked. It executes different types of script code at different times. It does not execute functions as the Web page loads. Instead, it waits for an event that you associate with a function to execute them instead. When an object on the Web page fires an event, the browser looks up the function associated with that event in the symbol table, and then executes it. Also, any time a script invokes a function, the browser looks it up in the symbol table to find the code.

Example 7.1

As another illustration of a JavaScript event and an event handler, this example uses a JavaScript mouse click event of a text element on a page to respond with a dialogue box containing the message 'JavaScript is fun.' The JavaScript code, using the NotePad editor, is displayed in Listing 7.1 and the output, using IE, is displayed in Figure 7.5.

Listing 7.1 JavaScript code for mouse click event handler

```
<html>

<!-- Example illustrating the use of JavaScript Mouse
events  -->

<head>
<title> Another JavaScript example illustrating the onClick
event </title>
</head>
<body>


   <a href ="next.html"
     onClick ="alert('JavaScript is fun!!');"

     <b> Click here to discover something about JavaScript
</b></a>
</body>
</html>
```

Figure 7.5
JavaScript output
for mouse click
event handler
from Listing 7.1

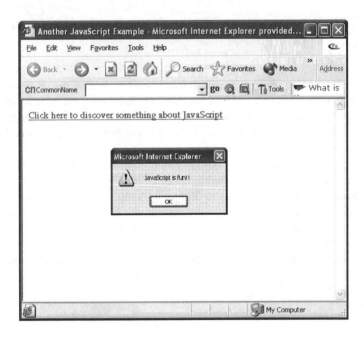

Basic JavaScript language constructs

JavaScript is an **object-oriented programming (OOP) language**.

A programming **object** contains **data characteristics** and **functions** (programming code). This idea is borrowed from our experience of 'real-world' objects. A television, for example, contains data characteristics, such as the size of the screen, the colour of the television and so on, and has functions that make the television operate, such as a control to turn the television on or off, a control to turn the volume up, a control to alter the colour contrast and so on. These aspects of a real-world television can be applied to objects that are used in the JavaScript language. Of course, JavaScript objects are confined to the domain of the World Wide Web (see the next section on the Domain Object Model).

The Domain Object Model (DOM)

The **Domain Object Model (DOM)** is a hierarchy of objects 'built in' to and recognized by the JavaScript language. The DOM is a W3C specification and the more recent recommendations relate to XML DOM (see Chapter 10) with the aim of providing a standard programming interface for a wide variety of applications.

The XML DOM is designed to be used with any programming language and/or any operating system. With it, a programmer can create an XML document, navigate its structure and add, modify or delete its elements. One of the most commonly used objects in JavaScript programs is the document object. It represents the content of a browser's window. Thus, any type of information that is displayed in a Web page is part of the document object.

NOTE

The DOM is technically separate from JavaScript. This means that the JavaScript language specification does not specify the nature of the DOM. As a consequence, Microsoft and Netscape have each developed their own individual DOM and they are not identical. However, recent versions of their browsers have converged to the W3C specification.

Object methods

The functions associated with objects are also known as **methods**. Most Web pages contain some textual information and JavaScript contains built-in methods called **write()** and **writeln()** that enable text to be added to a Web page. Both methods perform the same function that adding text to a standard XHTML file does. They are very similar – the difference between them being that the **writeln()** method also adds a carriage return after a line of text finishes.

To use, or **execute**, these methods, you would make a '**call**' to the object's method. To do this, a standard object reference syntax is used – append the method to the object with a full stop and include any arguments between the method's parentheses.

For example, suppose we wanted to include a statement in a JavaScript program that would display the text string 'This is my first JavaScript code'. We would write the JavaScript statement for this as follows:

```
document.write("This is my first JavaScript code")
```

NOTE

The effect of the above statement would not be to cause a carriage return after the line finishes as the **write()** method, rather than the **writeln()** method, has been used.

Creating objects

The above examples use built-in JavaScript objects and methods. However, there are times when you may want to create your own objects to use in a JavaScript program. Suppose, for example, you wanted to create a new instance of an object type that represents a car, perhaps your own car. Let us call it **myCar**. You could do so by using the following JavaScript statement:

```
MyCar=new Object()
```

Creating properties associated with the new object

The following statements would define properties associated with this new object called **myCar** in the JavaScript language:

```
MyCar.make="Ford";
MyCar.model="Fiesta";
```

```
MyCar.fueltype="Diesel";
MyCar.enginesize="1800";
```

These statements say that the make of my car is a Ford, the model is a Fiesta, it runs on diesel and has an engine size of 1800 cc.

Creating methods associated with the new object

The following statement might define a method associated with **myCar** that causes the horn to toot:

```
MyCar.toot;
```

The following statement might define a method associated with **myCar** that turns the lights on:

```
MyCar.lights;
```

It is beyond the scope of this book to complete a detailed study of the JavaScript language, but some simple examples will be explored in the following sections to get you acquainted with the object-oriented programming paradigm that is prevalent in most Web languages. I refer you to Gosselin (2000), Flanagan (1999) and Deitel and Deitel (1999) for more detailed coverage of the JavaScript language.

Some tips for Web programming

The following tips may help make both client-side and server-side Web programming a little easier.

- Ensure that you set the browser preferences so that script debugging is enabled and notification is given of script errors when they occur. This can be done by using the menu option 'Tools / Internet Options' and then setting the relevant checkboxes, if you are using Internet Explorer (see Figure 7.6). If you are using the Netscape browser, type 'JavaScript' in the location box. An example of an error dialogue box using the IE browser is given in Figure 7.7.

- Watch your spelling of the names of object properties. Remember, if you create your own object properties and misspell, then the computer will think that you are creating another.

NOTE

The dialogue box shown in Figure 7.7 displays the line number and position in the line where the error has occurred. The type and the nature of the error are shown in the ensuing dialogue box. In the example given, the object is required.

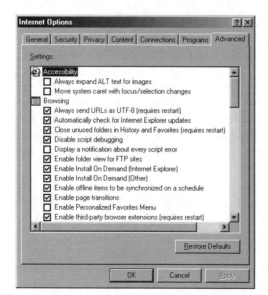

Figure 7.6
Setting
preferences for
script debugging
on a Netscape
browser.

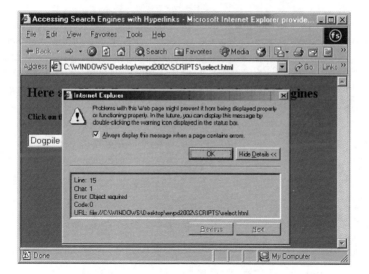

Figure 7.7
Example of a
JavaScript error
message when
using an IE
browser

Specifying a default scripting language

You can specify a default scripting language for an XHTML file and forget about
specifying it within each <script> tag. You use the <meta> tag at the beginning
of your XHTML file. Set HTTP-EQUIV to Content-Script-Type and set content
to the MIME type of the scripting language you're using. For example, the following
tag sets the default language for the XHTML document to VBScript:

```
<meta http-equiv="Content-Script-Type"
content="text/vbscript">
```

Handling non-scripting browsers with `noscript`

With the release of Navigator 3.0, Netscape introduced several new XHTML tags, including `<noscript>`.

The purpose of a `<noscript>` block is similar to that of `<noframes>` – it identifies an XHTML block for processing by a browser that doesn't support scripting. However, `<noscript>` is not part of the XHTML standard and neither is it supported by IE, so it has failed to be adopted by other browsers. Fortunately, there is another way that works across all browsers. It relies on a unique attribute of JavaScript.

Handling comments with non-scripting browsers

While the JavaScript interpreter looks inside the `comment` tag block for its `script` code, it has the unique function that, once it encounters a comment end tag `(-->)`, it ignores everything else on that line. Non-JavaScript browsers, on the other hand, pick up the processing after the comment closes and interpret the rest of the line as valid XHTML.

This means that you can place an empty comment `(<!-- -->)` at the beginning of a line inside the `<script>` tag and get an XHTML statement that JavaScript (and browser) ignores, but displays to non-scripting browsers. This effectively creates the equivalent of a `<noscript>` ... `</noscript>` block, as demonstrated in Listing 7.2. Some older browsers require the single line comment `symbx II` before a block ends, hence its inclusion in the blocks.

Listing 7.2 Creating a non-script block using comments

```
<script language ="JavaScript">
<!-- begin hide
script browsers will process this
end hide -->
</script >

<script language ="JavaScript">
<!-- -->Non-script browsers will not process this
</script >
```

NOTE Even though the text in the second `<script>` block is intended for browsers that do not support scripting, it is necessary to specify `JavaScript` as the scripting language because Internet Explorer requires that the language attribute be given when using the `script` tag.

Example 7.2

This is a different type of example, showing how JavaScript can be used to make pages **dynamic**. More on dynamic pages will be covered later in this chapter.

A **dynamic page** is one that contains instructions to tell the browser to behave differently every time the page is loaded. In this particular example, we use JavaScript to display the current date and time, along with suitable text. This is clearly going to produce a different result every time the page is loaded.

The program works by calling a function named `printDetails()` in the `<head>` section. The function is called from the `<script>` tag written in the `<body>` section. Notice how the `comment` tags have been inserted around the `script` tags to ensure non-rendering with non-JavaScript – compatible browsers (see Listing 7.3). The output from this program is shown in Figure 7.8.

Listing 7.3 Creating a dynamic page for JavaScript – compatible browsers

```
<?xml version="1.0" encoding="iso-8859-1"?>
<!DOCTYPE html PUBLIC "-//W3C//DTD XHTML 1.0
Transitional//EN"
"http://www.w3.org/TR/xhtml1/DTD/xhtml1-transitional.dtd">
<html xmlns="http://www.w3.org/1999/xhtml">


<head>
<title>JavaScript Date and Time Document</title>
<script language="JavaScript">
function printDetails()
{
document.writeln("<h1>Good day!</h1>")
document.writeln("<h2>Date and Time Details</h2>")
document.writeln()
document.write("<h3> The Date and Time is:")
document.write(new Date())
}
</script>
</head>


<body>
<script>


<!--
printDetails()
//-->
</script>
</body>
</html>
```

You will see that the `document.write()` and `document.writeln()` methods have been used to send the text argument contained in quotes `"..."` to the document to be displayed in the browser window. Notice how XHTML elements are used to format and lay out the text, such as `<h1>` and `<h2>`.

Displaying the text

The effect of the first three `document.writeln()` statements in the function will render the text exactly as if it were contained in the `<body>` section of the program. The next two `document.write()` statements cause the date and time to be displayed. The first writes the text 'The Date and Time is:' before displaying the actual date and time. A `writeln()` method has not been used because we want the actual date and time to follow on the same line.

Displaying the date and time

The date and time are then dynamically found by making a call to the `Date()` object. This is a built-in JavaScript object that creates a new instance of the class by writing the argument of the `document.write()` object as `new Date`. This is not written inside quote marks because we want the actual value of the `Date` rather than displaying a literal text string. This is then written to the `document` and so becomes visible in the browser window. Notice that the date is displayed, followed by the time, followed by UTC 2004. This refers to the Universal Coordinated Time display format.

Example 7.3

This example is a variation on Example 7.2, this time using JavaScript to place the current date and time separately in the NeoPlanet browser window.

The code is shown in Listing 7.4. Notice that the script begins with the `<script> language="javaScript">` line in HTML. This tells HTML that what follows is a JavaScript program. Also notice that the script code is placed in the `<head>` section of the program. The `<head>` section only has been included in this listing.

The program works by breaking down the `Date()` object into its component parts of the day, month, year, time in hours and time in seconds. As in the previous example, the new `Date()` object is created, and the hours component is created by the statement:

```
var hoursElapsed = theTimeNow.getHours()
```

This statement defines a new variable called `hoursElapsed`, which takes the hours from the `getHours()` method of `theTimeNow` object.

Listing 7.4 JavaScript code for placing the date and time separately in the browser window

```
<head>
<script language ="JavaScript">
var theTimeNow   = new Date()
var hoursElapsed = theTimeNow.getHours()
var minsElapsed =theTimeNow.getMinutes()
var monthnow = theTimeNow.getMonth()
var yearnow = theTimeNow.getYear()
var daynow = theTimeNow.getDay()
document.write( "<h6>");
document.write( "<h3>" + "The date now is: " +
             daynow + ":" + monthnow + ":"+ yearnow +
                "</h3>");
document.write( "<h3>" + "The time now is: " +
             hoursElapsed + ":" + minsElapsed +
                "</h3>");
</script>
</head>
```

The other components are created in a similar way. The `document.write()` and `document.writeln()`, as in the previous example, are used to output the required data in the browser window. The output, using the NeoPlanet browser, is shown in Figure 7.9.

Figure 7.9
The output for
program shown in
Listing 7.4

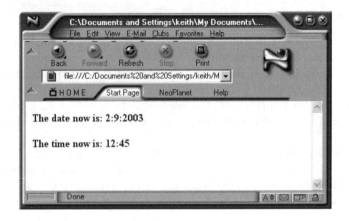

Adding Java applications to your Web pages

Many people confuse Java and JavaScript, thinking that they are the same thing – they are not!

Java is a programming language with powerful Web applications. It was developed by Sun Microsystems (http://java.sun.com). A detailed study of Java is beyond the scope of this book, so the following sections give a brief overview. For more detailed study, see Farrell (2002), Bates (2000) and Deitel and Deitel (1999).

Unlike JavaScript, Java is a compiled, standalone, general-purpose language. Despite being general purpose, it is used in many Web applications because Java programs are portable – meaning that they can be used with operating systems other than the one that was used to create them. This works by using a so-called **Java Virtual Machine (JVM)**, which compiles the Java code into executable code on the user's machine. When you pass Java source code to the Java compiler, it turns it into something called **bytecode**. This is not machine language, but any machine that has the JVM installed can read this bytecode and convert it into machine code and run it irrespective of other aspects of the machine. This means that such Java programs could be created on a Windows PC and yet run on a Macintosh, Linux or any other operating system environment (see Figure 7.10). This would be extremely difficult to do without the JVM because different computers have their own, sometimes different, internal architectures.

A JVM and compiler are included in the major IE and Netscape browsers, which means that Java applications can run on Web pages. If you intend using other browsers with Java, you may have to download a Java plug-in.

The Java programs that run within Web pages are called **applets**. These applets provide a way for Web page users' to interact with the page. They are fast because they run on the client's machine. Web page applets offer true online interaction with the viewer and can be used for a wide variety of tasks, including verification of security data, such as banking online or, perhaps, an applet could be used to calculate the lowest personal loan rate offered by a range of financial institutions.

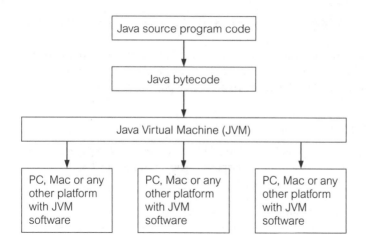

Figure 7.10
The Java Virtual
Machine (JVM)
architecture

The case for Java on the Web

The reason for Java's popularity on the Web is that it has better support for networking than almost any other programming language (Bates, 2000; McBride and McBride 2001). The majority of the time, Java is used to run applets to give client-side functionality, although Java programs are now also frequently used to achieve server-side functionality by means of Java **servlets**, which are briefly discussed later in this chapter.

Using Java applets in Web pages

A Java-enabled browser recognizes a special hypertext tag called an `applet`. When downloading a Web page containing an `applet` tag, the Java-enabled browser knows that a special kind of Java program called an `applet` is associated with that Web page. The browser then downloads another file of information, as named in an attribute of the `applet` tag (see the example in Listing 7.5 below), that describes the execution of that applet. This file of information is then written in bytecodes.

The Java-enabled browser interprets these bytecodes and runs them as an executable program on the user's computer. This execution of content on the user's host is what sets Java content apart from the hypertext and other multimedia content of the Web.

The process of using executable content in a Java-enabled browser, for the user, is seamless. The downloading and start of the execution of content happen automatically. The user does not specifically have to request this content or start its execution. Also, as will be explored more in the next chapter, this executable content is platform-independent – that is, Java programmers need not create separate versions of the applets for different computer platforms, as long as the user has a Java interpreter (or Java-enabled browser) installed on his or her computer.

Adding Java applications to your Web pages

There are several basic ways in which to add Java applets (programs) to your Web pages. The first is an extension that Netscape and other companies rolled into their browsers as the Java language first became popular by using the <applet> tag.

The <applet> tag

The <applet> tag can be used to add Java applets to Web pages. The basic format for the <applet> tag for this purpose is shown in Listing 7.5.

Listing 7.5 The format for the <applet> tag

```
<?xml version="1.0" encoding="iso-8859-1"?>
<!DOCTYPE html PUBLIC "-//W3C//DTD XHTML 1.0
Transitional//EN"
"http://www.w3.org/TR/xhtml1/DTD/xhtml1-transitional.dtd">
<html xmlns="http://www.w3.org/1999/xhtml">
<head>
<title>Untitled Document</title>
</head>
<body>
<applet code = "filename.class"
            width ="number"
            height = "number"
            align = "direction">
<param name = "name" value="number/string">
<img src="URL" alt="text" />
</applet>
</body>
</html>
```

In Listing 7.5, the code attribute specifies the Java applet file name, the height and width attributes are just numbers that represent the dimensions in pixels for the applet window on your Web page and the align attribute has the values left, right and center, top and bottom.

Using parameters

The <param> tag for <applet> refers to any parameter elements that you use in your program.

Parameters enable values to be passed from XHTML into applets. This means that your applet can be reused to get different effects. For example, if you created a board game applet, you might want to set different board colours and so on. Using parameters with the `applet` tag lets you customize different aspects of it. Parameters enable your Java applet to recognize and deal with the incoming data.

The `<img>` tag allows you to add the URL to an image for display in browsers that are not Java-enabled.

An example of the use of the `<applet>...</applet>` tag is:

```
<applet   code =" http://www.free-
applets.com/BreakOut/BreakOut.html "
                    width ="20"
                    height ="20"
                    align = "left">
      <param name = "Speed"  value = "6">
      <img src  = "nojava.gif"  alt = "This applet requires
a Java-enabled browser"/>
  </applet >
```

Example of adding Java applets

The following example is one of the many free applets available – a version of the old classic arcade game, Breakout. It was written by Louis Schiano and includes sound effects (although they cannot be appreciated without running the applet in a browser) and plenty of user-customizable options. The code is shown in Listing 7.6, and a screenshot of the output is shown in Figure 7.11.

Listing 7.6 The code for Breakout game applet

```
<html>
<head>
<body>
<h3>This applet was written by Louis Schiano</h3>
<h3>This applet has been added using the applet tag in
XHTML</h3>

<applet code = "breakout.class "
                        width = "466"
                        height = "457"
                        align =  "left">

</applet>
</body>
</html>
```

Figure 7.11
Output of
Breakout game

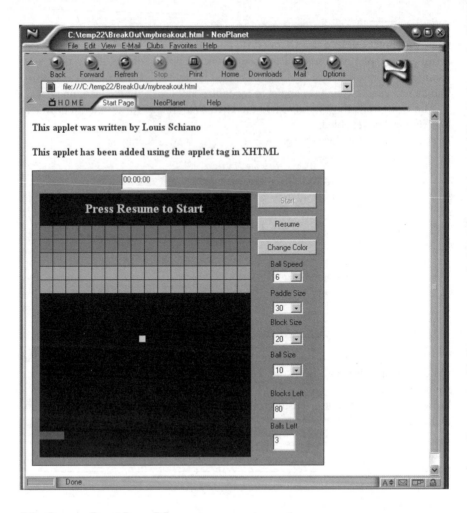

Figure 7.11
Output of
Breakout game

Using ActiveX components

ActiveX is by Microsoft and seen as the Microsoft competitor to Java. Like Java applets, ActiveX applications could include anything from calendars to animated buttons and virtual reality. Several ActiveX components are freely available from some websites (go to www.activex.com). Alternatively, as with Java, you can create your own.

To include your own ActiveX component in your Web page, you can use the `<object>` tag. Authoring tools, such as Dreamweaver, let you drop ActiveX components directly on to your Web pages.

Static and dynamic Web pages

Static Web pages

A **static** Web page is one the content of which consists of HTML that is exactly determined by the author of the page. Static Web pages have an extension .htm or .html. The content of such Web pages is determined before the request was made by the browser to the server. An example of a static Web page is shown in Figure 7.12.

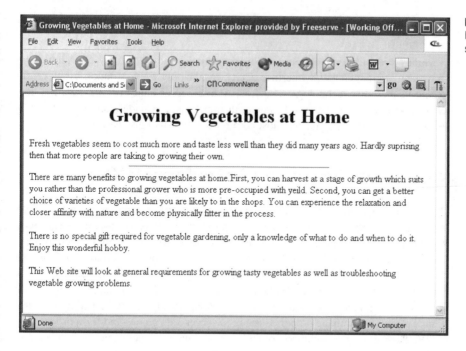

Figure 7.12
Example of a
static Web page

Dynamic Web pages

A **dynamic** Web page is one the content of which is not determined solely by the author, but, instead, is generated dynamically on request. Dynamic XHTML pages contain instructions that tell the browser to behave differently every time the page is loaded. For example, suppose you wanted to display the current time on your Web page. You could not use HTML to insert the time into the page because the user will request the page at some random time in the future. In other words, you know that the user will request the page, but you do not know what time that will be. Hard-coding the time will always quote the same time, which would be wrong. As we cannot hard-code the HTML *before* the page is requested, a method is required to generate the HTML *after* the page is requested – that is, a means of replacing the hard-coded HTML with a set of instructions using some other language, which will be used to generate HTML for the page at the time the user requests the page, whenever that might be, giving the correct time.

The same would apply to someone who, for example, wants to view the contents of a DIY retailer's database on a server. Clearly, the database is constantly changing, with customers buying and the DIY retailer restocking items. Therefore, a customer Web query would have to be dynamically generated. Server-side scripting languages would have to be developed for this purpose. Again, a scripting language such as JavaScript could be used for this purpose. This could be implemented using a client-side or server-side script. Server-side scripting requires knowledge of the **Common Gateway Interface (CGI)**, which is covered in the next section.

Server-side technologies

Several server-side technologies are now becoming common on the Web. A few years ago, the Common Gateway Interface (CGI) was the only viable solution. However, in recent years, other technologies, such as Active Server Pages (ASP), Java Servlets (JSP) and PHP are beginning to make an impact and provide alternatives to CGI. However, CGI is still by far the most common, so we shall discuss it first.

Common Gateway Interface (CGI)

The **Common Gateway Interface (CGI)** is a standard protocol via which applications interact with Web servers. The CGI provides a relatively straightforward way for 'clients' – that is, browsers – to interact indirectly with applications such as databases, spreadsheets and so on. In order to do this, a script is required, enabling it to interact with the required application – called a **CGI script**. Such server-side scripts are often written in a language called **Perl**, as well as other languages, such as **C** or C++. CGI scripts are the traditional method for performing a wide variety of functions ranging from image map processing to server-side games and form processing.

Web server implementations of CGI act as a gateway between the user request and the data that it requires. It does this by first creating a new process in which the program will be run (see Figure 7.13). The program will then load the required program and any required runtime environments and environmental variables to support the running of the application. Finally, it will pass in a request object and invoke the program. When the program is finished, the Web server will read the response from standard output.

Figure 7.13
Architecture of the Common Gateway Interface (CGI)

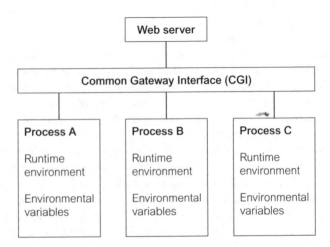

The big problem with CGI is that it takes one process at a time – each requiring its own runtime environment, variables and programs. Each process also requires its own allocation of memory. Thus, during periods of heavy traffic, CGI is vulnerable to potential crashes.

To overcome the deficiencies of CGI, alternative technologies have been developed, such as ASP, JSP and PHP.

The **Perl language** has established itself as the de facto standard for CGI programming, but it was originally intended for reporting purposes. Perl runs on several platforms, it is also relatively easy to modify and run.

NOTE

Active Server Pages (ASP)

This is a Web technology developed by Microsoft that combines XHTML, scripting and server-side components in one file called an **ASP**. ASP was first developed in the fall of 1996, and has now established itself as one of the leading server technologies. The main benefits of using ASP are that the web page is not created until required by the user and the page is not dependent on the browser that is used (see Figure 7.14).

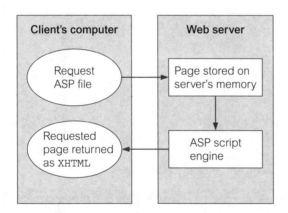

Figure 7.14
How ASP works

How ASP works

To understand how ASP works, consider what happens when a client types a URL into the browser.

The process begins when the browser requests an ASP page from the server. The server recognizes any file with an '.asp' extension and sends it to the ASP script engine (see Figure 7.14) for processing.

Next, the ASP engine generates an XHTML Web page at the specified place and time that page is accessed before sending it back to the client. Therefore, when the client views the source of an ASP file, it looks very similar to a standard XHTML file. ASP is an interpreter that executes specially marked lines of VBScript or other scripting languages embedded within XHTML.

Scripting languages used for ASP

An ASP can be written using JavaScript or VBScript. Via the scripting, the ASP can access server-side components. These components can be written in any language, as long as it presents a **COM Interface (Microsoft's component specification)**, although VBScript has become the de facto standard for ASP scripting.

An advantage of ASP is that everything is executed on the server. This helps to ensure that the pages are browser-independent, limited only by what the server can do. Some of the advantages and disadvantages of using a technology like ASP is displayed in Table 7.2.

The structure of ASP

ASP scripts are normally written in VBScript and contained within the <% and %> tags, and can, as with JavaScript, be mixed with XHTML. Thus, the following ASP script displays the time on the Web server.

```
<html>
<head>
<title> Welcome to ASP</title>
</head>
<body>
<h2>Welcome to ASP</h2>
The time now is: <%=Time %>
</body>
</html>
```

Table 7.2 The advantages and disadvantages of ASP

ASP advantages	ASP disadvantages
The ASP engine does not depend on a single language because the ASP engine does not execute the code you write	Technology confined to Microsoft servers, although ASP ports can be handled with plug-ins, etc.
ASP is browser-independent because it is executed on the Web server and generates pure HTML. Therefore, the client machine does not need to conform to any particular browser	ASP is an interpreted, not a compiled, language, so it is slower than compiled solutions

In order to publish ASP pages, you will need a Web server that supports ASP. The Microsoft IIS Web server is the obvious choice as it was specifically designed to run on Microsoft technology and is bundled with the IIS Web server. However, there are other Web servers that do support ASP. For more information, go to http://www.sum.com./software/chilisoft/index.html

Java Server Pages (JSP)

JSP is very much like ASP, in that JSP is a server-side technology that is embedded into the Web pages. With a Java-enabled server, a programmer can write so-called **servlets** that can produce dynamic Web content in the same way that ASP can.

JSP is a derivative of the Sun Java product, so it is a proprietary product.

PHP

Originally called Personal Home Page, PHP's name changed later to PHP Hypertext Preprocessor. **PHP**, like ASP and JSP, provides an alternative server-side technology to CGI.

PHP is an architecture-neutral, portable, server-side HTML scripting language. It is faster than Java, because it requires no virtual machine. Moreover, PHP has the advantage that it runs on many servers because it is non-proprietary. It runs on both Apache and Microsoft servers.

Using PHP is similar to using ASP. PHP pages are, like ASP, embedded into HTML pages using special tags. PHP code begins with <? and ends with ?> and is also not browser-dependent.

The advantages of PHP include that it:

■ is an open-source and non-proprietary language and available for free as a download

■ uses an easily learned syntax, based on the C language syntax

■ delivers broad database connectivity, including support for MySQL, Informix and Oracle.

Summary of the main languages used for client- and server-side programming

Table 7.3 summarizes the characteristics of the main client-side scripting languages that are in common use, while Table 7.4 summarizes the server-side technologies in common use.

Table 7.3 Summary of client-side scripting languages

Language	JavaScript	VBScript	Java
Uses	Client-side scripting	Client- and server-side	Client- and server-side
Compiled/Interpreted	Interpreted	Interpreted	Compiled into bytecode
Restrictions	Works with both main browsers	Works with IE only	Requires installation of JVM, so is quite slow. Different browsers support Java to differing degrees
Vendor	Netscape	Microsoft	Sun Microsystems Inc.
Uses	General purpose	General purpose	Mainly interactive Web pages

Table 7.4 Summary of server-side technologies

Technology	PHP	ASP	JSP	CGI
Uses	Server-side dynamic scripting	Mostly server-side scripting	Client- and server-side	Server-side, although PerlScript used for client-side work
Compiled/ interpreted	Interpreted	Interpreted	Compiled into bytecode	Compiled
Restrictions	Works with most servers	Works well with Microsoft servers, but has to be tweaked to work with others	Requires installation of JVM on client machine	Works with all servers
Vendor	Open source	Microsoft	Sun Microsystems	Non-proprietary
Main benefits	Good database connectivity. PHP is also open sourceand uses the familiar C systax	Good database connectivity with Microsoft Access	Java Servlets more efficient and easier to use than CGI	CGI is very portable and can be written in many languages

Summary

- Scripting languages can be server- or client-side.
- The two most commonly used client-side scripting languages are JavaScript and VBScript.
- JavaScript has established itself as the de facto standard for client-side scripting.

- JavaScript is case-sensitive – use lower case for JavaScript statements.

- JavaScript source files are contained within the `<script>...</script>` tags.

- You can specify which language is being used by means of the `language` attribute in the `<script>` tag.

- XHTML documents can contain inline – or embedded – JavaScript code or JavaScript source files.

- It is more common for scripts to be written in the `<head>` section of a program by using functions. A function is a self-contained block of JavaScript statements that will be executed when it is called from a JavaScript statement in a `<script>...</script>` block, in the `<body>` part of the document.

- To hide JavaScript code from non-compatible browsers, you can use the `comment` tags `<!--...-->`. JavaScript-compatible browsers will execute the code as normal, while non-compatible browsers will treat the comments as usual – that is, they will not display them in the browser.

- Java is a language that requires the installation of a Java Virtual Machine (JVM).

- Java applets – small Java programs – can be used for client-side or server-side processing tasks.

- Java applets can be incorporated into XHTML documents by using the `<applet> </applet>` container tags.

- There are several options for server-side programming, including CGI, ASP, PHP and JSP.

- CGI is still the most commonly used server-side technology and CGI scripts are normally written in the Perl language.

- ASP is a Microsoft-based technology that creates dynamic Web pages – normally using the VBScript language – converted to HTML format ready to be returned to the browser.

- ASP files use an '.asp' extension.

- PHP is a non-proprietary programming environment for creating dynamic Web pages, suitable for use on all servers. It combines well with the MySQL database application (see Chapter 13).

- PHP files use a '.php' extension.

Exercises

1   Explain the difference between a client-side and a server-side scripting language.

2   What are the conditions for which you would choose to use a client-side scripting language in preference to a server-side one?

3   What is the de facto standard language for client-side scripting?

4   Give two examples of JavaScript events.

5   Give two examples of Web page objects.

6   Write the JavaScript event handler code to display a message box containing the words 'Good day' for the `onMouseOver` event.

7   When would it be appropriate to use an inline JavaScript as opposed to a JavaScript source program?

8 Create an XHTML document as follows. Include in the document the title 'My first JavaScript task'. Create a JavaScript source file in the document that will output the line 'Hello World'.

9 State the main differences between CGI, ASP and PHP.

10 What are the benefits and problems associated with using Java for client-side processing tasks?

11 What is a Java applet? What XHTML tag is used to insert a Java applet into a Web page?

12 What tag would be used to insert an ActiveX control into a Web page?

13 PetHelp is a UK-based pet and animal welfare charity that is in the process of setting up a website for providing help with finding new homes for abandoned pets, as well as educational information regarding the welfare of animals. The charity also hopes to raise funds via its website. Describe three potential uses for client-side scripting and three potential uses for server-side scripting for this website.

14 What type of scripting is the VBScript language mostly used for?

Chapter

8

Cascading Style Sheets (CSS)

In this chapter you will learn:

- to understand the role of CSS
- to write style sheet rules and understand the ways in which they can be combined
- to be aware of the ways in which CSS can be applied to XHTML documents
- to understand the term **inheritance** and how the cascade works
- to understand how classes can be applied to groups of elements
- to apply CSS to other Web media, such as printing
- to be aware of browser limitations with regard to CSS
- CSS and JavaScript
- CSS tools
- an introduction to DHTML.

Introduction

Many believe that the appearance of a Web document – the colour, font, layout – are as important as the textual content of the document itself. However, as we have seen in earlier chapters, HTML was never designed to be used to control the appearance of a Web document. HTML was primarily designed to mark up the structural parts of documents, such as headings, lists, hypertext links and so on. In the very early days of the Web – when the Web community was small – appearance was not that important, but, as the Web rapidly expanded, the desire to produce professional-looking pages became very important.

HTML has evolved by adding a plethora of appearance elements, but no separation of layout from content, making it difficult to develop and maintain Web pages.

CSS has been recommended by the W3C to, among other things, enable the style and layout of the document to be specified separately. This separate document is called a **style sheet**. Thus, CSS will foster the use of a clean, structured markup code free of any tags associated with layout. That way, not only is there a better chance of all browsers displaying your document properly but also, if you want to change such things as the font of text displayed in a Web document, you could edit the style sheet, thus circumventing the need to meddle with the XHTML code.

The whole impetus behind the birth of XHTML is the desire not to use HTML for layout any more. Instead, use HTML tags to do things such as create a link, make a table or whatever, but leave the layout to CSS. As an example, let us suppose that you wanted to carry out repetitive formatting tasks, such as indenting the first line of each new paragraph using a set of Web pages. This could be done by designing a style sheet to be externally defined to apply to a number of Web pages. Alternatively, a style sheet could be applied to either a section or the whole of a single Web page. Style sheets – or Cascading Style Sheets(CSS) as they are more correctly known – are one of the most exciting features in the tool kit of the website developer. As with Web technologies, the W3C has been responsible for the evolution of CSS.

Another point to make about CSS is that browsers interpret HTML elements in such a way that the results cannot always be predicted. For example, a browser will always render an h1 heading larger than an h2 one, but the actual size will depend on the browser. CSS is a technology that gives the designer more precise control over how the text appears on the Web page. Moreover, CSS enables the separation of structure from presentation and simplifies the process of maintaining and modifying a document's layout.

CSS and the W3C

The W3C released the first recommendation for Cascading Style Sheets – Level 1 (CSS1) – in December 1996. This specification gave support to about 50 elements and went some way towards the goal of CSS to separate presentation from content.

An improved specification was released in May 1998, when the W3C adopted CSS2. CSS2 expands on the capabilities of CSS1 by giving precise support to content positioning. This is a big leap forward for the Web designer because not only can the Web designer now guarantee how the page will look in a browser, but, when CSS2 is combined with JavaScript, sophisticated animation becomes possible – known as Dynamic HTML. Moreover, CSS2 goes some way towards fulfilling the accessibility goals of the W3C that we talked about in Chapter 1 because it supports a variety of other media, such as Braille devices and audio media.

Browser support was a little slow but both of the main browsers – NN 7 and IE 6 – now support CSS2 extensively. Browser support for CSS is something that we will look at in more detail later in this chapter, but first, we look at how to use and edit style sheets.

Creating and editing style sheets

You can create and edit a style sheet in the same way that you would an XHTML document – that is, by using a text editor, such as WordPad, then typing the style sheet instructions directly into the document window. Alternatively – as we will see in Chapter 9 – some tools, such as Dreamweaver, use a built-in CSS template editor for creating style sheets.

CSS syntax

CSS code uses a different syntax to XHTML. A CSS consists of **rules**. A **rule** is simply a statement that defines the stylistic aspects of one or more elements. For example, suppose we wanted to create a rule that required all elements that were h1 – heading level 1 – to be colour red. This rule would be written in the following way using CSS:

```
h1 {color : red}
```

CSS rule syntax consists of two parts.

- The **selector part**, which is the part before the curly brace referring to the element(s) the required style is to be applied to. In the example given, h1 is the selector.
- The **declaration part**, which is the part within the curly brace that declares the style that is to be applied to the selector – in this case, making the heading red. The notation used for doing this consists of two parts separated by a colon. The part before the colon is called the **property**. The part after the colon is called the **value** because it refers to the value that the property is to take (in this case, red).

The expression `color : red` is called an **assignment** as the colour of the selected item is being assigned the colour red.

NOTE

As another example, the rule shown below will set the typeface for list item elements to which it is applied in a serif font.

```
li {font-family : serif}
```

Before we look at the scope for applying rules to elements, we need to be familiar with some techniques for combining selectors in more complicated rules.

Self-assessment exercise

Write a CSS rule that will assign the colour blue to level 3 headings.

Setting multiple properties in a single rule

It is possible to write style sheet rules so that they apply more than one style characteristic to an element. For example, we may want to set a heading level 1 – h1 – to both the colour red and a serif font. This could be written in two rules as:

```
h1 {color : red}
h1 {font-family : serif}
```

However, we can achieve the same effect faster by grouping both these declarations into a single semicolon-separated list, as follows:

```
h1 {color: red ; font-family: serif}:
```

Thus, to set multiple property values for an element in a rule, simply separate each assignment using semicolons.

In this example, the browser displays each occurrence of the `<h1>` tag using the colour red and a serif font. For all other properties, the browser uses the default values.

Grouping selectors together in a single rule

It is possible to write CSS rules that define a similar style for several tags. For example, we may want to make the paragraph, unordered list and level 1 headings all a 12-point font size. This could be written in three rules as:

```
p {font-size: 12pt}
ul {font-size: 12pt}
li {font-size: 12pt}
```

However, instead of writing these as three separate rules, we could write a single CSS rule by using the following syntax:

```
p, ul, li {font-size: 12pt}
```

In general, when you have a similar style to be applied to several tags, you can group the selectors together and define a single rule for them as a group by separating each selector in the list with a comma.

Defining parent–child relationships in rules

With XHTML style sheets, you can be very specific about when a style is to be applied to a tag. For example, you may want to define two styles for the `<li>` tag – one that's applied when it is a child of the `<ul>` tag and another when it is a child of the `<ol>` tag. We can do this by using **contextual selectors**.

Contextual selectors

Contextual selectors define the exact sequence of elements to which a style will be applied. In other words, you can specify that a style applies to a particular tag, such as `<li>`, only if it is a child of the `<ol>` tag, as follows:

```
ol li {list-style-type: decimal}
```

You can also specify that a particular style applies to the `<li>` tag only if it is a child of the `<ul>`tag, as follows:

```
ul li {list-style-type: square}
```

Note that the list of selectors here have not been separated with a comma. If they were, this would cause all the tags in the list to have the rule assigned to them.

Applying CSS to XHTML pages

Having studied the CSS syntax, the next question that arises is: how do we include style sheets in Web page documents? There are three ways to do this:

- by linking an external style sheet to your XHTML document
- by embedding a style sheet within an XHTML document
- by applying CSS-style rules to a section of a document.

In a strict XHTML document, you should only use linked external style sheets because they separate document content from presentation. Transitional XHTML documents, on the other hand, can use linked, embedded or inline styles. It is therefore recommended that you use only linked style sheets if you are conforming to strict XHTML.

Linking an external CSS style sheet to your XHTML document

The most common way in which CSS style sheets are used is to link one page or more in a website to an external style sheet. The external style sheet is a text file, just like an HTML file, but it must be given a .css extension instead of .html. The file itself will consist of a number of CSS rules, such as:

```
h1 {color: blue}
```

The rules can then be executed within an XHTML document by linking the required XHTML document to the style sheet (see Figure 8.1).

Figure 8.1
Attaching an external CSS style sheet to an XHTML document to execute the rules

To link an external CSS file to an XHTML document, you need to use the `<link>` tag within the `<head>` section of the target XHTML page. The `link` tag must be written in the following way:

```
<link rel = "stylesheet" href = "mystyle" type = "text/css">
```

The attribute `rel = "stylesheet"` tells the browser that the link is relative to a style sheet. This means that the style sheet file is assumed to be in the same directory as the source XHTML file. The attribute `href = "mystyle"` is the URL of the requested file. This file, as already stated, should have a .css extension. The attribute `type = "text/css"` tells the browser that the linked external file is a .text/.css file.

Example 8.1

Let us apply an external style sheet to the XHTML file that was written in Figure 6.3 of Chapter 6. You may recall that this was an example illustrating the use of a diagnostic table for growing spinach. Pages had also been written for diagnosing growing problems with onions and lettuce, so this would be a good time to apply an external style sheet, as uniform style rules can be applied to all of these documents.

We will apply the following style rules to these documents:

■ all h1 headings should be colour blue and in a sans serif font
■ all table headings should be colour red and in bold
■ all table data items should be centred in the data cell.

The style sheet containing these rules – shown in Figure 8.2 – will accomplish this. This file has been named "veg_tables.css". Note the first line in this file is a comment. Stylesheet comments are written in this manner.

Figure 8.2
The style sheet CSS file veg_tables.css

```
veg_tables - Notepad
File  Edit  Format  View  Help
/* An external stylesheet example css file written by Keith Darlington June 02 */

h1     { text-color: blue; font-family: sans-serif }

th     { color: red;
             font-weight: bold}

td     { text-align: center }
```

Figure 8.3
Effect of the external style sheet on the spinach_ex.html file

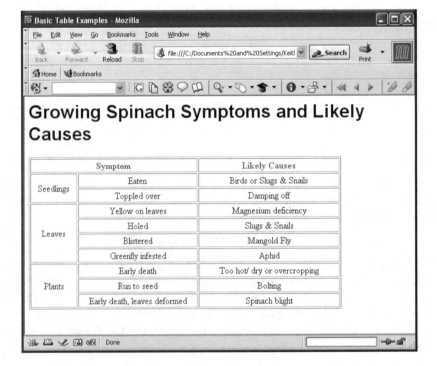

Basic Table Examples - Mozilla
File Edit View Go Bookmarks Tools Window Help
Back Forward Reload Stop   file:///C:/Documents%20and%20Settings/Keitl   Search Print
Home Bookmarks

Growing Spinach Symptoms and Likely Causes

	Symptom	Likely Causes
Seedlings	Eaten	Birds or Slugs & Snails
	Toppled over	Damping off
Leaves	Yellow on leaves	Magnesium deficiency
	Holed	Slugs & Snails
	Blistered	Mangold Fly
	Greenfly infested	Aphid
Plants	Early death	Too hot/ dry or overcropping
	Run to seed	Bolting
	Early death, leaves deformed	Spinach blight

Done

Having written the external style sheet file, we now only need to edit the vegetable table XHTML files that we called spinach_ex.html, onion_ex.html and lettuce_ex.html to include the following tag in the <head> section:

```
<link rel ="stylesheet" href = "veg_tables.css" type =
"text/css" / >
```

The effect of adding this line will be to set up the link to the external style sheet and, thus, alter the appearance of the Web page to include the effect of the style rules. See Listing 8.1, which displays a part of the spinach_ex.html file that includes the <link> tag.

Figure 8.3 shows the effect of the style sheet on the spinach_ex.html file.

This example exemplifies the power of CSS in that, if a change needs to be made to the appearance of all the vegetable pages, then you only need to make the change in the external style sheet. This can save a great deal of time, especially when dealing with large websites.

Listing 8.1 Amended spinach_ex.html file

```
spinach_ex - Notepad
File  Edit  Format  View  Help
<head>
<title>Basic Table Examples</title>
<link rel ="stylesheet" href = "veg_tables.css" type = "text/css" / >
</head>
<body>
<h1> Growing Spinach Symptoms and Likely Causes </h1>
<table border="2" width="558">
  <tr>
    <th colspan ="2" width="354">Symptom</th>
    <th width="247">Likely Causes</th>
  </tr>

  <tr>
    <td rowspan ="2">Seedlings</td>
    <td>Eaten </td>
    <td>Birds or Slugs & Snails</td>
  </tr>

  <tr>
    <td>Toppled over</td>
    <td>Damping off</td>
  </tr>

  <tr>
    <td rowspan ="4" >Leaves</td>
    <td>Yellow on Leaves</td>
    <td>Magnesium deficiency</td>
  </tr>

  <tr>
    <td>Holed</td>
    <td>Slugs & Snails</td>
  </tr>

  <tr>
    <td>Blistered</td>
    <td>Mangold Fly</td>
```

Embedding a style sheet within an XHTML document

You do not have to store your style sheet rules in a separate file, you can embed them within an XHTML file. This means that the style rules within an embedded style sheet only affect the XHTML within that file. Thus, you can't embed a style sheet in an XHTML file and expect to use that across multiple XHTML files without copying the style sheet rules into each file.

To embed a CSS style sheet into an XHTML file, simply enclose the style rules within the `<style>` ... `</style>` tags within the `<head>` section. The following example shows how CSS rules can be embedded within an XHTML document:

```
<head>
<style type = "text/css">
h1 {color : blue}
p{font-size : 10pt}
li {text-color : red}
</style>
</head>
```

In the above example, the style attribute `type = "text/css"` is optional, but, nevertheless, should be included because it specifies the MIME type. This means that it identifies the style sheet language so that browsers not supporting style sheets or the specified language won't display the contents of the `<style>` container. For CSS, it is set it to `"text/css"`.

Listing 8.2 A template for embedding a style sheet in an XHTML file

```
<?xml version = "1.0"?>
<!DOCTYPE html PUBLIC "-//WC3//DTD XHTML 1.0 Transitional //EN"
"http://www.w3.org/TR/xhtml11/DTD/xhtml11-transitional.dtd">
<html xmlns = "http://www.w3.org/1999/xhtml">


<head>
<style type ="text/css">
 Style definitions go here
</style>
</head>


<body>
...
</body>
</html>
```

The rules that follow the `<style>` tag just state that all `h1` headers will be coloured blue and all paragraphs will be in a 10-point font size (the default font is assumed).

Hence, a template for a `<style>` container to embed a style sheet in your XHTML file will look something like that shown in Listing 8.2.

For example, if the style rules are:

```
h1 {color : blue}
p{font-size : 10pt}
li {text-color : red}
```

and these have been applied to the `list_exam.html` file that was described in Chapter 5 – you may recall that it illustrated the use of XHTML list elements – the complete listing, including the embedded rules, is as shown in Listing 8.3.

Listing 8.3 Embedded CSS rules

```
list_exam_stylesheet - Notepad
File  Edit  Format  View  Help

<!-- Example using lists with embeded style sheetDate Feb 2002   -->

<html>
    <head>
        <title>List Processing Example using nested unordered lists</ti
        <style type = "text/css">
        h1 {color: blue}
        li {color:red}
        </style>

    </head>

    <body>

        <h1>My favourite Rock Groups and tracks:</h1>
        <ul>
            <li>REM</li>
            <li>U2
                <ul>
                    <li>It's a beautiful day</li>
                    <li>One love</li>
                    <li>The sweetest thing</li>
                </ul>
            </li>
            <li>Rush</li>
            <li>Phil Collins</li>
            <li>Manic Street Preachers</li>
        </ul>

    </body>
</html>
```

The effect of the style sheet is to produce the output shown in Figure 8.4.

Defining styles inline

Inline styles are ones that you can apply to a specific portion of a Web document. You can, for example, use inline styles to quickly change the appearance of a single XHTML tag. You can also use them to give precedence to a style for a particular tag (more on precedence rules later in this chapter). For example, if you've defined an embedded style sheet that sets the colour of the `<h1>` tag to blue, you can set the colour of a specific element, using the `<h1>` tag, to red.

Figure 8.4
Output in IE 6
showing the
effects of the
embedded style
sheet

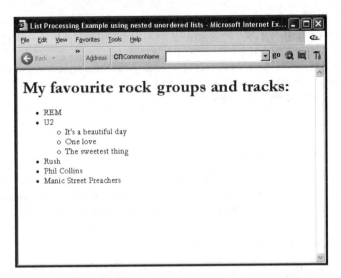

With inline styles, you define a tag's style within the tag itself. You can do this by using the `style` attribute, which is supported by all `body` tags. To define an inline style, add the `style` attribute to the tag you want to change the style of and set its value to the string representing the style definition, like this:

```
<h1 style="color : blue">
```

NOTE

Inline style sheets are not recommended by the W3C because they assimilate style with content. However, inline style sheets can be very useful sometimes for overriding inherited styles in external or embedded style sheets (some examples of this are given later in this chapter).

Using `<div>` and `<span>` when applying style to a section of a document

You can use inline styles with the `<div>` tag to set the style for an entire block of XHTML within your document. This works because of the concept of **inheritance**, which you will learn about later in this section. For example, if you want to change the text colour of an entire block of tags to blue, you can put those tags in the `<div>` container and define a style for the `<div>` tag that sets the text colour to blue. It looks like this:

```
<div style="color : blue">
  <h1>This is a heading</h1>
    <p>This is a paragraph. It will look blue in the user's
browser</p>
  ...
  </div>
```

Using `<div>...</div>` provides a means of applying styles to whole sections of a document. You can also use `<span>...</span>` instead of a `<div>  </div>`

Listing 8.4 Code for applying different styles using inline style

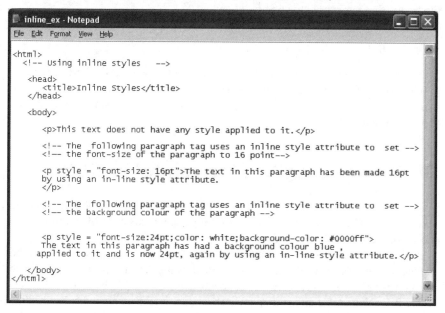

```
inline_ex - Notepad
File  Edit  Format  View  Help

<html>
  <!-- Using inline styles    -->

  <head>
     <title>Inline Styles</title>
  </head>

  <body>

     <p>This text does not have any style applied to it.</p>

     <!-- The  following paragraph tag uses an inline style attribute to  set -->
     <!-- the font-size of the paragraph to 16 point-->

     <p style = "font-size: 16pt">The text in this paragraph has been made 16pt
     by using an in-line style attribute.
     </p>

     <!-- The  following paragraph tag uses an inline style attribute to  set -->
     <!-- the background colour of the paragraph -->


     <p style = "font-size:24pt;color: white;background-color: #0000ff">
     The text in this paragraph has had a background colour blue ,
     applied to it and is now 24pt, again by using an in-line style attribute.</p>

  </body>
</html>
```

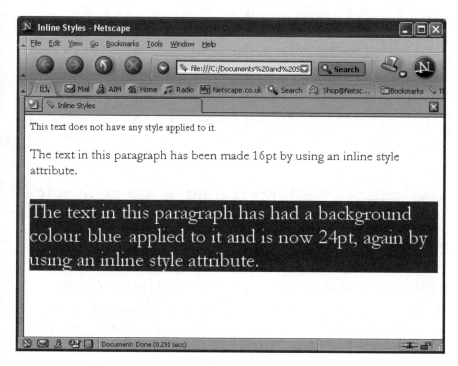

Figure 8.5
Screenshot in
Netscape 7 of
output of inline
style of Listing 8.4

container, but `div` should only be used when a style is to be applied to a section or block. A `span` tag is used to contain inline text.

Example 8.2

This example shows how inline styles could be used with CSS. Different paragraphs have different styles that are applied by the `style` attribute. The XHTML file name is `inline_ex.html` (see Listing. 8.4) and the output, using Netscape 7, is shown in Figure 8.5.

Understanding the 'cascade' in CSS

Many people wonder why the word 'cascading' is included in the term Cascading Style Sheets! The term actually refers to the possible existence of multiple style sheets for a given Web XHTML document.

   In the previous sections, we have seen the various ways in which CSS can be applied to your Web page documents – external, embedded and inline. You can use any combination of these methods to control how your Web page looks (see Figure 8.6). Notice that an external style sheet, along with an embedded and inline sheet, can be applied to an XHTML document. The question then arises – what rules of precedence will the browser apply to executing the style sheets? We will look into this in the next sections.

Figure 8.6
Precedence for
conflicting styles

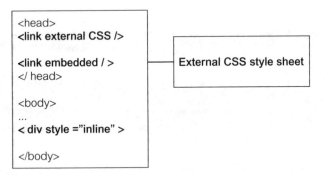

The browser's interpretation of the style rules

The browser follows a certain set of rules to determine the precedence of styles – their cascading order. The rules are:

1 **inline** styles always take precedence over **embedded** style sheets

2 **embedded** style sheets always take precedence over **linked** style sheets.

What this means is that the most specific level is always given priority. That is, when properties conflict, the browser chooses the property from the most specific style. External styles are not as specific as internal styles as they are in a separate file. For example, if an external style sheet were to set all paragraph fonts to Times and an inline style tag in the target Web page were to set an individual paragraph font to Impact, then the Impact font would win the conflict and be displayed in the browser because the inline tag is more specifically applied.

Sources of style sheets

There are three sources of control of style sheets.

1 **Web developer style sheets** These are what we have been looking at already in this chapter – external, embedded and inline style sheets.

2 **Browser default style sheets** Any browser must have its own inbuilt style sheet that defines how each element is going to be displayed. Otherwise, in the absence of Web developer style sheets, everything – including paragraphs, lists, bold text and so on – would look the same. The browser style sheet will assign **default styles** in the absence of anything given by the developer.

3 **User style sheets** The user can, if required, assign style preferences while viewing Web pages. For example, a user could change the text font for viewing Web pages to Blackadder ITC in IE 6. This could be done by choosing `Menu/Internet Options/General` and then pressing the `Fonts...` button to select from the display shown in Figure 8.7.

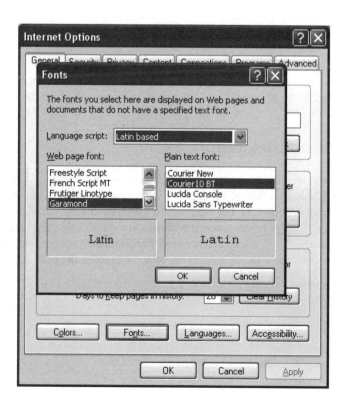

Figure 8.7
User setting style sheet via browser controls

Precedence for style sheet sources

Given that style sheets can arise from various sources, then the question arises, what are the precedence rules for conflicting style sheet sources? The answer, with some exceptions, is as follows:

- the author's style sheet overrides the user's style sheet
- the user's style sheet overrides the browser's default values.

The above rules are intuitive – one would expect the user to have more power than the browser in choosing their own preference. After all, a user who, for example, suffers from visual impairment will be the best judge of what colour combinations suit their needs. On the other hand, you could say that the author's expert choice should succeed over that of the Web page user. After all, the website designer will surely know what combinations of colours, text, layout and so on will make the site look its best.

Using the keyword 'important'

You can override the usual order of precedence for a rule by using the keyword 'important'. In the following example, the assignment of 'red' to the property colour and the assignment of sans serif to the property font family are marked as 'important':

```
h1 {color: red ! important font-weight: bold font-family:
sans serif ! important}
```

Because both these attributes are marked as important, the browser will not override these styles. If, however, two competing style sheets mark the same property as important but the styles are different, the rules in the previous sections apply.

Understanding inheritance

Inheritance is another important issue to consider when designing CSS. To understand how inheritance works, remember that XHTML document tags inherit certain properties from their parents. For example, all the tags within the <body> tag, such as the <p> and <ul> tags, inherit certain properties from the <body> tag, such as the text colour. Similarly, the <li> tag inherits properties from the <ul> tag that contains it.

Now, consider the following fragment of an XHTML document:

```
<style type ="text/css">
p {color : blue}
</style>
<body>
<p>Hello. This is a paragraph of text. <em>This text is
emphasized</em> </p>
</body>
```

We can see that this style sheet listing sets the colour for the <p> tag in the body to blue. There is no definition for the <em> tag and, therefore, you might expect the text in the <em> tag to change back to the default colour – black. However, that would not happen because the <em> is within the container tag <p> (try this on your computer and you should get the result shown in Figure 8.8 but will be able to see that it is still colour blue). The <em> tag is called the **child** of the **parent** <p> tag, and the <em> tag inherits the colour property from the <p> tag. The <em> tag is said to **inherit** the properties of the <p> tag.

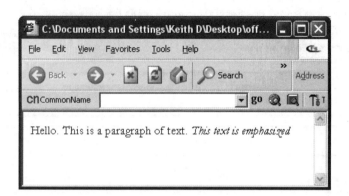

Figure 8.8
Inheritance at work in the <p> tag

Working with classes in style sheets

For more style flexibility, the selector of a style rule can have multiple style declarations, called **classes**.

Let us take an example to illustrate how these work. Say we wanted to add a number of Web pages to our vegetable website, containing individual pages of growing information for each vegetable, such as tomatoes, spinach, lettuce and so on. Suppose that, for each vegetable page, we wanted to display consistent sections, as shown in the fragment given in Figure 8.9.

In the text shown in Figure 8.9, it is required that the division beginning with the heading 'In the Kitchen' has a blue background and that the 'tip' division is displayed using blue text, surrounded by a thick border. The division showing the growing season is displayed with red text and, again, surrounded by a thick border. Finally, the division at the bottom of the page is a copyright division that uses smaller text, displayed in the colour purple.

If we wanted to create several such pages that would consistently use these categories by referencing CSS styles, the task would be made easier if we were to identify these categories as selectors, referred to by category names. We can do this by creating **class names** for each of these style variations. A **class** defines a style variation that you refer to in a specific occurrence of a tag using the class attribute.

Creating a class is very much like defining a style, the only difference being that you must add an arbitrary class name to the end of the tag, separating it with a full stop. For example, you can define three variations of the h1 style, and then refer to

Figure 8.9
Categories of style
applied to
different divisions
in each vegetable
page

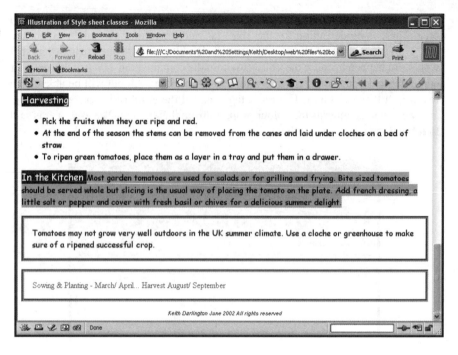

each one in the appropriate context, thus:

```
h1.blue {color : blue}
h1.black {color : black}
h1.red {color : red}
```

Then, when adding the `<h1>` tag to your XHTML document, you can set the `class` attribute to indicate exactly which style you're using:

```
<h1 class = "black">Red Heading</h1>
```

If we look at Figure 8.9, we can see the effects of style rules using classes that have been created for a number of categories, including the gardening tip. The class style rule for the tip sets the text colour to blue, and sets a border around the text that can be applied to any part of the body of a document and would be written as:

```
.tip { color : blue; margin-bottom : 1em; border-style :
groove; border-width : thick; padding : 1em; text}
```

To reference this class in an XHTML document, we would write the tag syntax in the following way, treating this class as an attribute:

```
<p class = tip> Tomatoes may not grow very well outdoors in
the UK summer climate. Use a cloche or greenhouse to make
sure of a ripened successful crop. </p>
```

A class has been created for each of the categories `season`, `copyright` and `kitchen`. The style sheet rules that have been applied to Figure 8.9 are shown in Listing 8.5 as an embedded style sheet.

Listing 8.5 Class style rules for page shown in Figure 8.9

```
f89 - Notepad

File Edit Format View Help

<!-- Using style sheet classes    -->

<html xmlns = "http://www.w3.org/1999/xhtml">
<html>

<head>

<style>
body {font-family: comic sans ms}
h1 {text-align:center;color:purple; font-family: Blackadder ITC; text-decoration: underline}
.tip {color:blue; margin-bottom: 1em;  border-style: groove; border-width: thick;
  padding: 1em; text}

.season {color: red; margin-bottom: 1em;  border-style: groove; border-width: thick;
  padding: 1em; font-family:trebuchet}

span.category {font-size: 1.2em; background: #990000; color: #FFFFFF}

span.kitchen {background-color:lightblue}

div.intro {background-color:pink; font-size:1.1em;margin-right:35em}

div.copyright {text-align: center;color:purple; font: italic 8pt arial, helvetica, serif}
</style>

</head>

<body>
```

The next rule can be applied to any `body` tag. Omitting a tag name before the dot means that it can be applied to anything, not just a `<div>` tag, as in the previous example.

```
.tip {color : blue; margin-bottom : 1em; border-style :
groove; border-width : thick; padding : 1em}
```

The above style rule contains several attribute values apart from the text colour blue. We have a border position, border style, border width and **padding**, which is the amount of space to leave between the text and border (see note below).

Using classes should make website maintenance a great deal easier, for, if the developer is writing content that uses class names, the code is likely to become more readable and, thus, more maintainable.

A complete study of CSS is beyond the scope of this book. However, a full CSS style reference is included in Appendix 1.

NOTE

ID class selectors

Class selectors give us the power to apply a style to every occurrence of an element. Sometimes, you may need to specify style rules for individual elements.

When this is the case, you can assign an ID attribute for setting such style rules. A style rule containing an ID selector begins with a #. A simple example is:

```
# underline    {text-decoration : underline}
```

If this is within the XHTML, the element with the underline ID, as shown below, will be displayed as underlined text. However, because it is an ID selector, it can only be shown once per page.

```
<p id="underline"> This text will appear as underlined.
</p>
```

NOTE

With regard to inheritance, the ID selector has a higher priority than the class selector.

Pseudo class selectors

So far, we have examined a range of selectors that can be applied to the structure of the XHTML document. These include type selectors that apply to XHTML elements, such as h1 headings, and attribute selectors, such as class or ID selectors – div.intro or #underline being examples.

None of these selectors, however, provides a technique for indicating the different colours for the status of a link. This is because the status of the link is determined by the browser. Hyperlinks defined with the anchor tag can have four different states – selected, visited, unvisited and hover.

Pseudo classes are known as **external type selectors** and were created to extend the capabilities of CSS to deal with selectors of the anchor tag colour states type. Pseudo classes are not attribute selectors as class and ID are – after all, an anchor tag hyperlink state colour is not a class. At the present time, only the anchor tag has external style capabilities, although others may be added in later versions of CSS.

You can create styles like that shown in Listing 8.6 (a style sheet file called pseudo.css) so that a browser can display each link state with a different colour and set other properties, such as text decoration. Note that a colon is used to separate the XHTML selector from its pseudo class.

Listing 8.6 Pseudo class style sheet

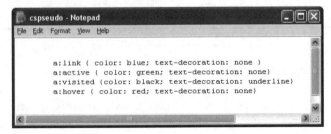

Notice, too, from Listing 8.6 that when this style sheet is applied, as shown in Figure 8.10, the `a: hover {color: red; text-decoration: none}` rule means that the text link 'My favourite search engines' will not be underlined when the mouse hovers over the link. On the other hand, the `a:visited {color: black; text-decoration: underline}` rule is going to cause the text link 'My favourite search engines' to be underlined when the link has been visited (see the output of this in Figure 8.11), because the text decoration property for this link has been set to underline.

Figure 8.10
The effect of the hover style sheet rule

Figure 8.11
The effect of the visited style sheet rule after visiting

Units of style sheet measurements

We saw earlier in this chapter that the `font-size` property can be specified by using em units. The em unit is a relative printing measurement. For any given font or size, an em is equal to the width of the capital letter 'M'. The size of the em is equivalent to the font size of that element. This means that if the default font size is 10-point, then stating a text size of 3 em would result in a 30-point text size – that is, 3 times the default text size. This means that the style rule given below will set all h1 headings to three times the default text size:

```
h1 {font-size:3 em}
```

Other units for specifying font size and other properties can be used, along with the abbreviations shown in Table 8.1.

Table 8.1 Units of measurement for CSS

Unit	Abbreviation	Comments
Pixel	px	A relative unit depending on the size of the monitor
Point	pt	An absolute unit – 72 points = 1 inch
Pica	pc	Another absolute unit – 12 points = 1 inch
Centimetre	cm	An absolute metric unit
Millimetre	mm	Another absolute metric unit
Inch	in	Another absolute unit of measurement
Em	em	A relative unit, varying according to the width of a capital letter M in the current font in that font size
Percentage	%	Relative to the base font size

CSS supports a wide range of both absolute and relative units and percentages. Absolute units are of fixed size and so can use measurements such as millimetres or points. Relative units can vary in proportion to the user's display size, such as pixels or ems. Refer to the table to get a full understanding of the meanings of the alternative units.

Categories of style properties

Style properties can be applied to any of the following categories of elements.

- *Font properties* Examples here would be the font family giving control over the font name or font size. For example, body {font-family: impact} would result in the text in the body of the document being displayed in Impact.
- *Text properties* Examples of text properties would be text alignment – right justify, centre, and so on – or letter spacing.
  For example, h1 {text-align: center} would result in all h1 headings being centred.
- *Background properties* Examples are the specification of the colour and background for images.
- *Printed style sheet properties* These add features to precisely control the placement of elements in the display. Examples are given later.
- *Classification properties* Examples would be properties that specify the display characteristics of lists and other elements at inline or block level.

- *Box properties* These specify characteristics for sections of text, at the paragraph level.
- *Positioning properties* These control the placement of elements in the display.

Positioning properties and CSS2

As stated earlier in this chapter, **content positioning** is one of the main features of CSS2. It provides a big leap forward for the Web designer because it is possible now to guarantee how the page will appear in a browser. Moreover, when CSS2 is combined with JavaScript, sophisticated animation becomes feasible as we will see later in this chapter.

In this section, we will look at some examples of content positioning. We begin by demonstrating how CSS can be used to create useful text effects that, hitherto, would only have been possible by creating graphic versions using tools such as Photoshop. As we will see, CSS renders all of this unnecessary.

Example 8.3

Suppose we wanted to create a logo as shown in Figure 8.12. The logo is coloured green and has a shadow that is coloured yellow. If we look at the style sheet to define the rules for this text (see Listing 8.7), we can see that the rule with the ID class selector called `logotext` – `#logotext {position: absolute; z-index: 2; left: 1px; top:31px; color: #008080; }` – is to be positioned exactly 1 pixel from the left of the window and 31 pixels from the top of the window and coloured green (#008080). Note that the `z-index` property is set to 2, which makes it appear closer to the viewer.

Figure 8.12
Example of content positioning using CSS to specify text effects

The second rule sets the ID class selector to name `logoshadow` – `#logoshadow {position: absolute; z-index: 1; left: 5px; top:35px; color: #FFFF00; }` – and the element specified by this rule will be positioned 5 pixels from the left of the window and 35 pixels from the top of it. The `z-index` property is set to 1, which means that it has a lower visibility compared to that set in the previous rule – it is set behind the green rule. The colour rendered to the element by this rule is set to yellow (#FFFFOO).

If we now look at Listing 8.8, we can see that the `<div>` tag contains a reference to the attribute called `logoarea`. The `<div>` contains two `<span>` tags that contain the text to be styled. These tags will, therefore, inherit all the properties from the `logoarea` rule. The first `<span>` references the ID class selector called `logotext`. The second `<span>` references the ID class selector called `logoshadow`. As they are ID selectors, they can be displayed only once on a Web page. This is very likely to be the case when it comes to rendering objects such as this one.

Listing 8.7 The Content positioning CSS file specifying the appearance of the logo

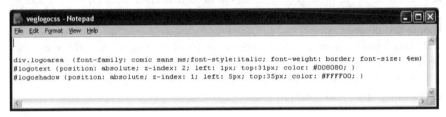

```
div.logoarea  (font-family: comic sans ms;font-style:italic; font-weight: border; font-size: 4em)
#logotext (position: absolute; z-index: 2; left: 1px; top:31px; color: #008080; )
#logoshadow (position: absolute; z-index: 1; left: 5px; top:35px; color: #FFFF00; )
```

Listing 8.8 The content positioning CSS file specifying the location of the logo on the Web page

```html
<html>
<head>
<title> Using Positioning Properties in CSS </title>
<link rel="stylesheet" type="text/css"
href="veglogocss.css" />
</head>

<body>
<div class ="logoarea">
<span id = "logotext"> Vegetable Expert </span>
<span id = "logoshadow"> Vegetable Expert </span>
</div>
</body>
</html>
```

Case study: Using CSS with the vegetable website

Before closing this section on CSS, let us see how CSS classes can be applied to the vegetable website that we discussed earlier.

The classes section in this chapter briefly looked at how several Web pages could be constructed with the use of CSS and classes. The screenshots in Figures 8.13 and 8.14 display sections of the vegetable growing description page for tomatoes and Figure 8.15 displays a fragment of the spinach vegetable growing description. All of these pages are linked to the external style sheet shown in Listing 8.9. Figure 8.16 displays the same fragment using the Netscape browser.

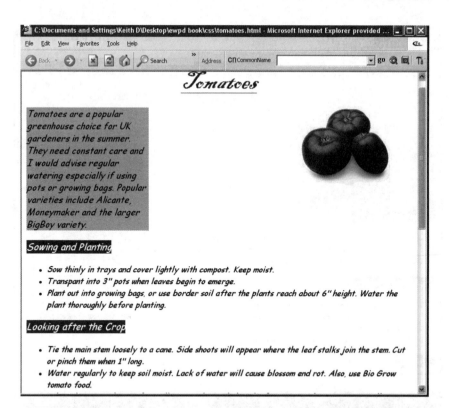

Figure 8.13
Fragment of the top part of the tomatoes page on the vegetable website

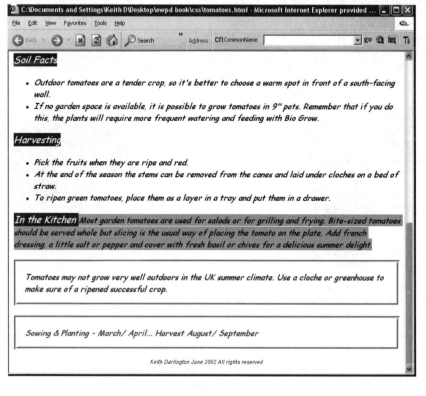

Figure 8.14
Fragment of lower part of the tomatoes page

Figure 8.15
Fragment of top
part of the
spinach page on
an IE 6 browser

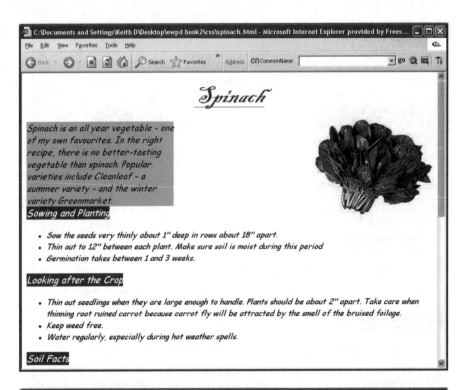

Figure 8.16
Output of the
spinach page on
a Netscape 7
browser

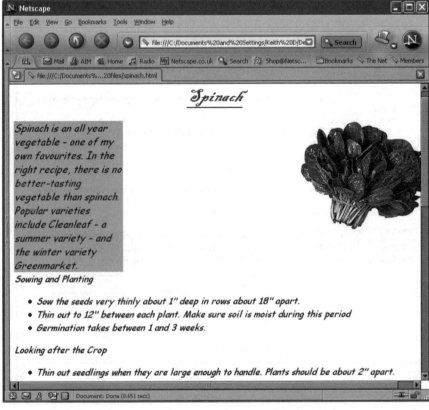

Notice that this style sheet contains many style definitions with classes. The border styles, for example, are rendered on Figure 8.14 because that part of the screenshot is visible. The effects of the other styles are visible on the other fragments where we see the top parts of the pages.

Listing 8.9 External style sheet for the vegetable website

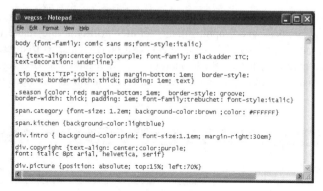

Browser support for CSS

Netscape 7 and IE 6 both provide extensive support for virtually all style sheet features. However, there may be differences in the way in which they display pages. Notice, for example, the way that the spinach.html Web page is displayed in each of these browsers (see Figures 8.15 and 8.16).

Netscape 6 and IE 5 provide support for most style sheet features, apart from perhaps printer layout and non-standard word spacing. IE 3 and 4 and Netscape 4 support some aspects of CSS, including font formatting, colour, margins, borders and positioning. Netscape 4 interprets some style features differently to IE, such as margins and borders.

As Table 8.2 shows, virtually all browsers now give some CSS support, with even the WebTV browser supporting some features! The table also summarizes the older browsers' support for CSS.

Table 8.2 Browsers' support for CSS

Browsers	CSS support
Microsoft IE 3	Limited CSS1
Netscape 4, IE 4, Opera 4	CSS1
Above Netscape 6, IE 5, Mozilla 1.3 and Opera 5	CSS2

Using CSS for other media

CSS allows Web authors the scope to create media-specific styles for a single document. For example, printer-specific styles could be created or styles that could be applied to handheld or Braille media. In the next section we focus on how to create style sheets for printouts.

Creating style sheets for printouts

Printer-specific style sheets are very popular because navigation bars, advertising banners and unnecessary graphic images clutter printouts and make them much harder to read. Printer-specific style sheets can be designed to free pages of such clutter. For example, Figure 8.18 displays a CSS printer-friendly version of the Web page displayed in Figure 8.17. Notice that all the clutter has been removed!

Figure 8.17
A typical Web
page with clutter

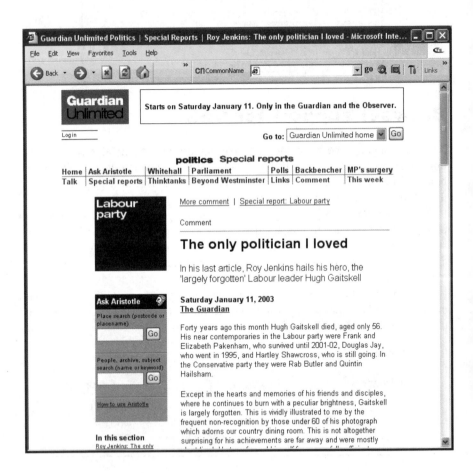

Some website designers create printer-specific pages by writing separate 'printer-friendly versions' of the same page, but this can be very time-consuming. Creating a CSS printer-specific style sheet offers an alternative way for authors to create style sheets that are medium-specific.

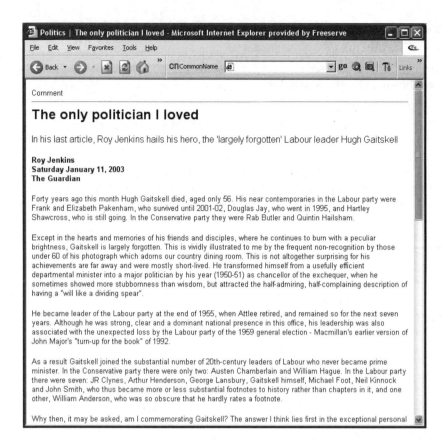

Figure 8.18
The printer-
friendly version of
the same Web
page –
decluttered

To do this, two style sheet rules must be created: one appropriate to screen display, the other appropriate to print. To associate a style sheet with a particular XHTML page, you then need to use the `media` attribute. This makes it possible to style a single page for screen or print output or both. The next section illustrates how this is done.

Using the `link` element with the `media` attribute

To style a single page for both screen and print media, we can add the `media` attribute to the `link` element:

```
<link rel="stylesheet" type"text/css" href="print.css"
media="print">

<link rel="stylesheet" type"text/css" href="screen.css"
media="screen">
```

In the first line, we see that the `media` attribute has been assigned the value `"print"`. This means that this style will be used when the document is to be printed. These styles will have no effect on the display of the document when viewed using a monitor, audio browser or any other non-printing device.

Example of restyling for print

We will use the tomatoes.html, described earlier in this chapter, to create a printer-friendly CSS version (see Figure 8.13). You may recall that this file was linked to the following vegcss.css stylesheet:

```
/* screen display styles */
body {font-family: comic sans ms;font-style:italic}
h1 {text-align:center;color:purple; font-family: Blackadder
ITC; text-decoration: underline}
.tip {text:"TIP";color: blue; margin-bottom: 1em;  border-
style: groove; border-width: thick; padding: 1em; text}
.season {color: red; margin-bottom: 1em;  border-style:
groove;
border-width: thick; padding: 1em;
font-family:trebuchet:
font-style:italic}
span.category {font-size: 1.2em; background-color:brown
;color: #FFFFFF}
span.kitchen {background-color:lightblue}
div.intro { background-color:pink; font-size:1.1em; margin-
right:30em}
div.copyright {text-align: center;color:purple; font:
italic 8pt arial, helvetica, serif}
div.picture {position: absolute; top:15%; left:70%}
```

Creating the printer-friendly version

To do this, we will choose a simple, conventional print style with all the text in black against a white background, without the picture of the tomatoes (see Figure 8.19). This means that the original style sheet rule in the vegcss.css file:

```
div.picture {position: absolute; top:15%; left:70%}
```

would be rewritten as:

```
div.picture {display: none} /* i.e. remove picture for print
```

Similarly, the `tip` and `season` class rules need to be rewritten so that the borders are removed and other similar adjustments made to the other class rules. Notice that the `h1` element has been retained, the copyright class remains centre aligned and both the intro class font size and category class are kept at 1.2 em. The completed style sheet is called vegprintcss.css and written as follows:

```
/* printing style rules for vegcss style sheet */
body {font-family: times;font-style: normal}
body {font-family: times;font-style: normal}
h1 {text-align:center; text-decoration: underline}
span.category {font-size: 1.2em; text-decoration:
underline}
```

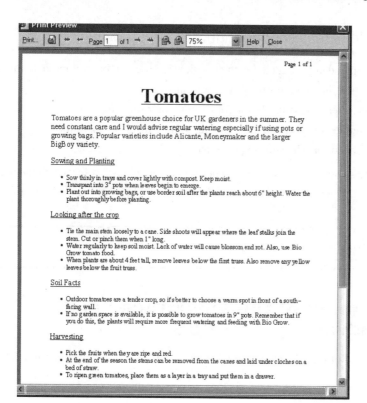

Figure 8.19
Printer-friendly
version of the
tomatoes.html file

```
div.intro {font-size: 1.2em}
div.copyright {text-align: center;font: italic 8pt arial,
helvetica, serif}
div.picture {display:none}
```

Now, to the <head> section of the tomatoes.html document, we must add the following link elements:

```
<link rel="stylesheet" type"text/css"
     href="vegcss.css" media="screen">
<link rel="stylesheet" type"text/css"
     href="vegprintcss.css" media="print">
```

The effect of these changes is that we get the plain and simple document shown in Figure 8.19 when printed.

Of course, the simple examples provided here are just a beginning. There is almost no limit to what can be done with alternative media style sheets. Pages that can be styled for regular screen output, printing, legible display on handheld devices and special styles for the blind are just some of the many possibilities. There are currently ten defined media types:

- *all* suitable for all devices
- *aural* intended for speech synthesizers
- *Braille* intended for Braille tactile feedback devices

- *embossed* intended for paged Braille printers
- *handheld* intended for hand-held devices
- *print* intended for paged documents viewed onscreen in print preview mode
- *projection* intended for projected presentations
- *screen* intended primarily for colour computer screens
- *tty* intended for portable devices with limited display capabilities
- *ty* intended for television-type devices.

The names chosen for CSS media types reflect target devices for which the relevant properties make sense. See www.w3.org/TR/REC-CSS2/media.html for more information on media types.

NOTE   Media type names are case-insensitive.

Summary of the advantages and disadvantages of CSS

A summary of the advantages and disadvantages of CSS is given in Table 8.3.

Table 8.3 Summary of the advantages and disadvantages of CSS

Advantages of CSS	Disadvantages of CSS
Smaller, faster pages can be produced because, as we have already seen, style sheets can contain the layout code in a separate, externally linked file	Lack of early browser support, although all the latest browsers support CSS
More production control – changes in layout characteristics throughout all the pages on the site can be implemented by changing the external style sheet document	Additional learning curve required for the website developer
The website developer has more design control, as with traditional print typesetting, from control of text fonts, text layout, positioning, to use of colours and much more. This clearly leads to greater consistency and fewer layout mistakes	Browser differences. Developer has to check to see how pages are rendered on a range of browsers as properties can be interpreted differently
Greater user control now available by giving choices such as printer-friendly document formats	
CSS can make Web pages more readable for those with disabilities, such as visually impaired users	

CSS checking

You can check the syntax and style of your CSS with a variety of tools available at various websites, such as at www.htmlhelp.com/tools/csscheck. You can normally check your CSS syntax by entering the site's URL or by directly inputting the style sheet (see Figure 8.20). In Figure 8.20, you will notice that a style sheet is being checked directly via the 'Direct input of style sheet' dialogue box. The user can click the 'Check it!' button when ready.

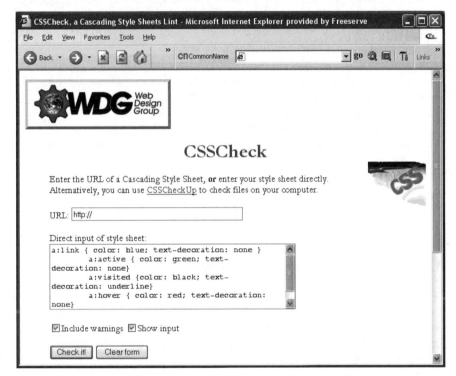

Figure 8.20
Checking the syntax of a CSS style sheet on a checking website

Combining CSS with JavaScript

JavaScript is compatible with CSS in the sense that it can be used to access and operate CSS properties. You need to be aware, though, of the differences in the ways that properties are written. In CSS, properties are always written in lower case and words are separated by hyphens, but when you use them in JavaScript, you will have to remove the hyphens and capitalize the first letter of every word in the property name, save the *first* word, which must stay in lower case. For example, the CSS property `font-size` would be written in a JavaScript reference as `fontSize`.

CSS and accessibility

As stated previously, the W3C has shown determination in expanding accessibility so that disabled users can have access to the Web. Its website includes a document entitled 'Web Content Accessibility Guidelines 2.0', issued as a working draft in July 2004. This includes help and advice for website designers covering everything, with guidelines, checklists, frequently asked questions, alternative browsers for accessibility and much more. The following is taken verbatim from the W3C's website:

Several CSS features make the Web more accessible to users with disabilities:

- *Properties to control font appearance allow authors to eliminate inaccessible bit-mapped text images.*
- *Positioning properties allow authors to eliminate markup tricks (e.g., invisible images) to force layout.*
- *The semantics of !important rules mean that users with particular presentation requirements can override the author's style sheets.*
- *The new 'inherit' value for all properties improves cascading generality and allows for easier and more consistent style tuning.*
- *Improved media support, including media groups and the Braille, embossed, and tty media types, will allow users and authors to tailor pages to those devices.*
- *Aural properties give control over voice and audio output.*
- *The attribute selectors, 'attr()' function, and 'content' property give access to alternate content.*
- *Counters and section/paragraph numbering can improve document navigability and save on indenting spacing (important for Braille devices). The 'word-spacing' and 'text-indent' properties also eliminate the need for extra white space in the document.*

Checking for accessibility

You can check the accessibility of your Web pages by using the Bobby site (see Figure 8.21). This free service allows you to test Web pages and help expose and repair obstacles to accessibility, encouraging compliance with existing accessibility guidelines from the W3C's recommendations. Visit: http://bobby.watchfire.com/bobby/html/en/index.jsp

NOTE The W3C site – at www.w3.org/wai – provides guidelines on how to make your site more accessible.

CSS Web tools

Many Web tools now give extensive support to CSS, including Dreamweaver, but we will explore the ways in which Dreamweaver can use style sheets in Chapter 13. Some dedicated CSS tools are also available, including the following.

- **TopStyle Pro (www.bradsoft.com/topstyle)** provides a very easy-to-use XHTML and CSS editor. The user interface contains a number of windowpanes (see Figure 8.22). The left-hand upper pane is where the style sheet is edited. The

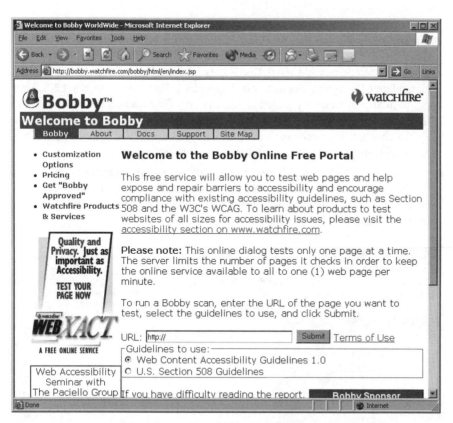

Figure 8.21
The Bobby
accessibility
checker

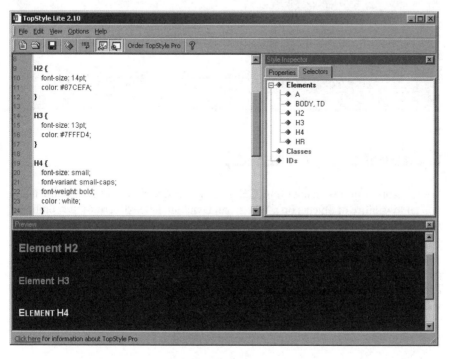

Figure 8.22
The TopStyle Pro
CSS editor in use

upper right-hand pane gives the user access to specific selectors, classes and so on. The lower windowpane lets the user preview the effects of any styles without the need of a browser. This software includes many features, among them one that can upgrade any old HTML documents by replacing outdated markup with equivalent CSS styling. For example, it can convert all <font> tags to CSS. This program also includes integrated access to HTML Tidy – a tool that lets you validate and reformat your HTML. TopStyle Pro also enables access to an HTML syntax checker. The user can also see which styles are related to some XHTML tag and which are related to the current HTML tag or CSS selector.

■ **CoffeeCup StyleSheet Maker (www.coffeecup.com/stylesheet-maker)** is another useful tool for editing CSS (see Figure 8.23). This is another dedicated style sheet editor that lets you construct Cascading Style Sheets, giving control over text placement, fonts, backgrounds and so on.

Figure 8.23
The CoffeeCup
StyleSheet Maker
in use

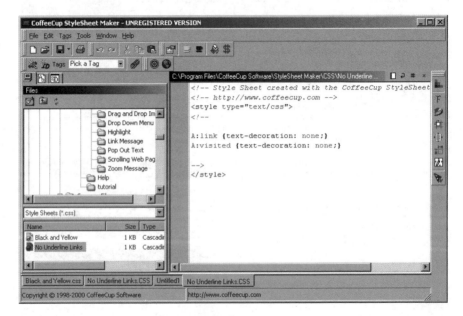

Dynamic HTML (DHTML)

We saw earlier in this chapter how CSS2 can be used to precisely control the position and visibility of objects on a Web page. Dynamic HTML describes the combination of XHTML, style sheets and scripts, which allows documents to be animated.

Dynamic HTML allows a Web page to change after it is loaded into the browser – this means that there doesn't have to be any communication with the Web server for an update. You can think of it as animated XHTML. For example, a piece of text can change from one size or colour to another, a graphic can move from one location to another, all in response to some kind of user action, such as clicking a button.

Dynamic XHTML gives authors creative control so that they can manipulate any page element and change styles, positioning and content at any time. It provides a richer, more dynamic experience on Web pages, making them more like dynamic applications and less like static content. Dynamic HTML presents richly formatted pages and lets you interact with the content on those pages without having to download additional content from the server. This means that a page can respond immediately to user actions, such as a mouse click, without having to retrieve an entire new page from the server.

The Document Object Model (DOM)

DHTML is a combination of three technologies – CSS, JavaScript and the DOM (Document Object Model). The DOM exposes every element of an XHTML page to a scripting language such as JavaScript.

The DOM is a hierarchy that begins with a Window object. Descendants of Window then include the document object as well as the frame object. The document object refers to the XHTML page and everything in it. All objects on the XHTML page, such as forms or images, will themselves contain descendent objects – that is, the form will usually contain radio buttons, text fields and so on. Scripting languages enable the page designer to reference each object by naming each one, from the root to the branch, and separating their names with full stops. In the following example, the mypic.gif image of the document is referenced:

```
document.images["mypic.gif"]
```

The W3C published its latest recommendations for the DOM – called DOM1 – which most browsers now conform to. These include Netscape 6 and IE 5.5, as well as Opera 5, MacIE 5, and Mozilla 1.4. Earlier versions of Netscape and IE used their own proprietary DOMs. For example, Netscape V4 used the layer tag for the implementation of DHTML, but this was discontinued in Netscape 6. The earlier versions of IE were based mostly on exposing CSS element attributes to scripts, which is the current recommendation from the W3C.

Implementing DHTML

The three main components of DHTML authoring are:

1 **positioning** precisely placing blocks of content on the page and, if desired, moving these blocks around – strictly speaking this is a subset of style modifications

2 **style modifications** on-the-fly altering of the aesthetics of the content on the page

3 **event handling** how to relate user events to changes in positioning or other style modifications.

Example 8.4

This example uses JavaScript to create **image substitution** – also called **rollovers** – to implement DHTML. This code will create rollover graphics that animate when the mouse pointer moves over them. The code in this example will change (or swap)

Figure 8.24
Before the
`onMouseOver`
event

Figure 8.25
After the
`onMouseOver`
event

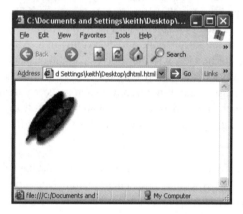

the `.src` (image file name) property of an object representing an `<img>` tag, thus causing the browser to display a different image at the tag's screen position without reloading the entire page. The event that will trigger this action will be the `onMouseOver` event.

To achieve this effect, you will need two images to produce the swap. In this case, two GIF images of vegetables have been used – one called `eggplant.gif` and the other `peas.gif`.

The code works by defining a JavaScript function called `changepic` that will swap one image for another. The body of the code then uses an anchor tag to link to "nopage.html", a dummy page with the `onClick = "return false"` being used to return no page. Next, the `onMouseOver = "changepic('veg', peas)"` event will make a call to the function `changepic` to swap the images `eggplant.gif` and `peas.gif`. When the mouse has passed out, the code `onMouseOut = "changepic ('veg', eggplant)"` is executed, making another call to the `changepic` function, this time to change the images back. Thus, during the time that the mouse passes over the `eggplant.gif` file, it will be replaced by `peas.gif` (see Figure 8.24), but when the mouse passes out of the file, it will change back to `eggplant.gif` (see Figure 8.25). The script's code is shown in Listing 8.10:

Listing 8.10 The rollover code

```
<html>
<head>
<script language ="JavaScript">
eggplant = new Image(64,32); eggplant.src = 'eggplant.gif';


peas = new Image(64,32); peas.src = 'peas.gif';


function changepic (imgTagName, imgObj)
{
if (document.images) {
document.images[imgTagName].src = imgObj.src}
}
</script>
</head>
<body>
<a href="nopage.html"
onClick="return false"
onMouseOver = "changepic('veg', peas)"
onMouseOut = "changepic('veg', eggplant)"
>
<img name = "veg" border = "0" src = "eggplant.gif" width =
"100" height = "100">
</a>
</body>
</html>
```

Web resources

The following are worth visiting for more on CSS.
www.w3.org/TR/REC-CSS2/media.html   Look here for the WC3 specification containing CSS properties and examples.

www.jalfrezi.com/fstyles.htm   Very handy site giving plenty of examples of how CSS are used to enhance website design.

www.web-weaving.net   Again, a very handy site, containing many useful articles on CSS.

www.westciv.com   A useful tutorial on CSS.

www.w3.org/Markup/Guide/Style   An introduction to CSS by Dave Raggett (see Figure 8.26).

Figure 8.26
Dave Raggett's
CSS tutorial

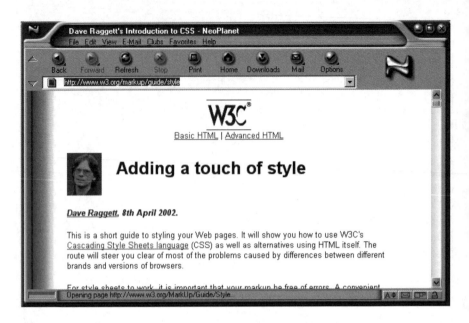

Summary

- Cascading Style Sheets (CSS) enable Web designers to maintain the same look and feel across all pages on a website.

- CSS enable the separation of style from content.

- CSS syntax is different to that of XHTML and consists of rules that define the stylistic aspects of one or more page elements.

- CSS can be linked to your XHTML documents externally, internally or by embedding CSS rules within a section of an XHTML document.

- The term 'cascading' refers to the possible existence of multiple style sheets for a given Web document.

- Rules of precedence pertaining to the cascade are that inline styles take precedence over embedded sheets, and embedded sheets take precedence over external style sheets.

- The order of precedence for a rule can be overridden by using the keyword 'important'.

- Precedence rules also apply to style sheet sources. An author's style sheet overrides a user's style sheet, and a user's style sheet overrides the browser's default values.

- Classes add more flexibility to style rules in that a style rule can have multiple style declarations.

- CSS can be applied to other media, including printouts, Braille, aural and others.

- Several CSS-based dedicated software tools are in widespread use, as well as being extensively supported by authoring tools, such as Dreamweaver and FrontPage.

- DHTML is a combination of CSS, JavaScript and the DOM, giving XHTML authors the opportunity to manipulate page elements to produce pages that let you interact with the content.

Exercises

1   Explain what a CSS rule is and how it differs from XHTML syntax.

2   Describe the ways in which CSS can be linked to an XHTML document.

3   Explain why the term 'cascading' is used in CSS.

4   Describe the anatomy of a CSS rule referring to the selector and declaration parts. Show how the syntax of a rule would be amended to include:

   a   setting more than one property value to a selector
   b   applying the same property value to more than one selector
   c   applying a rule to a contextual selector.

5   Write a CSS rule that makes all level 2 headings text font size 12.

6   Write a CSS rule that makes all level 2 headings text font size 12 and colours it green.

7   Write a CSS rule that makes all level 2 headings and paragraph elements text font size 12 with a sans serif font and colours it red.

8   Write a CSS rule that makes the font style of all occurrences of ordered list elements that are contained within a definition list italic.

9   Write a CSS rule that makes all level 2 headings text font size 12, font Courier and colours it red.

10 Describe, giving examples, the difference between inheritance and a cascade. What are the rules of priority for inheritance? What are the rules of precedence for the browser, user and developer?

11 Study the following XHTML file. Predict the output, then check your prediction by running the file using an IE 6 browser.

```
<html>
<head>

<style>
h1 {color: red}
h3 {color: blue}
</style>

</head>

<body>
<h1>This is header 1</h1>
<h3>This is header 3</h3>
</body>

</html>
```

12 Create a CSS rule that sets all <h2> elements to bold text, twice the default font size.

13 Write a CSS rule that creates a class selector that can be applied to a document division called split. The rule should make all text font Impact and place a border around it.

14 Write a CSS external style sheet that contains the rule that makes all text font size 12, sets the text font to Courier and colours the font red. Create a Web page that includes some text, which references this external style sheet, and test that the style sheet rule works using your browser.

15 Go to the external style sheet called vegcss.css on the resources website. Modify this style sheet so that the background colour is set to light blue. Also, modify the text colour of the tip class so that it is now black.

Chapter

9

Multimedia and the WWW

In this chapter you will learn about the:

- role of multimedia on the Web
- difference between digital and analogue data
- range of graphics formats used on the Web
- principles of graphic design for the Web
- principles of audio and video design for the Web
- techniques for inserting XHTML multimedia tags into Web pages
- Portable Document Format (PDF) for the Web.

Introduction

Before the birth of the Windows operating system in the early 1990s, the personal computer world was a predominantly text-based medium. The WWW was, therefore, originally created as a text-only medium. Remember, XHTML is an acronym for Extensible Hyper*text* Markup Language – not Extensible Hyper*media* Markup Language. However, when Marc Andreessen and Eric Bina added the `<img>` image tag to their Mosaic browser in 1993, the impact was huge because graphic capability became possible on the Web.

The age of multimedia on the Web – that is, the inclusion of graphics, video and sound on Web pages – was born. Multimedia as the name suggests, offers users of the Web many other means of media communication apart from text. Multimedia provides communication methods that include text, graphics, animation, video, music and the spoken word. Multimedia provides the Web designer with a fascinating resource. A traditional painter can only use painting media such as water-colours, oils, acrylics, pastels and so on, but the website designer can call on text, graphics, sound, video, numerical information and so on. Together, these enrich the means of communication for the user and go some way towards fulfilling the accessibility goals of the W3C, because multimedia also offers alternative ways of communicating. So, for example, visually impaired users may prefer to communicate by means of the spoken word and this is now possible.

The W3C's site at www.w3.org/wai provides information about its Web Accessibility Initiative (WAI) and offers guidelines on how to make your site more accessible.

Analogue and digital devices

Despite the benefits of multimedia, its inclusion in online Web pages has never been easy. This is because using multimedia often requires the conversion from an **analogue** to a **digital** format. The computer is a digital device – all processing is reduced to a series of digits – the binary digits 0 and 1. On the other hand, devices for capturing, copying and playing sound, such as cassette recorders, or devices for copying and reproducing video images, such as video recorders, or devices used for reproducing photographs, such as cameras, have traditionally been analogue devices. This means that they make an analogous copy of the image that has been copied. When you hear the sound of a human voice on a cassette recorder, for example, you are hearing a copy of the waveform of that human voice being played.

To get an idea of what a sound waveform looks like, Figure 9.1 displays a digital waveform of me attempting to sing accompanied by a guitar. This image was taken using the sound-editing tool Cool Edit (see later in this chapter). Similarly, when you see a photograph of yourself taken by a non-digital camera, you are seeing an image that records and transmits the light patterns in the same waveform as the image received at the camera when the picture was taken. The same sort of thing happens with a video recorder and other analogue devices.

A computer, on the other hand, does not take an analogue copy of the original. Instead, it converts the image into a series of **bits** – binary digits. For example, in copying a sound waveform, a computer will sample the analogue sound many times per second. This sampling process gives the computer, at each sample, the pitch or frequency of the sound, and the volume or loudness of the sound. However, to get a very close representation of the analogue copy of the waveform, a computer will typically sample at 44,100 per second and from this produce an (approximate) digital representation of the analogue waveform. This means that a computer would need to store 44,100 numerical values every second. Each numerical value is usually represented using a range of 16 bits – called **16-bit sampling**. A typical 3-minute song, therefore, would consume approximately $3 \times 60 \times 44,100 = 7,938,000 \times 16$ bits, or $7,938,000 \times 16/8$ bytes = approximately 16 mB memory, in pure wave form.

Storing data in this way is clearly memory-hungry. Fortunately, as we will see later, there are compression techniques now available that can reduce this substantially. Later on in this chapter we will look at some software tools that can be used for this task as well as editing the sound, video and other digital multimedia files. Nonetheless, a great deal of memory is still consumed. The same thing happens, to some extent, when you store graphic images, animation and video originals in digital computer format. The point to remember is that – apart from textual information – multimedia is memory-hungry and, clearly, the larger the file size is, the longer it will take to travel over a Web connection. The normal dial-up modem Web connection sends data at a maximum speed of about 56,000 bits per second. This means that a 1-mB file (1,000,000 bytes) will take a minimum of $1,000,000 \times 8/56,000 = 143$ seconds, or almost 2.38 minutes. In practice, it would take longer because modems rarely run at the maximum speed and, in any case, the Internet connection transmits data in packets, slowing the transfer of data even more.

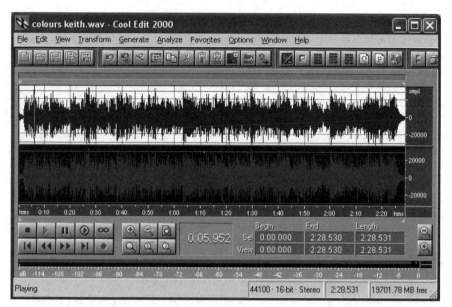

Figure 9.1
A digital copy of a human voice waveform

Problems with multimedia and the Web

From the previous section, it is clear that the major impediment to the implementation of multimedia on the Web has been **bandwidth** – the speed of the transfer of online data. In the mid-1990s, modem speeds of 33.6 k and even 14.4 k were typical and were just not fast enough to sustain users' attention on the screen when graphic or sound images could take several minutes to download. The 56-k modem sound and video is still not really viable. Figure 9.2 gives a one-dimensional chart indicating the relative speeds of each of the types of media.

In more recent years, high-speed **broadband** Internet access is becoming fairly common for both business and home users. Broadband access does reduce the bandwidth problem. Nevertheless, there is still a high proportion of users who use dial-up modem access facilities, so, if you want to include multimedia on your site and ensure that it is inclusive, then you might need to think about alternatives for slower-access users. For example, it might be that you offer text alternative pages for users with slower access speeds.

The next section looks at some aspects of using graphic images on the Web. Sound and video follow later in this chapter.

Figure 9.2
Indication of the
relative transfer
speeds for
different types of
media

Fast transfer		Slow transfer	
Text	Graphics	Sound	Video

The role of graphics on the Web

Some people see Web graphics as serving a decorative purpose. This is a mistake because graphics convey valuable information about a site, as well as adding to its visual appeal. A good illustration of the power of graphics is given by Figure 9.3 of the Corbis home page (http://pro.corbis.com).

Research (Nielson/NetRatings 2002) has shown that the average surfer on the Web is more likely to stay with a site when it contains some graphic appeal than if it doesn't. The Web designer needs to think carefully how, when and where to use graphics on Web pages, however. An essential prerequisite of this is a basic understanding of the theories of colour and image representation on the computer.

Figure 9.3
Example of the
appeal of
graphics – the
Corbis home page
on a Netscape 7
browser

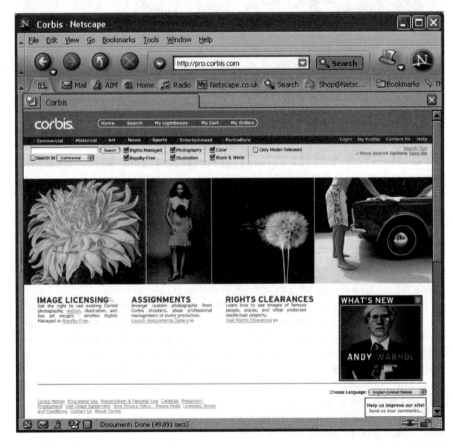

How graphic images are displayed

When you see a graphic on your computer screen, what you're really seeing is a collection of coloured screen **pixels**. The word pixel is a term constructed from the words 'picture element'.

Each pixel contains a colour and brightness value that, taken together with lots of others, produces a meaningful image. Each monitor or display will have a capacity to display many pixels on the screen. Think of a pixel as occupying a dot in a matrix of two dimensions – after all, monitors display images in two dimensions. All of these dots fill up the display and, as each can have a different colour and brightness, it follows that coloured images can be reproduced.

The quality of the image will depend in part on the number of pixels that can be displayed – this is known as the **resolution** of the display. Also, as each pixel contributes to the appearance of the image on the screen, the image file has to contain information on how to reproduce that collection of pixels onscreen. This is accomplished by describing the pixels' properties mathematically and storing these descriptions in the file. However, there is no unique way to mathematically describe image data. Such data can be described in many different ways and, hence, there are many possible image file formats, as we have seen. Fortunately, each of these formats can be classified as being one of two types – a **bitmapped**, or **raster**, **graphic** or a **vector graphic**. The next two sections examine the specific details of each type.

Bitmapped or raster graphics

With a bitmapped graphic, information about each pixel is stored as a sequence of bits in the file. Depending on the storage formats, these bits could represent colours, brightness or some other visual characteristic of the pixel. What's important is that each sequence of bits tells the computer how to paint the pixel on the screen.

Bitmaps are something of a natural format because they store information in exactly the same way the computer displays it on a monitor. This means that the program rendering the image has to do very little processing. It just reads in the data and passes that information along to the screen drivers, which, in turn, display the pixels on the monitor.

Vector graphics

A vector graphic file contains mathematical information that is used to redraw the image on the screen. A vector file is actually a small program that describes the position, length and direction of lines. Unlike a bitmapped file, a vector file contains instructions about how to draw the pixels, rather than information about the pixels themselves. When a computer displays a vector image file, it reads in the redrawing instructions and follows them.

This might sound like a lot of unnecessary processing, but there is an important advantage to this approach.

It is that you can rescale the image to new sizes without loss of resolution because there's no fixed relationship between how it is defined in the file and the pixel-by-pixel image on the screen. When you try to resize a bitmapped file, you often get a loss of resolution that detracts from the image. Vector graphic formats are typically used for images with distinct geometric shapes. Computer-Aided Design (CAD) drawings are examples of this type of image.

The advantages and disadvantages of bitmap and vector graphics

Choosing whether to use a vector or raster image depends on a number of issues. Each type of graphics has its own strengths. Table 9.1 shows a comparison of each method of representation.

Table 9.1 Comparison of bitmapped and vector graphics

Bitmapped	Vector
Delivers higher-quality viewing at normal screen resolution	Zooming capabilities possible because of the nature of vector formats
Best format for photographic display of images	Produces a more compact file size than bitmapped image
Most common format for direct browser viewing	Highest quality for print formats
Can be used to implement links containing image maps	Easy object editing
A bitmapped image is more difficult to convert to digital format because of its size	Animation via Flash

Colour on the Web

The importance of colour

Colour is a powerful visual prompt to the Web page reader. A bright colour calls attention to an element on a page; a dull colour can have the opposite effect.

Before we look at good practices for using colour on Web pages, we need to understand how colour is used on the digital computer and the Web.

Understanding computer and Web colour

Computer monitors display colour by mixing three primary colours – red, green and blue. Each of these is known as a **colour channel**. An intensity range varying from 0 to 100 per cent can be expressed for each channel. Colours vary depending on the monitor specification and users' preferences.

There are differences between the way in which colour is displayed on a monitor and the way it is displayed on canvas. When you work with paint on canvas, every colour that you create is a combination of red, yellow and blue. For example, combining red and yellow in equal proportions produces orange. These three columns are known as **primary colours**. Also, when you put paint on to a white canvas, each colour that you add darkens the overall picture. This is called **subtractive colour** because each colour added *subtracts* from the lightness of the final colour.

In contrast, when you display colour onscreen, each colour added *adds* to the lightness of the final colour because, unlike the painted canvas, which is absorbing light, a computer monitor is generating light and, therefore, the colour we see on a screen is obtained by the addition of colours. This means that when the computer mixes colours, the outcome is going to be different from that of colour mixing on a canvas. Computer monitors use three primary colours to do this – red, green and blue, which is known as **RGB**. Combining these three primary colours at full strength will produce pure white light. This takes a little getting used to, but means, for example, that when you mix red and green at full strength on a computer monitor, you will get yellow.

The RGB colour system

Each of the RGB colours has a channel that can take a value between being completely absent (0 per cent) and completely present (100 per cent) – corresponding to two bits, 0 and 1. Assuming only these possibilities, the range of colours that could be displayed would be $2 \times 2 \times 2 = 8$. However, if there are 6 possible states for each channel, then there are $2^6 = 216$ possible colour combinations. These are known as **Websafe colours**.

The numbers of data bits that are used to create colour on the Web are called **colour depth**. This factor determines the number of colours that a monitor can display. Monitors typically display 16- or 24-bit colour depth. A 24-bit colour depth means that you can store approximately any colour in the range 0 to 16 million colours. As a general rule, you should aim to keep the colour depth as low as possible for the image that you are using. For GIF images, 256 colours is sufficient, but this would be inadequate for displaying colour photographs.

Although many monitors display 24-bit colour depth, many do not. If a browser tries to display 24-bit colour depth on an 8-bit monitor, it will have fewer colours to work with than was intended. The browser will try to approximate to the colour that it is closest to the one it is trying to display. When a monitor cannot display a colour, it attempts to re-create the colour by combining two or more other colours in the pixels on the display. Clearly, if the monitor resolution is low, then the effect will be to see speckles. This is known as **dithering**.

RGB and hexadecimal colour codes

All RGB decimal numbers can be expressed as hexadecimal numbers (base 16). For example, (0,0,255) can be written as (00,00,FF) or 0000FF. The hash symbol # preceeds hexadecimal numbers when used in XHTML.

Some characteristics of coloured images

Before we look in detail at the graphic formats that are used on the Web, we need to be aware of some colour characteristics that affect the display of images on the Web.

■ *Alpha channels*
Alpha channels are a way in which to associate variable transparency with an image. We already know that the three visible colour channels are red, green and blue. These are the colours of light and are mixed in specific values to output the TrueColor spectrum of light. In addition, some bitmaps can also store 256 levels of transparency. They have an ability to incorporate something called an 'A' **channel**, or **alpha channel**. This is a mask represented in 256 colours of the greyscale spectrum. While white stands for 100 per cent opaque, black represents 100 per cent transparent and the shades of grey in between represent varying degrees of transparency. This 'A' channel is known as the alpha channel.

■ *Gamma correction*
Gamma correction is the ability to correct for differences in how computer monitors interpret colour values. This has long been a problem with Web images rendered on Macintosh monitors, where Web images tend to look too light compared to those on other PCs. However, this problem doesn't just apply to Macintosh computers for sometimes a PC-created image will not display correctly on all PCs.

■ *Alias*
The term alias refers to an image that has jagged edges. These rough edges appear because the text or graphic has a curved or angled edge that still has to be displayed using the square pixels. Aliasing can be resolved by doing something called **anti-aliasing**, causing a slight blur to be added to the edges of objects and graphics to smooth out the edges.

■ *Transparency*
A transparent image is one where its background colour or images show through the transparent pixels. Transparency is particularly useful for images that appear on a patterned background.

■ *Interlacing*
Download times for some images can sometimes seem too long. Interlacing is a technique that gives the viewer of the graphic a lower-quality definition image before it is fully defined. When you store an image in an interlaced format, non-adjacent parts of the image are stored together. As the image is decoded, pixels from all over the image are filled in rather than being filled in row by row. The result is that the image appears to 'fade on' to the page, as if it were being revealed from behind Venetian blinds. This permits the user to get a sense of the entire image right away, instead of having to wait for the whole thing to be read in from top to bottom. It usually takes several passes for the image to fade in completely.

■ *Dithering*
Dithering is the process of juxtaposing pixels of two colours to create the illusion that a third colour is present. An example of this is an image with only black and white in the colour palette. By combining black and white pixels in complicated patterns, we can create the illusion of grey-valued pixels. An illustration of dithering is given with the two images of the cat shown in Figures 9.4a and 9.4b.

Figure 9.4a
Cat image stored
in 256-colour GIF
format

Figure 9.4b
Cat image stored
in JPEG format

The dithering causes darker areas in the GIF image, which lack definition, as displayed in the JPEG image shown in Figure 9.4b.

One way in which to deal with dithering is for Web designers to use the so-called 'Websafe palette'. This consists of 216 colours that will not dither or shift when used on 8-bit monitors.

Web graphics formats

As stated in Chapter 4, when you focus your attention on Web graphics, the vast number of usable graphic storage formats quickly reduces to two or three.

The **Graphics Interchange Format**, or **GIF**, is a proprietary format that was developed by CompuServe in 1987 to store graphics used over its network. CompuServe can thus charge licence fees to companies that open and save files in the GIF format.

The **JPEG** format came about more recently and takes its name from the Joint Photographic Experts Group that agreed the format, which was intended to be free to everyone. However, in 2002, Forgent Networks (www.fact-index.com/f/fo/ forgent_networks.html) asserted that it owns, and will enforce patent rights on, the JPEG format. The JPEG committee reacted with the following statement and is preparing a new format – JPEG 2000 – to overcome the problems:

> *It has always been a strong goal of the JPEG committee that its standards should be implementable in their baseline form without payment of royalty and licence fees, and the committee would like to record their disappointment that some organizations appear to be working in conflict with this goal. Considerable time has been spent in committee in attempting to either arrange licensing on these terms, or in avoiding existing intellectual property, and many hundreds of organizations and academic communities have supported us in our work.*
>
> *The up and coming JPEG 2000 standard has been prepared along these lines, and agreement reached with over 20 large organizations holding many patents in this area to allow use of their intellectual property in connection with the standard without payment of licence fees or royalties.*

Both GIF and JPEG are bitmapped formats, but another – PNG – offers support for vector storage formats and is becoming the standard. The specifics of each of these formats, and instances of when you would want to use one over the other, are discussed in the following sections.

The graphic interchange format (GIF)

Transparent GIFs

GIF supports many effects that are desirable on Web pages. Chief among these is **transparency**. In a **transparent GIF**, you can designate one colour to be the transparent colour. Then, whenever the GIF is rendered onscreen, pixels painted with the transparent colour will actually be painted with the colour of the page background. This gives the illusion of the pixels being transparant as they allow what's behind them to show through. The advantage of transparent GIFs is that they make a graphic appear to float freely on a page. Many graphics programs available today come with support for creating transparent GIFs.

Interlaced GIFs

GIF supports interlacing. When you store a GIF in an **interlaced format**, non-adjacent parts of the image are stored together. As the GIF is decoded, pixels from all over the image are filled in rather than being filled in row by row. The result is that the image appears to 'fade on' to the page, as if it were being revealed from behind Venetian blinds. This permits the user to get a sense of the entire image right away, instead of having to wait for the whole thing to be read in from top to bottom. It usually takes several passes for the image to fade in completely.

Animated GIFs

The first animations that appeared on the Web required a great deal of effort. Using an approach introduced by Netscape called **server push**, it was possible to create an animation by having a server literally push several images down an open HTTP connection. When presented in sequence on the browser screen, these images create the illusion of animation. Setting this up required knowledge of the Common Gateway Interface (CGI) and some type of programming language. As most digital media graphic artists do not have knowledge of CGI programming, producing a Web animation often required collaboration between the artists and the server administrator. In short, it was very complicated.

GIF, however, supports image animation. The GIF 89a standard supports multiple images stored in the same file. Furthermore, you could place instructions in the file header that describe how the images should be presented. Creating animated GIFs has since become fairly easy with the advent of software tools such as the GIF Construction Set (available at www.mindworkshop.com). In this program, you can specify the individual GIF files that make up the animation and presentation instructions in a set of dialogue boxes. When you're finished with the setup, the program will create the animated GIF file using the information you've specified. Other animation tools include Animation Shop (see Figure 9.5), a tool that is marketed with Paint Shop Pro (www.jasc.com).

Most browsers support the GIF89a standard. While other browsers support one feature or another, Navigator 2.0 and Explorer 3.0 (and later versions of both) also support the standard's ability to store more than just a single image. Note that interlacing and transparency are supported by GIF89a. In fact, GIF89a also supports storing timing data, so that the speed at which successive images are displayed can be controlled. This makes it possible to create flip-book-like animations that store as a single image file and do not require helper applications or plug-ins to view them.

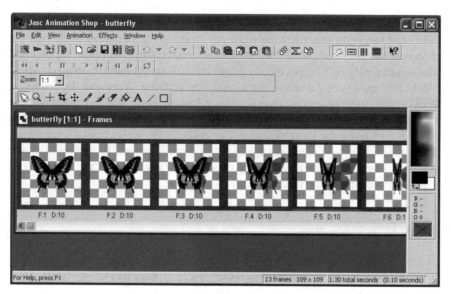

Figure 9.5
Using Jasc
Animation Shop

While other animation file types, such as QuickTime, require helper applications or plug-ins to run, animated GIFs are totally self-contained. The file downloads once and plays from the computer's disk cache. From the perspective of XHTML, an animated GIF is no different to any other image. The steps required for creating an animated GIF are:

1 create each separate frame in the sequence as a separate graphic file (see Figure 9.5 for an illustration of how frames are used to create the effect of animation)

2 glue the individual frames together with control blocks between each frame – the blocks instruct the browser how many 100ths of a second to wait before loading the next frame

3 add a final block that instructs the browser to start over at the beginning in the case of a looping animation.

There are many other GIF animation tools available – some as free shareware. Some examples are:

∎ GIF Construction Set (for Windows) by Alchemy Mindworks
∎ GIF Animator by Ulead Systems.

The JPEG format

The JPEG format, briefly described in Chapter 4, is a set of formats that supports full-colour and greyscale images and stores them in compressed form. JPEG stores colour information at 24 bits per pixel, allowing an image to contain over 16.7 million colours. This makes it the natural format of choice for photographs on the Web.

How JPEG works

JPEG can handle so many colours while still keeping file sizes reasonable because it compresses the image data. You even have some control over how big or small the file ultimately is. You can specify a high level of compression to get a very small file, but the quality of the image onscreen will be reduced. When you decompress a JPEG image, there is always some amount of loss, meaning that the image will not look the way it did originally. Fortunately, JPEG's compression/decompression scheme is such that the lost image data tends to be in the higher colour frequencies, where it is harder for the human eye to detect the differences. In spite of this loss, you can still use JPEG to achieve compression ratios between 10:1 and 20:1 without appreciable change in the image.

The PNG format

The **Portable Network Graphics (PNG)** – pronounced 'ping' – format has been defined as a network standard by the W3C. PNG is described by the W3C as 'an extensible file format for the lossless, portable, well-compressed storage of raster (bitmapped) images'.

PNG provides a patent-free replacement for the GIF format. CompuServe developed the GIF format and GIF uses the proprietary LZW compression scheme owned by the Unisys Corporation. Any graphics tool developer who makes software that saves in GIF format must pay a royalty to Unisys and CompuServe, but this is no longer necessary with the PNG format.

Many other features are supported by the PNG format, including a full range of colour depths, sophisticated image transparency, better interlacing and automatic gamma corrections.

The PNG format was designed to replace the older and simpler GIF format, but, like JPEG, is capable of storing high-resolution images. For the Web, PNG really has three main advantages over GIF. They are that it:

- supports alpha channels – whereas GIF supports single-channel transparency, so any pixel can be either transparent or opaque, PNG allows up to 254 levels of partial transparency

- compresses better than GIF in most cases – the PNG format uses a lossless compression scheme that is capable of compressing files about 30 per cent smaller than the GIF format and its progressive feature enables browsers to load the first pass much more quickly than the first pass of an interlaced GIF file

- can hold a short text description of the image's content with the image, which allows Internet search engines to search for images based on these embedded text descriptions.

Problems with GIF

Unfortunately, not all of PNG's graphic format's features are supported by all the major Web browsers. At the time of writing, Internet Explorer 5 for Macintosh, Netscape 6 for Macintosh and Netscape 6 for Windows all support many features of the PNG format, including full alpha channel transparency. Internet Explorer 6 for Windows partially supports PNG but does not support PNG alpha channel transparency. So, it is currently Microsoft's support that is preventing the widespread adoption of PNG on the Web.

Other graphics formats

Several other emerging formats are beginning to make an impact on the Web, so they are briefly described below.

- **JPEG 2000** is an updated JPEG format providing better compression. This format uses the suffix `.jp2` and produces small file sizes without any noticeable loss of quality. Unfortunately, there is little in the way of browser support. As at the time of writing, there is no direct browser support for .jp2 files, although support from some vendors is provided via plug-ins. For example, Adobe provides a plug-in with Photoshop Elements software. JPEG 2000 offers new ways to deal with compressed images. With it, it is possible to extract various resolutions, qualities, components or spatial regions without decompressing the entire file. Visit www.crc.ricoh.com/~gormish/jpeg2000.html for more information.

∎ **SVG** stands for **Scalable Vector Graphics** and is a language for describing two-dimensional graphics in XML. It allows for three types of graphic objects – vector graphic shapes (such as paths consisting of straight lines and curves), images and text. Graphical objects can be grouped, styled, transformed and composited into previously rendered objects. The feature set includes nested transformations, clipping paths, alpha masks, filter effects and template objects. SVG drawings can be interactive and dynamic animations. For more information, visit www.w3.org/Graphics/SVG/SVG-Implementations.html

Finding graphics online

There are many sites on the Web that provide royalty-free graphics that you can download and use on your own site.

Importing images to use on the Web

There are several ways in which the Web designer can import images into Paint, Photoshop or image manipulation software before importing them on to the Web.

∎ *Scanners*   provide a relatively cheap means of importing images into digital format so that they can then be used on the Web. A desktop scanner works by shining white light across a printed usage so that an electronic copy of it is received by the scanner's charged couple device (CCD). This chip records the image and transfers it to a digital file. Scanners are usually bundled with image manipulation software to edit the converted file.

∎ *Picture CD*   Images can be scanned on to a CD in digital format when you process conventional photographic film at photographic laboratories for an extra charge. The digital CD would often contain easy-to-use tools that would help you to zoom in to or crop images, reduce red-eye and so on.

∎ *Digital video cameras*   can be used to create both digital still images and video. They can be connected to a PC via a firewire interface, but with some difficulty.

∎ *Digital still cameras*   are increasingly popular for downloading images taken directly with the camera on to a computer. Images can be saved directly on to a PC's hard disk by using a USB port. Various removable memory cards are available for storing the images.

Optimization for the Web

Many image creation tools include facilities to save documents for the Web. The File/Save for Web ... in Photoshop is an example. The same option is available in **ImageReady**, **Fireworks**, **Illustrator** and many other tools.

Preparing an image for the Web, as already stated, requires rendering it in a suitable file format. There are two essential requirements for images that are going to be used on Web pages. The first is that they must be in a form that can be displayed by browsers – that is in the GIF, JPEG or PNG formats. They must also be of a suitable size for transmission on the Web in the fastest possible time. Clearly, the larger the file, the longer the download time, so optimization implies reducing the file size. This is why file formats such as **TIFF** and bitmaps are ruled out. In the case of the bitmapped format, each pixel occupies an average of almost 2 bytes of memory – far too much for the Web.

The optimization process, following on from choosing the `Save for Web` option, is made possible by using compression algorithms. An example is shown in Figure 9.6a and 9.6b. You can see that the same file has undergone compression so that it is reduced to less than 10 per cent of its original size.

Compressed files are either **lossless** or **lossy**. A **lossless image** is one where, when compressed, its inverse decompression will restore the original image completely – bit for bit. **Lossy algorithms**, on the other hand, work by discarding information, so if an image is compressed, then decompressed, the resulting image will not be the same as before the compression. The JPEG format is a lossy compressed format. However, tools that enable JPEG compression will normally provide a quality setting, so that you can trade off the quality against the size and, therefore, the download speed.

Figure 9.6a
Image before optimization – file size 6.39Mb

Figure 9.6b
The same file after invoking the Save for Web option file size 551 KB

Creating thumbnail images and galleries

A **thumbnail image** is a scaled-down 'preview' replica of the full-size image. As a thumbnail image is smaller than its full-size counterpart, it will load much faster and, therefore, can provide a means of viewing essential content in a programme. Thus, thumbnail galleries are very commonly used for presenting slide shows of photographs or art gallery displays on the Web. Figure 9.7 displays a thumbnail gallery of paintings. When a viewer clicks on a thumbnail image, the browser will open a window that contains the full-size image (see Figure 9.8). With a thumbnail gallery, the viewer can decide what they want to view.

Many Web tools offer support for the creation of thumbnail galleries. These include image manipulation tools such as Photoshop and authoring tools such as Dreamweaver.

Some audio issues

Adding audio to a Web page

There are several ways in which to add sound to a Web page. However, there are some factors that you need to consider before deciding on a format and method for

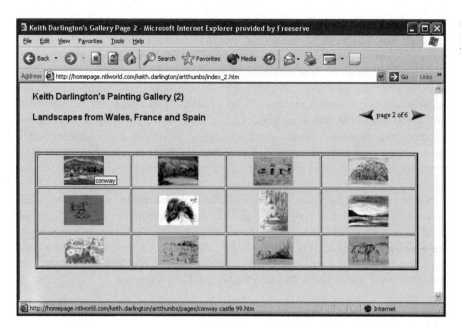

Figure 9.7
Example of a
thumbnail gallery

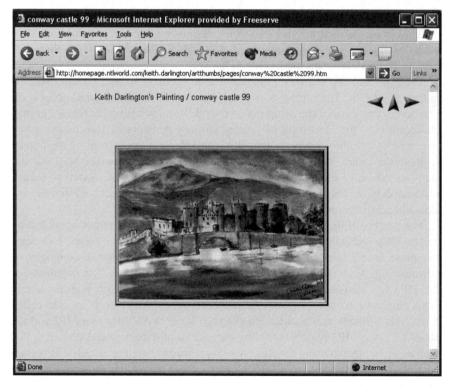

Figure 9.8
The full-size linked
image

adding sound. Not least, you need to be clear about its purpose. You also need to ask yourself why you are using sound and whether or not it is likely to improve users' experience of your website – sometimes sound can simply confuse users. You need to think carefully about your audience. From what age and social groups are the visitors to your site likely to come? Clearly, if your anticipated audience is in the elderly age range, then a rap music clip is probably inappropriate. You need to think, too, about the sound quality delivered. Sound files consume a great deal of memory and, therefore, compression is essential. However, using some compression schemes can lead to a degradation in the quality of the sound. Another thing that you need to give thought to is the differences in browsers' interpretations of sound.

Once you have given due thought to all these considerations, you need to decide how best to add sound to your Web page. The easiest is to make the audio file available for download. Place the file on the server and make a link to it, as would be the case with any other file. When users click on the file, it is downloaded to their desktops and played via an application such as RealPlayer or WinAmp. This sometimes means that the whole file is downloaded before it starts playing.

The MP3 sound format

As with graphic files, there are many formats that can be used to store sound files, including the **Microsoft wave (WAV)** and the **midi (MIDI)** format. However, it is the **MP3** (www.mp3.com) format that now dominates sound on the Internet. The success of MP3 is mainly due to its high level of compression – files are up to 10 per cent or less of their original size. Also, despite it being highly compressed, the sound quality is not severely compromised. It is therefore used for live radio broadcasts as well as musicians publishing on the Web.

The MP3 standard emerged from the **Motion Pictures Expert Group (MPEG)** in the early 1990s. The compression process is very different from traditional compression in that most of the compression in an MP3 comes from the science of psychoacoustics – the modelling of human auditory perception. The theory is that uncompressed audio sounds contain much data that isn't perceived by the human brain, so this unnecessary data is not included after compression. The MP3 encoder analyses the audio streams and compares them to mathematical models of human psychoacoustics. This is more processor-demanding than the familiar zip compression, but results in more efficient compression.

The success of the MP3 format has spawned much interest in music publishing on the Web, including websites dedicated to MP3 music (see Figure 9.9). Sites like these distribute commercially produced music that is subject to copyright, so downloading these files can sometimes breach copyright laws. The popularity of the MP3 has also led to a plethora of other audio tools on the Web, including www.musicmatch.com – a site that contains many tools, such as one called MusicMatch Jukebox, which lets you convert large WAV files into MP3 format. Other tools are MP3 players, enabling the user to play back sound files on a PC, such as those created using the RealOne Player format (see Figure 9.10). It is even possible to purchase dedicated MP3 players – these are similar in appearance to a Sony Walkman.

It would be unusual for musicians to record directly to MP3 format, even in digital studios. Recordings would normally be created in tape format and then transferred to MP3.

Figure 9.9
Website makes available music published in MP3 format on the Web

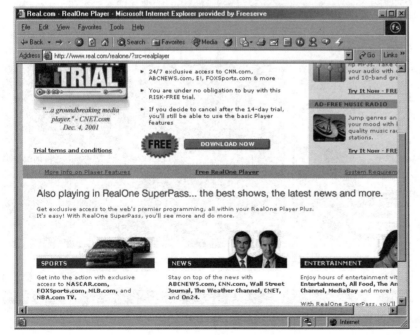

Figure 9.10
RealOne Player for playing sound files on a PC

Other audio formats

- **Musical Instrument Digital Interface (MIDI)** uses a `.mid` compressed file extension and is a format that is well suited to instrumental music. MIDI files are supported by many browsers and do not require a plug-in. Although MIDI sound quality is generally good, it would depend, in a large part, on the quality of the user's sound card. A small MIDI file can provide a long sound clip. MIDI files cannot be recorded directly, but musicians often synthesize such files using computer equipment with special hardware and software.

- **Waveform Extension (WAV)** is a natural, uncompressed format that uses the `.wav` extension. WAV files are Microsoft proprietary and have good sound quality, are supported by many browsers and do not require a plug-in. You can even record your own WAV files directly from a CD, tape, using a microphone and so on. However, the large file sizes severely restrict their use on the Web.

- **Audio Interchange File Format (AIFF)** files use an `.aif` extension. This format, like WAV, has good sound quality, can be played by most browsers and does not require a plug-in. You can also record AIFF files from a CD, tape, using a microphone and so on. However, the large file sizes severely limit the length of sound clips in this format that you can use on your Web pages.

- **Real Audio files** use a `.ra` extension. This is a format providing, in some cases, a higher degree of compression than MP3. Whole song files can be downloaded in a reasonable amount of time. Because the files can be 'streamed' from a normal Web server, users can begin listening to the sound before the file has completely downloaded and so, like MP3, this a popular format for live broadcasts. Users of this format must download and install the RealPlayer helper appli-

Figure 9.11
Screenshot of the RealPlayer

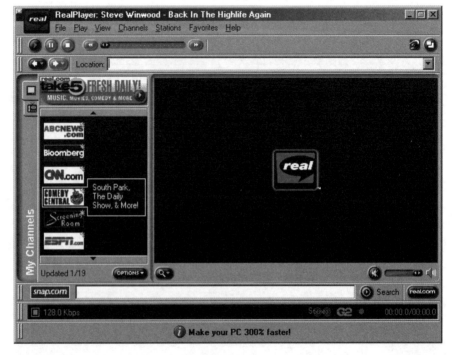

cation or plug-in in order to play these files. A screenshot of the RealPlayer is shown in Figure 9.11.

Streaming audio

Streaming is another method for delivering audio over the Web. Streaming differs from traditional downloading in that the file starts playing as soon as it begins downloading. Streaming is a constant updating of the buffer and can only be used when connected online. This is ideally suited to live broadcasts and so on. The file never downloads to the user's machine. Sites such as Live365 (www.live365.com) even let you create streams from MP3 sound files. The most well-used streaming format is RealAudio, which uses an `.ra` or `.ram` extension. Figure 9.12 displays the RealPlayer playing a live streaming session using the RealPlayer `.ram` format.

When to use streaming

Streaming sound files would be appropriate when the following conditions apply:

■ broadcasting a live event – streaming is clearly a necessity, for the only way the listener can hear the event live is in real time – that is, as it is being played

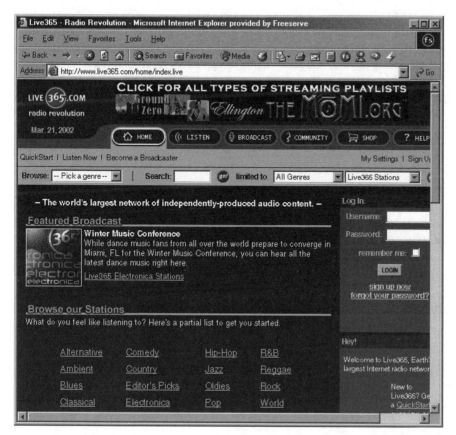

Figure 9.12
Live365's website, here using RealPlayer to play a live streaming session

- the sound requires large files – clearly, very large files take time to download and consume much hard disk space, so streaming may be the better option
- the distributor does not want to allow the file to be copied – a downloaded file can be copied; a streamed file cannot because it is not copied to the hard disk of the user's computer.

Website music

Many businesses, especially music companies or musicians, may want to incorporate music on their websites, but there are other reasons for wanting to do so. There have been numerous research studies that show music can affect a person's mood. Thus, it makes sense to use music if it induces the right type of mood in users of your site. The more at ease and relaxed they are, the more receptive they may be to your products and services. However, designers need to think carefully about one issue: is having music worth prolonging how long users have to wait for the site page to download? Clearly that is a decision only each site owner can make.

The Moving Picture Experts Group (MPEG) format

The **MPEG format** was established in 1988 with the mandate to develop standards for coded representations of moving pictures, audio and their various combinations. Since its birth, MPEG has been involved in an ongoing and evolving set of standards for the coding of video and audio digital compression. As virtually all technologically advanced countries in the world participate in defining these standards, MPEG ensures that the quality of video and audio after coding reaches an internationally acceptable level. There have been four phases in the evolution of the MPEG standard:

- *MPEG-1* was designed for coding video with only the Video CD and CD-I media formats at transmission speeds not greater than 1.5 million bits per second – called **MIPS**
- *MPEG-2* was designed for coding interlaced images at transmission rates substantially higher than MPEG-1 to about 4 MIPS – and this standard was also used for digital TV broadcasts
- *MPEG-3* was originally designed for high-definition TV (HDTV), but was merged with the MPEG-2 format when it became apparent that the MPEG-2 standard met the HDTV requirements (note that MPEG-3 is not the same as MP3 – MP3 uses MPEG-1 audio layer 3 files in order to achieve high compression)
- *MPEG-4* was designed to support speech and video synthesis and other artificial intelligence (AI) approaches to standards.

Inserting multimedia objects with XHTML

We have already seen that the <img> tag can be used to insert any valid graphic format on the Web. Early versions of HTML only provided the <img> tag for inserting media into HTML documents. While this tag has certainly proved worthwhile, it is restricted to image media, which severely limits its usefulness as richer and richer media find their way on to the Web. Thus, developers have been experimenting with ideas for dealing with new media on the Web ever since.

Several incompatible schemes – proprietary and otherwise – have been developed for inserting multimedia objects into Web pages. For example, Microsoft created the dynsrc attribute for video and audio, Netscape popularized the <embed> tag for compound document embedding and Sun created the <applet> tag for executable code. However, all have now been supplanted by the <object> tag. Even so, you may still find code that contains these elements. The future of developing multimedia elements for the Web, though, lies in the <object> tag, so choose from attributes that support this tag. Table 9.2 describes some of the most well-known attributes that you are likely to use with this tag and Example 9.1 shows the tag being used to incorporate a Macromedia Shockwave presentation. In the

Table 9.2 Some attributes of the object element

Object attribute	Purpose
id	Used to define a document identifier
type	This specifies the Internet media type for the data referenced by the data attribute in advance of actually retrieving it
data	This is a URL pointing to the object's data, for instance a GIF file for an image
name	This attribute provides a way to determine whether or not an object within a form block should participate in the 'submit' process
align	This attribute determines where to place the object on the browser display. The align attribute allows objects to be placed as part of the current text line or as a distinct unit, aligned to the left, right or centred
codebase	Some URL schemes used to identify implementations require an additional URL to find the implementation. Codebase allows you to specify that URL
codetype	Similar to the type attribute in that it specifies the Internet media type of the code referenced by the classid attribute in advance of actually retrieving it
classid	This is a URL that identifies an implementation for the object. In some object systems this is a class identifier
width	This gives the suggested width of a box enclosing the visible area of the object. The width is specified in pixels
height	This gives the suggested height of a box enclosing the visible area of the object. The height is specified in pixels
border	This attribute applies to the border shown when the object forms part of a hypertext link, as specified by an enclosing anchor element. The attribute specifies the suggested width of this border around the visible area of the object. The width is specified in pixels. As with previous uses of this attribute, border = 0 implies that no border will be displayed

sections that follow, we will look at how to incorporate sound and other multimedia components into XHTML code.

Example 9.1

The following XHTML code segment enables the viewing of a Macromedia Shockwave presentation using the object element. The attribute data specifies the file name – called myshockfile, which includes a .dcr (director) extension. The type attribute indicates the type of application file – that is, director. The other attributes – width and height – have been used to specify the width and height of the browser display area. Finally, the GIF image – called shockwvimage – will be displayed with the presentation.

```
<object data= "myshockfile.dcr"
        type="application/director"
        width = "288" height = "200">
<img src ="shockwvimage.gif" alt="Use Shockwave with this
app">
</object>
```

Using XHTML to add sound to a Web page

You can add sound to a Web page, assuming that you are using the MP3 format, by using the anchor tag with the href attribute. For example:

```
<a href = "guitarsolo.mp3"> Click here to download a guitar
solo. Note that this download will take about 25 minutes if
you are using a 56KB modem </a>
```

The music file described in the anchor tag above is an MP3 music file with a size of 4.3 mB. It is therefore suggested that this information be given to users before they decide whether or not to download the file for playing. If users download it, then they will need a player or plug-in to use the file. Many sites now use JavaScript programs to query the browser to find out what plug-ins are available. If one isn't found, then users are invited to download one.

NOTE   Different browsers handle sound files in very different and inconsistent ways. If you are considering incorporating sound on your website, make sure that you thoroughly check what the results are across the different browsers.

Embedding audio

Embedding audio is another way to render sound that incorporates the sound player directly into the page, but the sound only plays if visitors to your site have the appropriate plug-in for the chosen sound file.

Embed files if you want to use the sound as background music or more control over the sound presentation itself. For example, you can set the volume, how the player looks on the page and the beginning and ending points of the sound file. For a description of embedding an audio file using Dreamweaver, see Chapter 13.

Background sound

Background sound can be added to a Web page using the <bgsound> tag for IE and <embed> for Netscape at the beginning of the document. The basic background sound tags for each are:

```
<bgsound  = "audio.mp3">
<embed src ="audio.mp3" autostart = "true" hidden ="true">
</embed>
```

In these examples, a compulsory src attribute specifies the source of the sound. In this example, the source file is called audio.mp3.

Other background sound attributes

If you wish to loop the sound and provide a name for the sound link, use the following tags and attributes:

```
<bgsound src ="audio_kd.wav" name = "mysound" hidden=
"true" loop ="true" autostart = "true">

<embed src ="audio/kd.wav" autostart = "true" loop = "true"
hidden ="true"> </embed >
```

In the first tag description, the attribute name ="mysound" specifies a name for the sound link, while the loop ="true" causes the sound to be looped and the attribute autostart="true" will set the sound to start automatically on entry to the Web page.

If you want to make a player console visible, with a volume control, and specify height and width attributes for the player, you could use:

```
<embed src ="bitterblue.mp3" volume ="50" width="144"
height = "60" controls = "console"> </embed>
```

In the above tag description, the height attribute is set at 60 pixels, the width at 144 pixels, with the controls set to the console. The WinAmp player console is used in this example (see Figure 9.13).

Tips for using audio effectively on a website

Including sound on a website has many attractions, but it can also have adverse effects. The following points should be borne in mind when embedding sound in a website.

■ As a general rule, try not to force sound on to your Web audience. This means that it is best to avoid embedding sounds into your home page. If you must, then at least make sure that it is thoroughly tested with a range of browsers.

Figure 9.13
A player console
used with XHTML
sound tags

- Try to ensure that your sound sources are of a high quality with consistent volume. Avoid including sounds containing crackling or hissing resulting from the recording.

- Avoid creating monotonous loops. Make sure that the choice of sound does not distract or irritate users. They may not return.

- When using sound loops, try to include silent breaks or gentle fade-outs. Again, break down any monotony that might set in and adversely affect users' perceptions of the site.

Sound-editing software for creating sound files for the Web

As stated earlier in this chapter, sound often has to be captured from an analogue format, such as a tape recording, and transformed into digital format for use on a computer. However, once the audio source material has been converted, there are other things that have to be done before you can integrate the sound into a website.

Basic sound editing is required, such as removing unwanted noise in the recordings, adding digital sound effects, such as reverberation, and creating delay effects, as well as optimizing the sound files for the Web by using compression techniques and so on. Several commercially available sound editing tools are available for this purpose. They come in a variety of forms and some of them are briefly described below.

- *Sound Forge (www.sonicfoundry.com/main.asp)* is a product that has been developed by Sonic Foundry and includes many facilities, tools and effects for manipulating audio. It is well suited to audio editing and recording and effects processing. You can combine Sound Forge with any Windows-compatible sound card to create, record and edit audio files. It also has built-in support for video and CD burning and can save to a number of audio and video file formats, including WAV, WMA, RM, AVI and MP3.

- *Adobe Audition (www.adobe.com/products/audition/main.html)* is a profes-sional audio-editing environment. Designed for demanding audio and video professionals, Adobe Audition offers advanced audio mixing, editing and effects-processing capabilities. Formally known as Cool Edit, it is a popular product and is most often found in recording studios.

- *SoundEdit 16 (www.macromedia.com/software/sound)* from Macromedia is another popular digital audio application used in multimedia productions. SoundEdit contains standard audio-editing facilities, such as reverberation and delay, as well as cut and paste features. It is often bundled with software packages such as Director Studio and other Macromedia products.

Video on the Web

Video on the Web, like every other computer media, is digital. However, conventional video is analogue. Like sound and still images, therefore, a computer must digitize the analogue signals so that they become suitable for use on the Web.

The continuous analogue signals are converted into digital format by taking 30 snapshots per second. This process is called **digital video (DV)**. The snapshots are called **frames** and impose huge demands on computer memory, even for a relatively short video clip. Furthermore, video is usually accompanied by a soundtrack, which, again, slows down data transfer. This means that file compression is essential, but compression alone is not enough, so video clips seldom take up the full browser window space. Normally, a video clip on the Web would not exceed 320 pixels width × 240 pixels height. An illustration of a video on the Web is shown in Figure 9.14, from a golf tuition website.

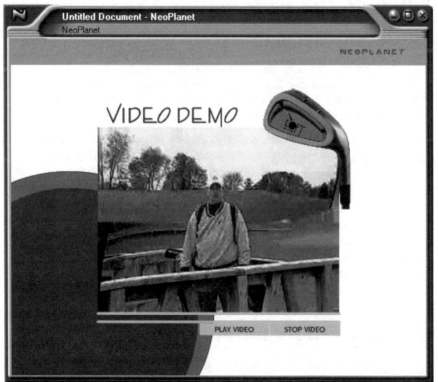

Figure 9.14
A video on the Web offering golf tuition

As with sound, you can download or stream video for playback. A video clip could be fully downloaded before it is viewed. A live video streaming clip is one that can be viewed as it is downloading.

Some video formats for the Web

Here are descriptions of some of the most popular video file formats.

- *The Moving Picture Experts Group (.mpg) format* is an International Standards Organization (ISO), high compression, very popular format. It is well supported by a range of players, including the Windows Media Player and Apple QuickTime player.
- *The QuickTime (.mov) format* is Apple's proprietary format, but is compatible with virtually all systems. It is also suitable for streaming video.
- *The Audio Video Interleaved (.avi) format* is Microsoft and Intel's proprietary format, suitable for displaying video files with sound. The .avi format can be used with the Windows Media Player or by using a QuickTime plug-in.
- *The Real Video (.ram) format* is RealNetwork's proprietary format, which can therefore be used with the RealPlayer. It is also suitable for streaming video.

Some advantages and disadvantages of video on the Web

Table 9.3 Advantages and disadvantages of video on the Web

Advantages	Disadvantages
Video can humanize aspects of communication that would sometimes be impossible using text and sound	Bandwidth can be major problem with video. Even if it is highly compressed, it is still a major problem
Video can provide another perspective in Web communications	Plug-ins cause much difficulty with video because of the range and the number that you might have to download. It is advisable to note those that have been downloaded
International viewers might gain a better understanding of video-based presentations than sites in another language based on text	

Software tools for video editing

Many established tools are available for video editing and they come in all shapes and sizes. At the lower end, there are tools such as Adobe's Premiere (www.adobe.com/premiere) – see Figure 9.15 and Pinnacle Studio (www. pinnaclesys.com), which run on both the PC and Macintosh and are designed for home and small business use. Both tools give support with storyboarding – a diagrammatic tool for planning the sequence of the video presentation, trim and arrange the clips using timelines and add titles, audio narration and music. At the upper end of the market, tools such as Avid Media (www.avid.com) provide for sophisticated television studio broadcasting as well as Web video broadcasts.

Figure 9.15
Adobe's Premiere for video editing

XHTML **for video**

Placing a video on a Web page is a lot like placing an image on the page. You must specify the src, width and height attributes. The common formats for video are avi and mov. An example of an XHTML tag with video is:

```
<embed src = "aimov.mov" width = "160" height  = "136"/>
```

In this example, a movie called "aimov.mov" is embedded and the movie is played in a window with a width ="160" and height ="136" pixels.

The Portable Document Format (PDF) on the Web

The Adobe **Portable Document Format** (.pdf) is a commonly used Web file format for rendering text and graphic-based documents. It is created and used by the

Adobe Acrobat software and is a particularly useful format because documents stored in this format will read in exactly the same way, irrespective of the browser used.

The Acrobat PDF format is probably the most widely known method for distributing portable documents, although other portable formats do exist. Based on Adobe's PostScript technology, Adobe PDF files can be viewed with browsers, providing the viewer has an Adobe reader and the necessary plug-ins.

The term portable documents refers to any sort of technology that allows you to distribute documents intact to users, without relying on the 'machine-dependent' nature of HTML. In other words, these are documents that can be viewed by the user, but only in one way. However, PDF documents cannot be reformatted to fit the needs of the user's Web browsing program or machine. The screenshot in Figure 9.16 shows a PDF document rendered on an IE browser.

Figure 9.16
A PDF format document as seen on an IE browser

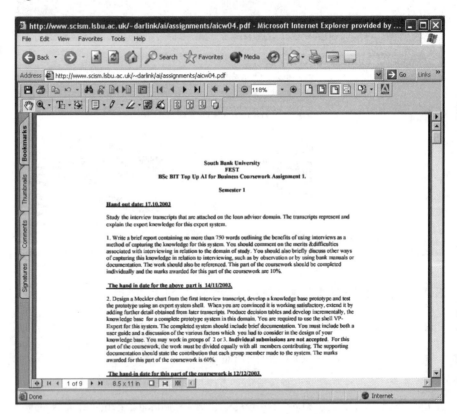

Adding PDFs to your website

Adobe distributes its Acrobat Reader free of charge and it can be downloaded from its website (www.adobe.com). However, Adobe Writer – the tool that creates Acrobat files – is not free.

Adobe Writer will enable you to create, lay out and save your files as PDF format files. If you plan to use PDF documents on your website, you might want to display a link to Adobe's website so that users can download the Adobe Reader if they do not already have it.

Adding an Acrobat file to your website takes nothing more than inserting a hyperlink with the appropriate extension. However, in order for the browser to accept these files, it needs to have the Adobe Acrobat reader set up properly as a viewer (or helper) application. In Netscape Navigator, for instance, this is accomplished via the 'Helpers' tab in Netscape's 'General Preferences' menu.

Other formats

Other file formats, such as the Microsoft Word format for text or the PowerPoint presentation file format, can provide a reasonable substitute to the Adobe PDF format. However, the alternative formats do not give you the same control over fonts and so on as the PDF format. At the same time, however, they do give you control over things like centring, text size, hard returns, font appearance (bold, italic, underlined) and similar attributes.

Among the formats that are an alternative to PDF are the following.

- *Microsoft Word* offers an easy way to distribute documents on the Web, as Word tends to be one of the most popular word processors and most other word processors can read Word's .doc files anyway. Fortunately, there's nothing special that you need to do to create a Word document that can be viewed on the Internet. The only requirement is that you use Microsoft Word to create them. Save the file with a .doc extension, just as Windows and DOS users normally would. Then, you can make it available as a hyperlink on your website, just as with any other multimedia file, as in the following example:

```
download the file in <a href="file.doc"> MS Word format
</a>.
```

- *Rich Text Format (.rtf)* is another interesting way to distribute formatted documents on the Web. This is also a Microsoft file format. It's designed to be more sophisticated than plain ASCII text, but less proprietary and complicated than word processing document types. Most word processors can create, view, print and save documents in this format. To make RTF format files available on your website, first save your document in your word processor as an RTF file with the extension .rtf. From there, all you have to do is include it in a hypertext link, such as the following:

```
<a href="myfile.rtf">Here's a copy of my special RTF
file.</a>
```

Summary of key points about PDFs

Adobe Acrobat is the most popular PDF format and adding PDF documents to your Web pages is as simple as creating a hyperlink. Acrobat files can be read with the free Acrobat viewer program that is suitable for most computer platforms.

Remember to point the user to the correct website for downloading the Adobe viewer software.

Multimedia websites resources

www.w3.org/Graphics/PNG/   Provides extensive information on the PNG graphics format.

www.faqs.org/faqs/jpeg-faq/part1/index.html   Provides answers to frequently asked questions about JPEG.

members.aol.com/royalef/gifanim.htm   Provides extensive information about the GIF format, including software tools for GIF animation.

www.webreference.com/dev/gifanim/tutorial.html   A GIF animation tutorial, including optimization techniques.

www.realplayer.com   The RealPlayer site contains many software tools for playing, editing and converting real audio format sound into MP3 and vice versa. A free MP3 player can also be downloaded.

www.angelfire.com/music2/MP3TUTORIAL/   This is an excellent tutorial for MP3, including many music downloads, music streams, artists' sites, and more.

http://webmonkey.wired.com/webmonkey/multimedia/video   A very good guide to using video on the Web. Includes digital video editing, Webcasting tools, interactive presentations with QuickTime and more.

www.streamingmediaworld.com/video/tutor/   A streaming video tutorial, including video editing for streaming and discussions of standards for video.

Summary

■ The word 'multimedia' refers to the combination of communication methods that can be used on the Web, such as text, graphics, video, sound and music.

■ To use multimedia on the Web frequently involves converting from analogue to digital format.

■ Images can be displayed using either bitmapped or vector graphics. With a bitmapped file, all the information about each pixel is stored as a sequence of bits in the file. A vector graphic file, on the other hand, contains mathematical information that is used to redraw the image on the screen.

■ There are three main graphic formats used for storing Web files. They are GIF, JPEG and PNG.

■ Use the three main Web graphic formats when the following conditions prevail.
   ■ Use GIF for low-resolution, everyday, coloured graphics and line art. GIF is well suited to animation and contains the transparency feature. Do not use GIF for high-resolution photographic work.
   ■ Use JPEG for photographic work. JPEG files are normally much larger than GIF ones, so lengthier download times are likely. Can use lossy compression to make files smaller.
   ■ PNG is now beginning to make an impression on the Web community, despite the fact that not all of its features are supported by all browsers. It has long been recommended by WC3. PNG offers support for transparency levels, colour correction controls and a lossless compression scheme.

- Some of the main problems associated with the implementation of colour on the Web are the following.

  - Dithering occurs when a colour is not available to use, so the colour is approximated by mixing pixels of similar colours that are available from the system's palette. The result of dithering is a random dot pattern, or noise, in the image. One way in which to deal with dithering is for Web designers to use the so-called 'Web-safe palette'. This consists of 216 colours that will not dither or shift when used on 8-bit monitors.

  - Aliasing sometimes renders itself as jagged, stair-stepped edges that appear between colours in a graphic image. This can be resolved by anti-aliasing, causing a slight blur to be added to the edges of objects and graphics to smooth out the edges.

- Sound can be added to a Web page using a number of formats, including MP3, MIDI, WAV and RA.

- MP3 is by far the most common format for non-streaming audio, while RA is the most common streaming 'live broadcast' audio format.

- Streaming audio on the Web allows listeners to begin listening before the file has completely downloaded.

- Sound can be embedded into XHTML pages by using the `<embed>...</embed>` tags. Background sound can be embedded by using the `<bgsound>...</bgsound>` tags.

- Several software tools can be used to edit sound for use on the Web. These include Cool Edit and Sound Forge.

- The main video formats for use on the Web are MPG, MOV, AVI, and RAM.

- Several software tools can be used for editing video for use on the Web. These include Premiere and Pinnacle Studio.

- The Adobe PDF format is a ubiquitous format for transmitting documents over the Web.

Exercises

1   Explain the role of digitization in the use of multimedia on the Web.

2   Name two household devices that are analogue and two that are digital.

3   Explain the difference between bitmapped and vector graphics.

4   Visit the website www.bbc.co.uk, then make a list of the different multimedia components that you have found on the site – sound, text, video, interactivity, graphics and so on.

5   Visit the www.mtv.com site. Make a list of the facilities available for the music buyer. Why is the inclusion of sound so important to this site?

6   Visit the Web page http://main.wgbh.org/wgbh/access/ to find out what multimedia can do to help disabled groups, such as visually impaired or deaf users.

7   Create a page that plays a background sound three times while displaying a background image as a watermark.

8   Add an AVI video clip to your page and have it play twice as the page loads, without showing controls.

9   Find two websites that use video to entertain. What do you think the sites that you have visited give the viewer that a non-video site could not give?

10   Find a website that uses video to educate the user in some way. Explain what difference the use of video makes to your understanding.

11   Create a simple Word document for distribution on your website. Download it over the Internet. If possible, use a different computer to download the Word document and view it in Word or the Word viewer. Does it look any different? If yes, in what ways?

10

Extensible Markup Language (XML)

In this chapter you will learn about:

- the concepts of XML
- the need for XML
- parsing XML and Document Type Definition (DTD)
- XML schema
- style sheet languages for XML
- XForms
- validating XML documents.

Introduction

XML – Extensible Markup Language – has established itself as the developers' language for the future of the Web. XML is a structured set of rules for how one might define any kind of data to be shared on the Web. It is called 'extensible' because it can be modified to suit any purpose and, as long as everyone uses it (the writer and an application program at the receiver's end), it can be adapted and used for many purposes, including describing the appearance of a Web page. Many in the Web community see XML as the most important technology used on the Web today.

It should be made clear from the outset that XML is not another version or replacement for HTML – both were designed with different goals in mind. The goal of HTML was to *display* information on the Web, whereas the primary goal of XML is to *describe* information on the Web. The purpose of XML is to structure, store and transmit information on the Web. It is also important to realize that, unlike HTML, XML by itself does not do anything, such as display or format the document. Neither does it use any predefined elements, as HTML does. Instead, you create or define your own elements and attributes. For example, if you wanted to describe the structure of supermarket shelf items, you could define tags and attributes as follows:

Listing 10.1 XML supermarket tags

```
<supermarketitems>
<item>
<name>Baked Beans</name>
<manufacturer> Heinz</manufacturer>
<size> small </size>
<cost>.45</cost>
</item>
<item>
<name>Corn Flakes</name>
<manufacturer> Kellogg's </manufacturer>
<size> medium </size>
<cost>.95 </cost>
</item>
<item>
<name>Biscuits</name>
<manufacturer> McVities </manufacturer>
<size>large</size>
<cost> 2.25 </cost>
</item>
</supermarketitems>
```

Note from Listing 10.1 that the tags here have been defined as <supermarketitems>, <item>, <name>, <manufacturer>, <size> and <cost>, which are not part of any HTML standard. In this example, we can see that the XML code contains data describing three supermarket items.

It should also be clear that these tags do not do anything other than store and structure information. If we wanted to format this data for a report or something like that, then we could use an XML style sheet language. We will come back to this example later in this chapter to see how this would be done after we have looked at the evolution of XML in a little more depth.

The rationale for Extensible Markup Language (XML)

HTML, as we have already seen in Chapter 5, has undergone several revisions, the latest being XHTML 2.0 (W3C, May 2003). The early versions of HTML included only elements for text formatting and displaying graphics. As the Web evolved and the number of users grew, so the demand grew for tags that not only improved the layout of text and graphics facilities but also delivered more sophisticated features, such as the implementation of forms, frames, dynamic behaviour, video, sound and so on.

Each new standard for HTML has added more features to the specification, which may or may not be implemented in a given browser. Frequently, a browser implements not only most of the features defined by the specification, but also a series of its own proprietary tags. The Netscape 4.0 layer tag is a case in point. This is an example of a tag that will not work on a Microsoft IE browser or even later versions of Netscape. Moreover, with the Web constantly evolving, the turnaround time required for the W3C to formulate new standards for HTML was too long.

The relationship between XML, HTML and SGML

The revision problem that has beleaguered HTML since its beginning led to the view that a new markup language was needed that could be implemented once and never need new revisions. However, instead of looking to a new markup language, the W3C decided to look back to the roots of HTML – that is, SGML.

This is because SGML is a **meta-language**. A **meta-language** is one for describing other languages. It allows you to create documents that describe themselves to their reader, such as documents containing newly defined tags and attributes.

HTML is not a meta-language – you cannot expand its vocabulary. In order to do this, a proposal needs to be submitted to and approved by the W3C.

SGML is a good general language for marking up all kinds of data, but, unfortunately, it is not really tailored to deployment in an environment like the Web because it does too much and is too big for this purpose.

The W3C realized that what was needed, then, was a scaled-down version of SGML, from which the W3C developed the specification for Extensible Markup Language (XML).

To summarize, SGML is a large extensible language and HTML is a non-extensible subset of SGML. XML can be seen as a middle point, with the network-centric non-extensible HTML on one end and the general-purpose extensible SGML on the other. The relationships between XML, HTML, XHTML and SGML are depicted in the Venn diagram shown in Figure 10.1.

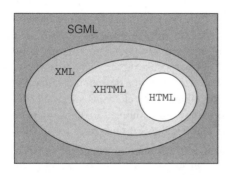

Figure 10.1
Venn diagram depicting the relationship between SGML, XML, XHTML and HTML

The design goals for XML

In designing XML, the W3C has taken into account several design goals. These goals define a plan for a markup language that fixes the evolution and compatibility problems that plagued HTML and is better than SGML in that it is geared for Internet deployment and is easier to use. The W3C defines the XML's goals on its website address (www.w3.org/TR/WD-xml-lang) as follows.

■ XML *shall be straightforwardly usable over the Internet.*

■ XML *shall support a wide variety of applications.*

■ XML *shall be compatible with* SGML.

■ *It shall be easy to write programs that process* XML *documents.*

■ *The number of optional features shall be kept to the absolute minimum.*

■ XML *documents shall be human-legible and reasonably clear.*

■ *The* XML *design should be prepared quickly.*

■ *The design of* XML *shall be formal and concise.*

■ XML *documents shall be easy to create.*

The major advantages of XML

There are three main advantages using XML over other markup languages.

■ The emphasis in XML is on descriptive rather than procedural markup. By 'descriptive', we mean that the markup elements themselves actually describe the structure of the document. For example, in Listing 10.1, we can see that the structure is a list of three supermarket items and details. This structure is implicitly contained in the markup. By contrast, procedural markup defines processing tasks to be carried out, such as, in HTML, the <b> </b> container is a command to make the text bold. However, a procedural task can be performed in an XML document by using programs called style sheets that are separate from the XML document, thus differentiating the descriptive markup from the procedural markup. This approach is consistent with the spirit of the W3C so often emphasized throughout this book.

■ XML documents can conform to a **document type**. The type of a document is formally defined by its constituent parts and their structure. The definition of a 'supermarket item', for example, might be that it consists of an 'item that has a name attribute associated with it, a "size" and "cost"'. Anything lacking a cost, for example, would not formally be a 'supermarket item'. If documents are of known types, a special-purpose program – called a **parser** – can check that any document claiming to be of that type does in fact conform to the specification. A parser can check that all and only elements specified for a particular document type are present, that they are combined in appropriate ways, correctly ordered and so forth. Document parsing is discussed in more detail later in this chapter.

■ XML is both hardware- and software-independent. A basic design goal of XML is that of ensuring that documents encoded according to its provisions can move from one hardware and software environment to another without any loss of information. All XML documents – irrespective of whatever language or writing system they employ – use the same underlying character encoding. The encoding is defined by the Unicode that was discussed in Chapter 5. This means that XML provides a method for not only communicating between different applications and different platforms in a standardized way but also for, in essence, defining new languages suitable for solving particular problems, such as in the domains of mathematics, business or multimedia, to name just three examples.

XML as a meta-language

DTD documents and style sheets enable us to define new XML-based languages specific to a given problem. HTML is the standard language for representing Web documents so all Web browsers know it and, when given an HTML document, can display it in a more or less standard fashion. The basic insight underlying XML was that it should be possible to define other languages, designed to solve other problems besides just displaying Web pages, in an equally standard fashion. Thus, XML is really a `meta-language`. In other words, it is a language for defining other languages. It has spawned the birth of many specific markup languages designed to solve specific problems. In the following sections, we will look at how XML is written and used on the Web.

Creating XML documents

As with XHTML (see Chapter 5), the first line in an XML document should be the processing instruction:

```
<?xml version="1.0" ?>
```

The W3C recommends that this declaration be included in all XHTML documents, although it is optional and only required when the character encoding of the document is other than the default UTF-8 or UTF-16.

You will recall from Chapter 5 that XHTML requires all tags to be enclosed within the `<html> </html>` container. This is called the root element and `html` should be the root element for all XHTML documents.

In the same way, XML requires that there must be one, and only one, root element for a document. The root element is the base element of a document, containing all the other elements in the document. In Listing 10.1, the root element is clearly `supermarketitem`, as it contains all the other elements in the listing. For example, look at the XML code below. The root element of this listing is clearly `<books>`:

```
<-- ! Sample XML Describing a Listing of Books -->

<books>
<heading>Great Web Design Books</heading>
<title>Learning Web Design </title>
<author>Jennifer Niedhurst </author>
```

```
<title>HTML - The Definitive Guide </title>
<author>Musciano & Kennedy </author>
<title>Cascading Style Sheets Complete </title>
<author>Busch Olsen </author>
</books>
```

Displaying XML using a browser

HTML describes to a browser the manner in which the HTML page should be displayed onscreen. However, that is not the purpose of an XML document. Rather, it simply serves to *describe* the data contained in the files. When an XML page is sent to a browser for onscreen display, it usually arrives with a style sheet or Document Type Definition (DTD) that tells the browser how to display the text. In the event that it doesn't, then it will probably be displayed as shown using the Mozilla Firefox browser in Figure 10.2. However, the same document displayed in Netscape 7.0 is shown in Figure 10.3. Notice that Netscape has made an attempt to display the content.

Figure 10.2
Listing 10.1 rendered on a Netscape 7 browser

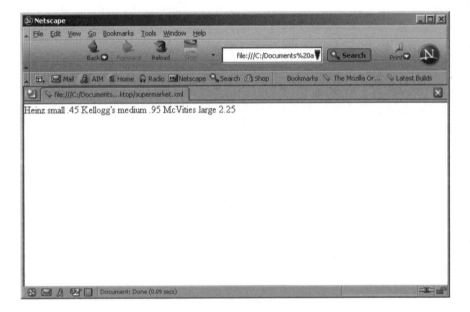

Rules for creating XML documents

XML documents must conform to the following rules.

■ Creating XML, like XHTML, requires that the tag structure be very rigid. All tags must either exist in pairs or announce to the browser that a closing tag is not present. For example, the <br> break tag does not have a closing tag, but, if used in XML, a closing tag would be required or XML would be told that it is not present.

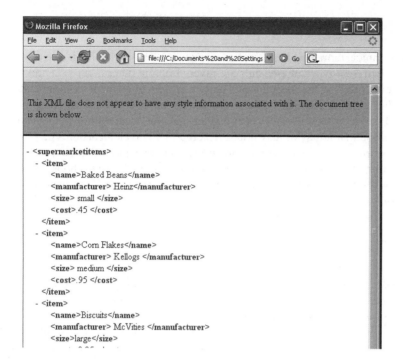

Figure 10.3
Listing 10.1
displayed on a
Mozilla Firefox
browser

To show that a tag stands alone, it would end with a trailing slash, indicating the lack of a closing tag. For example, we would write `<br></br>` as `<br/>`.

- XML also requires that all attribute values occur in quotation marks. For example, the following tag pair is incorrect: `<color value = red></color>`. Instead, you would have to write this as: `<color value = "red"></color >`. HTML itself originally asked the same of authors. However, it seems that, over time, authors realized that their omission didn't matter if they were using quotation marks and browsers stopped requiring them.

- XML is, like XHTML, case-sensitive. Make sure that all tags use lower-case characters and no capitalization is used in tag keywords or attributes.

- XML will not allow any illegal nesting of tags. This means that, for every open tag, its closing tag must appear at an unambiguous location. For instance, in the first example below, there is some ambiguity regarding which question is being closed by the first and then the second `</question>` tags. The listing below this demonstrates how the code should be written to ensure a valid nesting of tags.

Example of an invalid XML tag structure:

```
<title>Test</title>
<question>What is the average weight of a cat?
<question>What kind of cat?</question></question>
```

Example of a valid XML tag structure

```
<title>Test </title>
<question>What is the average weight of a cat? </question>
<question>What kind of cat?</question>
```

Elements

The technical term used in XML for a textual unit is **element** – that is, the text within a tag. Different types of elements are given different names, but XML provides no way of expressing the meaning of a particular type of element, other than its relationship to other element types. For example, all one can say about an element called <zok> is that instances of it may or may not occur within elements of type <poh> and that it may or may not be decomposed into elements of type <tis>. In other words, XML is unconcerned about the semantics of textual elements – these are application-dependent. It is up to the creators of XML code to choose intelligible names for the elements that they identify and define their proper use in text markup.

XML parsers

In order to process an XML document, a software program called a **parser** is required. The **parser** reads the document, checks its syntax, repairs any errors and allows access to the document's contents.

An XML document is considered **well formed** if it is syntactically correct – that is, the parser did not report any errors due to missing tags, overlapping tags and so on. Every XML document *must* be well formed and it is only going to be well formed if it conforms to the rules given earlier. If a document is well formed, the parser will display the document, such as Listing 10.1, like that shown in Figure 10.2 when using the Mozilla browser. The same document displayed in Netscape 7.0 is shown in Figure 10.3. Notice that Netscape has made an attempt to display the content. Both these browsers – in different ways – have attempted to display information without any knowledge of the rules concerning the elements in the super-market.xlm file. Knowledge of the elements can be provided by using a Document Type Definition (DTD).

The Document Type Definition (DTD)

As stated earlier, XML is a meta-language that lets you develop markup languages that obey certain rules. A DTD adds extra rules that state which elements can be used in the markup language, how they can be used with others and also what attributes and default values are usable. If we take the supermarket.xlm file, we know from Listing 10.1 that the tags have been defined as <supermarketitems>, <item>, <name>, <manufacturer>, <size> and <cost>. We can write a DTD file that codifies this information. The file called supermarket.dtd can be created, like any XML file, by using an ordinary text editor, such as NotePad, and is displayed in Listing 10.2. Notice that the syntax of this file is different to the syntax for XML documents.

Listing 10.2 The DTD supermarket file – `supermarket.dtd`

```
<!-- Top-level element, supermarkets contains a list of
supermarket items.-->
<!ELEMENT supermarketitems (item+)>

 <!--An item contains an optional name followed by a
manufacturer, size and cost.-->
<!ELEMENT item (name,manufacturer,size,cost)>

<!ELEMENT name              (#PCDATA)>
<!ELEMENT manufacturer      (#PCDATA)>
<!ELEMENT size              (#PCDATA)>
<!ELEMENT cost              (#PCDATA)>
```

The body of the DTD itself contains definitions in terms of elements and their attributes. The `<!ELEMENT supermarketitems (item+)>` line, for example, defines the DTD for `supermarketitems`. In effect, this line says that the `supermarketitems` element may contain one or more item elements – the '+' symbol indicates one or more. In more general terms, after the `<!ELEMENT` markup comes the element name, followed by its **content model**. In this declaration, the content model is seen to be `(item+)`. It states that a supermarket item has a name, manufacturer, size and cost. Each remaining element consists of parsed character data (`PCDATA`). This means that each remaining element can contain only text or numbers.

A DTD declares a set of allowed elements and allowed attributes for each element. These represent the permitted lexicon. No other element names or attributes are permitted.

NOTE

Accessing DTDs in XML documents

DTDs are linked into XML documents by using the document type declaration DOCTYPE in the linked XML document. To understand how this is used, notice that Listing 10.1 references `supermarket.dtd` using a document type declaration, as follows:

```
<!DOCTYPE supermarketitems SYSTEM "supermarket.dtd">
```

The DOCTYPE declaration above indicates that the Listing 10.1 document conforms to a DTD that is in a file called `supermarket.dtd`, with root element `supermarketitems`. There are other possible variations on this declaration, as we will see later.

Creating valid XML documents

When developing an XML file, that file can be defined as either valid, well formed or both. Valid XML files are those that have and follow a given Document Type Definition (DTD) such as the XML file shown in Listing 10.1.

NOTE

A well-formed XML file is one that can be used without a DTD. While a DTD is not required, a well-formed XML file must conform to the tag and attribute rules specified earlier in the section.

IE 5 uses a built-in parser called **msml**.

Using XML schema as an alternative to a DTD

XML document types can be defined using an XML schema instead of a DTD. Indeed, the XML schema is likely to replace the use of DTDs in the future. There are advantages to using XML schema as they are written in XML, which ensures more consistency in the code and the element structure is written so that it is easier to process using XML applications.

Writing schema files

Listing 10.3 displays an XML schema file corresponding to the supermarket DTD shown in Listing 10.2.

Notice first from Listing 10.3 that the statements in this file are XML statements and, therefore, the first statement defines the version of XML being used with the file.

If you study the remainder of the listing, there is a supermarketitems element, which is defined as being a sequence of item elements. Notice that a maxOccurs attribute has been set at "unbounded", meaning that there can be one or more item elements. The item element again consists of a sequence containing name, manufacturer, size and cost elements. Both the elements supermarketitems and item contain other elements, so **complex types** are used to define them. The elements name, manufacturer, size and cost, however, are defined as **simple types** because they are not divisible into further elements. Notice also that the tags are prefixed with xs: and the prologue section contains the tag:

```
<xs:schema xmlns:xs = "http://www.w3.org/2001/XMLSchema">
```

This schema element uses the familiar namespace attribute xmlns:xs.

Listing 10.3 XML schema file called `supermarket.xsd`

```
<?xml version = "1.0"?>
<xs:schema xmlns:xs = "http://www.w3.org/2001/XMLSchema">

    <xs:element name = "supermarketitems">
                         <xs:complexType>
                           <xs:sequence>
        <xs:element ref = "item" maxOccurs ="unbounded"/>
                           </xs:sequence>
                         </xs:complexType>
    </xs:element>

    <xs:element name = "item">
                         <xs:complexType>
                           <xs:sequence>
                                 <xs:element ref = "name"/>
                             <xs:element ref = "manufacturer"/>
                                 <xs:element ref = "size"/>
                                 <xs:element ref = "cost"/>
                           </xs:sequence>
                         </xs:complexType>
    </xs:element>

    <xs:element name = "name" type = "xs:string"/>
    <xs:element name = "manufacturer" type = "xs:string"/>
    <xs:element name = "size" type = "xs:string"/>
    <xs:element name = "cost" type = "xs:string"/>
</xs:schema>
```

Referencing a schema file

You do not reference an XML schema file from an XML file using the DOCTYPE declaration as you would when using a DTD. Instead, attributes of the root element of the document are used. For example, if the file in Listing 10.3 was saved as `super-market.xsd`, then this schema could be referenced using the following coding:

```
<?xml version = "1.0"?>
<supermarketitems xmlns: xsi =
"http://www.w3.org/2001/XMLSchema-instance"
Xsi:noNamespaceSchemaLocation = "supermarket.xsd">
..
</supermarketitems>
```

Using a CDATA section in XML

If your text in XML code contains the < character or & character – as program code often does – they could pose a problem in that their meanings could conflict with the intended meanings of the tags. To overcome this problem, you could define XML elements as a CDATA section. Everything inside a CDATA section is ignored by the parser. This gives you the opportunity to use these, or any other special characters, if you wish to do so in your XML code.

A CDATA section always starts with <![CDATA[and ends with]]>. For example, suppose you wanted to include a JavaScript section of code, such as that shown in Listing 10.4.

Listing 10.4 Illustrating CDATA with XML

```
<script>

<![CDATA[
function min(x,y)
        {
        if ( x< y && x > 0) then
        {
                     return true
        }
        else
         {
                     return false
        }
}
]]>
</script>
```

You will notice that all the occurrences of these special characters are ignored by the XML parser in Listing 10.4.

NOTE — A CDATA section must start with <![CDATA[and finish with]]>.

Moving from HTML to XML

You will have little trouble converting those files created with HTML to XML, if you have carefully developed the HTML. However, sloppy HTML needs some fixing due to XML's strong typing.

The first step in converting an HTML page to an XML one is making sure that the page is well formed. After this is done, you need to add a DTD to the XML document's header and ensure that it references one of the available HTML DTDs.

The HTML DTD tells the reader application how to deal with each of the tags that are part of the HTML specification.

Using style sheets with XML

Introduction

As previously stated, the purpose of XML is to capture the structure of the information to be displayed. However, there are times when you will want to view XML documents, in which case, you will probably want to add style or formatting characteristics. You can do this by using CSS or XSL. Both have been recommended by the W3C.

XML with CSS

In this section, we will look at a fairly simple example that illustrates how the supermarket.xml file can be used with a CSS file to achieve a suitable layout. Figure 10.4 shows how the supermarket file looks when it is externally linked to the CSS file shown in Listing 10.5.

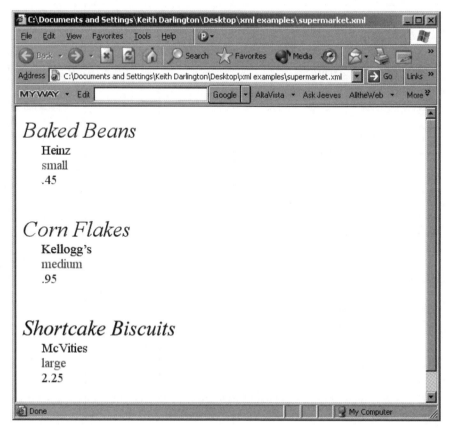

Figure 10.4
Supermarket XML file CSS style sheet displayed on an IE 6 browser

Listing 10.5 CSS file used with XML

```
supermarket - Notepad

File  Edit  Format  View  Help

supermarketitems
{
background-color: #ffffff;
width: 100%;
}
item
{
        display: block;
        margin-bottom: 30pt;
        margin-left: 0;
}

name
{
        display: block;
        color: #000000;
        font-size: 24pt;
        font-style:italic;
}

manufacturer
{
        display: block;
        color: #0000;
        margin-left: 20pt;
        font-size: 14pt;
}
        size
{
        display: block;
        margin-left: 20pt;
        color: #FF0000;
        font-size: 14pt;
}
        cost
{
        display: block;
        margin-left: 20pt;
        font-size: 14pt;
}
```

CSS selectors can be applied to XML elements in the same way that they can be applied to XHTML elements. Notice that the line:

```
<?xml-stylesheet type = "text/css" href =
"supermarket.css"?>
```

links the style sheet to the supermarket file as shown in Listing 10.6. The properties used in this CSS file will be familiar from Chapter 8.

Self-assessed exercise

Amend the CSS supermarket style sheet file as shown in Listing 10.5 so that the font applied to each name element is 20-point Arial.

Extensible Stylesheet Language (XSL)

CSS has the capabilities to format and style a document, but can do little more than this and, for this reason, a more sophisticated style sheet language has been created

Listing 10.6 XSL applied to an XML product

```
supermarket - Notepad                                      _ □ ×
File  Edit  Format  View  Help
<?xml version = "1.0"?>

<?xml-stylesheet type = "text/css" href = "supermarket.css"?>

<supermarketitems>
<item>
<name>Baked Beans</name>
<manufacturer> Heinz</manufacturer>
<size> small </size>
<cost>.45 </cost>
</item>
<item>
<name>Corn Flakes</name>
<manufacturer> Kellogg's </manufacturer>
<size> medium </size>
<cost>.95 </cost>
</item>
<item>
<name>Shortcake Biscuits</name>
<manufacturer> McVities </manufacturer>
<size>large</size>
<cost> 2.25 </cost>
</item>
</supermarketitems>
```

for use with XML. This is called **Extensible Stylesheet Language (XSL)** and was written specifically to work with XML.

XSL is superior to CSS because, by using it, you can transform a document before it is displayed. This gives tremendous scope for formatting XML documents. For example, you could transform an XML document to HTML for display purposes. You could also generate output for other media, such as WML for WAP phones (see Chapter 14) and so on.

If you want to link an XLM document to an XSL style sheet, you will need to include – as with the previous CSS example – a statement of the following form before the XML code:

```
<?xml:stylesheet type = "text/xsl" href = "super1.xsl"?>
```

Before we look at an example, there are some things that you need to know about XSL syntax. When you use XSL, you will often want to transform container and empty tags. The prefix xsl: is used before the XML tag name to indicate the use of the XSL namespace:

```
<xsl:stylesheet xmlns =
http://www.w3.org/1999/XSL/Transform version = "1.0">
```

Understanding the meaning of the XSL code in Listing 10.7

The code shown in the listing will transform the XML into HTML.

The purpose of the `<?xml version = "1.0"?>` tag has been described earlier in this chapter, but note that the `<xsl: stylesheet>` tag contains the version and namespace attributes. The version attribute – version="1.0" – indicates

Listing 10.7 XSL style sheet applied to supermarket file for transforming to HTML

```
super - Notepad                                                    _□×
File  Edit  Format  View  Help

<?xml version = "1.0"?>
<xsl:stylesheet version ="1.0" xmlns:xsl ="http://www.w3.org/1999/XSL/Transform'
  <xsl:template match = "supermarketitems">
    <html>
    <head>
      <title>Creating an HTML Document from the Supermarket XML file </title>
    </head>
    <body>
       <p><h3>List of Supermarket Items and Details</h3></p>
       <table border = "2">
       <tr>
          <th>Item Name</th>
          <th width ="100">Manufacturer </th>
          <th padding ="30">Size</th>
          <th>Cost</th>
       </tr>
       </table>

       <xsl:apply-templates/>
       </body>
    </html>
  </xsl:template>

  <xsl:template match = "item">

     <table border = "2">

        <tr>
            <td  width ="70">
               <xsl:value-of select = "name"/>
            </td>

            <td width ="100">
               <xsl:value-of select = "manufacturer"/>
            </td>
             <td width ="30">
               <xsl:value-of select = "size"/>
            </td>
             <td width ="30">
               <xsl:value-of select = "cost"/>
            </td>
        </tr>

     </table>
  </xsl:template>
```

version 1.0 compatibility. The xmlns:xsl attribute defines the :xsl prefix as referring to tags in the XSL namespace. If the xmlns attribute had no :xsl suffix, this would indicate that the default namespace for non-XSL tags would be XHTML.

The line <xsl: template match = "supermarketitems"> is an XSL template instruction – a **template** provides a pattern that can be matched for processing. Before the XSL applies the style sheet instructions, the first thing it looks for is a template that matches the root node. In the case of the supermarket file, the root node is "supermarketitems". The root node is also indicated by '/'.

After the template match on the root node, the HTML template begins with the html, head and body elements. Within the body, a table is created to render the headings for the table shown in Figure 10.5. The empty tag <xsl: apply-templates/> is used to tell the processor to match against stipulated tags in the source tree and insert the output into the result tree in a given location.

The next template match tag – <xsl: template match = "item"> – follows up by entering data into table cells, giving values from the <xsl: value-of > tags. For example, the <xsl: value-of select = "name"/> will return the

Figure 10.5
XSL applied to an
XML document

value of the `<name>` from the current template match, and so on, until the table of data is complete.

An application of XML: XForms

In this, the final section of this chapter on XML, we look at XForms – one of the many applications of XML.

XForms represent the next generation of HTML forms. The first version of XForms was released as a W3C recommendation during August 2003.

The standard XHTML forms (discussed in Chapter 6) are adequate as long as you have some knowledge of scripting. The problem is that many Web designers find scripting difficult and time-consuming to learn. Moreover, Web applications and e-commerce solutions have sparked the demand for better Web forms with richer interactions. Standard forms are also very device-dependent – running well only on desktop browsers, not always on other devices such as mobile phones, PDAs and so on, which is becoming a problem as their popularity has increased tremendously. XForms now provide a viable alternative to standard forms.

According to the W3C (www.w3.org/TR/2003/PR-xforms-20030801/slice1.html):

XForms 1.0 is the response to this demand, and provides a new platform-independent markup language for online interaction between a person (through an XForms Processor) and another, usually remote, agent. XForms are the successor to HTML forms, and benefit from the lessons learned from HTML forms.

The primary difference between XForms and HTML forms is that, with XForms, there is a separation between the data being collected and the markup of the controls collecting the individual values. By doing this, it becomes clear what is being submitted where. Using XForms also makes reuse of forms easier, as the underlying, essential part of a form is no longer irretrievably bound to the page it is used in.

A second major difference is that XForms, while designed to be integrated into XHTML, are no longer restricted to only being a part of that language, but can be integrated into any suitable markup language if desired – such as WML (see Chapter 14).

How XForms are used

In the XForms approach, forms are comprised of a section that describes what the form does – known as the **XForms model** – and another section that describes how the form is to be presented. The Listings 10.8 and 10.9 demonstrate how this works with the following example. It is a simple online payment form that might be rendered on the Web page segment as shown in Figure 10.6.

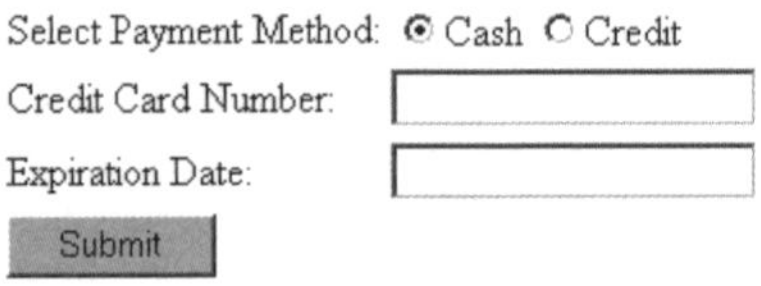

Figure 10.6
A simple online payment form as it is rendered on the Web page

Select Payment Method: ⦿ Cash ○ Credit
Credit Card Number: [   ]
Expiration Date: [   ]
[Submit]

By studying this layout, it is clear that we are collecting a value that represents whether cash or a credit card is being used for the transaction. If a credit card is being used, then its number and expiration date must be supplied in the form. This can be represented in an XForms `model` element, as shown in Listing 10.8.

The XForm model is defined by the container `<xforms:model>` `</xforms:model>`. An instance of the XForms model is then defined by the container `<xforms:instance></xforms:instance>`. The payment container says that three items of information are being collected and that they will be submitted using the URL in the `action` attribute.

The `method` attribute takes one of the possible values `"post"` or `"get"` and has the same meaning as it does with standard forms processing (covered in Chapter 6).

Note also the use of the `id` attribute taking the value `submit`. The XForms model would generally appear in the `head` section of a document.

Listing 10.8 Illustration of an XForms model

```
<xforms:model>
  <xforms:instance>
    <payment xmlns="">
      <method/>
      <cardno/>
      <expiry/>
    </payment>
  </xforms:instance>
  <xforms:submission action="http://example.com/submit"
method="post" id="submit" includenamespaceprefixes=""/>
</xforms:model>
```

With XForms, you can define a device-neutral, platform-independent set of form controls suitable for general-purpose use that can then be bound to the XForms model via the XForms by using the `ref` attribute (see Listing 10.9) in the controls section of the coding. In XHTML, this markup would typically appear within the body section.

Listing 10.9 Illustration of XForms section concerning the controls

```
<select1 ref = "method">
  <label>Select Payment Method:</label>
  <item>
    <label>Cash</label>
    <value>cash</value>
  </item>
  <item>
    <label>Credit</label>
    <value>cc</value>
  </item>
</select1>
<input ref="cardno">
  <label>Credit Card Number:</label>
</input>
<input ref="expiry">
  <label>Expiration Date:</label>
</input>
<submit submission="submit">
  <label>Submit</label>
</submit>
```

There are many advantages to using this approach to design. First, the user interface is not hard-coded to use radio buttons. This means that different devices (such as voice browsers) can render the concept of 'select one' as appropriate. Also, there is no need for the `form` element, as in HTML, and the corresponding markup for specifying form controls is simpler than for HTML forms.

XML **Web resources**

The following is a list of Web tutorial articles on XML.
www.xml.org   This is the industry portal for XML. This site gives access to many XML resources.

www.w3.org/pub/WWW/TR/   This is the WC3's XML specification document.

www.w3schools.com/xml/xml_editors.asp   A very good introduction to XML for both the beginner and experienced user. Included is an online editor which allows you to edit and experiment with XML code. There is also a quiz that tests your knowledge of the subject when you have completed the lessons.

http://msdn.microsoft.com/library/en-us/xmlsdk30/htm/xmtutxmltutorial.asp
A Microsoft XML tutorial covering all concepts of XML.

www.brics.dk/~amoeller   The XML RevolutionTechnologies for the future Web.

www.ibiblio.org/pub/sun-info/standards/xml/why/xmlapps.htm   Jon Bosak's (Sun Microsystems) article 'XML, Java and the future of the Web'. Quite an old article now, but still useful.

www.zvon.org/o_html/group_xml_newbie.html   Another useful XML tutorial called 'XML basics quick start', from ZVON.org, The Guide to the XML Galaxy.

www.computer.org/internet/xml/xml.tutorial.pdf   'Extending your Markup: An XML Tutorial' by André Bergholz (Stanford University), *IEEE Computing*, July/August 2000.

www.tei-c.org/Guidelines2/gentleintro.html   Another gentle introduction to XML.

Summary

■ XML stands for Extensible Markup Language and can be used to suit any purpose.

■ XML is, like XHTML, another descendant of SGML.

■ The goal of XML is to describe information on the Web. It does not use any predefined elements, like HTML, but lets the user define their own.

■ XML conforms to strict syntax rules.

■ An XML document is said to be well formed if it is syntactically correct. A parser is a program that checks to see if an XML document is well formed or not.

■ A Document Type Definition (DTD) can be used with XML to incorporate rules that state what elements, tags and attributes can be used with the user application. An XML document that conforms to its DTD is said to be valid.

■ XML document types can be defined using an XML schema instead of a DTD.

■ There are advantages to using XML schemas as they are written in XML, which ensures more consistency in code, and the element structure is written in such a way that it is easier to process using XML applications.

■ XML does not do anything by itself, but style languages can be used with XML such as CSS and XSL.

■ XForms is one of many applications of XML gaining popularity on the Web.

Exercises

1   Explain the meaning of the term meta-language and what advantages XML has over HTML as a result.

2   Explain the differences between the markup languages SGML, HTML and XML.

3   What is the difference between a well-formed document and a valid document? What is the purpose of a parser?

4   Explain the purpose of a CDATA section in an XML document.

5   Identify and correct the errors in the following XML code:

```
a   <?xml version = "1.0">
b   <2ton> weight </2ton>
c   <THEAMOUNT> 50 </THEAMOUNT>
d   <inequal> 5 > 4 </inequal>
e   <this><that> or the other </this></that>
f   <CDATA> Here it is!</CDATA>
g   <customer name = keith> big spender </customer>
h   <md cd>The Best of U2</my cd>
```

6   Use NotePad or some other text editor to create the `supermarket.xml` file as shown in Listing 10.1. Test the file using IE, Netscape and Opera browsers. Compare the output in each case.

7   Create an XML document that marks up the structure as shown in the structure chart in Figure 10.7 using the following data:

■ the course is Internet Computing, duration is three years, the level is BSc degree
■ the course is Business Information Technology, duration is two years, the level is HND.

Figure 10.7
Structure for XML document

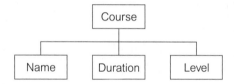

8   Create an XML document that marks up the details of the following music CD collection. One CD in the collection has been recorded by the group called the Stereophonics, the title of the CD is 'Word Gets Around' and the names of specimen tracks are 'A thousand trees', 'Looks like Chaplin' and 'Goldfish bowl'. Another CD in the collection is called 'Revolver', recorded by the Beatles, and contains the tracks 'Good day sunshine', 'Dr Robert' and 'Tomorrow never knows'. Check that the code is well formed by running it with the IE browser.

9   Write a CSS style sheet to apply to the XML document that you have created in question 8 to do the following: make the title 24-point Arial and colour each track title green. Place a border around the data.

10   Amend the CSS supermarket style sheet file as shown in Listing 10.5 so that the font applied to each size element is 14-point Times New Roman. Check the code using Netscape 6 and IE 6 browsers.

11   Write an XSL style sheet for question 8, so that the data is transformed into an HTML table containing the CD's title as a heading and then the track numbers 1, 2 and 3 in the first column and the corresponding track titles in the second column. Test the code using an IE 6 browser.

12   Use the Google search engine to find three websites that use different applications of XForms. Write a short paragraph summarizing each one.

Chapter

Introduction to Dreamweaver MX

In this chapter you will learn how to:

- set up your computer for a new Dreamweaver site
- define a local site
- choose a workspace layout
- make your Dreamweaver pages XHTML-compliant
- create and edit a new Web page using text and graphics
- set page properties
- create hyperlinks to other pages and check links
- add graphical images to a Web page
- connect to a remote site
- create an e-mail link
- embed audio and video files.

Introduction

This chapter provides an introduction to the steps involved in building a website using Dreamweaver. With it, you can develop a site from scratch fairly quickly – it is a rapid development tool. The approach taken in this book is version-independent, although reference will occasionally be made when differences in versions are important. The emphasis is on hands-on examples to help you understand how to define a local site and create, edit and link Web pages. The first of the three chapters focusing on Dreamweaver, here we will look at the fundamentals, including the use of templates for speed development. The next two chapters on Dreamweaver give a flavour of how more advanced features can be used, along with a description of how various Web technologies can be utilized.

As we have seen in earlier chapters, Web pages can be marked up by using a text editor, but this can be a time-consuming process. Dreamweaver is a WYSIWYG (what you see is what you get) Web development tool – meaning that it is not necessary for the Web designer to express commands in the form of HTML tags. The

Dreamweaver interface enables you to bypass HTML because Dreamweaver inserts the appropriate tags when required. This means that the designer can edit Web pages without having any contact with HTML. In practice, however, it often helps to have knowledge of HTML because sometimes fine-tuning at the HTML level becomes necessary if a particular technology is not supported. The Dreamweaver designer can flip from WYSIWYG development mode – called **Design View** – to HTML mode – called **Code View** – and edit in either mode. The designer can also convert documents from HTML to XHTML format if required.

Dreamweaver is much more than a WYSIWYG Web page editor, though. It is a complete professional website development tool, handling all the usual HTML components, including forms, tables, frames, layers, images and hyperlinks. It also includes JavaScript components and behaviours, and supports countless other Web technologies, including XML and CSS. It is also well equipped, with an array of site management facilities including a built-in FTP client, which can be used to upload sites as well as for team development support. Dreamweaver also contains an array of testing and checking facilities, including multiple browser-testing facilities, link checking and markup validation. Recent versions of Dreamweaver provide facilities for dynamic database connectivity applications using server technologies, such as ColdFusion, ASP, PHP and JSP (more on this in Chapter 13). As of the time of writing, Dreamweaver MX 2004 (see Figure 11.1) is the most recently released version in use and many examples using this version are included in this book, although many of the methods should also work with earlier versions with a minimum of tweaking.

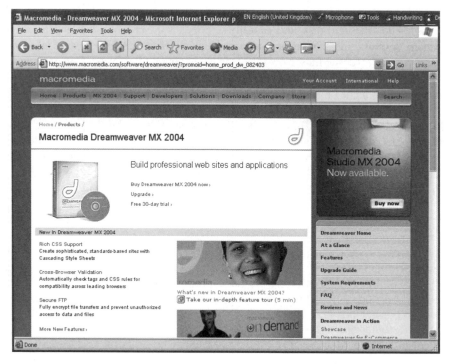

Figure 11.1
The Dreamweaver website

NOTE There are several versions of Dreamweaver available, including Dreamweaver 4, Dreamweaver Ultra Development, recently Dreamweaver MX written for use with the Windows XP operating system and, even more recently, MX 2004. This book has attempted to present the material in a version-independent manner, for many of the older features are similar to these new ones. However, some features may differ slightly in the ways that they are presented. If the items displayed on your system do not accord exactly with the screenshots here, don't panic for it could be due to version differences. However, the screenshot contents and the procedures should be roughly the same.

Setting up your computer for a new Dreamweaver site

Create a new folder for a new Dreamweaver site

Before you use Dreamweaver, it is good practice to begin by creating a new folder so that you can categorize the different file types, such as images, document pages and so on, so that you know exactly where they are stored on your machine. This will make future management of your site a little easier.

You should do this before you open Dreamweaver, creating a new folder in the root directory of your hard disk. To do this you will need to double-click the My Computer icon on the desktop if you are using the Windows operating system, then double-click the hard disk icon (usually C:). You will see a window appear containing several folders. You are going to add a new folder in which to store all your Dreamweaver website files. Now select the menu option File / New / Folder. A new folder should be visible in the window that has the name New Folder. You are going to change the name of this folder. Press the backspace key on the keyboard and type 'mysite'. You have now created a new folder called mysite (see Figure 11.2).

Now open the mysite folder by double-clicking on it. In this folder, create two new folders using the same method as above. Name them 'images' and 'documents'. The images folder will store graphic files related to your website. The documents folder will contain all the HTML files pertaining to your application, apart from the home page, which is usually named 'index.html' and should be stored in the mysite folder. The contents of mysite should now resemble Figure 11.3.

NOTE Some of the screenshots that follow may look a little different to your own. If this is the case, do not panic! It could be that you are using a different version of Dreamweaver or you might be using a different view of it, or even have your panels configured differently. In the following hands-on approach to Dreamweaver, I have tried to present the material in a version-independent manner, but inevitably there may be some differences. However, the screenshots shown here should bear some similarity to what you are seeing on your machine.

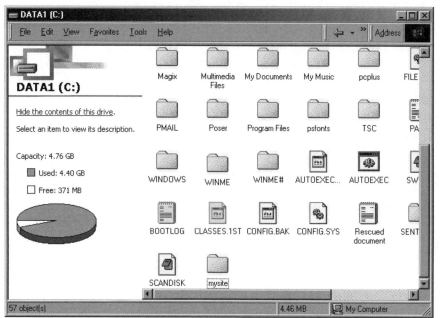

Figure 11.2
Creating a new folder called 'mysite'

Figure 11.3
The contents of the 'mysite' folder.

Setting up a site in Dreamweaver

Many new Dreamweaver users think that setting up a Dreamweaver site is something that takes place later on in the site development process, but they would be wrong. Setting up a site is something that needs to be done before you begin creating the pages. The reason is that Dreamweaver needs to know where your pages and other files are being stored so that it can set up the necessary links. Setting up a site tells Dreamweaver which hard disk folder the HTML files will be stored in, as well as where to find images and other associated Web files.

Starting Dreamweaver

Starting Dreamweaver will depend on the platform that you are using. If you are using the Microsoft Windows environment, select Macromedia from Start Menu / Programs in Windows. If you are using Macintosh Dreamweaver, then you can run the program from the Finder program.

Dreamweaver MX users: the workspace layout

If you are a Dreamweaver MX user, then you have a choice of two workspaces that you can use. If you are using MX for the first time, then you will be presented with a choice of two workspace layouts, as shown in Figure 11.4. For the purpose of maintaining version compatibility, I will use the Dreamweaver 4 layout throughout the remaining chapters about Dreamweaver to make it easier to follow for users with earlier versions. Once you have chosen a workspace, then this will open by default every time you use MX.

- *Dreamweaver 4 Workspace* is the workspace layout that we will use here to ensure maximum compatibility with earlier versions of Dreamweaver. In the Dreamweaver 4 workspace, each document is displayed in its own separate floating window. Panel groups are docked together, but are not docked into a larger application window. This layout is recommended for Dreamweaver 4 and Ultra Dev users who prefer to use a more familiar workspace.

- *Dreamweaver MX Workspace* is an integrated workspace called the Multiple Document Interface (MDI), in which all document windows and panels are integrated into one larger application window.

NOTE   If you are using Dreamweaver on the Macintosh, you will have to use the standard Dreamweaver 4 view. The MX view is not available for the Macintosh version.

Figure 11.4
The Dreamweaver
MX Workspace
layout

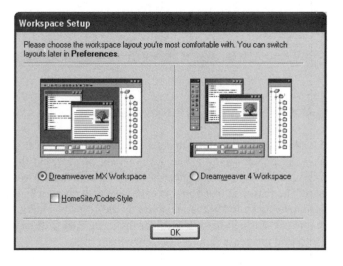

To switch to a different workspace after one has been selected

1 Choose Edit > Preferences ... (Ctrl U) from the menu.

2 A dialogue window will appear (see Figure 11.5) and from this window select the General category in the Category list on the left, if it isn't already selected.

3 Click the Change Workspace ... button.

4 Select a workspace layout and click OK.
An alert message appears to tell you that the new layout will appear after you restart Dreamweaver.

5 Click OK to dismiss the alert message.

6 Click OK again to close the Preferences dialogue box.

7 Exit Dreamweaver and restart to make the change take effect.

> **NOTE**
>
> Most Dreamweaver commands can be completed using shortcut keys on the keyboard. For example, step 1 above – Edit > Preferences ... – can be completed by holding down the Control key and pressing U. This is abbreviated as Ctrl U. Appendix 3 displays a complete list of Windows keyboard shortcuts for Dreamweaver commands for your reference.

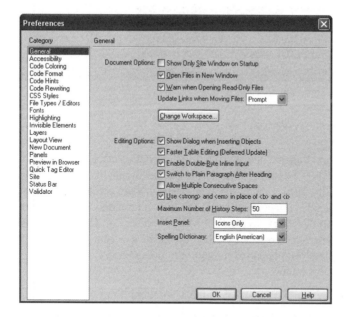

Figure 11.5
Changing the
workspace layout

Running and using Dreamweaver

As stated earlier, you can launch Dreamweaver by selecting Start / Programs / Macromedia Dreamweaver. After selection of your workspace layout, the screen will look something like that shown in Figure 11.6. Dreamweaver is suitable for different styles of working and can be customized as required. You will note that many windows are open for use – called **panels**. We will look at these in some detail later. The main work area is called the **document window** and displays the current Web page that is being created or edited. More on this follows in later sections. Before you start editing any pages for your website, you need to define your site.

Figure 11.6
The Dreamweaver
document window

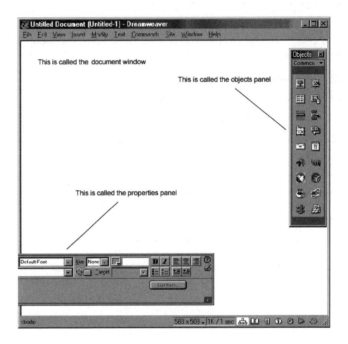

Defining your site

One of the first things a new user should do is define a site so that files can be properly managed by Dreamweaver during the development of your site. In order to build a website from scratch, the Web pages that are created will have to be stored on a local site. This means storing the files on a hard disk on a PC before the pages are placed on the World Wide Web via a Web server. The local website that you define will be mirrored exactly when uploaded to a remote site. The place where these files are stored is called a **local site** in Dreamweaver. To create a local site, follow the steps below.

1 In the Document window, select the Menu item Site / New Site.

2 A Site Definition wizard will appear, as shown in Figure 11.7 for Dreamweaver MX users. If you are using earlier versions of Dreamweaver, then you will see something slightly different, as shown in Figure 11.8. Note that, although these dialogue boxes may look different, they essentially fulfil the same function. That is, they allow the designer to specify where the site will be located on the hard drive and where it will be located on the server, as well as other relevant information.

3 In the site name field, type mysite (see Figure 11.7), then press the Next button.

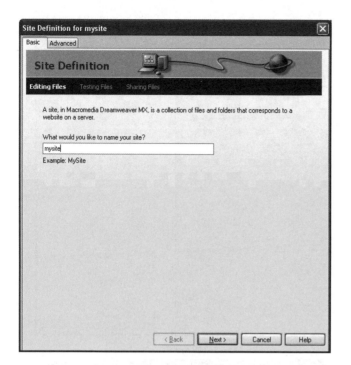

Figure 11.7
The site definition dialogue box for setting up a new site with Dreamweaver MX

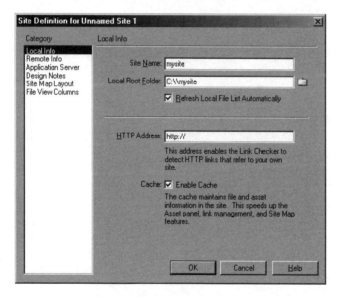

Figure 11.8
The site definition dialogue box for setting up a new site with earlier versions of Dreamweaver

4 The next dialogue box with Editing Files, Part 2 highlighted (see Figure 11.9) will appear. Leave 'No, I do not want to use a server technology' checked for the time being – this can always be changed later.

5 Press the Next button and, in the Editing Files, Part 3 dialogue box (see Figure 11.10), you will see an edit box with the label 'Where on your computer do you want to store your files?' Type C:\\mysite.

Figure 11.9
The site definition editing – Files, Part 2 dialogue box

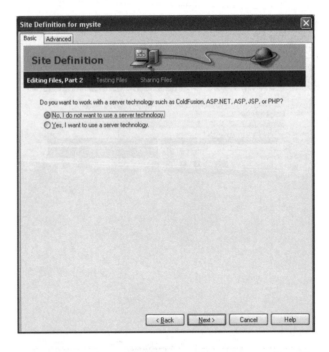

Figure 11.10
Site definition editing files, dialogue box Part 3

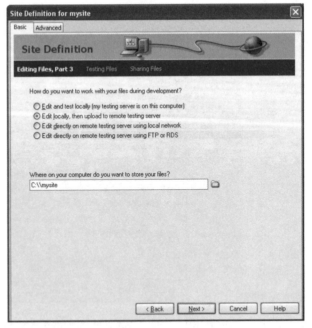

6 Press the Next button again. Another dialogue box will appear, as shown in Figure 11.11. The purpose of this box is to know what type of remote site you want to create. For the time being, we will leave this (we will return to it later on), so in the 'How do you connect to your remote server?' pull-down list box, select the 'I'll set this up later' option, then press the Next Button.

7 The task is now complete. Press the <u>D</u>one button, which you can see in the screenshot in Figure 11.12.

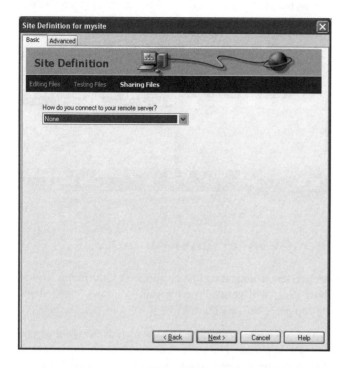

Figure 11.11
The Sharing Files
dialogue box

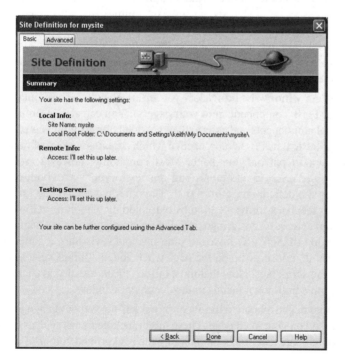

Figure 11.12
The Site Definition
Summary
dialogue box

You should now see the Site files window appear (see Figure 11.13). The right-hand side displays the contents of the local mysite folder, while the left-hand one displays the contents on the server, which is currently empty as no files have been uploaded.

Figure 11.13
The Site files
window

The Dreamweaver Environment

The Dreamweaver environment can be customized for different styles of working. However, most users will generally have four windows – called **panels** – open during the startup process (see Figure 11.6).

- The **document window**, as we have already seen, is the main work area that displays the current Web page being created or edited. The document window is the main editing window. Notice at the bottom of this window, moving from left to right, there is a <body> tag shown at the beginning. This lets the developer know the current tag that is being edited. After this, the value 583 × 508 indicates the screen resolution, the next box shows the value 1 K/1 sec, indicating the download time for the page. The next box shows the quick launcher panel, enabling other objects and so on to be loaded quickly.

- The **objects window** or **panel** lets you insert objects such as images, frames, scripts or Flash components into your page(s). You can also insert more complicated html components and externally embedded objects into your page using the **object palette**. It has eight tabs, each of which contains a group of things that you might want to put on your page. Most commonly, however, you'll use the object palette to add tables and images to your page, both of which are located in the default **common panel**. The other panels include **forms**, for creating user feedback forms, **head**, mostly for adding meta-information about your page, **characters**, for inserting special characters, such as the £ sign, **special** for the insertion of ActiveX, Java and plug-ins, and **invisibles**, a collection of elements that do not show up on the page when added – things such as comments, breaks, and script tags. Note that most of the objects are also available for selection from the pull-down menus in the document window.

- The **properties inspector window** or **panel** lets you set or change properties for objects used on your Web page. These might include things such as changing the font size of some text object or changing the background colour of an object.

- The **launcher window**, which, by clicking the buttons described below, enables you to access Dreamweaver's advanced page-creation tools and palettes.
  - The **site window**, as seen earlier, is used to manage your pages as an integrated site – creating pages, moving them, transferring pages to a server, handling version control and so on.
  - The **library palette**, used to manage components of your pages that are reused commonly. You can only use the library if you set your site up to work with Dreamweaver's site management tools.
  - The **style palette**, used to add CSS to your document.
  - The **behaviour inspector**, used primarily to add JavaScript events to elements.
  - The **timeline inspector**, used to govern animation and events that occur over time on your page.
  - The **hml inspector**, used to hand-edit the actual html code that Dreamweaver creates.

A variety of other panels can also be opened, as and when required, that can supply other facilities. These are called **floating panels**. Examples are CSS, Site Map, and History.

A brief overview of the Dreamweaver menu system

The menu system in Dreamweaver is easy to understand and most of the functionality offered by the palettes above is replicated by the menu. This means that there are usually two ways to carry out a task. You are advised to experiment with both methods – using the panels is normally a more direct way than using the menu. However, in this book, I will perform most tasks via the menu because this method is compatible with previous versions of Dreamweaver. The following list briefly describes the menu options.

- *File* This option contains the choices Open, New Save and Print HTML documents. There are many other options, including one called Importing and Exporting data. This lets you import or export from external sources, such as XML. A Convert option lets you select files to be converted into XHTML or other formats. A Preview in Browser option enables the testing of files in chosen browsers and many other options, some of which will be described in the following chapters.

- *Edit* This option provides the familiar Cut, Copy, Paste and Select All options, as well as many others. A Keyboard Shortcuts option allows for the customization of keyboard shortcuts for Dreamweaver commands, while a Preferences option allows the designer scope to customize the Dreamweaver environment to set all sorts of features.

- *View* This option provides options that enable the Dreamweaver user to view HTML or alternative views, or view/hide other options, such as guidelines or table borders and other desirable items.

- *Insert* This option includes all of the options that are available on the objects panel and is likely to be used a great deal by the Dreamweaver developer.

▪ *Modify*   This option allows you to change items that you have already placed on your page. For example, the Page Properties option allows you to change page characteristics, such as the background colour, page title and so on. The Table option allows you to change any characteristics of a table that has been inserted on your page, such as deleting a column, increase a row span and so on.

▪ *Text*   As the name suggests, this option contains items pertaining to text manipulation, such as setting font, size, style, formatting and so on.

▪ *Commands*   Many customized commands can be created by recording your own commands and then playing them back when required with this option. Moreover, a library of commands can be downloaded free from the Macromedia website.

▪ *Site*   This option, as expected, includes items pertaining to the creation and management of the site. These include Site Files for displaying files on the site, Site Map displaying the structure of the files, New Site for defining local and server files on your site and Edit Site, which gives options for editing files on a site.

▪ *Window*   This option provides scope for different views on panels and other windows that are used in Dreamweaver.

▪ *Help*   The help system can be launched any time from within Dreamweaver. As well as including extensive online help, you will also find a tutorial, access to website help and to the Dreamweaver Exchange, allowing you to exchange ideas with a community of users. There is also a code reference, which you can access via the Window/ Reference option from the menu to check for correctness of HTML tags or attributes or browser compatibility. An illustration of this is shown in Figure 11.14.

Figure 11.14
The code reference option within the help part of the menu

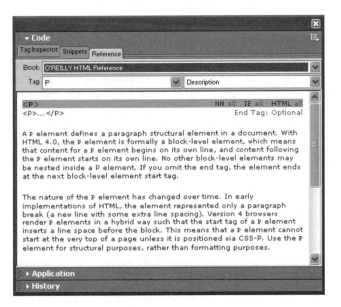

Working with other views in Dreamweaver

In versions of Dreamweaver before MX, you could display data in three ways:

- design view
- document view
- split view.

Split view displays design and code, while the default view is document. When working in design view, there are two different ways of viewing – layout and standard. The layout view gives the developer the facilities to design page layout, insert text and graphics. In standard view, it is possible to insert layers, frames, tables and apply other changes to a Web page – these options are not accessible in layout view.

Making Web pages XHTML-compliant

If you are using Dreamweaver MX, then you can make your web pages XHTML compliant. We have already made the case for XHTML in previous chapters so shall not go into it further here. Before we begin to create pages, we first look at how you can make new pages XMTML-compliant.

1 Select File / New from the Dreamweaver Menu. You will see the new document dialogue box appear (see Figure 11.15).

2 Click the Make Document XHTML Compliant checkbox (again, see Figure 11.15).

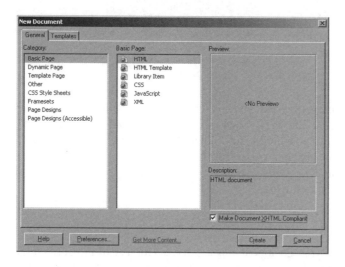

Figure 11.15
Making a new document
XHTML-compliant

Making an existing HTML page XHTML-compliant

1 Open the required document using File / Open ... (or Ctrl O) on the Menu.

2 If the document is not frame-based, then choose File / Convert / XHTML from the Menu. Otherwise, if it does contain frames, you will have to convert each frame using File / Convert / XHTML from the Menu, as well as the frameset document.

Making all pages XHTML-compliant by default

1 Select Edit / Preferences (or Dreamweaver / Preferences if you are using a Macintosh) and select the New Document category (see Figure 11.16).

2 Click the Make Document XHTML Compliant checkbox, as shown.

Figure 11.16
Making all pages
XHTML-compliant
by default

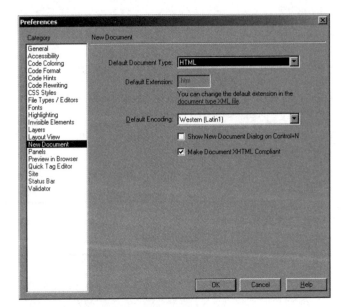

Setting page properties

The page properties dialogue box lets you change default values of page characteristics for your site pages, such as colours, fonts and so on. You can set the page properties by choosing Modify / Page Properties from the Menu. The page properties dialogue box appears, as shown in Figure 11.17.

You can change many characteristics using the page properties dialogue box, including the following.

Add a document title

The title of your document appears in the Title bar of the browser. Note that the document title is saved to a user's browser's favourite list. Moreover, some search

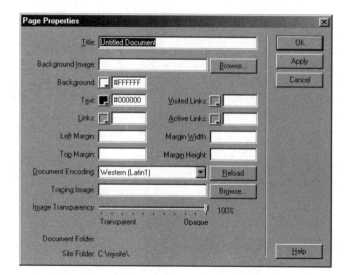

Figure 11.17
The page
properties
dialogue box

engines use the document title to retrieve Web documents (more on this later in the next chapter). The document title should, therefore, be memorable and contain the relevant keywords to describe its purpose.

To set a page title, just enter its name in the Title field of the page properties dialogue box and click the Apply button, on the right-hand side.

Changing text colours

Text on a page is, by default, black on a white background. To change text colour, click the Text box next to text to reveal a colour picker. The colour picker (see Figure 11.18) provides an opportunity to either select an available colour from the palette or use the colour wheel (second icon from the right along the top bar in Figure 11.18) to customize a required colour.

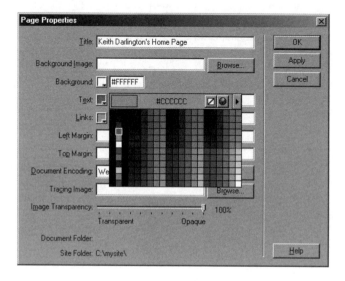

Figure 11.18
Selecting a colour
from the colour
picker

Background colours can be changed from the default colour (white) in the same way. Be careful, however, when deciding on the combination of text and background colours. Make sure that users are comfortable with the contrast. The default hyperlink colour is blue with a visited link normally in purple. These colours can also be changed, using the page properties dialogue box (see Figure 11.17).

As you can see from Figure 11.18, you can also change other Web page parameters in page properties. For example, background image, margins and transparency.

Creating Dreamweaver pages containing text and graphics

Entering text

Entering and formatting text using Dreamweaver is not very different from using a word processor, such as Microsoft Word. Just click the appropriate place in the document window to place the insertion point, then begin typing. Text entered is wrapped at the right side of a document, just like a word processor. Pressing the Enter/Return key on the keyboard starts a new paragraph. Dreamweaver also contains a spellchecker (see Text Menu, or Shift F7). Using the properties panel, you can modify the characteristics of text, such as font, size, colour and so on. Properties of any item selected on the page can be modified. Enter the text shown, using your own name and title, in Figure 11.19, highlight it and change its font size to +6 by using the Size pull-down list box in the properties panel.

Save the document using the File / Save As ... menu option. You should name the file 'index.html'. Dreamweaver will automatically save this file in the root directory of the mysite folder.

Adding graphic images to your Web pages

Next, we are going to include our graphic logo – named veg_logo – to the Web page and align it at the right-hand side of the page. To do this, place the cursor after the words 'The Vegetable Gardener' and click the images icon on the objects panel (at the top left-hand corner). A Select Image Source dialogue box, as shown in Figure 11.20, will appear. The image that is required (veg_logo) for this Web page is stored in the images folder of the mysite folder. Select this image and click the OK button. You will notice that the image is now displayed on the page as shown in Figure 11.21.

NOTE

If you are using MX Studio, it is possible to animate a graphic that's already in a page, providing it is a GIF graphic. To do this, select the graphic while in the standard window and click the Edit button in the Property Inspector. The graphic will automatically be loaded into Fireworks, which is your default graphics editor if you have the Studio bundle. (If you look closely, you'll notice the Editing From Dreamweaver text and images that signal you initiated the editing from Dreamweaver.)

Figure 11.19
Entering and
formatting text in
the home page

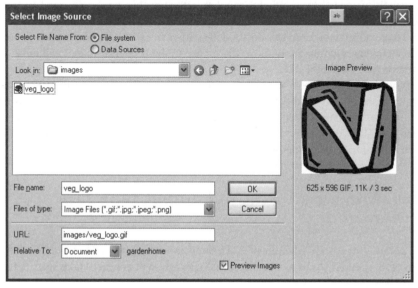

Figure 11.20
The Select Image
Source dialogue
box

Figure 11.21
Adding the
veg_logo image to
the Web page

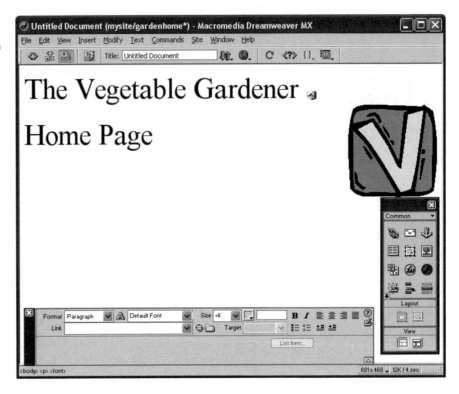

Adding a list of items

We are next going to add an unordered list of items. You will recall from Chapter 5 that an unordered list is one in which the items are not necessarily intended to be followed in the sequence in which they are written. Each item in an unordered list is usually preceded by a bullet symbol ●, although this can be changed to some other symbol if required.

To create an unordered list, position the cursor where the first list item is to go in the document window. Now move the mouse to the properties panel and click the list icon (see Figure 11.22).

You will notice that a ● bullet symbol has automatically been inserted in the position shown in Figure 11.22. You can now type the text. When you press the return key, another list item bullet will automatically be inserted, as can be seen in Figure 11.23. Continue to enter any remaining list items required and click the list icon in the properties panel when done to break out of insert list mode.

Creating a new HTML document type in Dreamweaver

To create a new HTML document in Dreamweaver, select the Menu option File / New File (Ctrl N). A New Document dialogue box will appear. Make sure that the

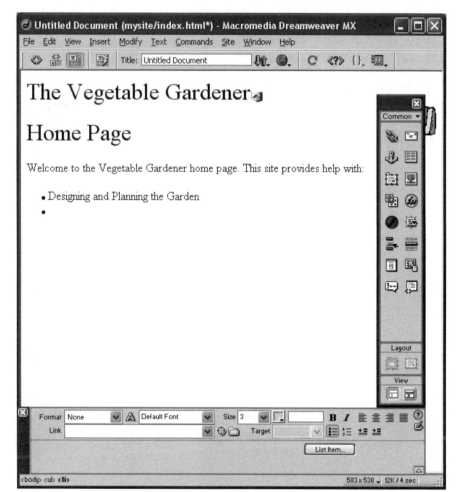

Figure 11.22
Selecting the list
icon from the
properties panel

Basic Page Category is selected, along with HTML, in the Basic Page type. Press the Create button and a new blank document will appear in the document window. Set the Title of the document to 'Designing and Planning the Garden', as shown in Figure 11.24, and save the document using the file name 'design.html'. Make sure that you save it in the documents folder of your site.

NOTE

If you are using MX, then the New Document dialogue box provides several types of documents from which you can create a new document. You will notice from Figure 11.25 that as well as being able to choose a blank HTML document, you can also create a template that will let you use a preset layout to enable you to produce professional-looking Web pages. Other document options can also be used from the New Document dialogue box. For example, you can use text-based documents, such as CSS or JavaScript. You can also choose dynamic page documents, such as PHP or ASP (see Chapter 13).

Figure 11.23
Bullets for new
lists items are
inserted
automatically
when you press
the return key

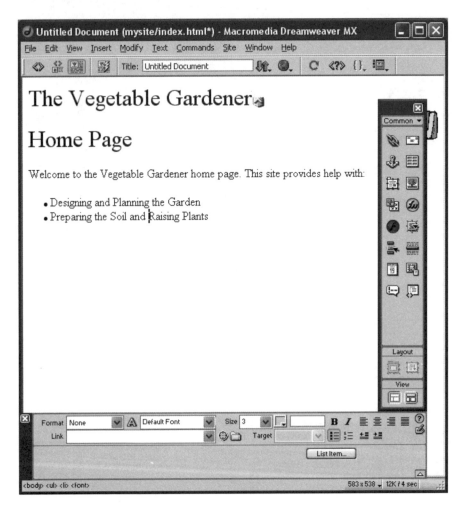

Adding hyperlinks to a Web page

We are now going to add hyperlinks from the home page to the two pages that are displayed as the list items. They are 'Designing and Planning the Garden', and 'Preparing the Soil and Raising Plants'. By way of illustration, the first list item will be linked to a local page while the second will be linked to an external URL.

Linking to a local page

The list item 'Designing and Planning the Garden' is going to be linked to the design.html page on mysite, so the file will have been stored in the documents folder of the local mysite. We will assume that the file name of this link is design.html. Make sure that if you are going to create a hyperlink to a local page, then that page exists and is placed in the documents folder, as we did in the previous section.

To set up the hyperlink, follow the steps below.

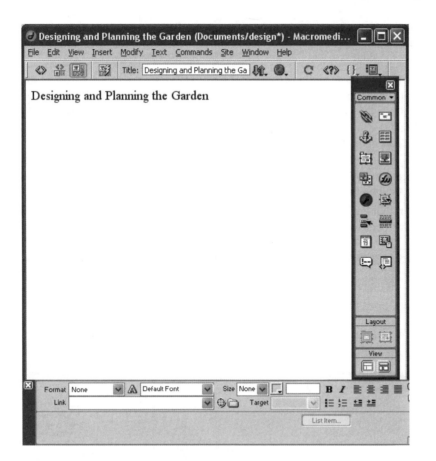

Figure 11.24
Setting the Title of
your new
document

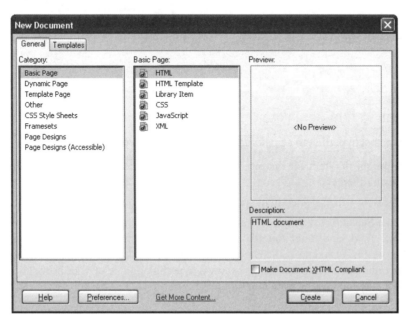

Figure 11.25
Choosing the
document type
from the New
Document
dialogue box –
here a blank HTML
document

1 Select the list item 'Designing and Planning the Garden', then click the 'point to file' wheel on the properties panel (this is to the left of the targets folder). Make sure that the Site window is visible to the right when doing this.

2 With the mouse held down, move the mouse over the right-hand pane of the site window and position the mouse over the file named design.html, then release the mouse (see Figure 11.26). You have now set up the link and the 'Designing and Planning the Garden' item in the index file should now be coloured blue – the default hyperlink colour. Alternatively, you can create a hyperlink by right-clicking the selected link and choosing the Make Link option from the pull-down menu. In the Select File dialogue box that follows, choose the file name required, as shown in Figure 11.27, and then press the OK button.

3 Test that the link works by using the Menu option File / Preview on the Browser. Save your work.

Figure 11.26
Adding hyperlinks
to a Web page

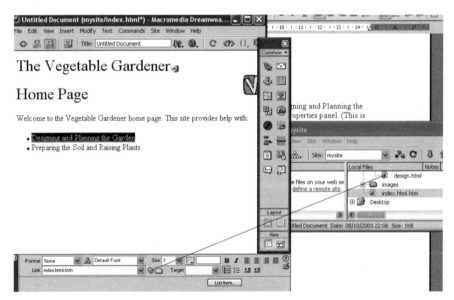

Creating a hyperlink to an external page

To create a hyperlink to an external URL, follow the steps below.

1 Highlight the item for linking. In this case, it is called 'Preparing the Soil and Raising Plants'.

2 Right-click the selected item and, from the pull-down menu, choose Make Link.

3 In the Select File dialogue box that appears, enter the full name of the URL in the URL field, and enter the file name of the URL in the File name box (see Figure 11.28) and press the OK button. You will see that the selected item is now blue and you should test that it is now a hyperlink on one of your browsers. The URL site link here is shown in Figure 11.29.

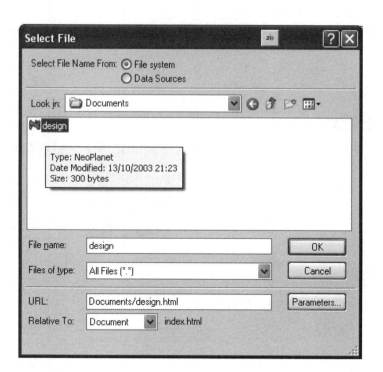

Figure 11.27
The Select File
dialogue box

Figure 11.28
Using the Select
File dialogue box
to create a
hyperlink

Figure 11.29
Testing the
hyperlinks works
on an IE browser

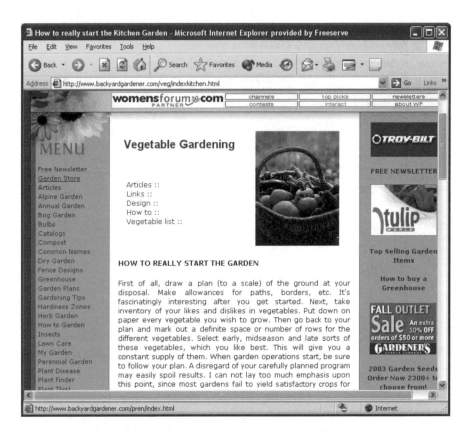

Uploading website files to the Web server using Dreamweaver

In order to upload your files from a local system, such as your PC, you will need **File Transfer Protocol (FTP)** software. The FTP is a protocol for moving files over the Internet from one computer to another. Examples of FTP software include **ws_ftp** for Windows and **Fetch** for the Macintosh. FTP functionality is also built into Dreamweaver. However, before you can upload files using Dreamweaver or any other FTP software, you will need to have the following information:

■ the FTP host name of your ISP Web server (host)

■ both the user ID and your password for access to your ISP, for security reasons.

How to upload a website using Dreamweaver

1 Select the Menu option Site / Edit Sites. From the dialogue box that appears, select `mysite` and press the Edit button.

2 From the familiar Site Definition wizard that follows, click the Advanced tab, whence you will see the Site Definition for mysite layout. Change the Local Info selection to Remote Info in the Category list. Then change the Access field from

None to FTP in the list box shown. You should now see a dialogue box as shown in Figure 11.30.

3 You must fill in the fields for the FTP Host, Login (user name) and Password for your server. When this is done, press the OK button.

4 You will now see the familiar Site window appear, which is divided into two windowpanes. In the right-hand pane are the local files and folders that you have created. The left-hand pane is called the Remote Site pane and is where your files will be stored when uploaded to the server. To upload the files from the Local Files folder, you will first need to press the 'connects to remote host' button, then press the 'put file(s)' button (see Figure 11.31).

5 The files will then be uploaded on to the Web server.

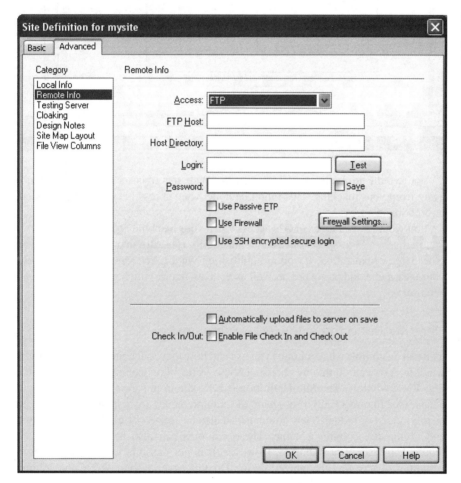

Figure 11.30
The FTP dialogue box in Dreamweaver

Methods of publishing

You can publish to a website using either FTP or **Local Area Network (LAN)** access.

Figure 11.31
The Site window
for transferring
files to and from
the server

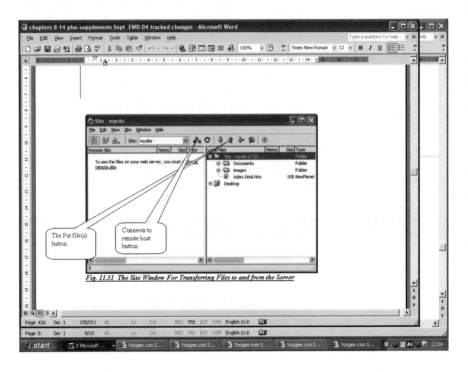

You would normally use FTP when the Web server is located some distance away from your machine. This might be done when access is via a dial-up modem or broadband access.

You would normally use LAN access when your machine is connected to a LAN via, perhaps, a high-speed Ethernet connection – typically in a university or some other large organization. If you are publishing via a LAN, you will need to know your user name and password, as well as the path name, which gives access to your Web server.

Reconfiguring the site window's columns

You can customize what columns you use and how they will appear in the Site View window. You can do this by choosing View / File View Columns from within the Site View window. The Site Definition (for mysite in this case) dialogue box will appear (see Figure 11.32). From here, the column names are displayed and they can be rearranged or hidden. New columns can also be created by clicking the + button and giving the column a name. These columns can also be removed later, if required, by using the – button. However, it is not possible to remove a built-in column – that is, one recognized by the Dreamweaver system. A created column can be associated with a design note by choosing a column name from the Column Name field and then associating it with an existing design note in the Associate with Design Note drop-down list box below it, shown in Figure 11.32.

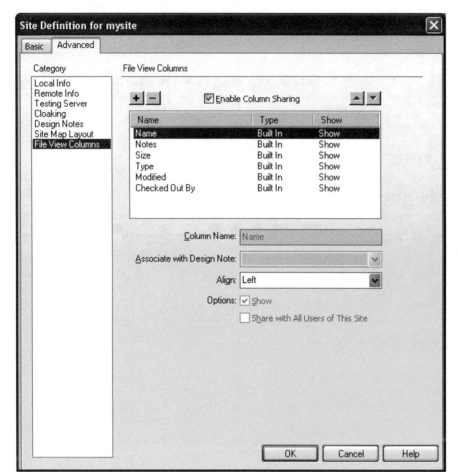

Figure 11.32
Reconfiguring the
site window's
column

Adding a Mailto link using Dreamweaver

Very often, it is quite useful to place a link on a Web page that allows a viewer to
send e-mail. This type of link is called a **mailto link**. To create a mailto link, follow
the steps given below:

1 Choose an appropriate label to refer to the e-mail link.
2 Next, click the Insert Email Link object from the object panel. A dialogue box
   then appears, as shown in Figure 11.33.

Figure 11.33
The Insert Email
Link dialogue box

3 Enter your e-mail address and click OK. The text on your Web page now looks just like a hyperlink, but links to your e-mail address instead of a Web page (see Figure 11.34).

Figure 11.34
The e-mail link as it appears on the Web page once it has been inserted

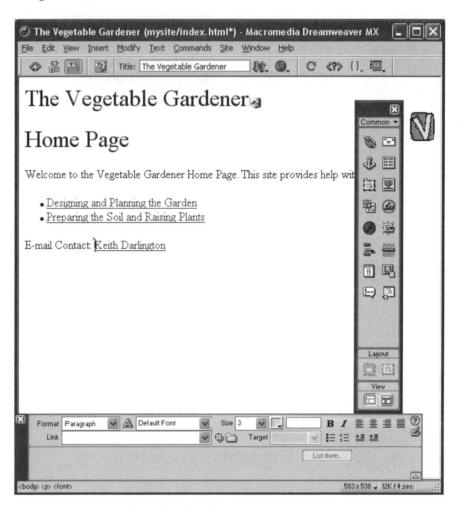

Setting up multiple browsers to preview Web pages

It is good practice to check your website pages on multiple browsers – or, at the very least, using IE and Netscape. You can set up Dreamweaver so that it can preview pages on a number of different browsers. To do this, take the following steps.

1 From the File menu, choose Preview in Browser, Edit Browser List.

2 The Preferences window will appear (see Figure 11.35). Click on the Browsers: + button to add a new browser.

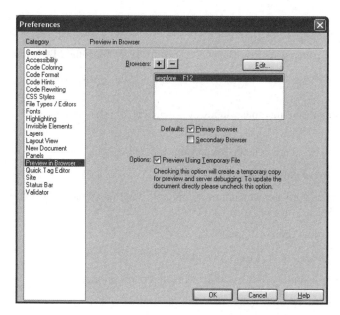

Figure 11.35
Using the Preview
in Browser list

3 In the Add Browser dialog box that appears (see Figure 11.36), enter the name of the browser that you wish to add in the Name: box. In this case, I have chosen Mozilla.exe. You will also need to show where this program is located in the Application: box.

4 Make sure that the Secondary browser box is ticked if you want to rank your choices of browser.

5 Click the OK button.

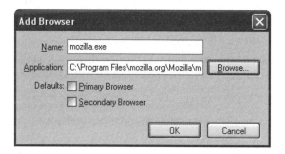

Figure 11.36
Choosing a new
browser

Summary

■ Dreamweaver is a Web-authoring tool used for building websites.

■ When using Dreamweaver, you should always create a site structure before beginning to design a new website.

■ You should always create a folder structure, too – beginning with a root folder that contains images and documents folders so that files can be arranged and easily found when required.

- The root folder is the main starting folder in Dreamweaver to use when building for your website.

- Dreamweaver MX provides for two workspace layouts – Dreamweaver 4 and the MX layout.

- Dreamweaver 4 layout is provided for users who are more familiar with an earlier version of Dreamweaver.

- The Dreamweaver environment contains four windows – document, objects, properties inspector and launcher.

- Dreamweaver commands can be entered via the Dreamweaver menu system.

- Web pages can be made XHTML-compliant with Dreamweaver.

- Entering text in the Dreamweaver document window is similar to entering text in any word processing program. What You See Is What You Get (WYSIWYG).

- HTML files can have the extension '.htm' or '.html'.

- A Web page title appears at the top of the browser window.

- The Preferences dialogue box enables you to customize Dreamweaver settings.

- You can set up Dreamweaver to test your website on multiple browsers.

- You can then preview your Web pages with your choice of browser.

Exercises

1 Describe the two layout views in Dreamweaver MX.

2 Explain the reason for having two layout views in Dreamweaver MX.

3 Briefly explain the benefits of creating Web pages using Dreamweaver, compared to writing XHTML code using a text editor.

4 List some differences between editing text in Dreamweaver and Word. Name some things that you can do with Word that you cannot do with Dreamweaver.

5 How would you use Dreamweaver to insert a graphic image for use in a Web page?

6 Describe two ways in which you can post from the local site to the remote site with Dreamweaver.

7 Use Dreamweaver to re-create exactly the page shown in Figure 11.37. The background colour is yellow. Use Dreamweaver to also create the linked pages shown – Rolls and Sandwiches, Burgers, and Kebabs and Pitta, but only include the title inside each page. Check the correctness of the links using your browser preview facility in Dreamweaver.

8 Use Dreamweaver to change the background colour of the page you created in question 7 to black and the foreground text colour to white. Also, change the list items to numerical items and move the main heading – Happy Grub on the Web – to the centre of the page.

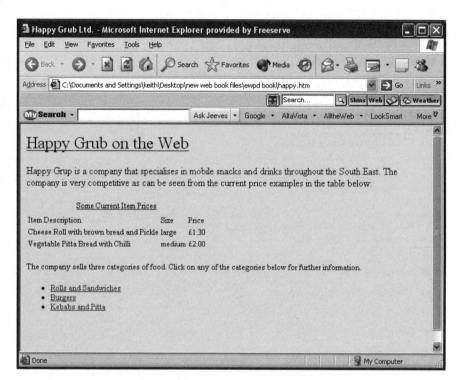

Figure 11.37
Page to be re-created for question 7

Intermediate Dreamweaver

In this chapter you will learn how to:

- use forms
- use tables
- use tables to enhance layout, using the layout view
- insert rollover images
- use meta-tags
- use behaviours and JavaScript
- use frames in Dreamweaver.

Introduction

The previous chapter looked at the basics of using Dreamweaver. In this chapter, we take things further by looking at how Dreamweaver can be used to implement some of the techniques that were studied in Chapter 6 and become acquainted with other useful procedures, including forms, tables and frames. The `<meta>` tag was encountered earlier, too, but here we see how it can be used to improve the chances of your site being found by a search engine, as well as how to implement animation using rollover images and behaviours using JavaScript.

Using forms with Dreamweaver

As we saw in Chapter 6, adding forms to your website can make it more interactive. Here we will look at how to use forms in Dreamweaver. You can construct a form by inserting text fields, buttons, checkboxes and other interactive elements on your page. Visitors to your site fill out the form and send it via a program called a form handler by clicking a submit button, where it will be processed by a script handler on the server. Figure 12.1 gives an example of a registration form.

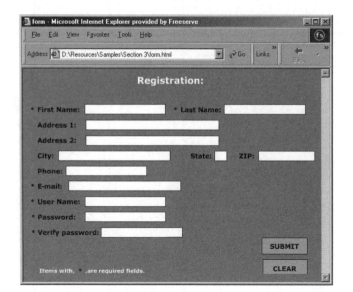

Figure 12.1
An example of a
registration form

When creating a form for use on your website, you should bear in mind the following points.

- Choose your form elements carefully. Creating a useful form requires you to think about the information you want to collect, as well as how you collect it.

- Think about your audience when creating the form. Make sure that you present the form clearly, with instructions at the beginning. Remember also that form-filling is time-consuming. People may take some persuading to complete a form. At the very least, you will need to reduce the effort required by the respondent to the absolute minimum. If you are looking for a high proportion of respondents, you might even have to consider offering incentives of some kind or another.

- Give careful thought to the layout and positioning of the elements that you use on the form. Think about when you should use each type of element. The sequence of questions should be logical and flow smoothly from one to the next.

Creating a form in Dreamweaver

You can set up a form using Dreamweaver on your Web page by following these steps.

1 Use the Insert / Form Menu option to insert a new form page. Notice that Dreamweaver adds a red dashed box to the top of the page to alert the user (see Figure 12.2).

2 Type in the address of the form handler in the properties panel in the Action field. Select either POST or GET in the list box called Method (the default is POST).

3 Change the default Form Name from Form1 to myForm.

Figure 12.2
Setting up a form
with Dreamweaver

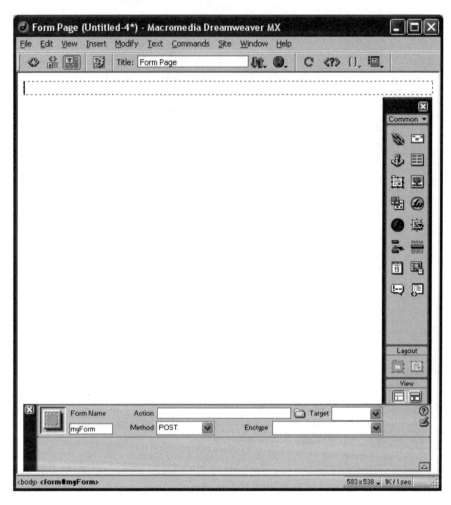

We will next add a number of components to the form. Figure 12.3 displays the components that will be added to this particular form. These include a name text field, a multiline text field, a pair of radio buttons and submit and clear buttons, for sending the form to the form handler.

Adding a text field

To add the username text field as shown in Figure 12.4, follow the steps shown below.

1 Click the mouse at the position in the document window where you want to insert the text field. You will notice that the cursor is placed inside the red dotted lines to signify the form area. You can move the cursor outside these lines if you wish. Type a label before you insert the text field so that users will know what kind of information to enter.

2 From the Menu, choose Insert / Form Objects.

Figure 12.3
Adding
components to a
form with
Dreamweaver

Figure 12.4
Adding a text field
to a form with
Dreamweaver

3 Select Text Field. Dreamweaver will now add a text field space on your form (see Figure 12.3).

4 In the properties inspector panel, type a name, such as username, for the text field (see Figure 12.4) and type Bloggs, Joe for the initial value of the field.

Adding a multiline text field

Next, we wish to add a multiline text field – you will recall that we called these text areas in Chapter 6. These are ideal when users are encouraged to submit comments about the website. To add the multiline text field:

1 from the Menu, select Insert / Form Objects / Text Field as before

2 in the properties panel, click the Multiline radio button (see Figure 12.5)

Figure 12.5
Adding a multiline
text field to a form
with Dreamweaver

3 adjust the width and height of the field using Char <u>W</u>idth and Num Lines (see Figure 12.5)

4 type a label for the multiline field above the field space – in this case 'Additional Comments:' (see Figure 12.3).

Adding radio buttons to the form

The next task is to add the gender radio buttons. This is what you need to do.

1 Position the cursor where you want the radio buttons to be displayed. Then type the label 'Gender'.

2 Choose the Menu option Insert / Form Objects / Radio Button.

3 A blank radio button will appear immediately after the label (see Figure 12.6). Type 'Male' in the Checked <u>V</u>alue box. In the properties panel, the Initial State is left <u>U</u>nchecked. This means that it will not be assumed true by default.

Figure 12.6
Adding a radio button to a form with Dreamweaver

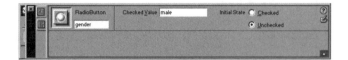

4 Repeat the process for the Female radio button. For this radio button, set the Initial State to Checked. This means that it will be assumed true by default. This seems to be a reasonable assumption as women form the majority of the population.

Adding buttons to a form

The final components that are required to be added to this form are the Submit and Clear buttons.

There are two types of behaviour that can follow from a button click on a form: submit or clear. Clicking the Submit button enables a user's data to be sent to the specified form handler. Clicking the Clear button resets all the elements on the form to their initial values.

To add the Submit and Clear buttons at the bottom of the form:

1 position the cursor where you want the radio buttons to be displayed

2 select from the Menu Insert / Form Objects / Button

3 a button will appear on the form – set this as a submit button by changing the Button Name to Submit in the properties panel (see Figure 12.7: you can also change the default label (Submit) to something else if you wish), then set the radio button Action to <u>S</u>ubmit form.

Figure 12.7
Adding a button to a form with Dreamweaver

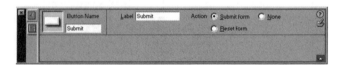

Do not forget to save your work regularly.

NOTE

Using tables with Dreamweaver

Tables can be used to present data on a Web page or create elaborate layouts. Each cell of the table can be used to hold Web page content in place. This technique is used to great effect to create white space and alignment options, as we saw in Chapter 6. Table borders in Dreamweaver can be made visible or invisible.

Some examples of the use of tables follow, beginning with the presentation of data on a page.

Inserting a table into your Web page

The first example that we shall look at presents data in the familiar rows and columns format. Suppose we wanted to create a table as shown in Figure 12.8 with just such a simple format. We will first need to create the table layout and then fill in the cells with the appropriate data afterwards. To do this, follow these steps.

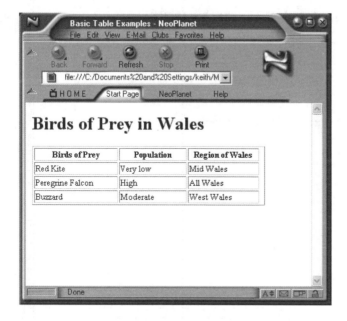

Figure 12.8
A simple table

1 Place your cursor where you want to insert the table.
2 Click the Insert Table button on the objects panel – the Insert Table dialogue box appears (see Figure 12.9).

Figure 12.9
The Insert Table
dialogue box

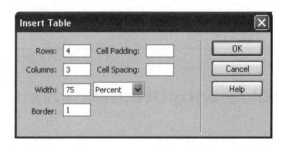

Figure 12.9
The Insert Table
dialogue box

3 Type the number of rows and columns in your table in the relevant boxes.

4 Type the width of your table (you can specify a percentage of window width if you wish).

5 Type a border size in pixels. Also, click values of Cell Padding and Cell Spacing if you wish. Then, click OK.

Dreamweaver now inserts a default left-aligned empty table on your page (see Figure 12.10). The next task is to insert the contents into the table.

Figure 12.10
The empty table

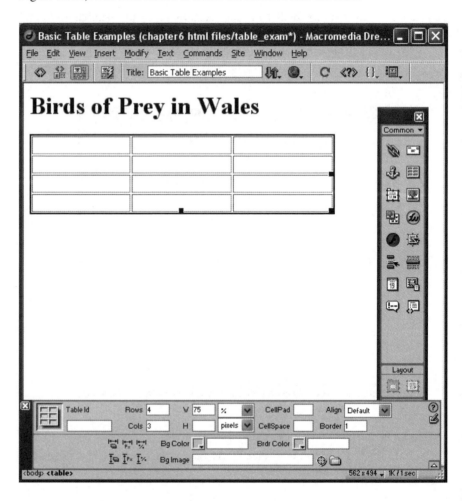

Inserting data into the table

When the empty table appears on your page, you can insert text into each cell as follows.

1 Click inside the first table cell (at the top, left-hand side).

2 Type in the text shown in Figure 12.8, using the tab key to move from one cell to the next. Do not worry about formatting text – Dreamweaver will wrap words around and extend cell widths to accommodate whatever you insert. Continue in this way until all the data has been entered. Note how the top row contains text headings.

3 In the event that you have too few rows or columns, you can change the row or column number by clicking the outline of the table. The properties panel then changes to the Table object and then you can change the value in the window. You can also change the column width by clicking the side edge and dragging it to the destination width.

The next example that we shall look at also presents data in the familiar rows and columns format. We will rebuild the example used in Chapter 6 about the symptoms of problems and their likely causes when growing spinach. The image is reproduced in Figure 12.11.

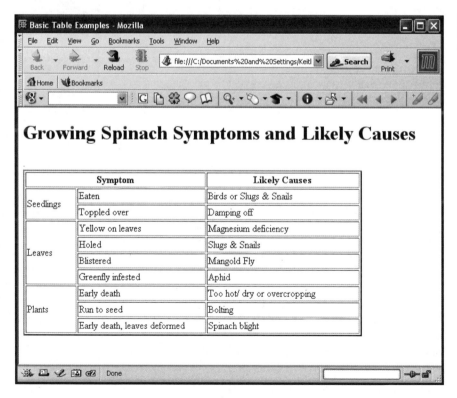

Figure 12.11
Finished table for spinach growing

Inside the figure:

Growing Spinach Symptoms and Likely Causes

	Symptom	Likely Causes
Seedlings	Eaten	Birds or Slugs & Snails
	Toppled over	Damping off
Leaves	Yellow on leaves	Magnesium deficiency
	Holed	Slugs & Snails
	Blistered	Mangold Fly
	Greenfly infested	Aphid
Plants	Early death	Too hot/ dry or overcropping
	Run to seed	Bolting
	Early death, leaves deformed	Spinach blight

This is clearly a more difficult example, in that the top row contains two merged column cells for the headings, then there are two merged row cells in the first column and so on.

To implement this table structure, we will first need to create a table using the maximum number of rows and columns in the table. We can see that, in this case, there are 10 rows and 3 columns. We create the table in the same way as the previous example to get the first stage of the table, as shown in Figure 12.12.

Figure 12.12
Merging the top first two columns in the first row

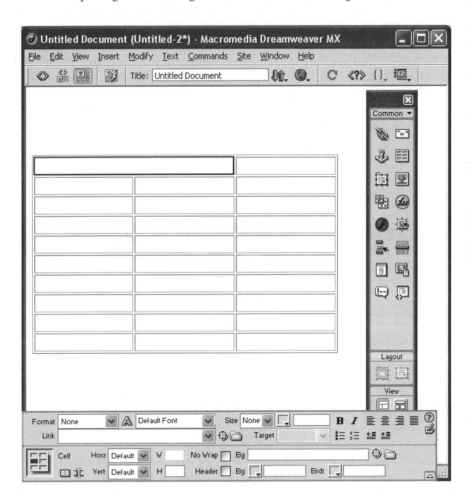

The data in this example, as you can see, contains two columns in row one spanning onto three columns in row two onwards, and the rows have been spanned in the ratio 2 : 4 : 3. We will first need to create the table layout to resemble Figure 12.11 and fill in the cells with the appropriate data afterwards. To do this, follow the steps below.

1 Place your cursor where you want to insert the table.

2 As with the previous example, click the Insert Table button on the objects panel – the Insert Table dialogue box appears.

3 Type the number of rows and columns in your table, as before.

4 Type the width of your table (you can specify a percentage of window width if you wish – in this example, 75 per cent is given).

5 Type a border size of 1 (pixel). Click OK.

6 As with the previous example, Dreamweaver now inserts a default left-aligned empty table on your page (see Figure 12.10). The next task will be to merge cells to create the structure shown in Figure 12.13.

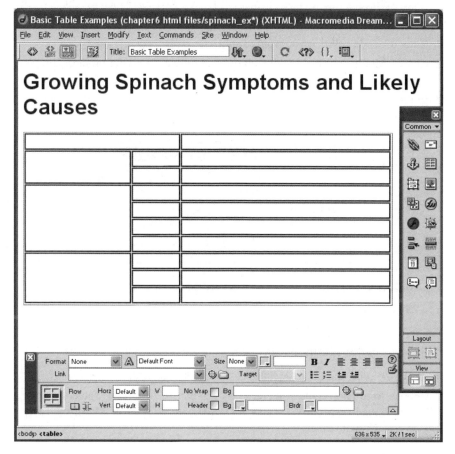

Figure 12.13
The empty table after it has been inserted into the Web page

NOTE

The table attributes Cell Spacing and Cell Padding were discussed in Chapter 6. They can be assigned values in the Insert Table dialogue box (see Figure 12.9), but in this particular example they have been left blank.

Merging cells in rows and columns

To merge the first two column cells in the first row:

1 select the two cells to be merged – in our example, the two adjacent cells in the first row, first two columns

2 from the Menu, select Modify / Table / Merge Cells (Ctrl Alt M).

You will see that the result will be the merged cell shown in Figure 12.12.

Splitting and increasing row span and column span

You can split cells (the reverse of spanning) in a table and/or increase the row span or column span of cells using Dreamweaver. To split cells, do the following.

1 Click the table cell that you want to split.

2 Choose Modify / Table / Split Cell or click the Split Cell button in the property inspector.

3 In the Split Cell dialogue box, specify how to split the cell (see Figure 12.14), then click OK.

Figure 12.14
The Split Cell
dialogue box

NOTE	You can only merge cells in rectangular contiguous locations.

To increase or decrease the number of rows or columns spanned by a cell:

1 Select the cell from the table that you want to be spanned.

2 Choose Modify / Table / Increase Row Span or Modify / Table / Increase Column Span or Modify / Table / Decrease Row Span or Modify / Table / Decrease Column Span.

Creating tables using Layout View

Tables are often used for organizing the layout of information on a Web page. Such tables would have their borders made invisible. It is better, however, to work in Layout View when creating a layout table. To do this, you need to:

1 click the Layout View button on the objects panel

2 click the Draw Layout Table button – the mouse cursor will now change to a +

3 click and drag to create a table – the outline of the table is now displayed

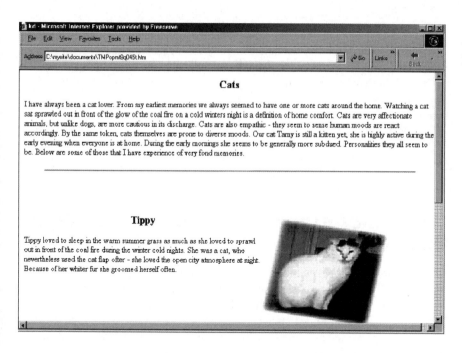

Figure 12.15
A layout table created in Layout View

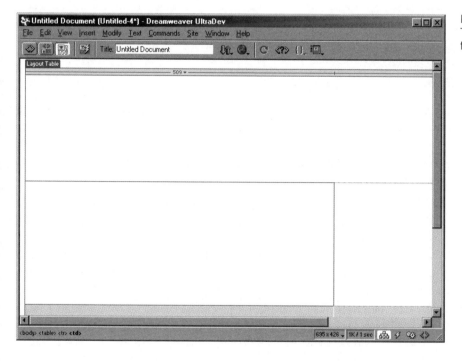

Figure 12.16
The layout table for Figure 12.15

4 add the content of your table, so you will need to create layout cells – click the Draw Layout Cell button

5 click and drag inside the table to create the required layout for the cell

6 click again to draw more cells

7 insert the content into your cells.

We are going to produce the table layout shown on the Web page in Figure 12.15. Figure 12.16 shows how the first three cells of the table were created before adding the content. The content added to this section of the page will include everything up to and including the photograph of the cat named Tamy.

Using meta-tags to help search engines find websites

Once you get your pages working on a Web server, you might want to make sure that potential visitors to your site can find them with search engines. Search engines are discussed in more detail in Chapter 14, but, for the purpose of this section, it is important to know that some search engines index all of the text on your page, while others only index the page title (this is why title page choice is so important!) or special keywords that you specify. This is done in the head section of an HTML document using so-called **meta-tags**.

Meta-tags can provide both descriptions and keywords about your Web page and, thus, make it easier for search engines to find your pages on the Web. Examples of such HTML meta-tags are shown below:

```
<meta name = "keywords"  content = " Vegetables, Gardening,
">

<meta name  = "description" content = "Green beans,
carrots, potatoes, swede, parsnips, lettuce, tomatoes,
cucumber, marrow, soil care, ">
```

Dreamweaver provides an easy way in which to enter description and keyword attributes into your Web pages.

Inserting meta-tag keywords and descriptions in Dreamweaver

1 To enter keywords in your meta-tags, choose the menu option Insert / Head Tags. Choose Keywords from the submenu. The Keywords dialogue box (see Figure 12.17) will appear.

2 Choose some keywords that do not appear in your title(s) or in the body of your page. Some examples of these can be seen in Figure 12.17. Press the OK button when done.

3 To enter descriptions in your meta-tags, choose the menu option Insert / Head Tags. Choose Description from the submenu. The description dialogue box will appear – it is very similar to the Keywords dialogue box.

Figure 12.17
The Keywords
dialogue box

4 In the Description dialogue box, describe the purpose of your page in two or three sentences – again, do not include descriptions included in the body of your page. Press the OK button when done.

Other methods for generating traffic to your website

There are several commercial sites available that provide a submission service – sometimes free. This means that you simply submit your site and it will be listed instantly in many search engines. The following are examples of sites offering this service.

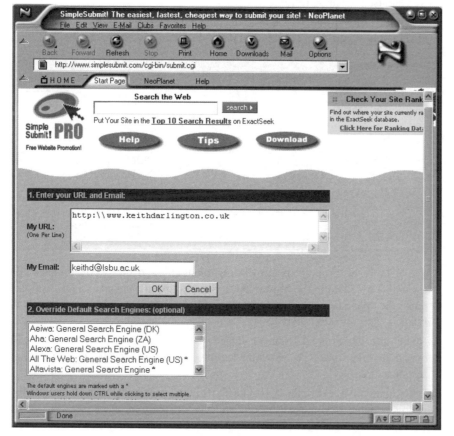

Figure 12.18
Screenshot
of simple
submit.com's
website for listing
your site on
search engines

- **simplesubmit.com (www.simplesubmit.com)** is a free service that will get your site listed in up to 17 search engines simultaneously. As you can see from the screenshot using the NeoPlanet browser in Figure 12.18, it is very simple to use, with the user only having to enter the URL for the home page of their site and their e-mail address for confirmation of receipt of the request.

- **Submit Express (www.submitexpress.com)** is another free service that gives access to over 40 search engines, including top names.

Using rollovers in Dreamweaver

A **rollover** is an image on a Web page that swaps with another image when the mouse pointer moves over it. This can result in an interesting interactive visual effect that can sometimes make your pages more appealing.

To create a rollover using Dreamweaver, you will need two images with exactly the same dimensions. We are going to create a rollover with movement of a 'lunch out' image. These are GIF images.

1. Open a new file and insert the title 'Vegetable Rollover'. Save the file in the documents folder of mysite. Place the cursor where you want the rollover images placed on the page (http://www.mccannas.com/free/freeart.htm is the free art website used for these rollovers).

2. Select the rollover image icon from the object panel. A dialogue box will appear, as shown in Figure 12.19. Name the image in the Image Name text field.

Figure 12.19
The Insert Rollover
Image dialogue
box

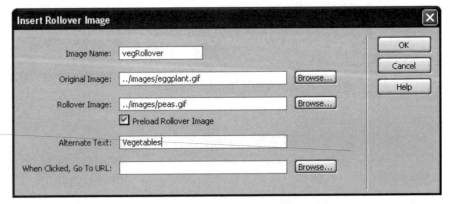

3. Select both the original image file (eggplant.gif) and the rollover image file (peas.gif) by clicking the browse buttons in the mysite/images folder. You can name the image using the Image Name field 'vegRollover'. This is not essential, but it is useful in case reference to it is required in the future.

4. Make sure the Preload Rollover Image checkbox is ticked because this will ensure that the images are downloaded into the viewer's cache, ensuring faster response times.

5. Enter alternative text in the Alternate Text field if you wish and add a link to the rollover image if you wish by clicking the Browse button or else type in an external website URL.

6 The dialogue box (Figure 12.19) is now complete. Click the OK button.

7 Preview the rollover on an IE or other browser(s) and run the mouse over the new image to check that it works. The before mouse skimming and after on mouse skimming should produce the two adjacent screenshots shown in Figure 12.20.

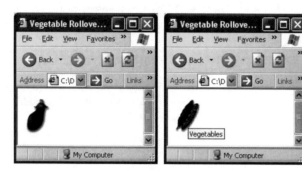

Figure 12.20
Previewing the rollover images

Using frames in Dreamweaver

Frames are another Web page concept that we also looked at in Chapter 6. To recap, **frames** provide a means of dividing your browser window into several smaller windows with the capacity to display different Web page(s) in each window. Each window is a separate HTML document. Recall also that a framed browser display can be created by dividing the document window into a set of vertical or horizontal windows or a combination of both.

If you intend building a frame-based website, it is important to think carefully about the number of frames to be used and the locations and proportions that will be assigned to each frame. Plan this stage on paper before committing the design to Dreamweaver.

NOTE

Creating a frameset in Dreamweaver

To create a frameset in Dreamweaver, you will need to divide the document window into two or more frames. You will also need to decide whether the division is to be vertical or horizontal or a combination of both.

Let us assume, for the purpose of the example that follows, that it will be vertical. Moreover, the example that is shown in Figure 12.21 consists of two vertical frames. The purpose of the left-hand-side narrow frame is to display the website navigation links. The right-hand-side one is to display the content that follows each link.

Figure 12.21
Dividing a page
into two vertical
frames with
Dreamweaver

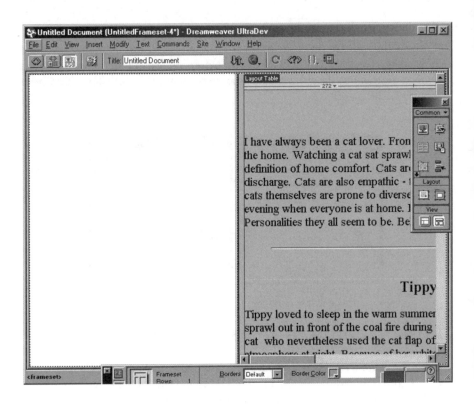

To divide the page into vertical frames, follow these steps.

1 From the document window, click the menu option Modify / Frameset / Split Frame Right.

2 The window splits into two frames. If content exists on the original page, it then shifts to the right-hand side, as shown in Figure 12.21.

Adding content to a frame

To add content to the left-hand frame, do the following.

1 Press the keyboard combination Alt-click (hold the Alt key down and click the left mouse button) inside the left-hand window to select it.

2 Click the folder icon to choose the HTML file for the page. A dialogue box will appear, as shown in Figure 12.22. Alternatively, you can type the content of the right-hand-side window. In this particular example, we might want to type some links to other HTML documents to appear in the left-hand window (see Figure 12.23).

3 Link the items in the right-hand-side window to other pages on the website as shown in Figure 12.23.

4 Preview the page and test the frame window links.

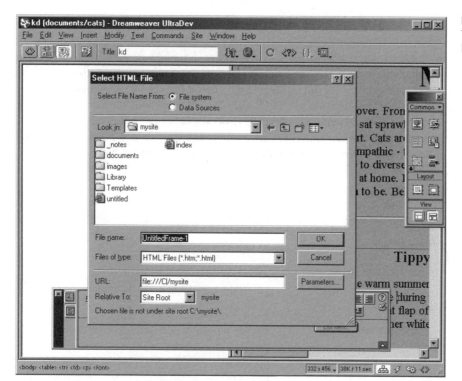

Figure 12.22
The select HTML
File dialogue box

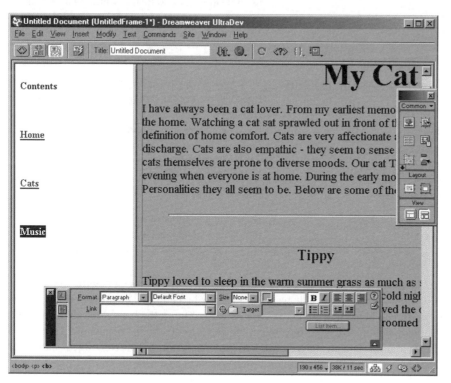

Figure 12.23
Entering the
navigation bar
items in the
left-hand frame

Dreamweaver behaviours

In Chapter 7, we saw how JavaScript and other scripting languages could be used to add interactivity to Web pages. **Behaviours** give you interactivity without the need to add coding in JavaScript as they do the coding for you. These behaviours could be the same things that we saw in Chapter 7, such as clicking the mouse or loading a page or typing a keyboard character. However, other behaviours that are specifically installed with Dreamweaver are possible and we will look at how to use some of these in the following section. Table 12.1 describes some of these.

Table 12.1 Some built-in Dreamweaver behaviours

Behaviours	Description of use
Swap image	Swaps the image source for another image source – that is, the rollover one. We have already seen that a rollover object is available on the object panel, but it can be implemented as a behaviour if required
Check browser	Getting a page to work with all browsers can be a formidable task, especially if you use style sheets. To overcome this problem you can use this behaviour to determine the browser being used by the user and then forward the user to a page that you might have built specifically for that browser
Open browser window	Opens a new browser window
Create a status bar message	When you pass your mouse cursor over a hyperlink on a page, that hyperlink destination URL will appear in the document window status bar. This behaviour will change that status bar message to one of your own choosing
Change property	Will change an object property
Play sound	Plays a sound
Check plug-in	Determines whether or not a user's browser has a particular plug-in installed

As already stated, Dreamweaver lets you create some behaviours without having to use JavaScript. When you want to attach a behaviour, Dreamweaver opens the appropriate behaviour dialogue box. After setting up the behaviour characteristics in the dialogue box, you must select the event to invoke the behaviour. To create a behaviour in Dreamweaver, we will use the example of creating a status bar message. Do this by taking the following steps.

1 Define the behaviour. In this case, we are going to create a status bar message to be linked to the 'Preparing the Soil and Raising Plants' hyperlink in the index.html page of mysite (see Figure 12.24).

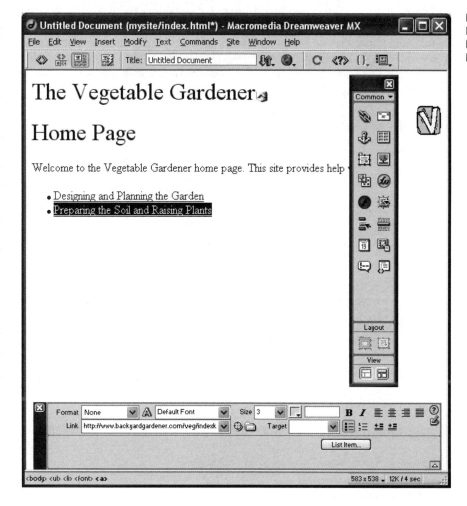

Figure 12.24
Defining a status
bar message
behaviour

2 Select an object from the document window that you want to link, so that the status bar message will appear when the mouse is skimmed over it. In this case, it is the object 'Preparing the Soil and Raising Plants' of the index.html page of mysite (see Figure 12.24).

3 Choose the menu option Window / Behaviors. You will see the Behaviors tab appear, as shown in Figure 12.25.

4 In the Behaviors tab, click the + key and, from the ensuing pull-down menu list that follows, select Set Text and click Set Text of Status Bar.

5 In the Set Text of Status Bar dialogue box that follows, enter the required text – in this case, I have used the message 'The Vegetable Expert website'.

Figure 12.25
The behaviors tab

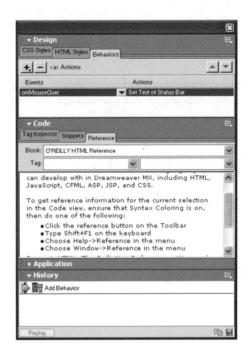

Figure 12.26
Screenshot of status bar behaviour operating

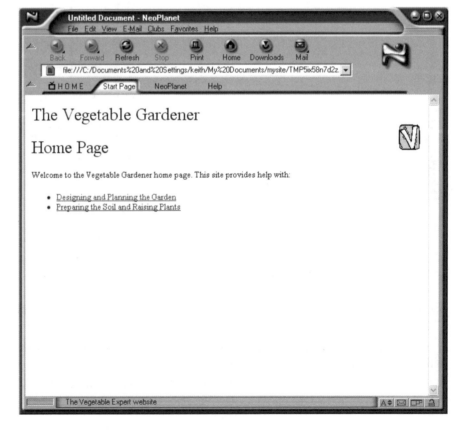

6 Test the behaviour. Check the behaviour with appropriate browsers. A screenshot of the working program is shown in Figure 12.26, where the message can be seen at the bottom of the screen.

You cannot attach behaviours to objects that are not appropriate for the object selected.

NOTE

Summary

■ Forms can be created easily in Dreamweaver to include text fields, buttons, checkboxes and other interative elements on your page.

■ Tables are often used to organize the layout of information on a Web page. Such tables would have their borders set to be invisible. To achieve this type of effect, you can use the Layout View in Dreamweaver.

■ Meta-tags enable search engines to locate and list your website.

■ Two name attribute values can be used with the meta-tag used in the head section of an XHTML document to help to get your site listed. They are 'keywords' and 'description'.

■ The history palette lets you view the commands applied to a Web page during the current editing session.

■ A rollover image changes when the user rolls the mouse over the image.

■ Frames provide a means of dividing your browser window into several smaller windows with the capacity to display different Web page(s) in each window.

■ To create a frameset in Dreamweaver, you will need to divide the document window into two or more frames. You will also need to decide if the division is to be vertical, horizontal or a combination of both.

■ JavaScript and other scripting languages can be used to add interactivity to Web pages.

■ Using Dreamweaver, behaviours can often give you interactivity without the need for coding in JavaScript. Behaviours can do the coding for you.

Exercises

Hands-on task

1 Consider the form shown in Figure 12.27. Use Dreamweaver to do the following:
   a   re-create the form to include all the checkboxes shown
   b   make all the labels on the form bold
   c   extend the form so that it includes Submit and Clear buttons.

Figure 12.27
Form for hands-on
task

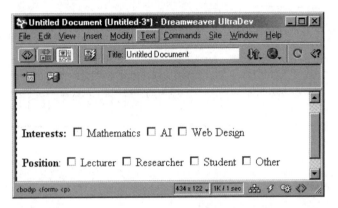

2   Create a form using Dreamweaver to collect user data of your choice. Prepare your form on paper before using Dreamweaver and give careful thought to the form's layout and the positioning of its components. Try to include on your form a variety of form objects, such as text fields, checkboxes, radio buttons and so on.

3   Create a Web page containing frames using Dreamweaver to implement the following structure. Create three horizontal windows in the ratio 3 : 1 : 1. The top window should be a heading window containing the message 'This is a heading'. The middle window should contain the message 'This is the middle' and the bottom window should contain the message 'This is the bottom'.

4   Use Dreamweaver to create an empty table entitled 'An Empty Table', consisting of four rows and two columns. Set the border of this table to 1 unit. Save the file using an appropriate file name and check the code using both the IE and Netscape browsers.

5   Create a Web page using Dreamweaver entitled 'Life in School'. Use meta-tags to include keywords and descriptions that describe your document.

Chapter

13

Improving productivity with Dreamweaver

In this chapter you will learn how to:

- use templates
- use the assets panel
- create library items
- make design notes
- use CSS
- use the HTML tag editor
- create clean HTML code in Dreamweaver
- use Dreamweaver layers
- use Flash buttons and rollover buttons
- use databases with Dreamweaver
- use other Dreamweaver features.

Introduction

This chapter looks at some advanced Dreamweaver techniques. Many of these – templates, assets and design notes – can improve productivity. Others, such as using Dreamweaver layers and Web databases, extend the functionality of Dreamweaver. In this chapter we will look in some detail at these and other advanced Dreamweaver techniques.

Using templates

Quality websites often have a consistent layout or background colour or style. However, in the early days of the Web, site developers would spend a long time re-creating tasks to render a consistent style across all the pages on a site. Fortunately, Dreamweaver templates provide the means to achieve this consistency without much effort.

A **template** is a model for a design. In Dreamweaver, templates are master documents from which other documents can be created. The idea is that, instead of opening a blank document with very little or no formatting, you open instead the required template.

Dreamweaver template documents contain the extension '.dtl' rather than '.html'.

A template document has sections that are non-editable and other sections that are editable. When each new document is created from the template, it has the same editable and non-editable regions as the others. Templates can be applied across a site and created in much the same way as a Dreamweaver page is created.

Creating a new template

1 Choose the File / New menu option. If you are using MX, you will be prompted to select a document type – choose Template. If you are using an earlier version of Dreamweaver, you can select New Template from the File menu.

Figure 13.1
Creating a new
template with
editable and
non-editable
regions

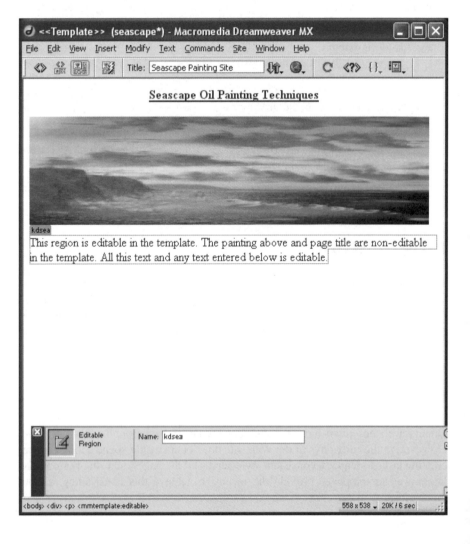

2 Choose the Modify / Page Properties menu option to choose a colour scheme or to set any other page characteristics for the template, such as the page title.

3 Add content to the page that you want to stay invariant (for example, it may be a graphic logo in the top right-hand corner or a custom home button at the bottom left-hand side of the page or a navigation bar on the left-hand side of the page).

4 To make other sections of your template editable, select a section of the template that you will want to be able to change by highlighting with the mouse. You need to give careful thought to the choice of editable and non-editable areas – remember, a non-editable area cannot be changed when defined in a template file.

5 Choose Insert / Template Objects / New Editable Region from the main menu. In the dialogue box that follows, you will need to name the editable region. In the example shown in Figure 13.1, the page title and seascape painting are to remain as fixed parts of the template page.

6 When complete, choose File / Save As Template and give the template a name, such as my_site_template (see Figure 13.1).

Using your template to create new pages

1 Select File / New from the menu. Choose the Templates tab from the ensuing New Document dialogue box and select the required template (see Figure 13.2).

2 Click on the site and template that you want from the dialogue box and click the Create button.

3 Edit the editable sections as required (see Figure 13.3) and save.

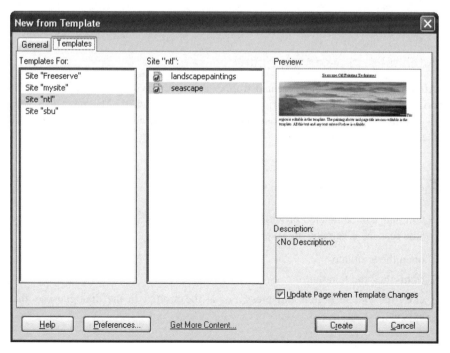

Figure 13.2
Selecting a template for use with a new document

Figure 13.3
Creating a New
Page based on a
Template

If you modify a template and save the changes, then you will be prompted by a dialogue box asking if you want to update all documents that use that template in your site.

Attaching pages to templates

After a new page has been created from a template, it will remain attached to the original template unless specifically separated or detached. The new document maintains a connection to previous pages in a site so alterations affect all pages with the same template, as before.

Deleting a template

A template can be deleted providing it is not being used by Web pages in memory, for the reasons given above. To delete a template:

1 open the template

2 right-click the template

3 click the Delete button and press Yes at the prompt in the dialogue box that appears.

If you are deleting a template, then you will also need to detach it (see next section) from Web pages that were created using it or else the editable regions will remain and suggest that the Web pages are still attached to the deleted template.

Detaching a template

You can detach a template from a Web page by following these three steps:

1 open the Web page that you want to detach from the template
2 from the menu, select Modify/ Templates / Detach from Template
3 Save the Web page.

The assets panel

The assets panel was introduced in Dreamweaver 4.0. Assets provide a way to organize your files according to type – graphics, templates and so on – within your site. These file elements include images, background, text colours, external URLs, included scripts, Flash movies, Shockwave content and many more file types.

Once you define your site using Site / New Site from the menu, all of these types of elements are automatically added to the proper tabs in the assets panel.

Using the assets panel

To view the assets panel, open it using Window / Assets from the menu. The icons on the left-hand side show the various assets, including images, Flash, Shockwave,

Figure 13.4
The Colors tab in the assets panel, listing all colours used on your website with hexadecimal value, RGB number and if they are Websafe or not

templates and so on. The panel also has a Colors tab, which is where all of the colours on your site are stored, including colours for text, backgrounds and links. It is a site-specific colour palette.

Click the tiny colour wheel on the left. You'll see a list of all the colours within your site (see Figure 13.4). You can drag those colours to selected text. If you select a particular colour, its combined hexadecimal value and RGB number appear. You are also notified if the colour is Websafe or not.

Library items

At the beginning of this chapter we saw how templates can be used to maintain consistency of page layout. What happens, though, if we want a technique to enable us to repeat the occurrences of elements in Web pages? For example, suppose we want to repeat the occurrence of a navigation bar or perhaps an organization's logo throughout a website.

Dreamweaver includes a feature called **library items** that helps you to insert repeating elements into every Web page you create. With one command, you can update and maintain library items efficiently and productively. In this section, we will see how to use this Dreamweaver feature.

Features of the library include the following useful capabilities:

- any item that goes into the body of your Web page can be nominated as a library item
- library items can be edited at any time (as with templates, Dreamweaver will let you choose whether to update the website immediately or postpone the update until later)
- once created, library items can be placed instantly on any Web page in your site, without you having to retype, reinsert or reformat text and graphics.

Creating library items

To create a library item, take the following steps.

1 Open the library panel by using Modify/ Library/ Add Objects to Library. You will see a library panel appear (see Figure 13.5).

2 Create a page that contains the item(s) you want to capture, then select the item(s) by highlighting.

3 In the library panel, name the library item.

4 Press the Enter key.

NOTE   When you create library item(s), Dreamweaver creates a folder called 'library' in the current site for storing library items. A library item file uses the extension '.lbi'.

Amending library items

You can amend library item(s) as you like. If you make a change to a library item, though, then all pages that use this item will be changed.

1 Open the library panel using Modify/ Library/ Add Objects to Library.

2 Highlight the required library item and double-click. The library item will be displayed in a Dreamweaver document window.

3 Make the required changes and, from the menu, select File/ Save.

4 Click the Update button. This will then update all the pages that are currently using the library item.

Figure 13.5
The library panel

Making design notes

During the development of a website with Dreamweaver, you can attach useful information, such as editing history and author names, to your Web pages using Dreamweaver **design notes**.

This is a very handy facility for team projects because the development status of page(s) can be updated following modifications. Even individual developers can benefit as the design notes can be stored for future reference on the PC.

To create design notes, follow the procedure described below.

1 Open the Web page to which you wish to attach design notes.

2 Click File / Design Notes.

3 A Design Notes dialogue box will appear. Enter a status for the page by clicking the pull-down list, as shown in Figure 13.6. This includes a number of values, including draft, revisions or final, corresponding to the version status of the document.

4 Type any notes that you wish to enter for the page into the Notes box, as shown in Figure 13.6. You can also include the date by clicking the date icon – this is just above the right-hand side of the Notes box (see Figure 13.6).

5 If you want your notes to be shown whenever the file is opened, you can click the checkbox below the Notes box.

6 Now click the All Info tab of the Design Notes dialogue box (see Figure 13.6) and you will then see the All Info tab (see Figure 13.7). To append new information to the design notes, click +. You can remove information by clicking the – key.

Viewing design notes

You can view design notes once they have been created by clicking File / Design Notes when a page is open in the document window. The Design Notes for that file will then open.

NOTE

Design notes are stored separately from the HTML files. Dreamweaver actually stores the information for design notes as XML files in a folder called "_notes". You might have noticed this folder created already in your local Dreamweaver files folder.

Figure 13.6
The design notes dialogue box

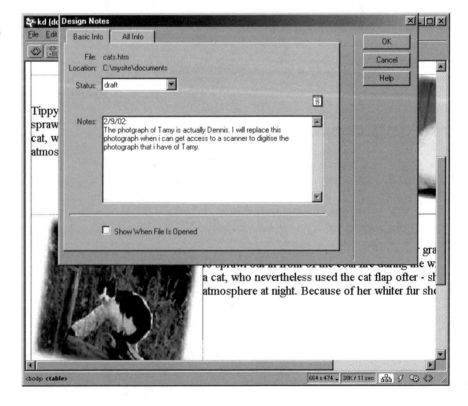

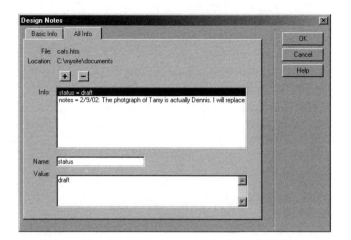

Figure 13.7
Using the Design
Notes All Info tab

Using CSS with Dreamweaver

In Chapter 8, we saw how CSS can provide a mechanism to create formatting rules
for your Web pages. They also make the maintenance of a website easier because
many pages can link to a single set of style rules. We saw, too, that website
designers can embed style rules within a page or part of a page, create an external
style sheet and link that to a page as required.

To create an external style sheet using Dreamweaver, follow the steps below.

1 Click Text / CSS styles / New CSS Style.
2 A New CSS Style dialogue box will appear, as shown in Figure 13.8. Leave the
   default selection as (New Style Sheet File) and click the OK button. Note that you
   can select a class, CSS selector or redefine an HTML tag. Ensure that the Use CSS
   Selector radio button is checked in Type. Note that you can also assign a name to
   a new style.

Figure 13.8
The New CSS
Style dialogue box

3 From the Save Style Sheet File As dialogue box that will now appear (see
   Figure 13.9), select where you want the external style sheet to be stored in your
   local files folder.
4 Name the style sheet file. In the example shown in Figure 13.9, I have named the
   file mysheet.css.

Figure 13.9
The Save Style
Sheet File As
dialogue box

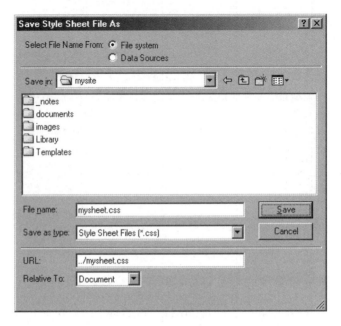

5 Click the Save button in the Save Style Sheet File As dialogue box.

6 From the Style Definition for the named file dialogue box that will then appear (see Figure 13.10), choose a style category. Notice that there are all the categories of CSS2 styles, including Type, Background, Box, Border, List and Positioning. When you select a category, the appropriate rules appear on the right.

7 Define your style information, then click OK.

Figure 13.10
The Style
Definition for
mysheet.css
dialogue box

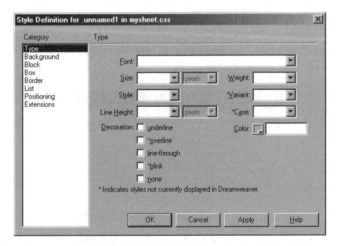

NOTE   When you attach a style sheet to a page in Dreamweaver, you can either browse for the file in your local site folder or enter an external URL. This last option means that you would be linking to a style sheet on another website.

How to link HTML tags to CSS style rules

To link an HTML tag to CSS style rules, follow the procedure set out below.

1 Click Text / CSS styles / New CSS Style.

2 From the New CSS Style dialogue box, select the Redefine HTML Tag radio button (see Figure 13.11). You will see a list of HTML tags in the Tag box that will appear. Select the tag that you want to apply the style sheet to.

3 Name the style sheet file, as in the steps above.

4 From the Style Definition for the named file dialogue box, choose a style category. Notice there are all the categories of CSS2 styles, including Type, Background, Box, Border, List and Positioning. When you select a category, the appropriate rules appear on the right.

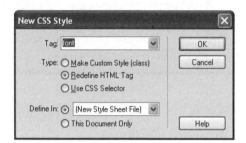

Figure 13.11
Choosing the Redefine HTML Tag radio button in the New CSS Style dialogue box

How to attach an external style sheet

To attach an external style sheet to a Web page, follow the steps given below.

1 Open the page to which you want to attach the style sheet.

2 Click Text / CSS Styles / Attach Style Sheet from the menu.

3 From the Select Style Sheet File dialogue box that appears (see Figure 13.12), select the external style sheet you want. That style sheet will now be attached to the nominated HTML file.

Using classes in Dreamweaver

You will recall from Chapter 8 that you can define custom style rules with CSS that you can apply to many different types of content on your page. These rules are known as **classes**. For example, you can create a style rule that turns the first and last paragraphs of text on a page red and then colours the centre paragraphs black. CSS classes can also be created, edited and applied to HTML documents in Dreamweaver, as described below.

Figure 13.12
The Select Style
Sheet File
dialogue box
being used to
attach an external
style sheet to a
Web page

Creating a CSS class in Dreamweaver

1 Click Text / CSS styles / New CSS Style.

2 In the New CSS Style dialogue box that appears (see Figure 13.13), click the Make Custom Style (class) radio button.

3 Name the class. In this example, we have called it .redpargh – an abbreviation of red paragraph. We will create an embedded style sheet to background colour the first paragraph red. Remember, from Chapter 8, that class names must begin with a full stop.

4 Select the radio button This Document Only if you wish to create an embedded style sheet and click OK. Otherwise, choose (New Style Sheet File) if you want to use an external style sheet.

5 You will now see another dialogue box appear – called CSS Style Definition for .redpargh (see Figure 13.14). Select the style information required from this dialogue box. That is, choose the Background Color category, then, using the colour palette, set the colour to red.

Figure 13.13
Using the New
CSS Style
dialogue box to
create a custom
CSS class

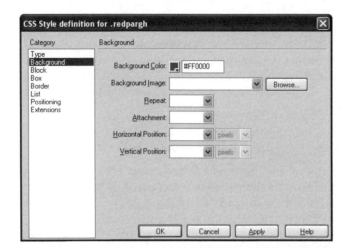

Figure 13.14
Setting the style
information for the
.redpargh CSS
class in the CSS
Style definition
dialogue box

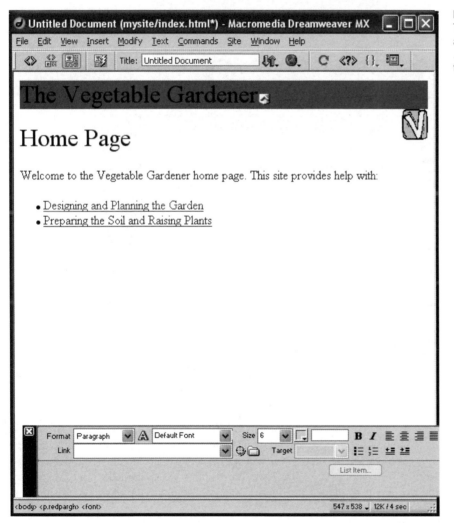

Figure 13.15
The result of
attaching the
.redpargh class to
the Web page

Attaching the style sheet to the embedded file

To attach the style sheet to the embedded file, choose Text / CSS Styles / redpargh. Note that redpargh will be available on the submenu list because this class has already been created and is therefore available for use with the page. Figure 13.15 displays the change resulting from attaching the .redpargh class to the document.

Another example of using a Dreamweaver CSS class

The following example shows how Dreamweaver CSS can be used to create and apply an external style sheet class to a text-based document to improve its readability by making the text larger. To do this, a class called .big has been created. Figure 13.16 displays the document before enlargement and Figure 13.17 displays the New CSS Style dialogue box, with the new class called .big applied to a (New Style Sheet File).

Figure 13.16
The document before applying the external style sheet .big class

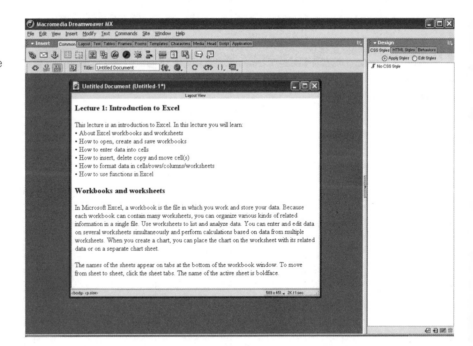

As with the previous example, the CSS Style Definition for the style sheet class dialogue box will appear and allow us to define the style rules to be applied to the .big class. In Figure 13.18, you will see that the Font chosen is the Times New Roman serif with a large size font. When this style is applied to the first half of the document displayed in Figure 13.16, you can see the result is as shown in Figure 13.19.

Figure 13.17
Using the New CSS Style dialogue box to create a class called .big

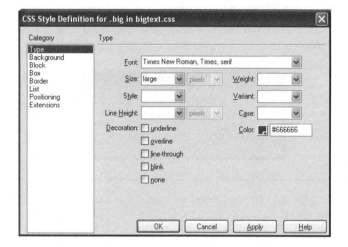

Figure 13.18
CSS Style Definition for the style sheet class called .big

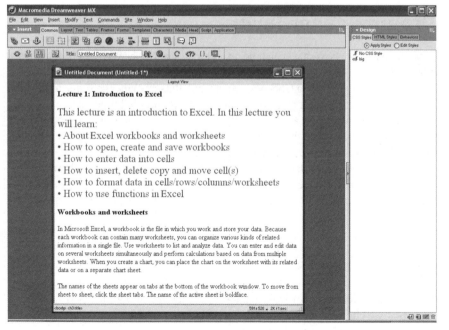

Figure 13.19
The .big class applied to the first half of the document shown in Figure 13.16

Converting CSS to HTML tags

Sometimes, you might want to convert CSS styles to HTML format so that you can have a site version that can be viewed by those whose browsers do not support CSS. You can make CSS formatting viewable on 3.0 browsers by taking the following steps.

1 Choose File / Convert to 3.0 Browser Compatible from the menu.

2 In the ensuing dialogue box – Convert to 3.0 Browser Compatible – if you leave the Both radio button selected (see Figure 13.20), then, as well as converting CSS to HTML markup, all layers will converted to tables (layers are covered next).

3 Click the OK button and Dreamweaver will open the converted file in a new, untitled window.

Figure 13.20
The Convert to 3.0
Browser
Compatible
dialogue box

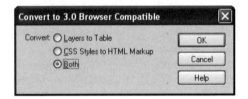

NOTE   Not all CSS styles can be converted to HTML – for example, positioning style attributes have no equivalent in HTML. Hence, not all CSS styles can be converted to CSS.

Dreamweaver layers

Layers are floating boxes that can hold text, graphics and other Web page components. These are not the same layers that are used in graphics software, such as Photoshop.

Layers are created using CSS positioning and, thus, provide the scope to position an element precisely on a page by means of point and click operations. You can place layers anywhere on a page, stack one on top of another, overlap portions of them and do many other things with them. Furthermore, layers can even be animated using **timelines**, which are means of implementing the animation.

Layers are only supported by IE 4+ and Netscape 4+ and there are also some discrepancies arising from the way in which layers are supported. So, thought has to be given to what browsers your users are likely to be using when you are considering layers.

Creating layers

To create a basic layer, you will need to select the menu option Insert / Layer. A layer box will be visible – see the rectangular box in the top left-hand side of the document window in Figure 13.21. This figure displays the layer in the UltraDev version of Dreamweaver. If you are going to be working with layers, then you will also need to open the layers panel. To do this, select Window / Others / Layers from the menu (see Figure 13.21). The layers panel is visible in the right-hand side of the document window. You will draw your layer in the rectangular box area in the top left-hand side of the document window as shown. The layers panel currently contains no layers because we have not drawn any as yet.

> When you create a layer, Dreamweaver inserts the `div` tag in your document by default to create the layer. However, you can change this default value, if you wish, to the `span` tag instead.

NOTE

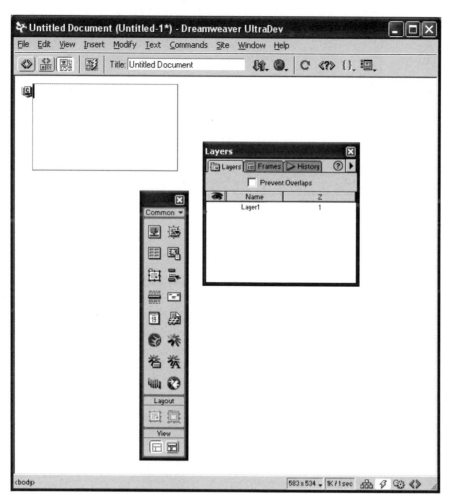

Figure 13.21
The layers panel

Adjusting the size of a layer

The size of a layer is set as a default value in Dreamweaver's Preferences dialogue box (see Figure 3.22). You can change the layer's size by choosing Edit / Preferences from the menu. Click the Layers category on the left-hand side of the dialogue box and you will see a list of the various layer parameters that you can change. These include the visibility, width, height and background colour of the layers.

Figure 13.22
Setting the layer's
parameters

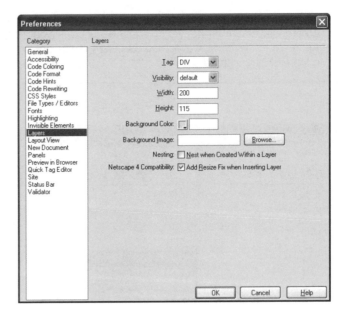

Adding content to the layer

To add content to a layer, you will first need to click inside the layer, then type in the required text or insert an image or include any other form of content that is required. You can also drag objects into a layer. Figure 13.23 displays the text layer with its content, 'This is too much!', in the document window and it appears blurry because of the way in which the message has overlapped. In the history panel, the layer activity is displayed in Figure 13.23. This is the result of slightly overlapping two layers with the same text message. Many other interesting text effects can be achieved using layers.

Setting a layer's properties

You can view a layer's properties in the properties inspector panel (see Figure 13.24). The properties are as follows.

■ **Layer ID**   You may need to assign an ID to a layer so that it can be identified for scripting behaviours or something else.

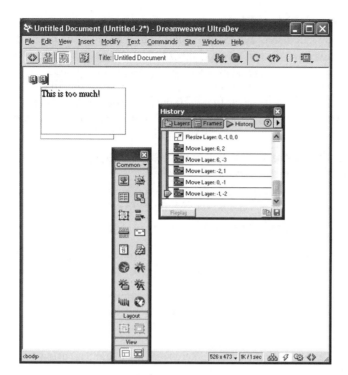

Figure 13.23
Two overlapping
layers have been
added to the
document window
to create blurry
text

- **L and T** Define the position (all in pixels) of a layer relative to the top left-hand corner of the Web page. If you have a layer that is nested in another layer, the L and T will relate to the Left and Top of the parent page.

- **W and H** Display the width and height of your layer. These values can be changed in the properties inspector panel.

- **Z-index** Controls the visibility of overlapping layers or sets the stacking order. The Z-index was defined in Chapter 8, when we looked at positioning. A layer with a higher Z-index will appear above a layer with a lower Z-index. The stacking order can be changed by resetting the Z-index box.

- **Bg Image** You can select a background image for a layer using this property.

- **Bg Color** As with Bg Image, you can select the background colour of a layer.

Figure 13.24
Seeing the layer's
properties in the
properties
inspector

- **Vis**   This property determines the visibility property of the layer when the page loads. You can also change layer visibility to turn layers on or off dynamically along a timeline. Vis can take a number of possible option values as follows:
  - **Visible**   displays the layer whatever the parent's properties
  - **Hidden**   will hide the layer, whatever the parent's properties
  - **Inherit**   causes the layer to inherit the properties of the parent
  - **Default**   will take the value 'Visible', unless the layer is nested, in which case it will inherit the value of the parent layer.
- **Tag**   This property enables you to select your layer as a DIV or a SPAN tag from the pull-down list.
- **Overflow**   This occurs when the layer's content exceeds the layer's dimensions. Overflow options can be set as follows from the pull-down list:
  - **Visible**   shows overflow content
  - **Hidden**   hides overflow content
  - **Scroll**   provides scroll bars to view overflow content
  - **Auto**   provides scroll bars where needed to view overflowing content.

Dreamweaver and HTML

As we have seen in earlier chapters, Web pages are marked up using HTML. We have used a text editor to create HTML Web pages, but creating and writing tags can be a time-consuming process. Dreamweaver is a WYSIWYG (what you see is what you get) Web development tool. The Dreamweaver interface enables you to bypass HTML by inserting the appropriate tags when required. This means that the designer can edit Web pages without having any contact with HTML.

In practice, however, it often helps to have knowledge of HTML because sometimes fine-tuning at the HTML level becomes necessary if a particular technology is not supported. The Dreamweaver environment allows the designer to flip from WYSIWYG development mode – called **Design View** – to HTML mode – called **Code View** – and edit in either mode and convert documents from HTML to XHTML format if required. To flip from Design View to Code View in Dreamweaver MX, select View / Switch View (or Ctrl +) from the menu, as shown in Figure 13.25.

Dreamweaver lets you view and amend HTML tags as a two-way process. For example, you can write page elements using the WYSIWYG environment and then view or amend the HTML page in the Code Inspector window. Moreover, the code generated by Dreamweaver can be made XHTML-compliant. However, all sorts of things tend to happen to a Web page during development, such as reformatting an element or deleting one. This can result in HTML code generated by Dreamweaver being less than optimal. Fortunately, Dreamweaver provides a Clean Up HTML code command. This command can not only improve the quality of code in your page, but also remove non-essential tags, such as comments.

Creating clean HTML code in Dreamweaver

You can optimize the HTML in your pages created with Dreamweaver by deleting

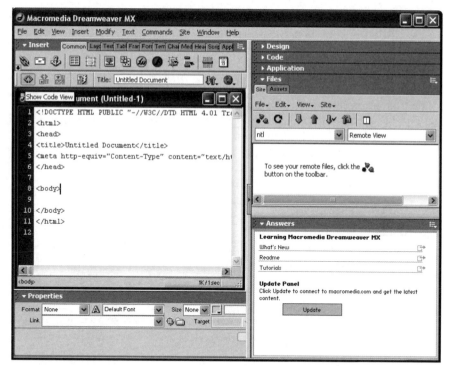

Figure 13.25
Flipping from
Design View to
Code View in
Dreamweaver MX

> Clean Up HTML cannot be applied to an entire site, but, rather, only one page at a time. It is therefore advisable to use this command when a page has been completely finished.

NOTE

non-functional tags. The purpose of doing this is to reduce the amount of code and improve the readability of the HTML file. To use the Clean Up command:

1 open the Web page that you want to use the Clean Up command on
2 click Commands / Clean Up HTML – the Clean Up HTML dialogue box appears (see Figure 13.26)
3 turn on/off any checkboxes as required for the options you want.

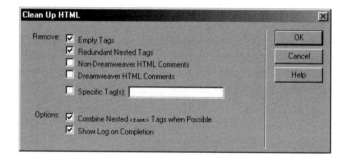

Figure 13.26
The Clean Up
HTML dialogue box

The meanings of the checkboxes in the Clean Up HTML dialogue box

- An **Empty Tag** is one that does nothing. Empty tags can appear in Dreamweaver pages. To understand why, suppose we were to delete the 'My Cats Page' heading on the Web page shown in Figure 13.27. If the page is open and we click the Code Inspector icon – < > – at the top left-hand side of the page, then the HTML tag containing the heading will appear, as we can see in Figure 13.27. When the relevant item is highlighted and deleted, you will notice that the align ="center" tag will remain, despite the removal of the heading. Notice that the default for this checkbox is ticked (see Figure 13.26).

Figure 13.27
Example of an empty tag as this heading has been deleted

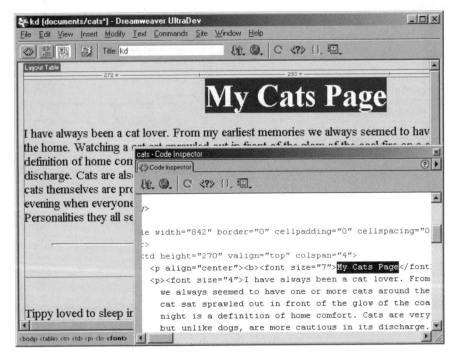

- **Redundant Nested Tags** are those that appear within other tags of the same type. For example, <I> This is <I> Italic</I></I>. This sometimes happens if you find yourself un-italicizing an italicized tag.

- **Non-Dreamweaver HTML Comments** are those deleted that were not originally inserted using Dreamweaver. Remember, comments are inserted to aid the readability of the HTML and have no impact on the rendering of tags on the Web page. Dreamweaver HTML Comments deletes any comments inserted by someone using Dreamweaver. Note that Dreamweaver relies on comments in some of its features, such as behaviours. So, choosing this option can sometimes have harmful effects.

- **Specific Tag(s)** deletes HTML tags that you specify – if you wanted to delete all occurrences of the blockquote tag, for example.

Using Check In/Check Out

After a website has been created and is online, future maintenance is inevitable. This might happen because you want to add new content or change the site layout, such as changing colours or images. If you are part of a team with individual responsibilities, then clearly you will want to keep track of who has worked on a file, so that you will avoid any duplication of effort. This becomes particularly important if you are working with team members who might be scattered around at different locations.

Check In/Check Out is a Dreamweaver feature that supports this form of file management. The basic idea is that each team member can monitor file usage because each user records what has been done, when and by whom. Moreover, when you are editing files, you can 'check them out' of the site so that other team members would be prevented from using them at the same time. This feature can even be used by one person – maybe someone who uses a computer for updating at home and work – because you can enter different Check In/Check Out names depending on which computer you are working on. Then you will know where the most recent changes are located should you forget to check a file back in.

The following steps illustrate how to use this feature.

1 Go to Site / Edit Sites ...

2 Select the required site and click the Edit button.

3 When the Site Definition dialogue box appears, click the Next button four times to select the defaults until you see the Sharing Files, Part 2 dialogue box (see Figure 13.28).

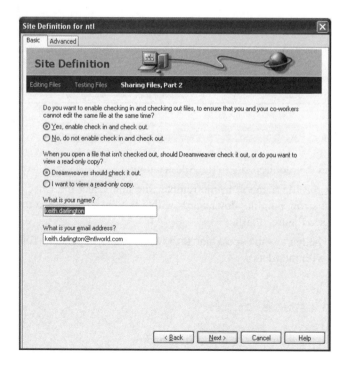

Figure 13.28
The Sharing Files, Part 2 dialogue box

4 Click the Yes, enable check in and check out radio button and you will see the additional text boxes appear, prompting you to input your user name and an e-mail address.

5 Type in your user name and an e-mail address.

6 Make sure that the Dreamweaver should check it out radio button is also selected, then click the Next button.

7 The Site Definition Summary dialogue box will appear (see Figure 13.29), which should include notification that Check-in/Check-out has been enabled. Click the Done button, and click the Done button in the Edit Sites dialogue box.

Figure 13.29
The Site Definition
Summary
dialogue box

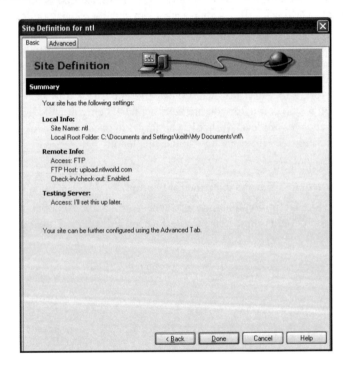

How to check out a remote file

1 Connect to the required site in the Site window.

2 Highlight the file name(s) in the remote Site and select the Check Out File(s) button (an arrow pointing downwards with a tick by it) along the top of the Site window (see Figure 13.30).

3 Choose whether or not you want to download any dependent files – such as images – with the file(s).

How to check in files

1 Connect to the required site in the Site window.

2 Highlight the file name(s) in the local Site and select the Check In File(s) button (an arrow pointing upwards to the right of the Check Out File(s) button described above) along the top of the Site window.

3 Choose whether or not you want to upload any dependent files – such as images – with the file(s).

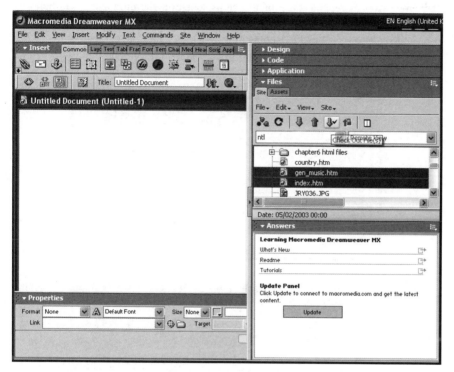

Figure 13.30
Checking out files
in the Site window

Automating tasks with Dreamweaver

You may sometimes, while creating documents, want to perform the same task several times. You can use the history panel to do this as it lets you see the commands that you have applied to the Web page since it was opened – rather like a video camera that has traced each of your steps.

You can view the history panel by selecting the menu option Window / Others / History (or Shift F10). The panel shown in Figure 13.31 is displaying some layer operations that have been completed in the document window. To repeat a series of steps, you can replay the steps in the history panel.

Repeating steps using the history panel

1 To use the history panel, you will need to record commands and then view these in the history panel window. To record commands, choose the menu option Commands / Start Recording. This means that every keystroke is then recorded

for playback until you choose to stop the recorder. The steps themselves are played back exactly as they were recorded – mistakes as well, which is why it is important to plan and use this facility carefully.

2 Some mouse movements cannot be recorded, such as clicking and dragging the mouse. Dreamweaver will notify you of this if you attempt these actions.

3 If you want to repeat some of the steps, position the cursor in the document window where you want the activity repeated, then highlight the steps that you want to repeat and click the Replay button in the history panel (see Figure 13.32). Notice in Figure 13.32 that the steps to be repeated have been highlighted in the history panel in the bottom right-hand pane.

Figure 13.31
A history panel where layer operations have been recorded

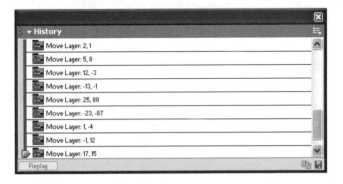

Figure 13.32
The highlighted steps to be repeated in the history panel

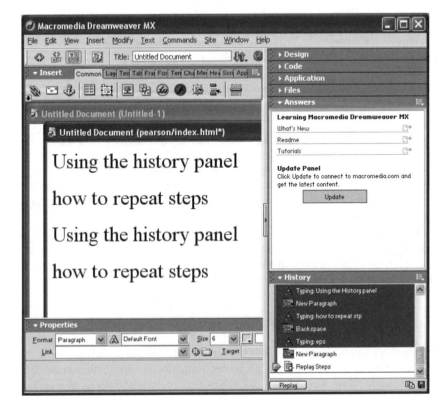

Flash and Dreamweaver

Dreamweaver 4 introduced a library of Flash rollover buttons that could be used in Dreamweaver applications. There is still much debate in the Web development community about whether or not Flash buttons should be used at all. The main reason for this is that a Flash plug-in is required with a browser incorporating Flash components. However, the numbers of browsers that do not support the plug-in are diminishing rapidly and, being a vector-based application, Flash files tend to be smaller than bitmap files so generally download faster. Dreamweaver users can now use off-the-shelf buttons and create Flash tests to use directly in Web pages.

Inserting a Flash rollover button

You will need to save a document before you can add a Flash rollover button to it. Then you can add your button as follows.

1 Open your document in Dreamweaver and place the cursor where you require the Flash file to be inserted.

2 From the menu, select Insert / Interactive Images / Flash Button to open the Insert Flash Button dialogue box (see Figure 13.33).

3 A list of button styles is offered to select from and each can be viewed, before selection, in the Sample box above the Style selection box.

4 Type in any button text that you want to appear in the Button Text box.

5 If you want to modify the default text style, select your preferred font and size.

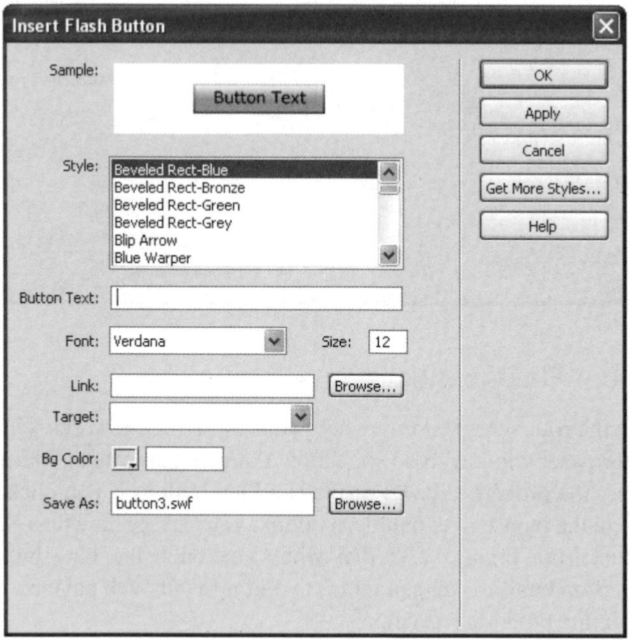

Figure 13.33
The Insert Flash Button dialogue box

6 Enter the URL that you want to link to the Flash button in the Link box.

7 Select a target from the Target list box only if you are using frames.

8 Click OK to save and exit to Dreamweaver.

NOTE If you want to select from more button styles, you can click the Get More Styles ... button on the right-hand side of the dialogue box shown in Figure 13.33. You will then be transferred to the Macromedia website and the Dreamweaver Exchange (see Figure 13.34). You can then access a much larger online library.

Figure 13.34
The Dreamweaver
Exchange at
Macromedia's
website

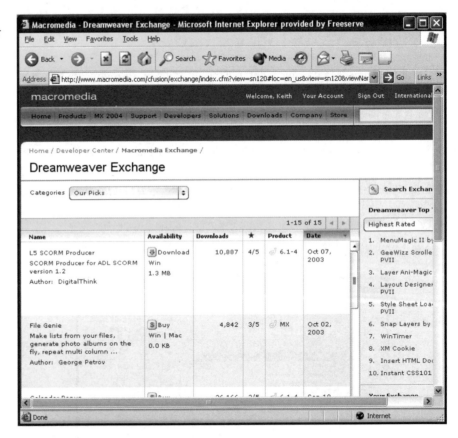

Testing your Flash button

You can test the rollover effect to see how your Flash button works without having to open the browser window to do so. You will notice that when a Flash button has been selected, the properties panel displays a Play button. If you click this button and then move the mouse over the Flash button, you can see how the rollover effect works. Notice from Figure 13.35 that when you click the Play button, it then changes to a Stop button. You can return to editing your Web page by clicking the Stop button in the properties panel.

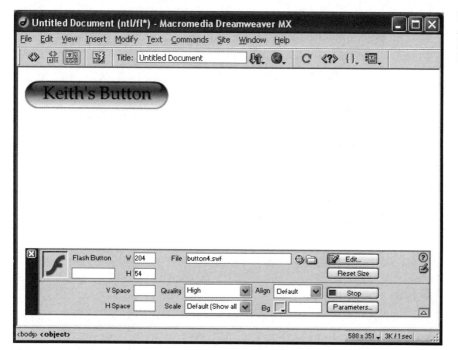

Figure 13.35
A Flash button
being tested in
Dreamweaver

NOTE

Figure 13.35 is showing the Stop button. This is because the screenshot has been displayed after the Play button has been invoked. Before invoking the Play button it will display Play instead of Stop in the bottom right-hand corner of the Flash Button properties panel at the bottom of the screen.

Creating text using Flash

You can also create Flash text without having access to the Flash application in Dreamweaver. To do this, follow these steps.

1 Open your document in Dreamweaver and place the cursor where you require the Flash file to be inserted.

2 From the menu, select Insert / Interactive Images / Flash Text to open the Insert Flash Text dialogue box (see Figure 13.36).

3 Specify the text background colour – Bg Color – and Rollover Color using the color palettes as shown in Figure 13.36.

4 Enter the required text in the Text box. If you want to modify the default text style, select your preferred font and size.

5 Enter the URL that you want to link to the Flash text in the Link box.

6 Select a target from the Target list box only if you are using frames. Choose a file name to save your Flash text.

7 Click OK to save and exit to Dreamweaver.

Figure 13.36
The Insert Flash
Text dialogue box

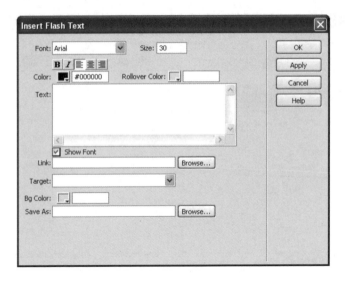

Testing your Flash text

As with Flash buttons, you can test if the Flash text areas are working without the need to run it on the browser. Notice that the properties panel displays a Play button (at the bottom right-hand side in Figure 13.37). If you click this button and then move the mouse over the Flash text, you can see how the rollover effect works. When you are happy with its working, click the Play button in the properties panel again and it will change to Stop. Notice that you can edit any Flash text by using the Edit... button in the properties panel. Clicking this button will transfer you to the dialogue box shown in Figure 13.36, then you can edit what you see in the Text box.

Figure 13.37
Testing Flash text
in Dreamweaver

Databases with Dreamweaver

In this section of the book, you will briefly see how to use Dreamweaver for dynamic database access with PHP/MySQL. PHP, as you will recall from Chapter 7, is a server-side scripting technology, while MySQL is a database application.

Database integration with websites enables content delivery that would not be possible with static Web pages as a database-driven website provides the user with dynamic content that depends on the query. This means that the user can obtain customized information delivered on the fly. For example, a user could request to view stock held in a musical instrument shop. If the customer was interested, say, in a purple bass guitar, the search query would return only the results fitting the query, so the user would not have to waste time searching through the entire database – which would be the option with static access.

Dreamweaver MX supports database integration with the Web. This section will focus on using the PHP/MySQL combination to create a dynamic database using Dreamweaver. To do this, you will create a simple database directly in MySQL, then use PHP with Dreamweaver to access the database. Beforehand, you will need to become familiar with some configuration issues regarding database access.

You can only use Dreamweaver MX or higher versions or the Dreamweaver 4 Ultra Development version to create dynamic database access – earlier versions do not have this facility.

NOTE

Accessing databases

Data stored in a database is normally stored in a proprietary format in the same way that text is in a word processor file, such as Word. A Web application, such as Dreamweaver, faces the same problem as any other application trying to access data in an unknown format – deciphering the data. Hence, a software interface is needed between your Web application and the database that allows the application and the database to communicate with each other.

ODBC (Open Database Connectivity) is a Microsoft standard interface that has the job of acting like an interpreter for communication between the database and the application. ODBC, as would be expected, works well with ASP and other server-based applications, such as ColdFusion. Other proprietary interfaces exist which fulfil the same purpose. For example, **JDBC (Java Database Connectivity)** is another interface that works with JSP and ColdFusion.

Each different database application will need a different program for this task called a **driver**. The purpose of drivers is to drive the interface between Dreamweaver and the database application. They are usually written by database vendors, such as Microsoft and Oracle. The ODBC drivers, which only run on the Windows platform, are automatically installed with Microsoft Office and Windows 2000. If you are using the MySQL, then an ODBC driver setup might not be necessary – it may be needed, though, if you are using some other database application.

Basic database concepts

In this section, we look at database concepts that we will need to know before we can apply them in Dreamweaver. We begin with the concept of a **record** – the building block of a database. A **record** is a collection of related data treated as a single entity. For example, a company employee would give rise to a database record. Each employee's database record would contain related data, such as the employee's name, address, age, salary, start date and so on. Each of these related pieces of information is called a **field** – a name field, an address field and so on. A collection of records that share the same fields is called a **table**, because this kind of information can easily be presented in table format – each column representing a field and each row a record. In fact, the word 'column' is synonymous with the word 'field', and the word 'row' is synonymous with the word 'record'.

A database can contain more than one table, each with a unique name. These tables can be related or independent from one another. A subset of data extracted from one or more tables is called a **recordset**. To create a recordset, you run a database query. A query consists of search criteria. For example, the query can specify that the only records to be included in the recordset are those where an employee earns more than a certain figure per annum. Alternatively, a query could assert that only certain columns be included in the recordset.

The standard query database language SQL can be used to do this. You can also use the open source MySQL query language to create and edit databases. **Open source** means that it has been developed by means of a public collaboration and is freely available. This is a perfect choice for those wishing to use the PHP application server for dynamic Web databases.

Using MySQL to create and edit databases

The MySQL software system can be downloaded from the website www.mysql.com (see Figure 13.38). When it has been downloaded and installed on your machine, you can use MySQL by using the monitor program. This is a client software program that enables you to create and use MySQL programs. To run this program, go to the bin directory which would be located in the MySQL folder. You will need to find out where this folder is located on your system. Inside the directory, you will find a file called MySQL.exe (see Figure 13.39). Open this file and you will see the monitor program open (see Figure 13.40).

Suppose you wanted to create a database to store some details of a CD music collection using MySQL. You can create a new database named cdcoll by using the mysql command from the monitor prompt:

```
mysql> create database cdcoll;
```

Now you need to tell MySQL that you are going to use this database before you can begin entering data into it. To do this, type the following command:

```
mysql> use database cdcoll;
```

Next, you need to describe the table format of the data in the cdcoll database. Let us assume that you want to store data in Artist and Title fields for each CD. You need to

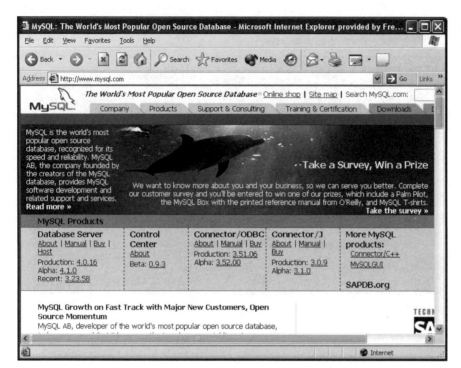

Figure 13.38
The MySQL
website

Figure 13.39
The MySQL bin
directory

Figure 13.40
The MySQL
monitor program
once it has
opened

tell MySQL how many characters are being stored in each field. Assign 20 characters
to the Artist field and 30 characters to the Title field. To do this, type the following:

```
mysql> create table items( Artist char(20), Title char(30) );
```

The above command tells MySQL to create a table called items that has two fields:
one called Artist, containing 20 characters, the other called Title, containing 30 characters. You can confirm the existence of the table by using the show tables command:

```
mysql> show tables;
```

Next, to enter data into the table, use the command:

```
mysql> insert into items values ( "U2", "Zoorama" );
```

See Figure 13.41 to view the response. You can add as many more music items to
the database as you like using this same command each time – that is:

```
mysql> insert into items values( "Stereophonics", "Word
gets around" );
```

Finally, to view the new records inserted, use the command:

```
mysql> select * from items;
```

See Figure 13.41 to view the output.

NOTE

The mysql program monitor is a DOS-based program. A Windows-based program
called WinMySQL Admin is also available for editing MySQL database files.

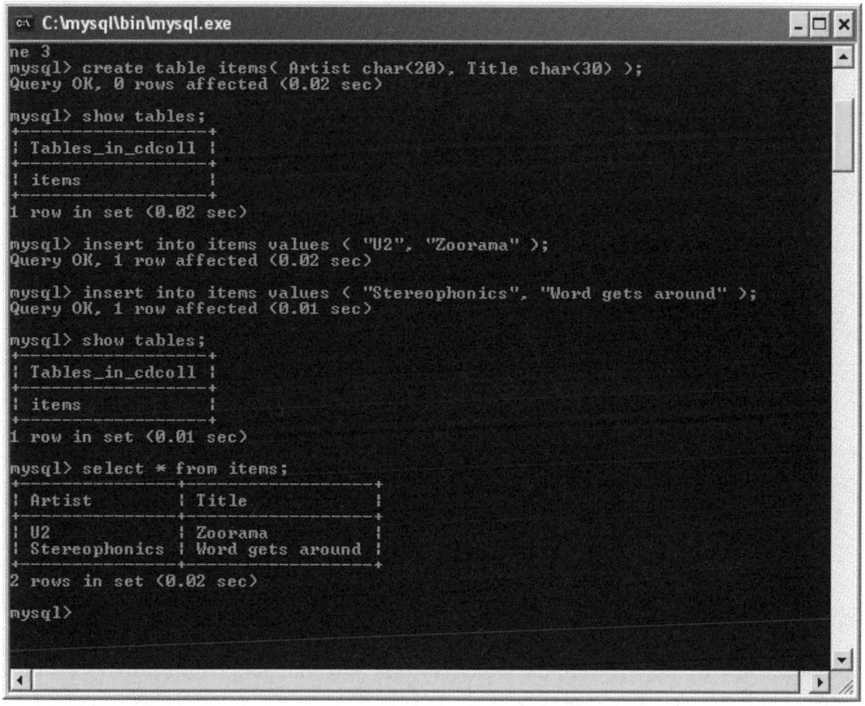

```
C:\mysql\bin\mysql.exe                                          _ □ ×

ne 3
mysql> create table items( Artist char(20), Title char(30) );
Query OK, 0 rows affected (0.02 sec)

mysql> show tables;
+------------------+
| Tables_in_cdcoll |
+------------------+
| items            |
+------------------+
1 row in set (0.02 sec)

mysql> insert into items values ( "U2", "Zoorama" );
Query OK, 1 row affected (0.02 sec)

mysql> insert into items values ( "Stereophonics", "Word gets around" );
Query OK, 1 row affected (0.01 sec)

mysql> show tables;
+------------------+
| Tables_in_cdcoll |
+------------------+
| items            |
+------------------+
1 row in set (0.01 sec)

mysql> select * from items;
+---------------+------------------+
| Artist        | Title            |
+---------------+------------------+
| U2            | Zoorama          |
| Stereophonics | Word gets around |
+---------------+------------------+
2 rows in set (0.02 sec)

mysql>
```

Figure 13.41
The MySQL monitor displaying the table containing the beginnings of a CD database

Creating a connection to a database from Dreamweaver

From the applications menu, click the databases tab, then click the + button.

Setting up a PHP in Dreamweaver

To use PHP with Dreamweaver, you will first need to set up site definitions for PHP within Dreamweaver, in the same way that you set up Dreamweaver for any other site. Before doing so, you will need to check with your ISP that it supports access to a PHP server and how you should configure the application server environment (visit www.macromedia.com/dreamweaver for more on this).

Once you have the necessary information, you can set up the site definition for using PHP as follows.

1 From the menu, choose Site / New Site..., then, from the Site Definition dialogue box that appears, select the Advanced tab. Choose Local Info in the Category box. Complete the boxes on the right as shown in Figure 13.42. Note that you must provide a name for your PHP site, the Local Root Folder box, where your local files will be stored, and the HTTP Address box, which will be obtained from your ISP. Click the Enable Cache box if you want to speed up processing of some features.

Figure 13.42
Completing the
Local Info Page of
the Site Definition
Dialog Box

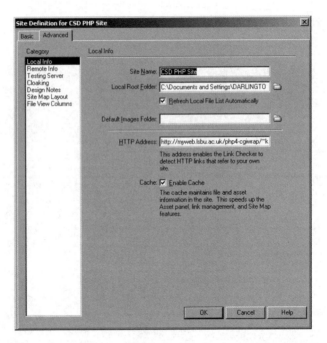

2 Next, click Remote Info in the Category box and change the pull-down list in the Access box to FTP – or Local/ Network if you are using LAN access (see Figure 13.43). You will need to complete the FTP Host, Host Directory, Login and Password boxes, all of which will be obtained via your ISP. You can enable some of the checkboxes, such as Enable File Check In and Check Out if you wish.

3 Next, click Testing Server in the Category box and change the Server Model pull-down list to PHP MySQL (see Figure 13.44). You will need to complete the FTP Host, Host Directory, Login and Password boxes, as with the Remote Info category in the last step. You must also complete the URL Prefix box in order to display live data. The Testing Server generates the dynamic content and so, before clicking the OK button, click the Test button. If a connection is made with the Testing Server, you will receive a message telling you that the connection was successful. Following a successful message, click the OK button.

Testing the PHP setup

Before setting up a connection to the MySQL database, you will need to check that the testing server is working correctly for running PHP scripts. To do this, you could try running a simple PHP in Dreamweaver. For example, the following PHP code finds today's date and prints it in the browser window. A detailed study of PHP is beyond the scope of this book, but the following PHP code is quite easy to follow:

```
<?PHP
    $today = date( "d-m-Y");
    print("Today's date is $today <BR>");
    print("Have a nice day!");
?>
```

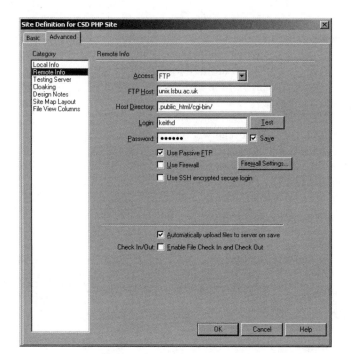

Figure 13.43
Completing the Remote Info page of the Site Definition dialogue box

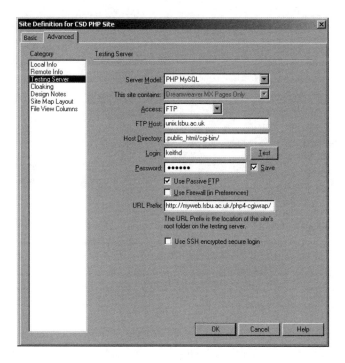

Figure 13.44
Completing the Testing Server category of the Site Definition dialogue box

The first line of the above code – `<?PHP` – marks the beginning of a PHP block of code and you will see that the block is terminated by the line `?>`. The line `$today = date( "d-m-Y");` assigns the current date to the variable called `$today` – notice that PHP lines of code are terminated with a semi-colon. The next line – `print("Today's date is $today <BR");` – tells PHP to print the message that contains today's date. The final code line tells PHP to print another message, which is 'Have a nice day!'

To insert this code into Dreamweaver, open a new document in the document window, switch to Code View by clicking View / Code on the menu, then insert the code between the `<body> </body>` tags (as shown in Figure 13.45). Now click the View / Switch to switch views back to Design View. You will notice that there is a PHP icon in the top left-hand corner of the screen. You can test the PHP connection by selecting View / Live Data from the menu. The output from this PHP code is shown in Figure 13.46.

Figure 13.45
Using Code View to insert a PHP file into Dreamweaver

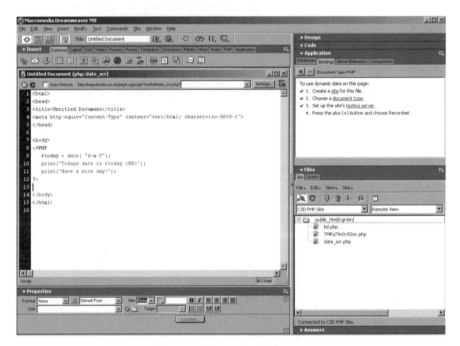

Creating a connection to a MySQL database

1 Select the Databases tab in the applications window, press the + button, then choose MySQL Connection from the pull-down menu list.
2 In the MySQL Connection dialogue box that follows (see Figure 13.47), complete the boxes, again using the information supplied by your ISP.

NOTE The password will not necessarily be the same as your ISP password because it will be your MySQL password.

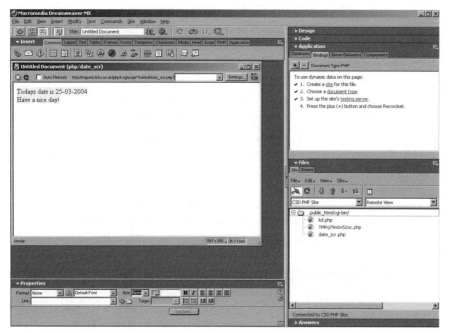

Figure 13.46
Output from the PHP code shown by clicking Live Data from the menu in Design View

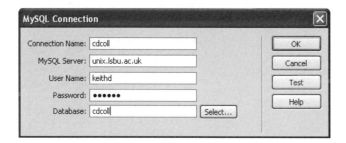

Figure 13.47
The MySQL Connection dialogue box

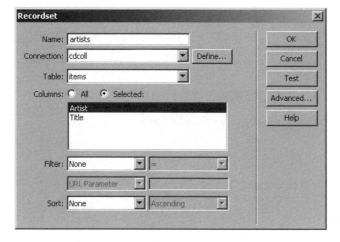

Figure 13.48
The Recordset dialogue box

3 When you have completed the data entry, click the Test button to test the connection. Click the OK button when the connection has been successful – a message telling you this will be displayed.

4 Choose the Bindings tab and, again, press the + button. From the pull-down menu list, choose Recordset.

5 In the Recordset dialogue box (see Figure 13.48), complete the boxes as shown. Note that, for this example, only the Artist column in the table has been selected.

6 Click the Test button and, if the connection is successful, you should see the Test SQL Statement dialogue box with the items displayed as shown in Figure 13.49.

7 Click the Application tab on the Insert toolbar and select the Dynamic Table icon from the submenu that appears (see Figure 13.51). You will see the Dynamic Table dialogue box appear (see Figure 13.50). Complete the boxes, as shown. Notice that, for this example, it is not necessary to change the Show 10 Records at a Time radio button because there are only two records in the database.

Figure 13.49
The Test SQL
Statement
dialogue box

Figure 13.50
The Dynamic
Table dialogue
box

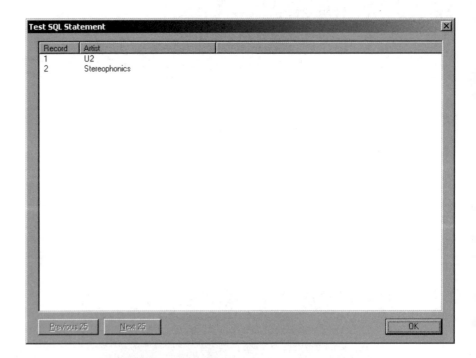

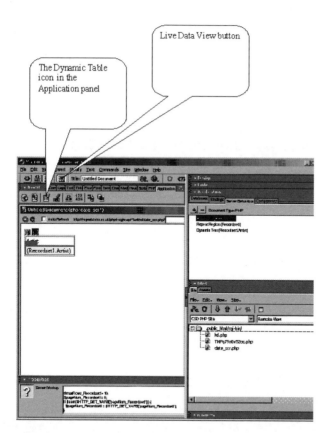

Figure 13.51
The dynamic table with placeholders displayed in the document window

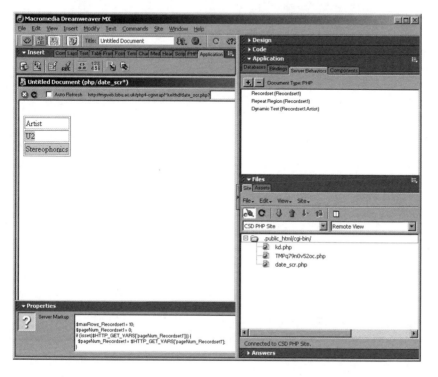

Figure 13.52
The dynamic table, with data, displayed in the document window

8 You will see that the dynamic table has been created in the document window (see Figure 13.51), but only displays dynamic placeholders. To populate the table with the actual data, click the Live Data View button (see Figure 13.51, or, from the menu, select View / Live Data). The table will become populated with the actual table data, as shown in Figure 13.52.

Other Dreamweaver features

There are countless other Dreamweaver features, including many that facilitate the efficient development and management of a Dreamweaver site. The next sections look at some of these features.

Dreamweaver extensions

You might wish for some feature when using Dreamweaver that isn't available. For example, you might wish that you had access to a custom icon on the objects panel – perhaps because you find in the nature of your work that you use a special component often. It would clearly be impossible for the software to incorporate every

Figure 13.53
Some Dreamweaver extensions available from the Dreamweaver Exchange Library on Macromedia's website

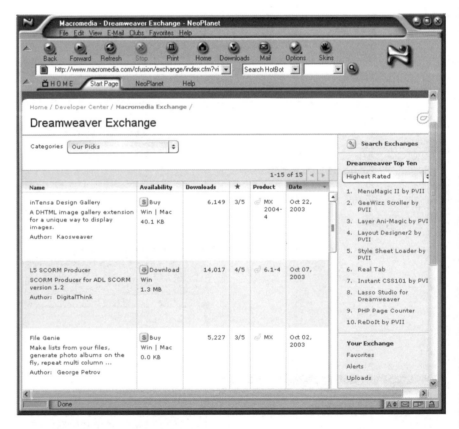

conceivable element, but the development spirit behind Dreamweaver is based on an **open architecture**. This means that Dreamweaver users can extend its functionality by writing their own components using XHTML. This is done by means of **extensions**. Dreamweaver extensions can be virtually anything, from adding a new icon to the objects panel to incorporating a new command in the commands menu. A good knowledge of XHTML is all that is required to write your own extensions, but, in any case, there is a vast library of off-the-shelf extensions available from Macromedia's Dreamweaver website (at www.macromedia.com/exchange, shown in Figure 13.53). There are many other sites on the Web that also provide extensions, such as http://webdesign.about.com/cs/dreamweaver/p/aadreamweaver.htm, which contains many Dreamweaver extensions, including an alphabetical case-changing extension that can convert text from upper to lower case and vice versa. Another example of an extension that is available is a very easy-to-use course-builder extension. This helps the user to create exams, check students' work and even incorporate timers for each question. Of course, this is a specialized example, but there are hundreds of others available, fitting all sorts of requirements. A more general example is a PHP page counter, which will set up a page counter on a Web page.

Many of the extensions that are developed and exchanged by Dreamweaver users are freely available.

NOTE

Changing keyboard shortcuts

One of the customizable features of Dreamweaver is the ability to change menus and keyboard shortcuts.

To do this, select Edit / Keyboard Shortcuts from the menu. A Keyboard Shortcuts dialogue box will appear, containing a set of shortcuts that you can tweak (see Figure 13.54). To change a shortcut, use the Current Set and, in Commands, the Menu Commands drop-down list to find the existing command that you want to change. Highlight the current shortcut and it appears in the Shortcuts field. To add a shortcut, click the Plus button and enter the new keystrokes that you want to use, which will be entered in the Press Key field. Click Change. You can also remove a shortcut by highlighting it and clicking the Minus button.

Dreamweaver and accessibility

The importance of accessibility has been briefly discussed earlier in Chapter 8. One of the central goals of the W3C is to make the Web accessible to disabled users. Dreamweaver supports many accessibility features that make it usable by people with disabilities, such as screen reader support, keyboard navigation and operating system accessibility support.

Figure 13.54
The Keyboard
Shortcuts
dialogue box

- A screen reader can recite text as it appears on the computer display, as well as reading other browser information, such as graphic descriptions on the page and so on. It would normally start reading from the top left-hand corner of the browser window.

- Using keyboard navigation facilities, it is possible to navigate through all the Dreamweaver panels using a keyboard only. All the Dreamweaver keyboard shortcuts are shown in Appendix 3.

Search and replace

The advanced search capabilities of Dreamweaver provide the developer with the scope to search and replace text or other items in XHTML or other documents.

You can launch the search and replace function from within the document window by using the menu option Edit/ Find and Replace (or Ctrl F), as shown in Figure 13.55. In the ensuing FindIn list box (see Figure 13.56), you can select Current Document, Entire Current Local Site, Selected Files in Site or even a Selected Folder. This is a very powerful facility because it means that you can do a global edit on all, or a selection, of files if necessary.

You can also launch this function from within a site window by using the same commands. The sitewide option is not the only feature that makes the search and replace function so impressive. There is also a great deal of flexibility in the scope for searching. You can use the Search For list box to do much of this. If you click this pull-down list box, you will see that there are three options.

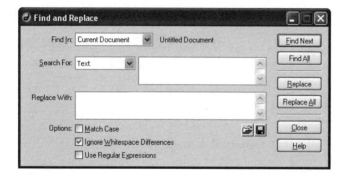

Figure 13.55
The Find and Replace dialogue box

- **The Text option**   This option lets you search for all occurrences of ordinary text. This means that the search will be such that any XHTML tags that interrupt the text string will be ignored. For example, searching for CBS www.cbsnews.com would find both CBS www.cbsnews.com and CBS `<a href="http://www.cbsnews.com/">cbsnews.com</a>`.

- **The Specific Tag option** (see Figure 13.56)   You can search for specific tags, attributes and values with this option. For example, you could find all the `<img>` tags in the entire site that have the width attribute of 50 and change them, delete them or add text within them.

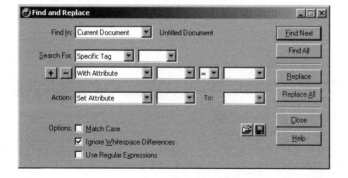

Figure 13.56
The Specific Tag option is used to search for text with defined tags, attributes and values

- **The Advanced Text option**   This gives you the choice to search for specific text inside or outside of a tag. You can limit your search by using the plus or minus buttons to list specific tags.

Other options in the Find and Replace dialogue box

You can see from Figure 13.56 that you can set other options, too, by means of the checkboxes at the bottom left-hand side of the Find and Replace dialogue box. The Match Case checkbox lets you do a case-sensitive search. The Ignore Whitespace Differences option, when selected, treats all white space as a single space for the purposes of matching. The Use Regular Expressions option causes certain characters and short strings (such as ?, *, \w, and \b) in your search string to be interpreted as normal expression operators. For example, a search for the b\w*\b rock will match both the big rock and the black rock.

Using audio and video with Dreamweaver

Using audio and video on the Web has already been discussed in some detail in Chapter 9, so, in this section, we will simply look at how to use audio and video in Dreamweaver.

Audio

You will recall from Chapter 9 that to use sound on Web pages usually involves beginning by using a sound-editing program to record, edit and store the sounds in a suitable format for the Web. The chosen format will depend on what type of sound you are using. If it is music, then the MP3 format is probably the best for the majority of users.

To embed an audio file, follow the steps given below.

1 In Design View, place the insertion point where you want to embed the file.

2 Select a plug-in by choosing Insert / Media / Plug-in from the menu.

3 In the properties inspector, click the folder icon to browse for the audio file or type the file's path and name in the Link field.

4 Enter the width and height by entering the values in the appropriate fields or by resizing the plug-in placeholder using the mouse resize mode in the document window (see Figure 13.57).

Figure 13.57
The audio file placeholder displayed in the document window

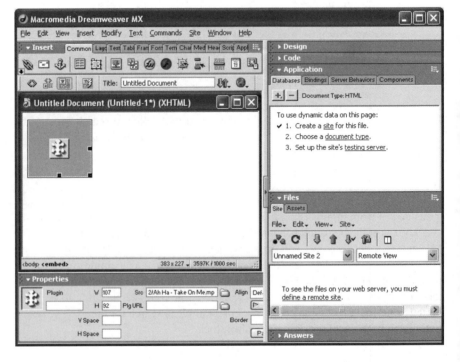

5 These values determine the size of the audio control display on the browser. For example, a width of 107 pixels and a height of 92 pixels are used in Figure 13.57 (see the properties inspector window) to see how the audio player appears in both Navigator and Internet Explorer. Note that you can sample the effect of this sound by previewing with your browser. Select File / Preview in Browser, as was described in Chapter 11.

If you are using streaming audio files, you will need to save them to a special folder. This special folder is on the streaming server and you will need to contact your ISP for further details.

NOTE

Video

The steps required to insert video files in Dreamweaver are very similar to those described for inserting audio files above.

1 In Design view, place the insertion point where you want to embed the video file.
2 Click the Plug-in button on the Objects panel or choose Insert / Media / Plug-in.
3 In the properties inspector window, click the folder icon to browse for the video file or type the file's path and name in the Link field.
4 Enter the width and height by entering the values in the appropriate fields or by resizing the plug-in placeholder using the mouse resize mode in the document window.
5 These values determine the size of the video control display on the browser (see see properties inspector window) to see how the audio player appears in both Navigator and Internet Explorer. View using the Preview in Browser facility, as described in step 5 above for audio.

Creating liquid pages using Dreamweaver

Liquid pages were briefly described in Chapter 3. A liquid page lets your Web page change as a user resizes the browser window. This means that the viewer should see no white space when the window is large nor scroll bars when the window is small.

Creating liquid pages is difficult when your pages contain tables that have multiple columns. However, Dreamweaver MX allows the developer to make such pages liquid by making a table column autostretch.

How to use Dreamweaver to autostretch a table column

1 Open your page containing the table, then switch to Layout View, as described in Chapter 12.
2 In Layout View, you will see a column width and a tiny drop-down arrow at the top of each column. Click the arrow on the column you want to make stretchy and

choose Make Column Autostretch (only one column can be set to autostretch). Instead of the number showing the width, you'll now see a wavy line at the top of the column. Dreamweaver automatically creates the spacer GIFs, which are denoted by the double bar on top of the column and are necessary to make this layout work. (If it's the first time that you're adding a spacer GIF to a site, a dialogue box will ask if you want to use an existing spacer GIF, let Dreamweaver create one or not use spacer GIFs at all.)

Managing links in Dreamweaver

Dreamweaver contains many features for managing website links. These are briefly described below.

Moving or renaming files

When you move or rename a file on a site, Dreamweaver will automatically update the links by displaying an Update Files dialogue box (see Figure 13.58). A list of files is displayed that are linked to the renamed or moved file. In Figure 13.58 there is only one file to be updated, named index.htm. Click the Update button if you want all the associated links to be updated.

Figure 13.58
The Update Files
dialogue box

Changing links sitewide

You can change the URL of a link throughout the site. To do this, from the Site menu, choose Change Link Sitewide..., and a Change Link Sitewide dialogue box will be displayed (see Figure 13.59). This box allows you to enter the old path and the new path.

The link checker

Site links can be checked by using the Link Checker. To do this, choose Check Links Sitewide... from the Site menu. Figure 13.60 displays three categories of links – broken links, orphaned links and external links. **Broken links** are the most serious and should be repaired. **Orphaned links**, as the name suggests, are those that do not

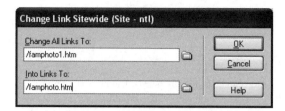

Figure 13.59
The Change Link
Sitewide dialogue
box

have any files linked to them. You will need to decide what you want to do with them, for they are taking up space in your site directories unnecessarily. Finally, **external links** are ones that Dreamweaver cannot check.

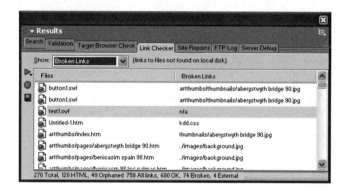

Figure 13.60
The Link Checker
tab, here showing
broken links

Summary

- Using templates can save development time and provide more consistency for site pages as templates enable website designers to use standard design components for all pages of a website.

- A template contains both editable and non-editable regions.

- When a template has been created, new Web pages can be created based on it.

- Templates can be edited and deleted.

- When a template is edited, a global change can be applied to all Web pages on a site that are based on that template.

- Assets provide a way to organize your files according to their type – graphics, templates and so on – within your site.

- Design notes provide a means of attaching useful information, such as editing history and author names, to your website during development.

- Library items make it possible to replicate sections of XHTML to enable easy editing and updating.

- Library items can be edited and deleted.

- Library items can also be detached and pasted on to a Web page to become a standard part of the page.

- CSS can be created and edited with Dreamweaver.

- CSS classes can also created and edited.

- Dreamweaver layers provide a means of adding floating boxes that can contain text, graphics and other Web page components.

- Dreamweaver provides a means of creating clean HTML code.

- Check In/Check Out is a facility that can assist with team project management by enabling team members to monitor site file activity because each can record what has been done, who has done it and when it was done.

- Flash buttons and text can be incorporated directly on to Web pages without having access to the Flash application.

- Dynamic databases can be created with versions above Dreamweaver MX or if you are using the Ultra Development version.

- Dreamweaver can be used with many server models, including PHP, ASP, JSP and ColdFusion.

- Before you can use Dreamweaver with a server model, you will need to set up a site using a testing server.

- Dreamweaver users can extend its functionality by writing their own HTML extensions or using ready-made extensions available at Macromedia's website in the Dreamweaver Exchange.

- A liquid page is one that resizes to suit each user's browser window.

- Liquid pages can be created using Dreamweaver.

Exercises

1 Create a Web page with two layers. Experiment with inserting images and text into the layers.

2 Create a style sheet in Dreamweaver that will colour the background of all level 4 headings on a Web page yellow.

3 Open a Dreamweaver page that you have created and view the page in Code View. Experiment with minor changes to the tags in Code View, paying particular attention to the Properties panel.

4 Create a template in Dreamweaver and practise making various objects editable – such as text, images, rollovers. Apply the template and check to see which objects can be marked as editable and which cannot.

5 Open a template that you have already created. Apply it to a newly created page and practise updating the new page. Check to see your newly edited page using Preview in Browser.

6 Create a library item and add it to a page that you have created in Dreamweaver. Close and re-open the library item and experiment with re-editing it. Check to see that the update has also been made on the connected page.

7 Practise running the Link Checker on a site that you have created in Dreamweaver. Are there any broken links listed? If so, study them and repair them if necessary. Check to see if you have any orphaned files. If so, remove them.

8   If you have access to PHP/MySQL, create a new database using the mysql monitor called 'cars'. Create a new table called cars_table and add the following structure, consisting of two fields called 'make' and 'model'. Now, add the following records:

   - Nissan Micra 1600
   - Ford Focus 1800
   - Citroën Picasso 2000

Test your PHP connection. Now set up a site using the method discussed earlier in this chapter and view the records in the document window in Dreamweaver. View the records using only the make of car.

Future technologies

In this chapter you will learn:

■ to understand alternative devices for the Web

■ WAP technology

■ search engine technology.

Introduction

The Web is a rapidly changing medium and Web content is being delivered to many alternative devices. Many of these will already be familiar to you, such as mobile phones and pagers. Web designers who design for users of these devices need to be aware of the technologies and markup languages relating to them.

This chapter briefly discusses some alternative Web devices. Also, given the importance of search engines to the Web, we briefly describe some commonly used search engines and the techniques that facilitate their operation.

Alternative devices for the Web

Most people's experience with the Web is via a desktop or laptop PC. However, many other devices support connection to the Web. Examples that come to mind are personal digital assistants (PDAs), mobile phones and pagers.

Alternative device design

In this section, we look at some of the alternative devices that are currently being primed for the Web. Here are some of the most commonly used ones at the time of writing.

Personal digital assistants (PDAs)

These are small wireless mobile computer devices that help people to manage their schedules and organize contact details. Figure 14.1 displays a typical PDA. On it is

Figure 14.1
A typical PDA
device

what is known as **Personal Information Management (PIM)** software. Some PDAs contain a modem connection and can handle e-mail and have Web-surfing capabilities. PDAs are available in all shapes and sizes. Some are pocket PCs that contain all the standard PDA features as well as providing games, sound and music facilities and even have the ability to edit Microsoft Office documents.

Palmtop PDAs are another type of wireless technology that work well with standard desktop software to make management of personal information easier.

Other types of wireless hand-held PDA devices provide modular attachments to other devices, such as PCs, printers, digital cameras, and so on.

All of these variants, however, generally offer some form of Web access, so the website designer should give careful consideration to the requirements of the PDA Web-surfing community.

Smart pagers

Smart pagers contain voice and paging communication facilities. They will also often contain PIM software, e-mail and Web browsers. Needless to say, screen space on these devices is very limited.

Set-top boxes

A set-top box is a device that gives access to Web TV (discussed briefly in Chapter 1) and, in doing so, enables an ordinary television set to become a user interface to the Internet and the television set to receive and decode digital television (DVT) broadcasts.

A set-top box is necessary to television viewers who wish to use their current analogue television sets to receive digital broadcasts. It contains a Web browser (which is really an HTTP client) and the Internet's main program, TCP/IP. A digital set-top box contains one or more microprocessors for running the operating system, possibly WindowsCE (see later), and for audio decoding and video streaming. Some set-top boxes even contain a hard drive for storing recorded television broadcasts, downloaded software and other applications.

Features of hand-held devices

Most of the newer technologies that support connection to the Web come in the form of hand-held devices, such as mobile phones, PDAs and pagers. Typically, these are devices that have

- small screen sizes, of, perhaps, 100 pixels high by 50 pixels wide (compare this with 800 pixels by 600 pixels for a standard monitor)
- text-based content that provides a maximum of about six lines of visible text at a time
- predominantly monochrome delivery, although 8-bit colour is beginning to make an impact
- wireless connections to the Internet.

Wireless technologies for the Web – WAP

The Hypertext Transfer Protocol (HTTP) was developed for land-based telecommunication links. This protocol is not well suited to managing wireless transmissions. The main reason for this is that sending wireless data via the HTTP protocol is very slow.

The **Wireless Application Protocol (WAP)**, however, was developed for and uses the client–server concept of the Internet. The **client** is the WAP-enabled device, such as a mobile phone or pager. The **server** is the normal Web server that is configured to serve WAP content as well. WAP requires the presence of two other conditions – a wireless network that aids satellite transmission and a WAP gateway that interprets Web content from the server and makes it suitable for transmission and interpretation on a WAP client.

WAP is the de facto standard for providing Internet and telephony services for mobile devices. WAP applications use a **micro browser** to view Web pages. This is a small piece of software that makes minimal demands on hardware, memory and CPU. Micro browsers display Web pages using a restricted markup language called **WML**.

NOTE   Micro browsers come in all versions, shapes and sizes and some compatibility problems can arise, just as they do with ordinary Web browsers.

The Wireless Markup Language (WML)

WML is another application of XML and is used to build content for the wireless world via WAP. WML is a markup language that is based on XML (Extensible Markup Language). The official WML specification has been developed and is maintained by the **WAP Forum** – an industry-wide consortium founded by Nokia, Phone.com, Motorola and Ericsson. This specification defines the syntax, variables and elements used in a valid WML file. The actual WML 1.1 Document Type Definition (DTD) is available for those familiar with XML at www.wapforum.org

Using WML

WML pages use the extension .wml and, being an application of XML, must conform to its stricter syntax. WML tags are text-based, but ones that would slow down communication with hand-held devices, such as images, are not a part of the WML language set. WML pages are often called **decks**. They are constructed as a set of **cards**, related to each other with links. When a WML page is accessed from a mobile phone, all the cards in the page are downloaded from the WAP server. Navigation between the cards is then carried out by the central processing unit inside the phone. An example of a WML page is shown in Listing 14.1.

Listing 14.1 A WML page

```
<?xml version="1.0"?>
<!DOCTYPE wml PUBLIC "-//WAPFORUM//DTD WML 1.1//EN"
"http://www.wapforum.org/DTD/wml_1.1.xml">


<wml>

<card id = " Card 1" title = "Rhiannon Page">
<p>
My name is Rhiannon.
</p>
</card>

<card id="Card 2 " title = " Amy Page  ">
<p>
My name is Amy.
</p>
</card>

<card id="Card 3 " title = " Katie Page  ">
<p>
My name is Katie.
</p>
</card>
</wml>
```

As you can see from the example in Listing 14.1, the WML document is an XML document. The DOCTYPE is defined as WML and the DTD is accessed at www.wapforum.org/DTD/wml_1.1.xml. The document content is inside the <wml>...</wml> tags. Each card in the document is inside <card>...</card> tags and paragraphs are inside

`<p>`...`</p>` tags. Each card element has an ID and a title. As noted above, `WML` pages are often called **decks**. A **deck** contains a set of **cards**. A **card** element can contain text, markup, links, input fields, tasks, images and more. Cards can be related to each other by means of links.

When a `WML` page is accessed from a mobile phone, all the cards in the page are downloaded from the `WAP` server. Navigation between the cards is done by the phone's computer inside the phone. This eliminates the need for any extra access trips to the server.

Search engines

The Web is a vast resource, containing some freely available information covering just about every subject imaginable. Yet, the sheer size of the Web can be a disadvantage because there is so much information out there that it isn't always easy to find what you are looking for.

Search engines provide a means of finding what you want. They are a very important resource for the website designer because, in such a rapidly changing field, it is important to have access to information regarding the most recent tools and technologies available.

The workings of search engines

There are two types of search mechanism in widespread use. They are **index-based**, such as AltaVista and Google, and **directory-based**, such as Yahoo.

The former work by maintaining an index of hundreds of millions of Web pages and use that index to find pages that match a set of user-specified keywords. The indices are created by software robots called **Webots**. They are sometimes called **spider-based search engines** because they employ special computer programs called spiders that follow links through the Web, sending everything they find back to a computer-compiled index.

Some search engines, such as `HotBot` (www.hotbot.com), have indexed most of the words on each page. This means that when you type in a word – perhaps, 'Oasis' – HotBot's search engine then looks through its index, finds all the pages with 'Oasis' on them, then puts the pages with the most mentions near the top of the list. The Google index is only updated once every three or four weeks, while other search engines, such as `Alltheweb` (www.alltheweb.com – see Figure 14.2), use indices that are updated more regularly.

The second type of search mechanism – the directory idea – was pioneered by Yahoo! and organizes links to Web pages in a **subject tree**. When you browse a subject tree, you start from the root of the tree and branch out to more specific topics. Each topic may then point to sub-topics below them. This idea is illustrated in Figure 14.3, using a small fragment of the topic tree from Yahoo! to find sporting information about Welsh Rugby Union. Because rugby is a sports topic, the topic to branch to is 'Sports and recreation' from which there are many sub-topics to go to,

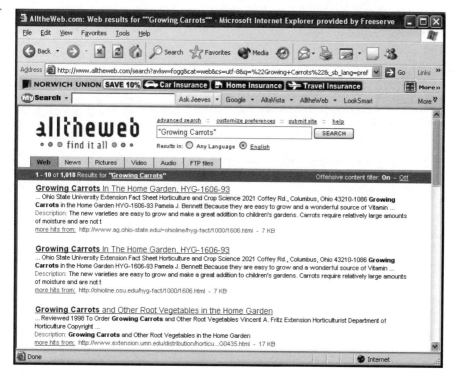

Figure 14.2
Results of
'Growing Carrots'
query using the
Alltheweb search
engine

Reproduced with
permission of Yahoo!
Inc. © 2004 by Yahoo!
Inc. YAHOO! and the
YAHOO! logo are
trademarks of Yahoo!
Inc.

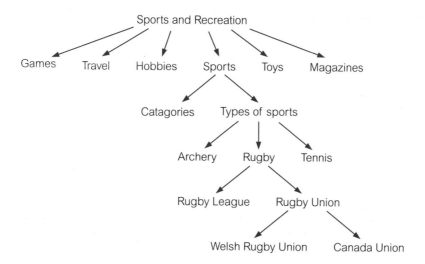

Figure 14.3
Fragment of a
directory's search
tree for the
subject Welsh
Rugby Union

including those shown. From here, the next decision point to move to is the 'Sports'
category, then, from the next level, the category chosen would be 'Types of sports'
and so on. Eventually, the search would be directed to the specific level called
'Welsh Rugby Union'.

Directories are compiled manually, unlike indices, which are generated automatically. Yahoo!'s subject tree organizes over 2 million documents. Each document is
added to the tree by people who check for its content and proper position in the tree

Figure 14.4
Searching Yahoo!
using a category
search for 'Welsh
Rugby'

Reproduced with
permission of Yahoo!
Inc. © 2004 by Yahoo!
Inc. YAHOO! and the
YAHOO! logo are
trademarks of Yahoo!
Inc.

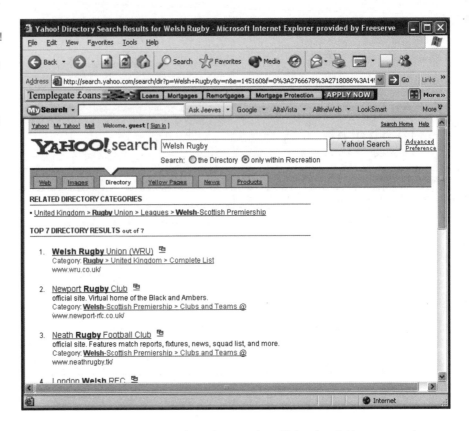

structure. Directory-based search engines, such as Yahoo! and About.com, give you
a choice between searching a tree or the Web (see Figure 14.4).

Using search engines on the Web

Despite the range of search engines available, it is often difficult to find relevant
information of interest on the Web. There are many ways in which you can improve
your searching. Here are a few ideas.

- The number of pages on the Web means that no search engine has managed to
  index even 50 per cent of those available. Try a range of search engines as they
  index different pages and another might have what you are looking for.

- If the search engine that you are using fails to deliver any expected results, then
  try different keywords. For example, if a query on show jumping failed to deliver
  results, then perhaps try the keyword 'equestrian event'.

- Experiment with different keywords in different queries. You might find that you
  need to refine your search queries by either broadening – to find a larger number
  of responses – or narrowing – to reduce the number of responses. You can normally use word filters that you will find in the **Advanced Search** section of a
  search engine. Figure 14.5 displays the Advanced Search page of the Lycos

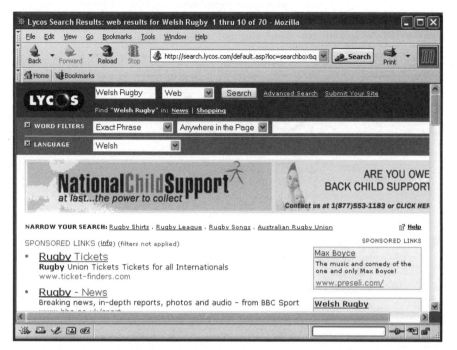

search engine. Notice how this query specifies an Exact Phrase search Anywhere in the Page and the language has been set to Welsh.

- Search engines vary in their ability to correctly interpret what you are after. It takes a great deal of practice to get the best out of any search engine and learn their quirks and weaknesses. Most will contain a search tips page providing detailed user help. Moreover, Boolean search operators may be different so check out relevant information from each search engine site.

- You might not be using the best search engine for a particular task. For example, Yahoo! is very good for general subject queries, because of its directory structure, while Google is much better for more specific queries, so choose a search engine that's best suited to the task.

- Many search engines offer specific searches for particular things. For example, Google provides newsgroup discussion listings (see Figure 14.6). Perhaps your own specific query is more likely to yield results within a newsgroup than via a search engine alone.

- Using Boolean operators can often dramatically improve your search when done properly. Of these, the 'and' and 'not' operators are often combined to give useful results. For example, suppose you were interested in references to growing vegetables, but not fruit, you could orientate your search accordingly by using these operators.

- Using exact phrase matching is also an effective searching technique. If you want your query to contain an exact phrase, insert double quotes around the text. For example, if you wanted to find exact match references to Tony Blair, you would insert "Tony Blair" into the search field of the search engine, then all the hits

Figure 14.6
Searching for
newsgroups with
Google

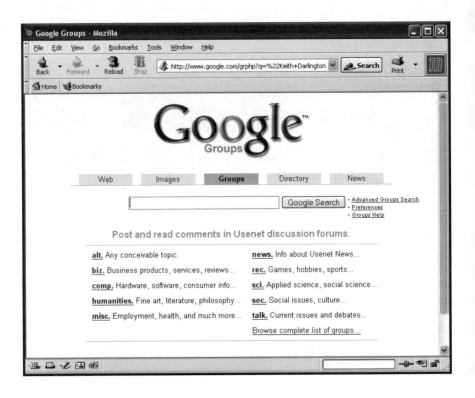

would contain the exact phrase Tony Blair, rather than some hits containing the
words Tony and Blair in the same document.

- Try to include words that define the context. For example, consider the word
  'equity'. Supposing we were interested in the organization called 'Equity', as
  opposed to the word 'equity' meaning even-handedness, then it may be better to
  use the search query 'equity organization' rather than just the word 'equity'.

- There are many other search techniques that can be applied to improve the quality
  of your search. For example, many search engines provide a title search capability. This means that pages will only be returned if they contain the queried text
  in the title of the document – that is, documents only including the text in the title
  bar of the browser. Doing a title search normally means prefixing the text with
  'title:'. For example, to do a title search on 'Growing carrots' in AltaVista, you
  would enter 'title: "Growing carrots" ' in the search field (see Figure 14.7). The
  hits then returned will only be those that contain the words 'Growing carrots' in
  the title of the document. Many other prefixes can be used in this way to direct
  your searches. Again, you will need to read the help or search tips sections.

Some popular search engines

- *Ask Jeeves* (www.ask.com) markets itself specifically as an easy-to-use, spoken
  language-like search engine, but it does often produce eccentric results.

- *AltaVista* (www.altavista.com) is one of the oldest and among the largest of the search sites on the Web. It is a good site for finding almost anything.

- *Yahoo!* (www.yahoo.com) is an acronym of 'You Always Have Other Options' and, as already stated, is a directory-based manually compiled search engine.

- *Lycos* (www.lycos.com) is one of the oldest search engines in use and has been watching the Web longer than any other major engine.

- *Webcrawler* (www.webcrawler.com) is a broad search system that works very fast – in fact, it is probably one of the fastest reply systems on the Web.

- *Excite* (www.excite.com) is another comprehensive online search site. Excite's search engine is freely available for inclusion on your own website. Excite is very good for finding scientific information.

- *Google* (www.google.com) – see below.

Google is now by far the most popular search engine. It was founded in 1998 by Larry Page and Sergey Brin and initially had a Web index of 25 million pages. Less than six years later, Google has indexed over 6 billion pages – 4 billion of which are Web pages. It has more than 200 million daily users in over 35 different languages. However, because of the way Google uses link data, it can actually return listings for additional pages that it has never actually visited.

The popularity of Google is partly due to its simplicity, speed and lack of clutter. Because of its technology, its results also often appear to be much more relevant than those of many of its competitors. This is because Google only indexes words that the user might see as being important. For instance, if a word is in bold, Google regards that word as being more important than one that is not in bold. Google also looks at the relationship between Web pages. If a major site links to a smaller site, that counts in the smaller site's favour. So, if you type 'Oasis' into Google, you are more likely to get the Oasis pop group than, say, the description of a desert. The billions of pages indexed by Google include many non-HTML formats, such as PDF files, Microsoft Office documents and other text-orientated material.

Meta-search engines

A **meta-search engine** is one that sends a user query to several search engines and then groups responses from each of them. For example, Dogpile (www.dogpile.com) is a meta-search engine, and Figure 14.8 displays a screenshot of the Dogpile output for the query 'Growing carrots'. Notice that the meta-search results can be ordered 'View By Relevance' or 'View By Search Engine' and that the Dogpile search includes Google, AltaVista, Overture and AskJeeves.

There are several other meta-search engines available, including KartOO (www.kartoo.com), 37 (www.37.com) and ProFusion (www.profusion.com).

A good meta-search engine saves you the time and effort of entering your query into many search engine sites yourself and should provide a complete set of hits from the most common websites.

Figure 14.8
Results of a search for 'Growing carrots' using the Dogpile meta-search engine

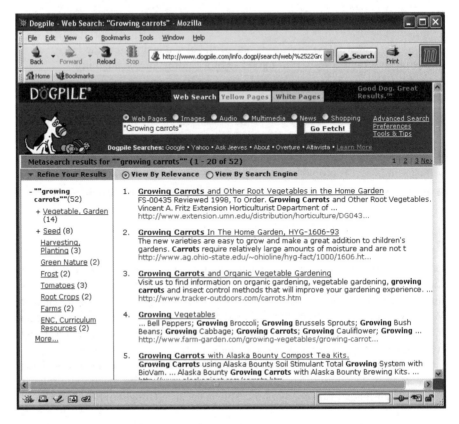

Specialized search engines

In the previous sections, we have discussed general search engines, but a range of special-purpose search engines is available. An example of a medical specialized search engine is Medsite, which is illustrated in Figure 14.9 (www.medsite.com). There are many other specialized search engines available. To find topic-specific searches, visit www.search.com

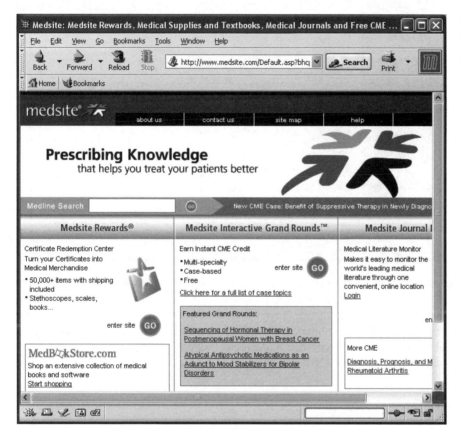

Figure 14.9
A specialized medical search engine – Medsite

Software repositories

In addition to search engines, there are several sites on the Web that provide a central clearing house for Internet-related applications. Many of these are being developed as low-cost shareware programs promoted by vendors of Web products and contain everything from JavaScript add-ins to HTML editors and browsers. For example, the Consummate Winsock Software (CWS) list (http://cws.internet.com) is – as its name implies – a complete collection of Internet-based software. The site combines a five-star rating system and extensive product reviews. CWS is a good site to visit to find out what is new and different in the Internet software world. Figure 14.10 displays a screenshot of CWS' product rating of the NeoPlanet 5.2 browser.

Figure 14.10
Screenshot of
CWS' website,
showing its
product rating of
the NeoPlanet 5.2
browser

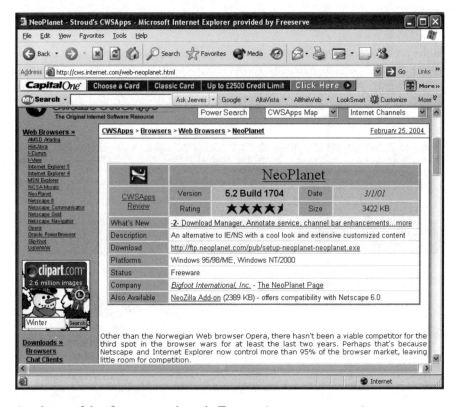

Another useful software repository is Tucows (www.tucows.com) – an acronym of 'The Ultimate Collection Of Winsock Software' – covering software for all platforms and requirements. Shareware (www.shareware.com) is another useful resource for Web developers. Unlike CWS and Tucows, which link one product to one download link, Shareware's download section presents a list of sites rated by reliability around the world.

Search engine resources

There is an abundance of search engine resources on the Web – almost too many to describe. The following should prove to be a very useful start.

**Search Engine Spiders, Crawlers and Indexers
(www.searchengineworld.com/spiders/index.htm)**   Provides an in-depth study on search spiders and how they index your page. The emphasis here is on increasing your site's ranking and visibility on the major search engines.

SearchEngineWatch (www.searchenginewatch.com)   One of the most comprehensive sources of information on the various search engines around the Web.

Search Engine World (www.searchengineworld.com)   A very useful search engine resource, containing reviews and many search engine articles of interest.

SearchEngineZ (www.searchenginez.com)   Again, very useful search engine resource, containing reviews and search engine articles.

WebmasterWorld Webmaster and Search Engine Glossary (www.webmasterworld.com/glossary)   Provides an extensive glossary of search engines.

Summary

- Many alternative devices are being primed for use on the Web. Examples include wireless devices, such as mobile phones, pagers and personal digital assistants (PDAs).

- The HTTP protocol is not suited to managing wireless transmissions because the speed of sending wireless data via this protocol is very slow.

- The Wireless Application Protocol (WAP) has been developed as a protocol for the wireless transmission of data over the web.

- WML, an application of XML, is a markup language that is used to build content via WAP.

- Alternative wireless devices, such as mobile phones and PDAs, are small hand-held devices and, therefore, image tags are not suited to markup language for them.

- WML pages are called decks and consist of cards. When a WML page is accessed from a device, all the cards in the page are downloaded from the WAP server.

- Search engines provide a means of finding information on the Web.

- There are two types of search engine in widespread use. They are index-based, such as Google, and directory-based, such as Yahoo!

- Index-based search engines work by maintaining an index of pages and that index is then used to find pages that match a set of user-specified keywords.

- Directory-based search engines, on the other hand, organize links to Web pages in a subject tree.

- Despite the range of search engines on the Web, it is often difficult to find relevant information because of the volume of websites online. There are many techniques available to improve searching – you are advised to gain familiarity with the techniques described in this chapter.

Exercises

1   Briefly, describe the function of a PDA.

2   What are the difficulties of using the HTTP protocol for mobile devices?

3   Explain the difference between a spider-based search and a directory-based search.

4   Use the Google search engine, go to the Advanced Search page and find out what the Froogle Product Search is used for. Use an example to illustrate your answer.

5   Enter the Google search engine and select the Groups tag to access the Usenet service. Find the alt.arts group and, from that, read the alt.arts.poetry page. Find out what is

meant by a thread. Now, go back to the main Groups page and browse other groups that you might find of interest.

6   Are all search engines likely to return the same results? Use Google, Yahoo! and Lycos to search the query 'great drummers'. Compare the results. Were there any similarities? Briefly describe the main differences between the searches.

7   Briefly explain how a meta-search engine differs from a search engine.

8   How would you write a Google query to carry out a title search?

9   For what purpose would you use a software repository?

Site development resources

There exist many resources and ideas on the WWW that will help with the development of your website. Those described below are just a very small sample, but will give you a good idea about what can be found on the Web. Use a search engine to find other sites.

■ Templates are available in abundance on the Web. Instead of using the ready-made samples that come with Dreamweaver, you might like to look at http://planetplexus.com. There are some design templates available to download for developing commercial sites and others. There is also a variety of backgrounds available. You might also try www.freesitetemplates.com. This is another site containing free template downloads. Other sites of interest include:

- www.freelayouts.com
- www.freewebtemplates.com
- www.graphicsbydezign.com

■ Many very good sites containing background colours, buttons, graphics, bars, bullets and icons exist, with trial downloads. These include www.elated.com for buttons and icons.

■ Colour schemers – programs that create colour-matching schemes – are also in plentiful supply. Try www.colorschemer.com

■ It is possible to reduce page sizes. If your site is a little heavy on memory, why not try www.spinwave.com/demos.html. By optimizing your graphic GIF and JPEG files, you can reduce the memory required significantly and, by reducing the download time, increase traffic to your site.

Useful Dreamweaver resource webSites

www.macromedia.com/support/Dreamweaver   Macromedia Dreamweaver Support Centre.

www.arrakis.es/~andrewc/downloads/dream.htm   another site containing Dreamweaver resources, including downloads, tutorials and a variety of other resources.

www.dreamweaverfever.com a fairly humorous site, focused on Dreamweaver MX development. Again, there are plenty of tutorials and downloads, as well as free Dreamweaver extensions.

www.dreamweaverresources.com more Dreamweaver templates and other useful resources.

www.macromedia.com/support/documentation/en/dreamweaver Macromedia Dreamweaver documentation, including product manuals, release notes and tutorials.

www.macromedia.com/support/fireworks Fireworks Support Centre, with download.

www.macromedia.com/support/flash Flash Support Centre, with download.

http://webdesign.about.com/cs/dreamweaver/p/aadreamweaver.htm another very good resource site, containing many Dreamweaver extensions.

www.webmonkey.wired.com/webmonkey General Web and Dreamweaver resource.

Web tool resources

www.adobe.com Photoshop vendor and supplier of many Web-based products.

www.barebones.com/index.html Bare Bones HTML editor site.

www.briefhistory.com/footnotes John Naughton, *Observer* columnist, writes articles on the business side of the Web.

www.coolgraphics.com free graphics to download.

www.cuteftp.com FTP download, software and other Web development software.

www.free-backgrounds.com free background images site contains many useful categories.

www.graphxkingdom.com free clipart, icons, backgrounds, navigation bars and other graphic material.

www.htmlvalidator.com HTML, XHTML and CSS validator site.

http://home.erinet.com/web/technicalsupport/library/graphicstools.html has a wide range of graphic tools, including Photoshop and Fireworks components and many other graphic items.)

www.java-scripts.net free JavaScript with easy-to-follow installation instruction, along with a live demonstration available for each one.

www.killersites.com this site contains many good illustrations of successful Web design.

www.macromedia.com/support/documentation/en/dreamweaver Macromedia Dreamweaver documentation, including product manuals, release notes and tutorials.

www.macromedia.com/support/fireworks Fireworks support with downloads from Macromedia.

www.macromedia.com/support/flash Flash support with downloads from Macromedia.

www.norvig.com a site that contains technical papers, essays, reports, software, presentations, and other materials by Peter Norvig.

www.pnc.com.au/~bridgfam/wavepage.htm a collection of sounds for use on the Web.

http://reallybig.com as the name suggests, a large library of general resources, including website add-ons, such as chat bulletin boards, guestbooks, calendars, surveys/polls, search engines, shopping carts, as well as Web programming, JavaScript, CGI scripts, and so on.

www.specialweb.com/original again, an extensive library of utilities for Web designers, including wallpaper, backgrounds, lines/bars and much more.

www.windyweb.com a very useful general Web resource site that also contains many tutorials covering everything from JavaScript and CGI scripting to design tools and wizards.

Bibliography

Bates, Chris (2000) *Building Internet Applications*. Chichester: Wiley

Below, Richard (2001) *WWW*. Cambridge: Cambridge University Press

Brink, Tom, Gergle, Darren, and Wood, Scott (2001) *Usability for the Web*. San Francisco, California: Morgan Kaufmann

Bruce, Betsy (2001) *Dreamweaver 4 in 24 hours*. Indianapolis, Indiana: Sams

Busch, David (1998) *Cascading Style Sheets Complete*. New York: McGraw-Hill

Chapman, Nigel (2000) *Flash 5 Interactivity*. Chichester: Wiley

Chapman, N., and Chapman, J. (2004) *Digital Multimedia*, 2nd edn. Chichester: Wiley

Crowder, David, and Crowder, Rhonda (2001) *Mastering Dreamweaver 4 & Fireworks 4*. Almeda, California: Sybex Press

Deitel, H., Deitel, P., Nieto, T. R., and Sadhu, P. (2001) *XML: How to Program*. Englewood Cliffs, NJ: Prentice Hall

Deitel, Harvey, and Deitel, Paul (1999) *Java: How to program*. Englewood Cliffs, NJ: Prentice Hall

Deitel, Harvey, and Deitel, Paul (2000) *Internet and World Wide Web: How to program*. 2nd edn. Englewood Cliffs, NJ: Prentice Hall

Deitel, Harvey, and Deitel, Paul (2000) *E-Business and E-Commerce*. Englewood Cliffs, NJ: Prentice Hall

Deitel, Harvey, Deitel, Paul, Nieto, Tem P., and McPhie, David (2001) *Perl: How to program*. Englewood Cliffs, NJ: Prentice Hall

Dubinko, M. (2003) *XForms Essentials*. Sebastopol, California: O'Reilly

Farrell, J. (2002) *Java Programming*, 2nd edn. Florence, Kentucky: Thomson Learning

Flanagan, David (1998) *JavaScript: The definitive guide*, 3rd edn. Sebastopol, California: O'Reilly

Fleming, Jennifer (1998) *Web Navigation: Designing the user experience*. Sepastopol, California: O'Reilly

Gosselin, Don (2000) *JavaScript Introductory*. Florence, Kentucky: Thomson Learning

Holzschlag, M. E. (2001) *Using XHTML*. Indianapolis, Indiana: Que

Jadav, A. D. (2002) *Designing Usable Web Interfaces*. Harlow: Pearson Education

Lehnert, Wendy (2001) *Web 101: Making the Net work for you*. Harlow: Addison-Wesley

Lengel, James (2001) *Web Wizards Guide to Web Design*. Harlow: Pearson Education

Lengel, James (2004) *Web Wizards Guide to Dreamweaver*. Harlow: Pearson Education

Lie, Hakon, and Bos, Bert (1998) *Cascading Style Sheets*. Harlow: Addison-Wesley

McBride, P., and McBride, N. (2001) *HTML 4 Made Simple*. Oxford: Elsevier

McFarland, David (2001) *Dreamweaver 4: The missing manual*. Sebastopol, California: O'Reilly

Meyer, E. A. (2001) *Cascading Style Sheets: The definitive guide*. Sebastopol, California: O'Reilly

Meyers, Paul F. (1999) *The HTML Classroom*. Englewood Cliffs, NJ: Prentice Hall

Musciano, Chuck, and Kennedy, Bill (1998) *Using HTML: The definitive guide*, 3rd edn. Sebastopol, California: O'Reilly

Niedhurst, J. (2001) *Web Design in a Nutshell*, 2nd edn. Sebastopol, California: O'Reilly

Rule, Jeff (1999) *Dynamic HTML*. Harlow: Addison-Wesley

Schneider, F., Blachman, N., and Fredricksen, E. (2004) *How to do Everything with Google*. Emeryville, California: Osborne

Schneider, G. P., and Perry, J. T. (2001) *Electronic Commerce*, 2nd edn. Florence, Kentucky: Thomson Learning

Sklar, J. (2002) *Cascading Style Sheets*. Florence, Kentucky: Thomson Learning

Slaybough, M. (2002) *Professional Web Graphics*. Florence, Kentucky: Thomson Learning

Strauss, R., and Hogan, P. (2001) *Developing Effective Websites*. Oxford: Focal Press

Sybex Inc. (2001) *HTML Complete*. Almeda, California: Sybex Press

Turban, Efraim, McLean, Ephraim, and Wetherbe, James (2001) *IT for Management*, 3rd edn. Chichester: Wiley

Van Slyke, C., and Belanger, F. (2002) *E-Business Technologies*. Chichester: Wiley

Van Slyke, C., and Belanger, F. (2003) *E-Business Technologies*. Chichester: Wiley

Williamson, Heather, and Epstein, Bruce (2001) *Dreamweaver in a Nutshell*. Sebastopol, California: O'Reilly

Zeid, Ibrahim (2000) *Mastering the Internet and html*. Englewood Cliffs, NJ: Prentice Hall

Appendix 1: CSS reference

This reference lists the main categories of CSS properties, along with a description of each and the possible values that each property takes. The values in italics specify a type of value that is taken. For example, 'background-color' refers to a possible background colour value, such as yellow. A 'length' refers to a length in pixels. Other italic values used in the table refer to a list of possible values, such as 'border-style' refers to a possible list of styles. These include none (for no style), dotted, dashed, solid, double, groove, ridge, inset and outset. Many of these possible values are self-explanatory. Dotted renders the border as a series of dots, while dashed renders the border as a series of short lines. Solid refers to a solid border. Ridge creates the effect of the border being raised from the page, while groove creates the effect of the border being grooved. Inset creates a 3-D effect of the border being embedded in the page and outset does the opposite and creates a 3-D effect, of the border coming out of the surface. For a complete description of all values taken by CSS properties, visit W3C's website at www.w3.org/Style/CSS

Background properties

Property	Description	Possible values
background	A shorthand property for setting all background properties in one declaration	*background-color* *background-image* *background-repeat* *background-attachment* *background-position*
background-attachment	Sets whether a background image is fixed or scrolls with the rest of the page	scroll fixed
background-color	Sets the background colour of an element	*color-rgb* *color-hex* *color-name* transparent

Property	Description	Possible values
background-image	Sets an image as the background	*url* none
background-position	Sets the starting position of a background image	top left top center top right center left center center center right bottom left bottom center bottom right *x-% y-%* *x-pos y-pos*
background-repeat	Sets if/how a background image will be repeated	repeat repeat-x repeat-y no-repeat

Text display properties

Property	Description	Possible values
color	Sets the colour of a text	*color*
letter-spacing	Increases or decreases the space between characters	normal *length* (4 em)
text-align	Aligns the text in an element	left right center justify
text-decoration	Adds decoration to text, such as underline or blinking text	none underline overline line-through blink
text-indent	Indents the first line of text in an element (can use length – 4 em – or percentage proportion to specify amount)	*length* %

Property	Description	Possible values
text-shadow	Sets a shadow behind each letter	*none* *color* *length*
text-transform	Controls the letters in an element	none capitalize uppercase lowercase
white-space	Sets how white space inside an element is handled	normal pre nowrap
word-spacing	Increases or decreases the space between words	normal *length*

Text properties

Property	Description	Possible values
font	A shorthand property for setting all of the properties for a font in one declaration	*font-style* *font-variant* *font-weight* *font-size* *line-height* *font-family*
font-family	A prioritized list of font family names and/or generic family names for an element	*family-name* (such as Courier) *generic-family name* (such as serif)
font-size	Sets the size of a font	*absolute-size* *relative-size* *length* %
font-stretch	Condenses or expands the current font family	normal wider narrower ultra-condensed

Property	Description	Possible values
		extra-condensed condensed semi-condensed semi-expanded expanded extra-expanded ultra-expanded
font-style	Sets the style of the font	normal italic oblique
font-variant	Displays text in a small capitals font or a normal font	normal small-caps
font-weight	Sets the weight of a font	normal bold bolder lighter 100 200 300 400 500 600 700 800 900

Border and box properties

Property	Description	Possible values
border	A shorthand property for setting all of the properties for the four borders in one declaration	*border-width* *border-style* *border-color*
border-bottom	A shorthand property for setting all of the properties for the bottom border in one declaration	*border-bottom-width* *border-style* *border-color*
border-bottom-color	Sets the colour of the bottom border	*border-color*
border-bottom-style	Sets the style of the bottom border	*border-style*

Property	Description	Possible values
border-bottom-width	Sets the width of the bottom border	thin medium thick *length*
border-color	Sets the colour of the four borders. Can have from one to four colours	*color*
border-left	A shorthand property for setting all of the properties for the left border in one declaration	*border-left-width* *border-style* *border-color*
border-left-color	Sets the colour of the left border	*border-color*
border-left-style	Sets the style of the left border	*border-style*
border-left-width	Sets the width of the left border	thin medium thick *length*
border-right	A shorthand property for setting all of the properties for the right border in one declaration	*border-right-width* *border-style* *border-color*
border-right-color	Sets the colour of the right border	*border-color*
border-right-style	Sets the style of the right border	*border-style*
border-right-width	Sets the width of the right border	thin medium thick *length*
border-style	Sets the style of the four borders. Can have from one to four styles	none dotted dashed solid double groove ridge inset outset

Property	Description	Possible values
border-top	A shorthand property for setting all of the properties for the top border in one declaration	*border-top-width* *border-style* *border-color*
border-top-color	Sets the colour of the top border	*border-color*
border-top-style	Sets the style of the top border	*border-style*
border-top-width	Sets the width of the top border	thin medium thick *length*
border-width	A shorthand property for setting the width of the four borders in one declaration. Can have from one to four values	thin medium thick *length*
clear	Sets the sides of an element where other floating elements are not allowed	left right both none
float	Sets where an image or text will appear in another element	left right none
height	Sets the height of an element	auto *length* %
width	Sets the width of an element	auto *length* %

List properties

Property	Description	Possible values
list-style	A shorthand property for setting all of the properties for a list in one declaration	*list-style-type* *list-style-position* *list-style-image*

Property	Description	Possible values
list-style-image	Sets an image as the list item marker (it changes the appearance of the bulleted list marker by replacing it with an image)	*url* (specifies the location of the url)
list-style-position	Sets the position where the list item marker is placed in the list	inside (lines after the first one are not indented) outside (all lines in the item are indented)
list-style-type	Sets the type of the list item marker at the beginning of each list item	none disc circle square decimal decimal-leading-zero lower-roman (lower-case roman numerals) upper-roman (upper-case roman numerals) lower-alpha upper-alpha lower-greek lower-latin upper-latin

Margin properties

Property	Description	Possible values
margin	A shorthand property for setting the margin properties in one declaration	*margin-top* *margin-right* *margin-bottom* *margin-left*
margin-bottom	Sets the bottom margin of an element	auto *length* %
margin-left	Sets the left margin of an element	auto *length* %
margin-right	Sets the right margin of an element	auto *length* %

Property	Description	Possible values
margin-top	Sets the top margin of an element	auto *length* %

Padding properties

Property	Description	Possible values
padding	A shorthand property for setting all of the padding properties in one declaration	padding-top padding-right padding-bottom padding-left
padding-bottom	Sets the bottom padding of an element (can use length – 4 em – or percentage proportion to specify amount)	*length* %
padding-left	Sets the left padding of an element (can use length – 4 em – or percentage proportion to specify amount)	*length* %
padding-right	Sets the right padding of an element (can use length – 4 em – or percentage proportion to specify amount)	*length* %
padding-top	Sets the top padding of an element (can use length – 4 em – or percentage proportion to specify amount)	*length* %

Visual and positioning properties

Property	Description	Possible values
bottom	Sets how far the bottom edge of an element is above/below the bottom edge of the parent element	auto % *length*
clip	Sets the shape of an element. The element is clipped into this shape, and displayed	shape auto

Property	Description	Possible values
left	Sets how far the left edge of an element is to the right/left of the left edge of the parent element	auto % *length*
overflow	Sets what happens if the content of an element overflow, from its area	visible hidden scroll auto
right	Sets how far the right edge of an element is to the left/right of the right edge of the parent element	auto % *length*
top	Sets how far the top edge of an element is above/below the top edge of the parent element	auto % *length*
vertical-align	Sets the vertical alignment of an element	baseline sub super top text-top middle bottom text-bottom *length* %
position	Places an element in a static, relative, absolute or fixed position	static relative absolute fixed
visibility	Sets if an element should be visible or invisible	visible hidden collapse
z-index	Sets the stack order of an element	auto number

Table properties

Property	Description	Possible values
border-collapse	Sets the border model of a table – whether the borders of each cell merge together or separate to form two thinner borders	collapse (one border) separate (separate borders)
border-spacing	Sets the distance between the borders of adjacent cells (only for the 'separated borders' model)	*length*
caption-side	Sets the position of the caption according to the table	top bottom left right
empty-cells	Sets whether cells with no visible content should have borders or not (only for the 'separated borders' model)	show hide
table-layout	Sets the algorithm used to lay out the table	auto fixed

Appendix 2: XHTML reference

This appendix provides a complete reference of XHTML tags. A brief description of each tag is included, plus the non-core attributes associated with each tag. Deprecated tags and attributes are described, so that you will know what variant of XHTML they may be applied to. The core attributes are:

- class, which is an attribute that specifies a style (CSS) class controlling the appearance of the tag's content
- id, which specifies a uniquely defined reference name for a tag
- dir, which specifies the rendering direction for text – normally left to right (ltr), although it can be right to left (rtl)
- lang, which specifies the language for the tag's contents using an ISO code.

Tag syntax	Description	Possible attributes
<!--...-->	The comment tag is used to insert a comment in the source code. A comment will be ignored by the browser. The purpose of comments is to explain your code, which can help you when you edit the source code at a later date	None
<!DOCTYPE>	The <!DOCTYPE> declaration is the very first element in your document, before the <html> tag. This tag tells the browser which HTML or XHTML specification the document uses	
<a>	The <a> tag defines an anchor element. An anchor can be used to create a link to another document by using the href attribute or to create a link inside a document by using the name or id attribute	
<abbr>	Defines an abbreviation. Indicates an abbreviated form, such as 'Inc.', 'etc.'. By marking up abbreviations, you can give useful information to browsers, spellcheckers, translation systems and search engine indexers	title style

Tag syntax	Description	Possible attributes
`<acronym>`	Defines an acronym such as 'USA' and 'ARPA'. Marking up acronyms can provide useful information to browsers, spellcheckers and search engine indexers	`title` `style`
`<address>`	Defines an `address` element, perhaps of where someone lives. Normally renders in *italic* and most browsers will add a line break before and after the `address` element	As above
`<applet>`	Defines an applet, having its roots in Java applets. An XHTML deprecated tag, but still commonly used in non-strict code	`height`, `width`, `align`, `alt`, `archive`, `code`, `codebase`, `hspace`, `name`, `object`, `title`, `vspace`
`<area>`	Defines an area inside an image map. The `<area>` tag must always be nested within a `<map>` tag	`alt`, `coords`, `href`, `shape`, `target`, `nohref`
`<b>`	Defines bold text	
`<base/>`	Defines a base URL for all the links on a page. This tag must be used in the `<head>` section of an XHTML document	
`<basefont/>`	Defines a base font for the text used in a document. This is an XHTML deprecated tag, not to be used with strict code	`color`, `face`, `size`
`<bdo>`	Defines the direction of text display	
`<big>`	Defines big text	
`<blockquote>`	Defines the beginning of a long quotation. Can be a useful formatting tag because it creates whitespace on either side of the text enclosed within the tag container	`cite`
`<body>`	Defines the `body` element and contains all the page content tags. Note that the presentational attributes for use with this tag, such as `bgcolor`, are deprecated and cannot be used with strict XHTML code	`alink`, `bgcolor`, `background`, `link`, `text`, `vlink`
` `	Inserts a single line break – not the same as the `paragraph` tag. Use it to enter blank lines	
`<button>`	Defines a customized push button. Not the same as the button used with the input element on a form, in that you can insert content, such as an image, thereby using it as the button	

Tag syntax	Description	Possible attributes
`<caption>`	Defines a table caption. The `<caption>` tag must be inserted immediately after the `<table>` tag. Only one caption can be used with a table. The `align` attribute is now deprecated with this tag and cannot be used with strict XHTML	`align`
`<center>`	Defines centred horizontal text. This tag is deprecated and should not be used with strict XHTML code	
`<cite>`	Defines a citation. Not a deprecated tag, but style sheets recommended instead	
`<code>`	Defines computer code text. Not a deprecated tag, but style sheets recommended instead	
`<col>`	Defines attributes for table columns so that different column widths can be obtained. For this reason, use it only inside a `colgroup`	`align, char, charoff, span, valign, width`
`<colgroup>`	Defines groups of table columns so that groups of columns can be formatted. Can only be used inside a `table` element	Same as above
`<dd>`	Defines a definition description in a list	
`<del>`	Defines deleted text. Can be used with `<ins>` tag to describe updates to a document	`cite, datetime`
`<dir>`	Defines a directory list. This tag is deprecated and should not be used with strict XHTML code	`compact`
`<dfn>`	Defines a definition term. Not a deprecated tag, but style sheets recommended instead	
`<div>`	Defines a section in a document. The `align` attribute used with this tag is deprecated and should not be used with strict XHTML code	`align`
`<dl>`	Defines a definition list	
`<dt>`	Defines a definition term in a definition list	
`<em>`	Defines emphasized text. Not a deprecated tag, but style sheets recommended instead	
`<fieldset>`	Defines a field set, which draws a box around its containing elements	

Tag syntax	Description	Possible attributes
`<font>`	Defines the font face, size and colour of text. This tag is deprecated and should not be used with strict XHTML code	`color`, `face`, `size`
`<form>`	Defines a standard XHTML form for user input	`action`, `accept`, `method`, `accept-char`
`<frame>`	Defines a subwindow or frame	`src`, `frameborder`, `longdesc`, `name`, `noresize`, `scrolling`, `longdesc`, `marginheight`, `marginwidth`
`<frameset>`	Defines a set of frames, each holding a separate document. The `frameset` element specifies how many columns or rows there will be in it by using the `cols` or the `rows` attributes	`cols`, `rows`
`<h1>` to `<h6>`	Defines headings, `h1` being the largest and `h6` the smallest. The `align` attribute that is used with this tag is deprecated and should not be used with strict XHTML	`align`
`<head>`	Defines information about the document. The browser does not display the `head` tag details on the page. The following tags can be used in the head section: `<base>`, `<link>`, `<meta>`, `<script>`, `<style>` and `<title>`	`profile`
`<hr>`	Inserts a horizontal rule. All presentation attributes that are used with this tag (see right-hand column) are deprecated and should not be used with strict XHTML	`align`, `noshade`, `size`, `width`
`<html>`	Defines an HTML document. The `xmlns` attribute is required with the XHTML specification	`xmlns`
`<i>`	Defines italic text	
`<iframe>`	Defines an inline subwindow or frame	
`<img />`	Defines an image for use in a document. The `align`, `border`, `hspace` and `vspace` attributes of the `image` element are deprecated and should not be used with strict XHTML	`alt`, `src`, `align`, `border`, `hspace`, `vspace`, `height`, `ismap`, `longdesc`, `width`
`<input />`	Defines an `input` field where the user can enter data	`accept`, `align`, `alt`, `checked`, `maxlength`, `disabled`, `name`, `readonly`, `size`, `type`, `value`

Tag syntax	Description	Possible attributes
`<ins>`	Defines inserted text. Can be used with `<del>` tag to describe updates to a document	`cite`, `datetime`
`<kbd>`	Defines keyboard text. Not a deprecated tag, but style sheets recommended instead	
`<label>`	Defines a label for a form control. Clicking the text within the label element will toggle the control	`for`
`<legend>`	Defines a caption for a field set	`align`
`<li>`	Defines a list item. Used in both ordered (`<ol>`) and unordered lists (`<ul>`)	`type`, `value`
`<link>`	Defines the relationship between two linked documents	`href`, `hreflang`, `rel`, `media`, `charset`, `rev`, `target`, `type`
`<map>`	Defines an image map. The `<map>` tag does not define the regions – the `<area>` tag does that	`id`, `name`
`<menu>`	Defines a menu list. This tag (and the associated `compact` attribute) is deprecated and should not be used with strict XHTML code	`compact`
`<meta>`	Defines meta-information about your page. Very common when defining descriptions and keywords for search engines	`content`, `name`, `scheme`, `http-equiv`
`<noframes>`	Defines a `noframes` section to display text for browsers that do not handle frames. This tag is deprecated and should not be used with strict XHTML code	
`<noscript>`	The `noscript` element is used to define alternative content (text) if a script is not executed – used for older browsers that cannot interpret scripts	
`<object>`	Defines an embedded `object`. Generally used for adding multimedia to your XHTML page. Like the `<applet>` tag, this tag allows you to specify the data and parameters for objects inserted into HTML documents and the code that can be used to display/manipulate that data	`align`, `archive`, `border`, `classid`, `codebase`, `codetype`, `data`, `declare`, `type`, `height`, `hspace`, `name`, `standby`, `usemap`, `vspace`, `width`
`<ol>`	Defines an ordered list – one that uses some form of numerals to insert items	`compact`, `start`, `type`

Tag syntax	Description	Possible attributes
`<optgroup>`	Defines an option group. This element allows you to group choices. When you have a long list of options, groups of related choices are easier to handle	`label`, `disabled`
`<option>`	Defines an option in a drop-down list	`disabled`, `label`, `selected`, `value`
`<p>`	Defines a paragraph. The presentational attribute `align` is deprecated and should not be used with strict XHTML	`align`
`<param>`	Defines a parameter for an object. The `param` element allows you to specify the run-time settings for an object inserted into XHTML documents, such as Java applets	`name`, `type`, `value`, `valtype`, `id`
`<pre>`	Defines preformatted text. The text enclosed in the `pre` element usually preserves spaces and line breaks and so can be a useful formatting tag. The attribute `width` is deprecated and should not be used with strict XHTML	`width`
`<q>`	Defines a short quotation	`cite`
`<s>`	Defines strikethrough text. This tag is deprecated and should not be used with strict XHTML code. W3C recommends using the `<del>` tag instead	
`<samp>`	Defines sample computer code. Not a deprecated tag, but style sheets recommended instead	
`<script>`	Defines a script such as VBScript or JavaScript. The `language` attribute is deprecated and should not be used with strict XHTML code	`type`, `charset`, `defer`, `language`, `src`
`<select>`	Defines a selectable list for use with the `<form>` tag	`disabled`, `multiple`, `name`, `size`
`<small>`	Defines small text	
`<span>`	Defines an inline section in a document	
`<strike>`	Defines strikethrough text. This tag is deprecated and should not be used with strict XHTML code. W3C recommends using the `<del>` tag instead	
`<strong>`	Defines strong text. Not a deprecated tag, but style sheets now recommended instead	

Tag syntax	Description	Possible attributes
`<style>`	Defines a style (style sheet) definition. The `style` element goes in the `head` section	`type`, `media`
`<sub>`	Defines subscripted text	
`<sup>`	Defines superscripted text	
`<table>`	Defines a table in a document. Table headings, rows, cells and even other tables can be placed inside a `<table>` tag	`align`, `bgcolor`, `border`, `cellpadding`, `cellspacing`, `frame`, `rules`, `summary`, `width`
`<tbody>`	Defines a table `body`. The `thead`, `tfoot` and `tbody` elements enable you to group rows in a table. When you create a table, you might want to have a headings row, some rows with data and a row with totals at the bottom. This division enables browsers to support scrolling of table bodies independently of the table's heading and footer. A very useful feature of tables	`align`, `char`, `charoff`, `valign`
`<td>`	Defines a table cell. The `bgcolor`, `height`, `width` and `nowrap` attributes of the `td` element are deprecated and should not be used with strict XHTML	`abbr`, `align`, `width`, `nowrap`, `axis`, `char`, `charoff`, `colspan`, `headers`, `height`, `nospan`, `scope`, `valign`
`<textarea>`	Defines a text area. This is a multiline text input control that is used to enable the user to write text in the text area. In a text area, you can write an unlimited number of characters	`cols`, `rows`, `disabled`, `name`, `readonly`
`<tfoot>`	Defines a table footer (read as for `tbody`)	Same as for the `tbody` tag
`<th>`	Defines a table heading. The text within the `th` element usually renders in bold. The `bgcolor`, `height`, `width` and `nowrap` attributes of the `<th>` tag are deprecated and should not be used with strict XHTML	`bgcolor`, `height`, `width`, `nowrap`, `abbr`, `action`, `char`, `charoff`, `colspan`, `headers`, `rowspan`, `scope`
`<thead>`	Defines a table heading (read as for `tbody`)	Same as for the `tbody` tag
`<title>`	Defines the document title of an XHTML document	
`<tr>`	Defines a table row. The `bgcolor` attribute of the `<tr>` tag is deprecated and should not be used with strict XHTML	`align`, `char`, `charoff`, `valign`, `bgcolor`

Tag syntax	Description	Possible attributes
`<tt>`	Defines teletype text	
`<u>`	Defines underlined text. This tag is deprecated and should not be used with strict XHTML code	
`<ul>`	Defines an unordered list. Both the 'compact' and 'type' attributes of the `<ul>` tag are deprecated and should not be used with strict XHTML	`compact`, `type`
`<var>`	Defines a variable. Not a deprecated tag but style sheets recommended instead	
`<xmp>`	Defines preformatted text. Should use `<pre>` instead. This tag is deprecated and should not be used with strict XHTML code	

Appendix 3: Windows keyboard shortcuts for Dreamweaver commands

The Dreamweaver keyboard shortcuts can save much time. However, it is better to begin by using the mouse and only learn to use them as you gain more experience. The complete list of keyboard shortcuts is given below.

General editing shortcuts

Action	Shortcut
Cut	Control + X
Copy	Control + C
Paste	Control + V
Clear	Delete only
Bold	Control + B
Italic	Control + I
Undo	Control + Z
Redo	Control + Y
Select all	Control + A
Move to page up	Page up
Move to page down	Page down
Select to page up	Shift + Page up
Select to page down	Shift + Page down
Select line up/down	Shift + Up/Down
Move to start of line	Home
Move to end of line	End
Select to start of line	Shift + Home
Select to end of line	Shift + End
Go to previous paragraph	Control + Up
Go to next paragraph	Control + Down
Delete word left	Control + Backspace
Delete word right	Control + Delete
Select character left/right	Shift + Left/Right
Find and Replace	Control + F
Find next/find again	F3
Replace	Control + H
Copy HTML (in Design View)	Control + Shift + C

Paste HTML (in Design View)   Control + Shift + V
Preferences   Control + U

Managing files

Action	Shortcut
New document	Control + N
Open an HTML file	Control + O
Open in frame	Control + Shift + O
Close	Control + W
Save	Control + S
Save As	Control + Shift + S
Exit/Quit	Alt + F4 or Control + Q

Page views

Action	Shortcut
Layout View	Control + F6
Standard View	Control + Shift + F6
Live Data mode	Control + R
Live Data	Control + Shift + R
Switch to next document	Control + Tab
Switch to previous document	Control + Shift + Tab
Switch Design/Code Views	Control + '
Server debug	Control + Shift + G
Refresh Design View	F5 only

Viewing page elements

Action	Shortcut
Visual aids	Control + Shift + I
Show rulers	Control + Alt + R
Head content	Control + Shift + W
Show grid	Control + Alt + G
Snap to grid	Control + Alt + Shift + G
Page properties	Control + J
Selection properties	Control + Shift + J

Code editing shortcuts

Action	Shortcut
Switch to Design View	Control + '
Print code	Control + P

Validate markup	Shift + F6
Open quick tag editor	Control + T
Open snippets panel	Shift + F9
Show code hints	Control + Spacebar
Indent code	Control + Shift + >
Outdent code	Control + Shift + <
Insert tag	Control + E
Edit tag (in Design View)	Control + F5
Select parent tag	Control + [
Select child	Control +]
Balance braces	Control + '
Toggle breakpoint	Control + Alt + B
Go to line	Control + G
Move to top of code	Control + Home
Move to end of code	Control + End
Select to top of code	Control + Shift + Home
Select to end of code	Control + Shift + End

Text editing and images

Action	Shortcut
Create a new paragraph	Enter only
Insert a line break 	Shift + Enter
Insert a non-breaking space	Control + Shift + Spacebar
Select a word	Double-click
Add selected items to library	Control + Shift + B
Open and close property inspector	Control + Shift + J
Check spelling	Shift + F7
Change image source attribute	Double-click image, edit image in external editor

Formatting text

Action	Shortcut
Indent	Control + Alt +]
Outdent	Control + Alt + [
Paragraph format	Control + Shift + P
Apply headings 1–6	Control + 1 and so on to 6
Align left/centre/right/justify	Control + Alt + Shift + L/C/R/J
Edit style sheet	Control + Shift + E

Working in tables

Action	Shortcut
Select table	Control + A

Move to the next cell   Tab only
Move to the previous cell   Shift + Tab
Insert a row   Control + M
Add a row at end of table   Tab in the last cell
Delete the current row   Control + Shift + M
Insert a column   Control + Shift + A
Delete a column   Control + Shift + - (hyphen)
Merge selected table cells   Control + Alt + M
Split table cell   Control + Alt + S
Defer table update   Control + Spacebar
Increase column span   Control + Shift +]
Decrease column span   Control + Shift + [

Working in frames

Action	Shortcut
Select a frame	Alt-click in frame
Select next frame	Alt + Right arrow
Select previous frame	Alt + Left arrow
Select parent frame set	Alt + Up arrow
Select first child frame	Alt + Down arrow
Add a new frame to frame set	Select frame, then Alt and drag frame border

Working with layers

Action	Shortcut
Select a layer	Control + Shift-click
Select and move layer	Shift + Control-drag
Add or remove layer from selection	Shift-click layer
Move selected layer by pixels	Arrow keys
Resize selected layer by pixels	Control + Arrow keys
Toggle the display of the grid	Control + Alt + G
Snap to grid	Control + Shift + Alt + G
Align layers left	Control + Shift + 1
Align layers right	Control + Shift + 3
Align layers top	Control + Shift + 4
Align layers bottom	Control + Shift + 6
Make same width	Control + Shift + 7
Make same height	Control + Shift + 9

Inserting objects

Action	Shortcut
Any object (images and so on)	Drag file from Explorer to document window

Image	Control + Alt + I
Table	Control + Alt + T
Named anchor	Control + Alt + A

Getting help

Action	Shortcut
Using Dreamweaver help topics	F1 only
Using ColdFusion help topics	Control + F1
Reference	Shift + F1

Managing hyperlinks

Action	Shortcut
Check links sitewide	Control + F8
Check selected links	Shift + F8
Create hyperlink (select object)	Control + L
Remove hyperlink	Control + Shift + L

Previewing and debugging

Action	Shortcut
Preview in primary browser	F12
Preview in secondary browser	Shift + F12
Debug in primary browser	Alt + F12
Debug in secondary browser	Control + Alt + F12
Action shortcut connect/disconnect	Control + Alt + Shift + F5
Refresh	F5
Create new file	Control + Shift + N
Create new folder	Control + Alt + Shift + N
Open selection	Control + Shift + Alt + O
Delete file	Control + X
Copy file	Control + C
Paste file	Control + V
Duplicate file	Control + D
Rename file	F2
Get selected files	Control + Shift + D
Put selected files / folders to remote site	Control + Shift + U
Check out	Control + Alt + Shift + D
Check in	Control + Alt + Shift + U
View site map	Alt + F8
Refresh local pane	Shift + F5
Refresh remote pane	Alt + F5

Browser windows

Action	Shortcut
View site files	F8
Refresh local pane	Shift + F5
View as root	Control + Shift + R
Link to new file	Control + Shift + N
Link to existing file	Control + Shift + K
Change link	Control + L
Remove link	Control + Shift + L
Show/hide link	Control + Shift + Y
Show page titles	Control + Shift + T
Zoom in site map	Control + + (plus)
Zoom out site map	Control + - (hyphen)

Site management and FTP

Action	Shortcut
Insert bar	Control + F2
Properties	Control + F3
Answers	Alt + F1
CSS styles	Shift + F11
HTML styles	Control + F11
Behaviors	Shift + F3
Tag inspector	F9
Snippets	Shift + F9
Reference	Shift + F1
Databases	Control + Shift + F10
Bindings	Control + F10
Server behaviors	Control + F9
Components	Control + F7
Site	F8
Assets	F11
Results > Search	Control + Shift + F
Results > Validation	Control + Shift + F7
Results > Target browser check	Control + Shift + F8
Results > Link checker	Control + Shift + F9
Results > Site reports	Control + Shift + F11
Results > FTP log	Control + Shift + F12
Results > Server debug	Control + Shift + F5
Others > Code inspector	F10
Others > Frames	Shift + F2
Others > History	Shift + F10
Others > Layers	F2
Others > Sitespring	F7
Others > Timelines	Alt + F9
Show/Hide panels	F4

Index